Anonymous

The Doomed City!

Chicago during an appalling ordeal! The fire demon's carnival: the conflagrations in the West, South and North divisions : graphic sketches from the scene of the disaster

Anonymous

The Doomed City!

Chicago during an appalling ordeal! The fire demon's carnival: the conflagrations in the West, South and North divisions : graphic sketches from the scene of the disaster

ISBN/EAN: 9783337083229

Printed in Europe, USA, Canada, Australia, Japan

Cover: Foto ©ninafisch / pixelio.de

More available books at **www.hansebooks.com**

CHICAGO

DURING

AN APPALLING ORDEAL.

THE FIRE DEMON'S CARNIVAL.

The Conflagrations in West, South and North Divisions.

GRAPHIC SKETCHES FROM THE SCENE OF THE DISASTER.

Prepared and Written by a Journalist.

DETROIT:
PUBLISHED BY THE MICHIGAN NEWS COMPANY,
(W. E. TUNIS.)
1871.

HISTORY
OF THE
GREAT FIRE IN CHICAGO.

GRAPHIC DESCRIPTION OF THE TERRIBLE EVENT.

SCENES, INCIDENTS, ETC.

"ONLY a fire in the West Division."

This was the reply to anxious enquirers or perhaps disinterested curiosity-seekers, as a bright light burst upon the horizon and illumined the district situated between the southern bend of Chicago River and Jefferson Street.

Only a fire on the West Side—and despite the efforts of firemen, despite the genius of human skill and mechanism—four magnificent blocks—magnificent by reason of the wealth, industry and enterprise they represented—were reduced to ashes, only three or four structures remaining on the entire area. Vinegar Works, Planing Mills, Box Factories, Lumber Yards, Wagon Works—all were swept like paper from roof to foundation, and fully $500,000 sacrificed. Amongst the heavy losers were Messrs. Lull and Holmes, Gweigle, Sheriff & Sons, Chapin & Son, Pittsburg, Fort Wayne & Chicago Railway Co., Wilmington Coal Co., Boltzer & Co. On Jefferson Street a row of tenement houses were consumed, together with the chattels and personal property of dwellers therein, who narrowly escaped with their lives, while an unfortunate lady, Mrs. Margaret Hadley, was so blinded and smothered that she fell upon her face in the hall of her residence, and naught save a calcined, charred and ghastly skeleton remained to identify the ill-fated victim.

But it was only one life, only a loss of a few buildings, only a loss of half a million dollars. The Insurance Companies were responsible, were sound; let the merry bells ring instead of the loud fire alarms; let the gloom of an hour be cleared before the glowing progress of a prosperous people.

It ten hours the Western conflagration was forgotten; in ten hours a rich, enterprising, pleasure-loving people were sketching out their plans for Sunday amusement, recreation, and devotional exercises; the fashion of the city, the poor of the city, thousands gathered under the roofs of magnificent churches, which in the short space of a few hours were to fall before the resistless advance of the fire fiend; thousands entered their offices and finished some neglected task; thousands visited pleasure resorts or listened to the Orchestrion's jangled music, in a northern saloon; thousands promenaded the parks or visited their friends and arranged future speculative transactions; whilst in the evening Turner Hall—the great German Sacred Concert establishment—was packed with jubilant humanity. Then the Western Light Guard Band struck up an exquisite selection from the opera. What cared the gay masses for the howling of the wind or the mournful warning of the night before; let the poor feel,—let the rich enjoy themselves—proceed with the music, pass around the glorious *Rhein Wein*, and drown the hurricane's roar without, by strains of music more exquisite and fascinating than the famed breathings of the Æolian harp.

But there is an alarm of fire; the door keeper looks out; the manager runs down to listen; still the light is west—; miles away in fact—and the answer to enquiries is:—" Only a fire in the West Division." "Only a fire in the West Division" is re-echoed throughout the vast assemblage—and the music proceeds. But the din grows louder—the bells ring out a heart-rending peal—; the sky is radiant—and the people quietly ret're from their Sunday evening amusements. At the Sherman, Tremont, Briggs, Palmer and other hotels, successful speculators, bold operators, interested tourists are calmly discussing various questions more directly concerning themselves—when the "clang, clang, clang," of the bells arouses them. "Where is the fire?" "Oh, way up in the West Division, I think," answers the porter.

But the bells almost speak—there is something deathly, awful, supernatural in their wild appeal. The streets are crowded with anxious faces, running to the scene of disaster—running to meet the foe so rapidly advancing upon their fortunes—families and homes. God knows, if a veil could close out the black spot upon the memory of those who witnessed these awful scenes which followed, humanity would kneel submissively and crave the boon; heads which never before bowed would sink in Christian humility; voices which never spoke save to curse their Creator—would be raised to thank Him for his great goodness!

"Clang, clang, clang!"—and through streets, across squares, down every possible thoroughfare hundreds of excited people rushed; from the north-west section they came to assist the firemen and sufferers; from the river towards the west dense masses of people thronged, wildly screaming *fire, fire, fire*—whilst the south-west wind—blowing a perfect hurricane—hurled clouds of dust and other refuse into the eyes of the excited, yelling racing crowd. The roar and hiss of the fire after it had fairly started is indescribable; it seemed as though a large pent-up power had suddenly sundered the shackles which bound it and revengefully burst upon its victims. On the corner of De Koven and Jefferson streets, the scene paralyzed description; the fire had spread with the wind and darted off with the rapidity of lightning; in fact to trace legitimately its progress would be an impossibility. In half an hour two solid blocks of fire spread a ghastly radiance between Jefferson and Clinton streets north. The firemen—bruised, exhausted and over worked, tore down buildings, attempted to head off the fire to the north—but in vain; shrinking multitudes, the victims of temporary lunacy, wild with afright and excitement, closed together and gave vent to loud lamentations; they cursed and jostled each other, knocked one another down, trampled over females in their mad anxiety, when the flames, with electric rapidity, sped on in their work of mad destruction. Building after building, block after block, followed in quick succession; Taylor, Farquar, Polk and Ewing streets were soon in flames, whilst hundreds of unfortunates, sacrificing property and all earthly possessions—vacated the districts; many of these were Germans, a few Irish and others of foreign nationality. One unfortunate woman on Polk street was seen to appear at the upper window of a blazing building and wildly display a child, wrapped in a blanket, and—true to a mother's instinct—she would not part with the treasures of her heart, both perishing together. Another woman, issued from a building screaming at the top of her voice, tearing her hair and calling on God to curse and kill her; others, happily a majority, were collected calm and resigned; whilst retreating, they gazed on the magnificent buildings which boldly fronted the fire, as though to dispute its passage; there they felt confident, the conflagration must cease.

Cease!—scarce had this carnival of the fire fiend commenced; this was but as advanced lines of skirmishers to prepare the road for complete desolation, one column of fire held its way along Clinton and Canal street, the other along Clinton and Jefferson—moving north-west with a sullen, angry roar. Fire and wind coalesced—a bond of unity seemed established, and man stood abashed in the presence of the terrible progress accomplished.

"My God, the fire has broken out in the South," was heard from the lips of a citizen, and sure enough while the blanched and weary toilers, with bloody hands, burned faces and many with torn garments, had been checking the progress on the West Side, a suggestive light appeared in the vicinity of the Gas Works, between Adams and Monroe, and Wells and Market streets. Immediately there was a stampede in that direction, though the atmosphere by this time was stifling; the heat, dust, wind, burning cinders and scorching ground was almost unbearable; it was maddening. A myriad of burning cinders had been hurled over one-fifth of a mile, impregnating a wooden tenement situated as above described, and in an instant, with the rapidity of breath, the structure was wrapped from roof to foundation in a seething blanket of flame! The fire crackled and roared, leaping with demoniac exultation from roof to roof; buildings apparently uninjured suddenly steamed, smoked and in a moment flames darted from beneath the eaves, grappled with the windows, embraced the girders, and with a parting roar, sped on to other quarters. This was before one o'clock Monday morning, and as the flames leaped toward the miserable, grovelling district, popularly known as "Connolly's Patch;" that portion of the fire between Clinton and Canal streets, in the West Division, was making rapid headway, quickly engulphing the lumber yards, tenement houses, and buildings on Van Buren street, whilst the extreme western branch had reached West Harrison street, bordering the scene of the previous night's calamity.

Suddenly another cry of alarm was heard, and each heart sank as a bright light appeared in the vicinity of Adams' street, and engines, firemen and volunteers dashed toward the scene. "Connolly's patch" was now blazing with intense fury, dozens of unfortunates ran out in almost a nude condition; struggling females, crying children, groaning men, rushed in dozens from the fire-feeding shanties; but not all—many were unable to escape, being perfectly hemmed in. A poor man who got out with his hair almost singed to the skull, raised his hands above his head and cried piteously for his child. "She's in the back room—my God, my God—save poor Anne, my poor child!" but it was an entire impossibility, and as the roof fell in, and millions of sparks sprung from the grave of the child, the unfortunate man fell prostrate on the ground. The maddened sea of flame broke like waves over the devoted settlement; it darted in fiery arrows, or rolled like a blazing cylinder, then suddenly burst into shafts which cut with the seething precision of a reaper at his work; a perfect parapet of fire blocked many in their dwellings; one man rushed forward and was silently drawn down to his long home; others madly screamed for help—but the barrier was impassable and fully eight or ten perished in the space of as many seconds—some with curses, some with prayers upon their lips. In the neighborhood of LaSalle street, Monroe, Clark and Dearborn streets, very little anxiety was felt concerning buildings in these neighborhoods. Few dreamed that the exquisite creations of genius, the handsome, massive marble structures which had comprised the wealth, the hope, the pride of the mercantile community, would prove but pasteboard obstacles in checking the advancing flames. Whilst this fire was in progress, a junction of the western branch was rapidly approaching—by way of Jefferson street towards the VanBuren street bridge and Market street; but the intensest interest was created on the south line of Monroe street and running along Wells and Market street. On Monroe street, the stables of J. V. Farwell & Co., and the American Union Express Company, were next attacked. The shivering horses nestled closely together; they neighed with fear and stood tremblingly eyeing the advancing death fiend; very few escaped; not more perhaps than eight or ten out of a hundred powerful animals. It was a fearful sight; but man was suffering still greater afflictions. On—on to Wells street—the poor again attacked and poverty—in such a case—the sure courier of ruin and death—clung to its little store until the scorching cohorts drove it from what had ever been its stronghold. Old men and women, stout, stalwart men and little children, all alike quailed before the march of this terrible enemy. Sick and maimed, decrepit and crippled, many fell by the way and were speedily lapped up by tongues of flame only too ready for prey. And the firemen—noble, reckless, Spartan-like in their efforts—no praise, no eulogy would do them justice; they worked with the defiant energy of men who would assert their manhood and discharge their duties even at the sacrifice of life;

darting through windows whilst dense smoke and lava-like rivers of fire streamed from the roofs; scaling the summits of blazing edifices—God knows, had it been possible to subdue the wild onset of the flames, these men would have achieved a victory. But Providence had otherwise ordained—the extraordinary powers and perseverance of these noble fellows was an imperishable monument in the record of manhood's heroism. And now the Southern Division was alive to the threatened danger. The managers of the Sherman, Tremont, Briggs and other hotels, hastily warned their guests—and in these immense buildings scenes took place beggaring description. Guests rushed from their rooms forgetting money, papers, clothes and other property; sickly women were conveyed to the first flat; porters stumbled over trunks and trunks fell upon guests; some fell down the stairways, others attempted to pack their possessions; but such a state of trepidation were they in that many abandoned the attempt and dashed into the streets.

The flames steadily advanced towards the north branch of the river—crossing Maddison and rolling their ravaging columns down La Salle street—rapidly approaching the Pacific Hotel, and there another voice made known the fact that the fire had sprung across the river at Van Buren street—and was working southward. That Division was doomed, and strong men wept upon the shoulders of their friends as they were warned to seek safety in flight. Many dashed towards the North Division—having little confidence in the west; some went south—others stood to see the reward of a life's labor swept away in the space of a few minutes. This new branch which had thus partially deserted the West Division became a powerful adjunct to that which was working north and east, and what the first fire which visited "Connolly's Patch" had left, the new arrival swept before it—working toward La Salle street; and here the united demons—impelled by a furious wind, strengthened by the unison of force, sped on in their mad career, flames forming a perfect canopy of lurid sheets which passed like an archway over the streets, roaring, crackling and gurgling with almost human significance; they seemed to vie with each other in the work of destruction. Suddenly there was a frightful explosion; in some parts of the city a perfect shock as of an earthquake was experienced—the Gas retorts had exploded, and quickly following this the Government Store House and some barrels of gunpowder in a gunsmith's shop ignited—creating a perfect panic—whilst many fiends in human shape, in order to carry on their thieving and plundering operations, announced that certain buildings were about to be blown up with gunpowder, thus creating a wild confusion, causing many to be trampled under foot and seriously injured. Up to 2:30 A. M., no fear for the North Division was seriously felt, for the hissing monster sprang upon and clung to his prey in the South Division, whilst a wail went up as the Lakeside Publishing House and the grand Pacific Hotel were attacked. The Pacific Hotel was nearly completed—the site being a solid block of land having four distinct fronts on Quincy, Jackson, Clark and La Salle streets. The general style of architecture as observable on the exterior was Italian, presenting the general effect of broad spaces and bold, sweeping outlines. The principal fronts and returns were exquisitely wrought in the olive tinted sandstone of Ohio, from the Amherst quarries, and presenting a continuous cut stone front of over 750 feet, rising ninety-six feet from sidewalk to cornice—and six full stories above a splendid basement. The total height of the walls was 104 feet from the pavement. Added to these, there was a magnificent display of architecture on the upper floors. The attack made by the fire on this edifice was watched with considerable interest—the announcement having been made that it was fire-proof. Thousands of feet of lumber, however, were stacked within, and this rapidly ignited, and in a few minutes the stately building was wrapped in flames. All the walls and partitions above the solid stone foundation were bricked to the second floor, and the interior divisions carried with brick to the tops of the building. The exterior walls were twenty-four inches thick to the first story, thence twenty inches thick to the fourth story, thence sixteen inches the remaining two stories. A system of iron girders entirely encircled the building, resting on brick walls, these girders carrying the main partitions and supporting the bricking in of the partitions on each floor, thus constructed to prevent fire running from one side of the building to the other, through the joists. Gentlemen of great intelligence and experience had pronounced the main portions of the Pacific impervious to the action of fire; but the mad flames, the roaring sea of fire which dashed through and enveloped this grand triumph of architecture, melted the very stones with which it came in contact and hurled the stately piles to instantaneous destruction—and with it over half a million dollars. The hotel was not yet opened, and was owned by a large company.

At this point the city appeared like a boiling cauldron; viewed from any point there was a weird, impressive grandeur. In the west fire was still raging—thousands of tons of soft and chestnut coal transformed the scene into that of a volcanic eruption; in the north-east huge fires and flames darting upwards, illumined the Northern Division, while in the Southern Division the cries of escaping refugees, the screams of injured beings, the roar of the fire and the shock of falling ruins, called to mind historic descriptions of the days of Pompeii and Herculaneum. At the magnificent fire proof building of the TRIBUNE Office, many gathered to witness the fire from an eminence—one of the editors thus graphically describing the awful grandeur of the scene:—

"The sight from the windows of the *Tribune* Building was one the like of which few have ever seen. At fifteen minutes to 1 o'clock the view was like this: To the south-west rose a cloud of black smoke, which, colored with the lurid glare of the flames which caused it, presented a remarkable picture. Due west another column of fire and smoke arose, while the north was lighted with the flying cinders and destructive brands. In ten minutes more the whole horizon to the west, as far as could be seen from the windows, was a fiery cloud, with flames leaping up along the whole line, just showing their heads and subsiding from view like tongues of snakes. Five minutes more wrought a change. Peal after peal sounded from the Court House bell. The fire was on LaSalle street, had swept north, and the Chamber of Commerce began to belch forth smoke and flame from windows and ventilators. The east wing of the

Court House was alight; then the west wing, the tower was blazing on the South Side, and at 2 o'clock the whole building was in a sheet of flam. The Chamber of Commerce burned with a bright steady flame. The smoke in front grew denser for a minute or two, and then, bursting into a blaze from Monroe to Madison streets, proclaimed that Farewell Hall and the buildings north and south of it were on fire. At 10 minutes past 2 o'clock the Court House tower was a glorious sight. It stood a glowing, almost dazzling trellis-work, around which was wrapped a sheet—a winding sheet—of flame. At a quarter past two, the tower fell, and in two minutes more a crash announced the fall of the building. The windows of the office were hot, and the flames gave a light almost dazzling in its intensity. It became evident that the whole block from Clark to Dearborn, and from Monroe to Madison must go; that the block from Madison to Washington must follow: Portland Block was ablaze, while everything from Clark to Dearborn on Washington street was on fire. At 2:30 the fire was half way down Madison street; the wind blew a hurricane; the fire brands were hurled along the ground with incredible force against everything that stood in their way. Then the flames shot up in the rear of Reynold's Block, and then the *Tribune* Building seemed doomed. An effort was made to save the files, and other valuables, which were moved into the composing room, but the building stood like a rock, lashed on two sides by raging waves of flame, and it was abandoned. It was a fire proof building, and there were but a few who expected to see it stand the shock. The greatest possible anxiety was felt for it, as it was the key to the whole block, including McVicker's Theatre, and protecting State street, and Wabash and Michigan avenues north of Madison street. When the walls of Reynolds' Block fell, and Cobb's Building was no more, the prospects of its standing were good. Several persons went up stairs and found it cool and pleasant,—quite a refreshing haven from the hurricane of smoke, dust and cinders that assailed the eyes."

Now the fire seemed to fasten upon the stately rows of marble and stone on La Salle, Clark, Dearborn, and the southern end of State street, running east, and surging through lanes and avenues, skipping, leaping from building to building with ravenous rapidity. W. K. Nixon's building, Republic Life Insurance Company's building, Boone's Block, Andrews' Block, on the east side of LaSalle street, and Bryan's Block, Otis' building, Miller & Drew's insurance building, Oriental building, Mercantile building of D. S. Smith & Co., Union National Bank building, on the west side of La Salle, were smoking; then south again, towards the lake, the fiend sped on unmolested; buildings were blown up, but the flames cast firebrands for blocks ahead, the first intimation of fire being a burst of smoke from the eaves and windows; iron shutters were torn open or drawn apart, metal from the roofs poured a flood of scorching fluid to the earth, whilst tin was pulled up and cast in coils from its resting place. Westward on Washington street a terrifying sea of fire existed, the Nicholson pavement—although resisting the fire to a very great extent—was obliged to succumb, blazing under the feet of fleeing multitudes, many of whom cursed their lives and indulged in the utmost profanity. Massive stone melted under the mad embraces of the heat; it chipped off in blocks, cracked into fragments and shrunk from the advancing fiend; man and the fruits of his industrious ingenuity were alike helpless. Whilst the western side of the South Division was burning huge pieces of fired timber were cast forward towards Randolph street, and even before many of the buildings on LaSalle, Dearborn and other streets were on fire, the Court House and several structures were commencing to blaze, thus dividing the firemen and preventing anything like a perfect concentration of the score of steam engines at work.

Opposite the tunnel the great Court House loomed in terrible grandeur. Removed to a great degree from the surrounding fire, those in authority hesitated to allow the prisoners liberty; the latter yelled in fury, prayed, beseeched for clemency, charity, anything that could soften the hearts of their guards, and at last, when smoke issued from the roof, they were discharged, two persons guilty of murder being placed in custody and held by the police. Then the great bell of this splendid edifice seemed to speak: it sent forth the wildest alarm which had yet been heard; even as the fire smothered the cupola, great harsh, mournful sounds were heard from it—

"CLANG"—"CLANG"—"CLANG."

This marked the precinct and the danger,—and people shuddered as volumes of smoke passed through the windows of this stately edifice, and great shafts of flame and myriads of trembling cinders were caught by the wind and hurled as messengers of ruin towards adjacent structures. Many people sought refuge in the LaSalle Street Tunnel, carrying books, trunks and papers with them. But dense columns of smoke passing north and south, warned the fleeing masses; immense blocks of stone, falling with the quickness of lightning from the buildings, cut huge masses from the stoning of the tunnel, and tore away parts of the iron railing as though it were thread; to add to the misery of the unfortunates, thieves prowled around, stealing property, frightening women, and indulging in the lowest description of blackguardism. In fact, some quietly entered back premises and fitted suits of clothes, hats, boots and vests—displaying a refined nicety in selecting their costumes not often observable. The fiends should have been handcuffed one after another.

It was just previous to this that the Gas Works exploded, and when the fire crossed Monroe street, several voices cried:

"The fire has reached the Gas House—run, run for your lives!"

A frightfully confused scene followed; curses and profanity, shrieks of fear and pain, were cast from white lips and passed upon the wings of the hurricane.

Here stood a mother with her tender child pressed closely to her bosom, the little darling pouting its innocent lips and pressing its face to the only heart it knew. "Take the child away!" almost yelled the father, who was acting as though perfectly insane—"My God! do you want to be destroyed?! Run, run for your life!" And he seized the cringing, startled woman by the arm, forcing her towards Clark street.

On State Street, Field, Leiter & Co., had engines employed flooding the palatial building which they occupied, and many firmly believed that the structure would be saved; meanwhile hundreds of thousands of dollars in goods were removed, and a systematic arrangement of forces instituted. Then on the corner of State and Randolph streets volunteers and others mounted the roof of Ross & Gossage's building, risking their very lives in attempts to chop away the cornices, which they succeeded in doing, the multitude below cheering enthusiastically. But the labor availed little, for speedily the immense block was wrapped in fiery garb, and crumbled into ashes before the enemy's attack. It was heartrending to hear women calling for their children; they would seize a bystander by the arm, and between hysterical sobbings and shiverings anxiously implore aid in seeking the missing loved ones; so startled were the horses that at times they would break loose from their fetters and dash madly into the ruins of the fire—whilst tame pigeons—crossing the line of fire—were suddenly paralized by the heat and added their little carcases to appease the wrath of this devastating monster. Back towards the central portion of Wabash avenue frightful scenes had occurred—scenes too solemn, too striking to permit of any perfect description. In many places naught could be seen save jagged remains of buildings, and angles pointed their scarred edges to the sky; very few buildings stood; the Post Office almost dared the sea of fire to engulph it; with a roar as of the waves of ocean hurling their mighty power against a rock-bound coast—the flames darted for their prey; they rolled beneath the cornices, hissed and gurgled as they found light prey amid the boxes and drawers and papers; the revelry of pandemonium seemed to be rivalled in this earthly region, where the fire king held sway and passed the fiat of destruction upon this doomed city.

Up to Wabash avenue the crowd was immense—thousands of poor houseless wretches, driven from their homes, had sought refuge in this district; but shortly after 4 o'clock the cry came—" Fire spreading up the avenue!" and immediately there ensued a state of excitement beyond parallel. The fire was behind them—the vast prairie of palatial residences was as straw in checking the flames; dense clouds of smoke rolled above, whilst cinders, burning and igniting everything with which they came in contact, found resting places in many a happy home which was soon to be desolated.

"Oh, sir, I have lost my mother."

She was a child of nearly thirteen, who spoke, whilst her sobs told what sufferings the little one was enduring; dressed in fashionable apparel, with a light "cloud" upon her head—it seemed a crime that rough fellows should push, jostle and frighten her; "her mother!" perhaps the tie had been severed in this world, and we placed the poor little soul under charge of a friendly policeman, who, no doubt, did his utmost to restore her to her relatives. Now came a struggle for the pavement; thousands rushing south met thousands pressing northward; women were crushed and fainted in the collision; blasphemy, imprecations, drunken jokes and other orgies indicative of degradation, were indulged in. The rich jewels of a pampered beauty, or reigning belle, did not preserve her from contact with those of meaner origin or meaner position; both had hearts, feelings—both suffered and both were subdued. One lady ran about with several chains passed over her neck, her fingers covered with jewels, whilst another manifested that the ruling passion was strong even in death—for she was attempting to pull a "Saratoga" through the streets; the flames captured the valuable trunk with its reminiscences of fascinating flirtations and watering-place insanities, and the last seen of this estimable but unfortunate lady was toward the lake—where a friend met her in a very philosophical mood; she remarked to him:— "I don't thnk I shall go to the opera to-night," and she kept her word—Crosby's Opera House had been magnificently fitted up, over $70,000 having been spent upon it—the work being only completed and approved on Saturday night; it was to have been opened by Theodore Thomas with his Orchestra on that Monday evening which saw it in ruins.

At intervals of ten, fifteen or thirty minutes an explosion could be heard; homes were blown up. Only two engines were in this section, and these were powerless without water. After the conflagration had sped beyond Adams, Jackson and Van Buren, and had arrived at Congress street, a determined effort was made at Harrison street on the west line. Leaving the block between Congress, Harrison, State and Wabash avenue, as certain prey for the flames, effort was concentrated on the line of buildings on the north side of Harrison. On the corner of State was a wooden building which was too dangerous to be allowed to stand; it was therefore blown up. Adjoining on the east was a three-story double brick which met the same fate, and in a minute only the front walls remained. The effect of this was seen in a moment, and the fire was effectually checked, at least as far as the high-reaching flames were concerned. Between the brick house, just mentioned, and the church which occupied the corner of Wabash was a small frame building, this was a dangerous heap, and partook of similar treatment which reduced the next house; but not until after it had so far been enveloped in flames as to seriously endanger the Wabash avenue Methodist Church.

For once man's ingenuity baffled the devastating fire fiend; by the skillful removal of buildings the church was saved and here the first check proved successful; the fire continued burning on Congress street—the east three buildings being saved. The fire passed from Wabash Avenue corner to Congress street and No. 330 Wabash avenue received a gunpowder visitation leaving a gulph between the fire which even wind, cinders and fury could not overcome.

And thus the awful scene closed at that point. At 4 o'clock the position was this—the line in the South Division extended from above Harrison street northward to the main branch of the river. Eastward, Dearborn street had been reached by the fire—sweeping magnificent blocks and grand edifices rapidly before it. All hoped now that the city east of the river and east of Honor's Pool—which had been destroyed—would now be preserved. In the south all was quiet, in the east the fire seemed to be subdued.

But the fire had not yet ceased—the work was not yet accomplished

Shortly before 7 o'clock A. M., the wind springs up afresh; it lifts huge boards and fans the dying embers with its hurricane breath; it bursts and eddies and scatters tons of dust over all pedestrians, blinds the workmen, blinds those who are retreating, blinds the unfortunate homeless child and the heart broken mother—and God knows, the world would be a more charitable, more kindly disposed could all in it have witnessed the miseries of Monday, the 9th day of October 1871.

"The fire has started again in the Southern Division." This was the announcement which nearly maddened the distracted populace—for now the north was rapidly being destroyed—deaths were occurring every hour; honest men were being pillaged by thieving express men, hack drivers and rascally carriers—; people were tired, hungry, sleepy—and yet nothing could be procured to meet the demands of nature.

"Don't cry mother, don't cry," were words heard thousands of times that night passing from the lips of a child who felt the convulsive spasms pressed into her own hands and knew well the awful anguish which afflicted the one who nourished, loved and would protect her, even by sacrificing her life. But scenes such as these had occurred too often to excite emotion now.

The wind increased; livid coals were caught up and hurled upon the wooden structures across the street, and in a moment the fire had gained a foothold, and swept on once more to the northward and eastward. All that had been left untouched between Jackson and Madison streets, and between Dearbon street and the lake shore, was now doomed, and as the fury of the first hurricane of wind subsided, there came almost a lull, so that the fire began to work southward and westward.

Solemn and serious a task as it is to chronicle the misfortunes of a wealthy city by fire, it is a doubly melancholy duty to speak of DEATH, and to record His work of silent destruction. People dashed from wagons and killed, horses burned to cinders, women rushing for succor, with their clothes in flames. Men in dangerous positions leaping forty and even sixty feet, to be dashed to pieces on the pavement below. The *Tribune* reporter witnessed an intensely exciting leap from Speed's Block, on Dearborn street, by which a man met sudden death under the following circumstances: While Madison street south of Dearborn, and the west side of Dearborn were all ablaze, the spectators saw the lurid light appear in the rear windows of Speed's Block. Presently a man, who had apparently taken time to dress himself leisurely, appeared on the extension built up to the second story of two of the stores. He cooly looked down the thirty feet between him and the ground, while the excited crowd first cried jump, and then some of them more considerately looked for a ladder. A long plank was presently found and answered the same as a ladder, and was placed at once against the building, down which the man soon after slid. But while these preparations were going on, there suddenly appeared another man at a fourth story window of the building below, which had no projection, but was flush from the top to the ground—four stories and a basement. His escape by the stairway was evidently cut off, and he looked despairingly down the fifty feet between him and the ground. The crowd gathered frantically at the sight, for it was only a choice of death before him— by fire or being crushed to death by the fall. Senseless cries of jump! jump! went up from the crowd—senseless but full of sympathy, for the cry was absolutely agonizing. Then for a minute or two he disappeared, perhaps even less, but it seemed so long a time that the supposition was that he had fallen, suffocated with the smoke and heat. But no, he appears again. First he throws out a bed, then some bed-clothes, apparently; why, probably even he does not know. Again he looks down the dead, sheer wall of fifty feet below him. Then he mounts to the window-sill. His whole form appears, naked to the shirt, and his white limbs gleam against the dark wall in the bright light as he swings himself below the window. Somehow—how none can tell—he drops and catches upon the tops of the windows below him. He stoops and drops again, and seizes the frame with his hands, and his gleaming body once more straightens and hangs prone downward, and then drops instantly and accurately upon the window-sill of the third story. A shout, more of joy than applause, goes up from the breathless crowd, and those who had turned away their heads, not bearing to look upon him as he seemed about to drop to sudden and certain death, glanced up at him once more with a ray of hope at this daring and skilful feat. Into this window he crept to look, probably, for a stairway, but appeared again presently, for here only was the only avenue of escape, desperate and hopeless as it was. Once more he dropped his body, hanging by his hands. The crowd screamed and waved to him to swing himself over the projection from which the other man had just been rescued. He tried to do this, and vibrated like a pendulum from side to side, but could not reach far enough to throw himself upon its roof. Then he hung by one hand and looked down; rising the other hand, he took a fresh hold and swung from side to side once more to reach the roof. In vain; again he hung motionless by one hand, and slowly turned his head over his shoulder and gazed into the abyss below him. Then, gathering himself up, he let go his hold, and for a second a gleam of white shot down full forty feet to the basement. Of course it killed him. He was taken to a drug store near by, and died in ten minutes.

When the Ross building near State and Washington streets fell, a man with a wagon — occupied by himself and four others—reached the base of the edifice just as the walls fell; they five were crushed to atoms and remained beneath the tomb which covered them. One of them saw the ruins topple and uttered an exclamation—but was unable to escape. One of the *Tribune* reporters, wandering on the North Side, discovered, in the rear cellar of the dwelling next east of the Historical Society's building, the charred trunk of a human body, lying amid ruins of many wine bottles and the apparatus of a water-closet. There was much roasted flesh still clinging to the spine, but no clue to the identity, or even the sex of the victim, was obtainable. The house had been occupied by a German—the keeper of the Historical Building—but the body may have been that of some person who had strayed into (apparently) the upper chambers of his house, probably in pursuit of plunder. Two men were also found in the neighborhood of a livery stable near the Pacific Hotel, burned and charred so as to render recognition an impossibility; only a part of their legs and trowsers remained to establish the fact that they were human beings. Mr. Morehead perished in the building of Reyburn, Hunter & Co., whilst endeavoring to save books; he fell back smothered. One Wolf was roasted to death at 95 West Harrison street; whilst a drunken man, endeavoring to cross the base ball ground, was also destroyed. Six men were working on the corner of Clark and Madison streets, top of J. B. Chamber's store, and when the fire caught the lower part of the building were unable to get down, and equally unable to escape to adjoining buildings. They fell through the roof and were totally consumed, after uttering heart rending shrieks! A woman on State street was unable to escape from her room ; she acted frantically, slapping at the flames, screaming at the crowd, dancing, singing and holding her head with both hands; then with a haunting, despairing shriek she succumbed to the fire and smoke. Her son did all in his power to save her, but the solid, seething fire darted towards him, and roared with distracting fierceness; the fire held untrammeled mastery over the people; their little efforts were—so to speak—mocked and jeered at as he leaped from building to building twisted his emissaries throughout a block, and hurled for miles around huge masses of fired timber; the wind changed frequently, but the mission of desolation had to be accomplished, and man had to succumb to the sway of this maddened element. Many of the dead were gathered together and conveyed to the West Side; some were smothered—some had their skulls fractured, some had been burned to death—but all were victims of the terrible calamity.

Ere turning attention to the North Side it may not be out of place to enumerate a few of the prominent blocks and Buildings leveled to ashes in the Southern Division. Of course there were hundreds of other edifices, representing millions of dollars which are omitted: City National Bank, Illinois Savings' Institution, Western Fire and Marine, Telegraph Office, Chamber of Commerce, Merchants' Insurance Block, Ætna Insurance Block, First Methodist Church, St. Mary's (Catholic), First Presbyterian, Second Presbyterian, Trinity (Episcopal), St. Paul's (Universalist), Swedenborgian Church, Wabash Avenue Methodist (partially), Birch Block, Palmer Block, Michigan Southern Depot, Academy of Design, Chicago Academy of Music, Bryant & Stratton's Commercial College, Jewish Synagogue, Phoenix Club House, Mayo Block, Drake-Farewell Block, *Tribune* Block, *Journal* and *Times* Offices, Offices of the *Post, Mail* and *Staats Zeitung, Republican* Office, Lombard Block, Sturgess Block, Farewell Hall, Morrison Block Arcade Building, Stones Block, Armory, Hubbard Block, Chittenden Building, Root & Cady's, Lyon & Healy's, Smith & Nixon's, Kimball's, Bauer's & Molter's Music store, Metropolitan Hall and Music Hall. The list, of course, includes only a very few of the business blocks of the South Division, but such as prominently occur to us in recalling the former condition of these once busy streets. Terrance Block, Michigan Central Depot, Adams House, Massasoit House, City Hotel, Metropolitan Hotel, Tremont House, St. Jame's Hotel, Palmer House, Pacific Hotel, Bigelow House, Sherman House, Matteson House, Nevada Hotel, Brigg's House, Court House,

Gas Works, Crosby's Opera House, McVickor's Theatre, Hooley's Opera House, Wood's Museum, Dearborn Theatre, Shephard Block, Honore Block, Post Office and Post Office Block, Reynold's Block, McCormick's Block, the Western News Company's, S. C. Griggs & Co.'s, and W. B. Keen & Co.'s Book House, Manufacturer's National, German National, Mechanic's National, First National, Second National, Third National, Fourth National, Fifth National, Commercial National, National Bank of Commerce, Illinois National, Cook County National, Union National, Merchants' National, Merchants' and Farmers' Saving, Loan and Trust, Badger's Bank, etc., etc., etc.

During the raging of the fire, little attention was excited by the occurrence of accidents; maimed, wounded, sick, crippled—all had to take care of themselves, and without doubt hundreds of men, women and children sleep their last sleep amid the ashes of this awful conflagration.

Whilst the south-west and southern sections were smouldering ruins, the centre of attraction was the north side, the fire making rapid progress urged by a north-west wind and reaching Brush street. The bridge here was crowded with people and it was at once turned to prevent the flames making further headway.

Vain effort!

As though aware of its power the fire attacked the bridge, drove many into leaping wildly into the water and many into suffocation. The warehouse, lumber yards, coal beds, planing mills and every wooden structure for blocks around were soon darting forth jets of flame; towards the lake the fleeing, worried, heartbroken crowd wended their way. And we cannot better continue the narrative of the spreading of this fire than by relying upon the evidence of reporters from the Chicago press—more particularly the *Tribune:*

So little idea had the people living near the Historical Society Building on Ontario street, between Dearborn and Clark, of the terrible and utter ruin which the fire would work, but snatching up what valuables they could, they sought shelter in its cellar, which was unfortunately filled to a great extent with inflammable material. According to the statement of the Librarian of the Historical Society, William Cockran, who was there at the time, the following persons certainly sought refuge there. Old Colonel Stone and his wife, Mr. and Mrs. Able and their daughters, Mrs. De Pelgrom, teacher of French, Mr. and Mrs. Carpenter, musical people, Dr. Freer and family, the former having with him $1,000 worth of personal property belonging to Rush Medical College, two patients from the hospital in Mr. Richard's place, and John B. Girard and family. Mr. Cockran had hold of one end of a trunk, and Mrs. Gebler of the other. Her dress took fire, and he left her and ran for the stairs, leading from the cellar up stairs. He is certain that old Colonel Stone suffocated and, from the sudden inrush of dense smoke, there is cause for fear that nearly all the others who were in there shared the same fate, bewildered by the fumes, and unable to find their way out of a building with which they were unacquainted. Mr. Cockran ran up the cellar stairs and went into the reading-room on the ground floor, and thence hurried up into the library room. At that time there did not seem to be any symptoms of fire in the roof. Then, going down stairs again into the lecture and pamphlet room, he saw the flames rushing up stairs, and made his exit as hurriedly as possible. Nothing was saved from the building, not even the Emancipation Proclamation, and it is now an utter and hopeless wreck.

At Chicago avenue. It was 10 o'clock when the fire got to Chicago avenue, and all down Clark and Wells streets was in a state of terrible excitement. The fire had crossed the river at another point, or, rather, the flying sparks had set fire up near Ontario street. Encouraged by the absence of policemen, the roughs along on Kinzie street broke into the saloons there, and began seizing and drinking the liquor. Many others, at the very moment when they most needed all the self-possesion they had, worried themselves, and, in many cases, were surrounded by the flames and stifled by the smoke. Some were found lying on the sidewalk, and, since no one paid any particular attention to them, they met their fate there. Some women, and their children, lingered too long, and were either lost in the house, or compelled to jump out of the windows, and receiving injuries, remained where they were. The incredible rapidity of the flames passed all comprehension. They sprang from side to side of the street, and skipping extensive tracts, returned to complete their work Often before the flames had reached a house, the thick, black smoke began to roll out of the chimneys, the result of the action of the intense heat on the pine woodwork within. The Church of the Holy Name, which has a slate roof, was especially noticeable. From the crevices of the slates poured out eddying whirls of black smoke which, after rising a short height, burned for a moment with an intense flame, and then went out. At an early hour in the morning, it was possible to get teams, but it was not very long before they were all secured.

So soon as the people west of Clark began to see that there was no hope, and that the fire was really bound to go northward to an indefinite point, they turned all their minds to getting over to the West Division, where there was comparative safety from the flames, and plenty of vacant ground on which to encamp. So, since Chicago avenue bridge was useless, the whole tide turned toward Division, which, from Grove to Halsted, was untouched, and promised to remain so. It was not many minutes before a steady stream of carriages, drays, express wagons, and vehicles of every description were rushing pell mell across that bridge, interlocking and breaking, while the southern streets leading up to Division were jammed with wagons, which occasionally caught fire. The expressmen and draymen, stimulated by the immense prices they were receiving—$20 to $50 a load—drove their heavy teams recklessly forward breaking down the weaker teams and forcing their way across the river in order to return as soon as possible for another load. Sometimes they themselves came to grief, and then, unfastening their horses, tried to find another wagon.

The roads were filled with people crazed by excitement and liquor, or stupified by smoke, and no regard at all was paid to them by the drivers, so that at all those points numerous accidents were constantly occurring. One man was driving up Clark street with a heavy load when he fell from his seat and instantly broke his neck. The team was loaded with trunks marked "Barton Edsall." Mrs. Edsall was taken from her house in a half insensible condition, quite early in the morning. It will be remembered that her husband was murdered in his house the preceding Thursday night.

The wanderers crossing Division street either scattered themselves north or went straight west, while many encamped themselves upon Grove Island, which lies between the North Branch and Ogden Canal. When the trains moved a little west they found their way blocked by the cars of the Northwestern Road, which had been run up there to avoid the fire, and people were compelled to make long detours to get through them. Many, unable to force their way through the confusion at Division street, which was almost equal to that at the crossing of the Beresina, turned into the side streets, and made their way to North Avenue Bridge, where they were able to get out without great difficulty, though much hampered by the railroad trains after they got across there. Not only teams, but foot passengers, carrying in their arms children and some little articles of furniture or wearing apparel, wended their weary way in the same direction. One woman had nothing but a silk sack, and another was accompanied by a child, who had in its arms a couple of cats and a little dog, and crying itself, sobs out, "Don't cry, mamma." After getting out upon the prairie, they settled down wherever they could find room, some sitting in rocking chairs, and others upon blankets on the ground. None of them said anything, but all sat looking intently at the fire which was immediately before them. Many who had teams went as far west as the Artesian Well, where they encamped around the large pond, which supplied them with water. There they remained in the most forlorn and uncomfortable condition, which was aggravated by the rain, which began falling about 11 o'clock on Monday night, and which caused a change from the warm and comfortable temperature of the day, to the piercing chilliness of Tuesday morning.

Late on Monday evening, Chicago avenue bridge caught fire, and soon fell into the river. It was even then almost impossible to get over at Division street, on account of the teams which were even then crossing. Everywhere the wildest confusion was prevailing. Families were separated, and the members were vainly seeking for one another. One policeman picked up a three months' old child, which had been lost in some way. Since there was no use in facing the flames, the engines arranged themselves along the west bank of the North Branch, did the best they could all Monday in playing on the East and West Sides.

The fire went further and further north, taking both sides of North avenue, and continuing north.

The people living north of Chicago avenue and rather west of LaSalle street, were exceedingly hopeful that they would escape, and that the fire would drift steadily eastward, not expecting that it would make any progress against the steady and furious west wind. They also had great hopes in Chicago avenue, which is a 100 foot street. But the flames running up Clark street, catching Turner Hall and the new building north of it, worked west, and got into the brick blocks on the east side of La

Salle, and then jumped that street and got into the blocks on the west side. At about the same time it crossed Chicago avenue and caught McEwen's planing mill, on Wells, near Pearson, and then rushed on northward among the wooden buildings situated there, blowing them down almost before they were on fire. Numbers of the citizens seized what property they could, piling it on drays, which they sometimes dragged themselves, and took the goods thus temporarily received over to a vacant lot on Franklin street beyond Elm, where there was nothing but earth and green celery, and there bestowed their possessions in little heaps, with which the ground was soon covered. But this material with which the earth was cumbered was of the most incongruous and often inflammable nature. Irish women brought straw beds, and others piled up chairs, bureaux, trunks, and every conceivable article. It was not long before the cinders, falling in dense masses, began to make of the surface of this lot a succession of small bonfires, and the owners, having no water, and no means of covering with earth what they had, were either compelled to stamp out these flames or to let their stuff go, and confine themselves to regretting the useless waste of time, or to pick up the most portable article and march off with it. One man was seen marching off with a glass kerosene lamp, and after he had carried it about a block, he met a friend, who asked him what was the use of carrying a thing like that any further. He looked at it, observed that there did not seem to be much use in it, and tossed it away. Another man had secured a rickety and tremulous cart, to which was harnessed a rickety and tremulous horse, and in it had a beer safe, which with great regard for the property of others, he was carrying out of harm's way, on the prairie or elsewhere. Other men took their goods up to Lincoln Park, hoping that there, at least, they would be safe. But there, as elsewhere, the fury of the flames passed their comprehension, and everything stored there, as well as the trees, were swept away.

"God help us, where is this to stop?" groaned a father, as with his children in his arms he traveled the streets, now and again looking back with a manifestation of intense anxiety. On—on—on—towards the lake the unfortunate people crowded, shrinking as the roar of the fire-torrent neared them. On—on—on—to the beach, and still the serpentine monster left its devastating marks behind, and advanced on the forlorn battalions crouching in the sand, or crawling in the water. As the hiss and roar advanced, many drove their horses into the lake; women unused to fatigue, clasped their children to their breasts and prayed fervently to their Maker. Others laughed with the hollow glee of lunacy, others stood petrified, gazing upon the terrible sight before them.

These people were sandwiched between two walls of death!

To advance was to be destroyed by fire—to retreat—to meet a watery grave!

One man held his head under water at intervals, another bound his coat around his head and saturated it with water. Wagons were capsized, and many retreated beneath them for concealment, and thus baffled their foe until far in the distance. Wright's and Ogden's groves could be seen distinctly, although the fire had not yet reached that point.

The line of devastation could be distinctly traced north-east towards Newbury School House, gliding into Webster avenue in the vicinity of Lincoln Place, there the ravages spread eastward along Hulburt street, east of Orchard on to the lake, whilst the entire city south of Orchard was also destroyed.

As the day progressed, the misery of the unfortunate sufferers increased;—nothing to eat, nothing to wear, nothing to hope for save anxiety, danger, trouble and tribulation. From the corner of LaSalle street north, the desolation of this division was particularily noticable; in some cases the buildings had been reduced to ashes, and the wind, after scooping rubbish and all in a body, hurled it forward in a perfect blinding cloud. Division street was swept clean, not a stone remained which could have pointed to the spot where stood some well-known building. Sidewalks seem to have acted as fire conductors;—they burned rapidly, and frequently were instrumental in aiding the hellish work of destruction. A battered tower marked the North avenue Police Station, whilst the charred, browned walls of St. Michael's Church—a German place of worship—were particularily noticeable. The Alexean Hospital, the R. C. Church—both disappeared—leaving scarce a trace behind. Within these landmarks rubbish and tangled *debris* alone remained. From Sedgwick, along North avenue to Orchard, everything is gone, the Newbury School having been a barrier to the further progress westward of the flames.

In fact no casual reader, one who has not been through the ruins, and witnessed the gloom and bitterness occasioned by the fell destroyer, would credit the assertion that for miles south, miles north, miles east, nothing is to be seen save ruins, jagged corners of buildings, blazing heaps of coal, smouldering wheat and acres of battered machinery, grimy, red and useless. There one could see the Orphan Home; it had accomplished some good work in its day—nearly three hundred children had gathered to be educated by the self-sacrificing Sisters of Mercy. Here occurred a heart-rending scene; the children screamed, hid themselves, and wept aloud—their lamentations being heard by many without. Mr. Sullivan at once secured wagons and saved them from the horrible fate with which they were threatened. The spire of the Church of Holy Name remained—a blast of wind blowing the platforms down and severely injuring several men. Unity Church, where the Rev. Robert Collyer delivered so eloquent a sermon the night before—dwelling upon the destruction of Paris—now became a victim to the element more deadly than man's wrath, more potent than military heartlessness. At the Water Works Mr. Creiger was striving to protect the interests of the city—the roof alone being destroyed; Mr. Creiger was amazed when viewing the fire on Ohio street, to observe the flames heading out to the Works. Even the graves in the old cemetery were scorched—the tombstones blistered and scaled, and iron railings twisted into fantastic shapes. But why dwell upon the frightful work accomplished during Monday? Why call back the painful objects, the saddening experiences of that awful day? The man who, maddened by anxiety and suffering, prevailed upon his brain to conjure up the burning of Sodom and Gomorra—and to prophecy a similar destruction in the case of Chicago, deserved pity; hooted as he was, driven from his stand—he yet was less crazed than hundreds who ran or walked or spoke as though in a dream, and who superstitonsly thought what the unfortunate man was reckless enough to speak. And standing to view the rapidly melting streets, we can see whole families secreting themselves under bridges or sidewalks; clergymen of all denominations were striving to escape the work of general destruction—in fact—like death—the fire levelled all, and common disaster made men brothers.

It were useless to endeavor to classify the magnificent structures reduced to ashes on the North Side; happy homes were made desolate; the laugh of youth was turned into weeping; the plans for future enjoyment were defeated; the prattling infant in the cradle, the young mother full of hope—what a fearful comment on the uncertainty of human happiness. Millions of dollars represented now by crumbled ruins; households pampered in luxury and ease praying for an opportunity of concealing themselves, protecting themselves, with paupers, beggars and thieves; not a building to enter, scarce clothing to cover their forms; God in his great mercy would not have sent so great an affliction without mysteriously ordering it for some wise purpose.

The following were a few of the destroyed buildings in North Division: Revere Hotel, Ullich's Block, Ewing's Block, the Hatch House, the Humboldt House, Illinois Street Church, Armour, Dole & Co.'s Elevator, Hiram Wheeler's Elevator, the private residences of William B. Ogden, J. L. Stark, Isaac N. Arnold, J. K. Rice, George L. Dunlap, W. B. Houghtaling, Samuel Johnson, E. I. Tinkham, Thomas Mackin, the contractor, whose loss is from four to five hundred thousand dollars; George F. and Julian Rumsey, Edward Burling, A. H. Burley, O. F. Fuller, Dr. C. V. Dyer, G. W. Gondy, Obadiah Jackson, General Rucker, the new Diversey Block, near the Water Works, E. B. McCagg, Perry N. Smith, Philip Hoyne, Franklin Mosely, Lincoln, Pierson Street Primary, Elm Street Primary, and other school buildings, the Clarendon Hotel on Clark Street, the North Side Stables, from which nearly all the horses were saved, McCormick's Reaper Factory, the Chicago Sugar Refinery, the Galena Freight House, the Galena Elevator, Lill's and Sand's Breweries, the Tanneries along the North Branch, the German Theatre at the corner of Indiana and Wells streets, Unity, New England, and Westminster Churches, the Chapel of the Holy Name, the Cathedral, the Hospital of the Alexian Brothers, the Jewish Hospital on LaSalle street, the new Catholic one on the corner of Sedgwick and Elm, with the Convent of the Sisters of Mercy, the Chicago Historical Society, the Huron Street Station, the Bethel, Galena Depot, &c., &c.

IT IS TUESDAY.

No papers are issued. Where once stood the *Times* office, from whence issued one of the most fearless, dashing papers on the Continent, was now a ruin, Mr. Storey's loss being altogether immense. The *Tribune*, having secured Edwards' Directory Office on Canal street, West Side, coalesced with the *Journal*, for the time being, in fact all the printing offices nestled closely together on Canal and adjacent streets. West Division was crowded, as also portions of the South. There is a settled gloom observable; rich men on Saturday are poor to-day. They are not downhearted, however. They calmly talk the matter, each one wondering, speculating as to how his safe has "stood it." Selfish merchants in some cases are extortionate in prices; they ask 25 cents per pound for the commonest brand of sugar; they swindle on bread prices until a manifesto is issued forbidding them to sell for more than eight cents per loaf. One man hangs out his shingle, and a real *bona fide* shingle, too; on it is inscribed his name, and underneath, "wife, children, energy!" That is all he had left.

On the corner of Canal street business men discussed their losses; they were philosophical, but ever and anon the trembling lip, the uncertain nervous action, told too plainly that the heart felt what the lip failed to utter.

Here is Mr. Wentworth of the Michigan Central; he has been working hard, and evidently has borne his share of the fray.

"How much money have you?" asks his friend.

"Just four dollars," is the reply—and one-half goes to the anxious enquirer.

A gentleman who had been worth $300,000 stood viewing the destruction of his wealth in an elevator. Pointing towards a mountain of wet, smoldering wheat, he said: "This day I am not worth a dollar; this day a week ago I was possessed of $300,000.

Scenes such as these were frequent; men came down from their wealth-created positions, and removed the mantle of business courtesy and practical coldness which had too often frozen their hearts, and made them indifferent to the troubles and burdens of others less fortunate in the battle of life.

But now all were wounded, and able to practically test the effect of changes, reverses and afflictions upon the human heart.

During the day the following notices, proclamations, etc., were issued:

"1. All citizens are requested to exercise great caution in the use of fire in their dwellings and not to use kerosene lights at present, as the city will be without a full supply of water for probably two or three days.

2. The following bridges are passable, to wit: All bridges (except Van Buren and Adams streets) from Lake street south, and all bridges over the North Branch of the Chicago River.

3. All good citizens who are willing to serve, are requested to report at the corner of Anne and Washington streets, to be sworn in as special policemen.

Citizens are requested to organize a police for each block in the city, and to send reports of such organization to the police headquarters, corner of Union and West Madison streets.

All persons needing food will be relieved by applying at the following places:

At the corner of Ann and West Washington; Illinois Central Railroad roundhouse.

M. S. R. R.—Twenty-second street station.

C. B. & Q. R. R.—Canal street depot.

St. L. & A. R. R.—Near Sixteenth street.

C. & N. W. R. R.—Corner of Kinzie and Canal streets.

All the public schoolhouses, and at nearly all the churches.

4. Citizens are requested to avoid passing through the burnt districts until the dangerous walls left standing can be levelled.

5. All saloons are ordered be closed at 9 P. M. every day for one week, under a penalty of forfeiture of license.

6. The Common Council have this day by ordinance fixed the price of bread at eight (8) cents per loaf of twelve ounces, and at the same rate for loaves of a less or greater weight, and affixed a penalty of ten dollars for selling, or attempting to sell, bread at a greater rate within the next ten days.

7. Any hackman, expressman, drayman or teamster charging more than the regular fare will have his license revoked.

All citizens are requested to aid in preserving the peace, good order and good name of our city.

October 10, 1870.   R. B. MASON, Mayor."

"*Proclamation.*—Whereas, in the providence of God, to whose will we humbly submit, a terrible calamity has befallen our city, which demands of us our best efforts for the preservation of order, and the relief of the suffering:

"Be it known, that the faith and credit of the city of Chicago is hereby pledged for the necessary expenses for the relief of the suffering. Public order will be preserved. The police and special police now being appointed, will be responsible for the maintenance of the peace and the protection of property.

"All officers and men of the Fire Department and Health Department will act as special policemen without further notice. The Mayor and Comptroller will give vouchers for all supplies furnished by the different relief committees. The headquarters of the city government will be at the Congregational Church, corner of West Washington and Ann streets. All persons are warned against any acts tending to endanger property. All persons caught in any depredation will be immediately arrested.

"With the help of God order and peace and private property shall be preserved. The City Government and committees of citizens pledge themselves to the community to protect them, and prepare the way for a restoration of public and private welfare.

"It is believed the fire has spent its force, and all will soon be well."

"R. B. MASON, Mayor.
GEO. TAYLOR, Comptroller.
By R. B. MASON.
CHARLES C. P. HOLDEN,
President Common Council.
T. B. BROWN, President Board of Police."

Gov. Hayes, who had been in Chicago for three days, assisting in the work, issued the following suggestions:

"To the People of Ohio:

It is believed by the best informed citizens here that many thousands of the sufferers must be provided with the necessaries of life during the whole winter. Let the efforts to raise contributions be energetically pushed. Money, food, flour, pork, clothing and other articles not perishable should be collected as rapidly as possible, especially money, fuel and flour."

(Signed)   "R. B. HAYES."

Lieut. Gen. Sheridan issued the following order:

"HEADQUARTERS MILITARY DIVISION OF MISSOURI,
CHICAGO, October 12.

"To His Honor the Mayor:

The preservation of the peace and good order of the city having been intrusted to me by your Honor, I am happy to state that no case of outbreak or disorder has been reported. No authenticated attempt at incendiarism has reached me, and the people of the city are calm, quiet and well-disposed, The force at my disposal is ample to maintain order, should it be necessary to protect the district devastated by fire. Still I would suggest to citizens not to relax in their watchfulness until the smouldering fires of the burned buildings are entirely extinguished.

   (Signed)   P. H. SHERIDAN, Lieut. General."

Mayor Mason issued the following appeal:

"Clothing and all protection from the cold will be needed through the winter as well as now. Send forward in as large quantities as possible. Collect money and hold it subject to our order. Send in provisions that will keep. Cooked meats nearly spoil before we can distribute them. Aid arrives liberally. Now we want to husband our resources as much as possible, for a long winter is before us, and the suffering will continue until our laboring classes are again enabled to sustain their families.

   (Signed)   R. B. MASON, Mayor."

The Gov. of Missouri, in his proclamation to the people, said:

"Let us unite likewise in the most generous emulation, and extend the largest possible aid to them in this the hour of misfortune. I, therefore, recommend all counties, cities, towns and other corporations, to all business and charitable associations, and to the community at large, to take immediate steps to organize relief committees to express the deep sorrow which Missouri feels at this overwhelming affliction. It was only yesterday that they were united with you in congratulating you on your own soil and in your own chief city, whilst their own homes were being destroyed. Let us respond by throwing open wide our own doors to those who are without shelter, by sending bread and raiment at once, and by such contributions ward off further distress, as the generous heart of our own great State will be proud to transmit, in recognition, too, of the warm and intimate feeling that has heretofore so closely bound our citizens together. I cannot forbear to extend to all who have been thus stricken down in the midst of an unbounded prosperity, the sincerest sympathy of Missouri's sons and daughters in their distress.

Done at the city of Jefferson this 9th day of October, A. D. 1871.

                B. GRATZ BROWN,
                Governor of Missouri."

The following dispatch was received Oct. 12th, by Archbishop Spaulding:

"To Archbishop Spaulding, Chicago:

The cathedral, six churches, orphan asylums, hospitals, House of the Good Shepherd, schools, charitable institutions and Bishop's house are in ruins. Over 100,000 people are homeless. I beg you for a general collection in your church next Sunday. The Superintendent of the Tel-graph Company asks you to report this message to the Prelates of the country as our wires are too crowded and few. Request all remittances to be to yourself.

            THOS. FOLEY, Bishop of Chicago."

And from one end of the Continent to the other arrived assurances of aid and support.

It may be interesting in the future as a reference to know some of the prominent towns and cities which contributed to the fund for relief of sufferers. It would prove an impossibility to publish all these who poured into the Treasury their small or great contributions; thousands of individuals halved their finances and prayed Providence to help the stricken people. North, south, east, west—across the prairies or across the ocean—across mountain steeps or in the radiant valley—all came forward to prove that Charity was yet an attribute of man's nature. Here are the prominent ones:

City St. Louis	$ 50,000
Citizens of St. Louis	70,000
Pittsfield, Massachusetts	5,000
J. M. Gould, Santa Fe	425
Boston, Massachusetts (various contributions)	400,000
Kansas City, Missouri	10,000
Pittsburgh, Pennsylvania—citizens	200,000
City Council	100,000
Hamilton, Ontario	2,000
Patterson, New Jersey	7,000
First installment of Urbana, Ohio	1,000
Buffalo, New York	100,000
Indianapolis, Indiana	40,000
First National Bank, Greencastle, Indiana	2,000
Cincinnati, Ohio	225,000
Leavenworth, Kansas	10,000
Collin, Randall & Co., New York	1,000
Quincy, Illinois	15,000
Montreal Board of Trade	10,000
Meadville, Pennsylvania	3,000
Fort Wayne, Indiana	2,000
Jeffersonville, Indiana	1,000
Portland, Maine	20,000
Baltimore *American* subscription list	10,000
Watertown, Mass., in addition to the fifty cases of clothing	1,000
Rondout, New York	2,000
San Francisco Stock Exchange, in gold	8,000
Adams Express Company	10,000
Alex Martin	2,000
James Roosevelt, Hyde Park, New York	1,000
Lawrence, Kansas	10,000
Joseph Barrett & Co., Boston	1,000
Amsterdam, New York	8,000
D. S. Morgan & Co., London, England	5,000
Drexel, Morgan & Co., New York	5,000
City of Rochester and Monroe county, New York	70,000
Port Byron, New York	250
San Francisco subscriptions	25,000

Which they intend to add	$75,000
Standard Life Insurance Company, New York	1,000
Waynesville, Ohio	2,000
Toronto, Ontario, (gold)	10,000
N. E. Dodge, London, England	10,000
Citizens of Missouri	20,000
City of St. Joseph	3,000
County of Missouri	18,000
Syracuse, New York	25,000
Jeffersonville, Indiana	1,000
Police Department, Washington, D. C.	600
New Orleans, subscriptions incomplete	10,000
Mechanics Trade Exchange, Brooklyn	1,000
Haverhill, Massachusetts	10,000
Shaneetown, Illinois	5,000
Guardian Mutual Life Insurance Company, New York	1,000
Topeka, Kansas	5,000
Louisville	200,000
Naragansett Steamship Co	1,000
Oswego	12,000
Newark	30,000
Trenton	17,000
Rome, N. Y.	2,500
Palmyra, New York	3,000
Robinson, Shade & Co., New York	500
Employees of the Department of the Interior, Washington, D. C.	4,000
Manufacturers and Builders Fire Insurance Company	5,000
North British and Mercantile Fire Insurance Company, London	5,000
Employees of the Engraving and Printing Bureau, Washington	1,400
Ohio Falls Car Company, Jeffersonville, Indiana	1,000
Philadelphia	130,000
Whitman & Field, manufacturing company, Shelburg Mass	500
Jacksonville, Illinois	500
Protestant Episcopal General Convention, in session at Baltimore	2,000
Laflin Powder Company	1,000
Greencastle, Indiana, council appropriation	2,000
Manchester, New Hampshire	15,000
Henry Fawn, of New Haven, Connecticut	5,000
Terre Haute, Indiana	10,000
Bloomington, Illinois	15,000
Decatur, Illinois	5,000
Green Castle citizens	1,200
New York Gold Exchange	12,000
Alexander T. Stewart, New York	50,000
Erie, Pennsylvania	15,000

Detroit	$30,000
Baltimore	200,000
Concord, N. H	7,400
Lancaster, Pa	25,000
Mason City, Illinois	260
Danville, Illinois	1,750
Chelsea, Massachusetts	260
New York Cotton Exchange	5,000
Lafayette, Indiana	10,000
London, (Canada)	2,000
Lynn, Massachusetts	5,000
Keokuk, Iowa	6,350
Commercial Exchange Philadelphia	10,000
General Julius White, Evansville, Illinois	500
Industaial Exhibition Fair, Buffalo	6,000
Paris, Illinois	1,000

Up to Saturday night the 14th, the following figures were recognized as being a fair estimate of the subscriptions already raised:

LONDON, ENG., LIST OF SUBSCRIPTIONS.

	Amount.
Corporation of London	$ 5,000
Private citizens of London	35,000
Messrs. Baring, of London	5,000
Messrs. Rothschild of London	5,000
Messrs. Morgan, of London	5,000
Messrs. Brown, Shepley & Co., of London	5,000
Great Western Railway, of Canada, London	5,000
Grand Trunk Railway, of Canada, London	5,000
Liverpool Chamber of Commerce	2,000
American Chamber of Commerce, of Liverpool	1,300
Total (gold)	$73,800

Recapitulation.

Total to October 12 inclusive	$1,375,880.00
Received at New York *Herald* office	1,079.45
At Chamber of Commerce	48,266.15
At Stock Exchange	2,825.00
At Cotton Exchange	1,250.00
At Produce Exchange	3,314.00
Brooklyn	125,000.00
At Grocers' Board of Trade	33,053.00
Hardware trade	15,111.50
Fourth avenue and Twenty-eighth street	120.00
Union, Adams & Co	85.00
Miscellaneous city collections	47,262.20
Other cities (including Canada)	454,500.00
Europe	73,800.00
Clothing, &c., estimated	600,000.00

Hon E. C. Ingersoll, on behalf of the Illinois State Association, Washington, D. C., had forwarded by special messenger $3,727, and provisions, and sent more the next day. Omaha also raised a fund, whilst many of those mentioned added largely to these contributions during the past week. Food and clothing arrived in abundance—hundreds of cars conveyed it thither—whilst it was rumored in many cases parties secured the charity of committees, and after obtaining articles or passes on railways sold them; such cases, happily, were few and far between; a bitter lesson had been taught—let us hope it benefitted thousands who seldom before appeared thankful for the protecting hand of Providence.

It is Wednesday. The people desired to blot out the past—rub the old reckoning off the slate and commence anew. The *Tribune* had already furnished admirable reports, and we are indebted to the able reporters for the annexed pithy information.

Owing to the fact that the North Division was accessible only across Kinzie and Division street bridges and through the dark Lasalle street tunnel, passage through which was forbidden to teams, the people who yesterday visited that quarter of the city were chiefly those who had formerly lived there, and were hunting for shreds and scraps of property, or were trying to find the places where they had once lived and the property they had once owned. The great rush of visitors on foot and in carriages was across Randolph, Lake, and Madison street bridges into the South Division. People from the West Side, from lower down on the South Division, and strangers who had just reached the city, all turned in that direction, and wandered from point to point, often puzzled as to their whereabouts, and seeking in vain for old and familiar landmarks. The principal business in the South Division yesterday was the digging out of safes from the smoking buildings in which they were buried. Several persons were shrewd enough to make that a business, and they succeeded in getting all the work they wanted. A few ropes, shovels, levers, and occasionally a little water, made up the stock in trade. Some had gotten out their fourth safe by 2 o'clock, and were hunting around in search of other jobs. Many of the safes came up in excellent condition, while others were the most deplorable wrecks. One of Herring's lay on River street near Rush street bridge, the interior wood-work gone, and all the papers charred. The Harris safe of Deeffenbacher who is in the tobacco business on Water street, was also found to be worthless. It contained papers valued at about $40,000. Others were taken out which had apparently passed unharmed through the fiery trial. Others which had been opened were found to be in excellent condition. All things considered, they have stood rather better than was expected. Many which have been gotten out were not opened for a day or two, until they got somewhat cooled off. McVicker was working to get out his and they were also laboring on one or two other buildings.

Another business was started by a man in a cart, who drove down Randolph to the lake displaying a sign "Removal signs painted here," so that persons desirous of sticking up upon the ruins of their stores a notice of the places at which they intended to reopen business could do so. Nothing strikes the eye more favorably, in going near the South Side, than the great number of these little Bulletin Boards, which have been roughly lettered off with notices of removal, generally to Wabash avenue or to West Canal or Randolph streets, and they give abundant proof that the energies of the merchants have not been crushed out by the catastrophe which has befallen them.

On crossing the river at Madison street there is a vacancy on the north side of the street and nothing else, and with a few noticeable exceptions there remain but insignificant and one-story relics of once first-class buildings. Law's coal yard on the south side of the street is on fire, and even where the flames have not broken out, the white smoke is pouring out at a fearful rate. Some of it may, however, be saved, by the liberal and constant use of water. Beyond there, going east, there is practically nothing until the relics of the Otis Block are reached, at the corner of LaSalle and Madison. Just to the south on LaSalle, the walls of the Arcade building, which was immediately in the rear of the Farwell Hall, remain comparatively intact.

The *Tribune* was, by several hours, the last building in Chicago to survive the general destruction, and its magnificent fire-proof building was the last to succumb, although it had been surrounded by fire on two sides for about four hours. The building was a perfect model of architectural elegance, and had been constructed throughout with reference to safety and durability in case of fire. The ceilings were of corrugated iron, resting upon wrought iron "I" beams, while every partition wall in the entire structure was of brick. It was, in all respects, one of the most absolutely "fire-proof buildings ever erected. That is, it was fire-proof up to the date of its destruction. It was completed in April, 1869, at a cost of $225,000, and its contents were fully $100,000 more. Relying upon the integrity of their edifice, the *Tribune* Company had taken no insurance, although they have little cause to regret this neglect. In the corner of the first floor was the counting-room and business office, with a fire-proof vault for the safe keeping of records, valuables, etc. On the Madison and Dearborn street fronts were elegant stores of various kinds, all filled with stocks of goods. In the basement were the boilers and engines, two of Hoe's eight-cylinder presses, several folding machines, large quantities of printing paper, and a vast collection of miscellaneous machinery, tools, appliances and material necessary to the carrying on of a great newspaper.

The second and third floor of the building were devoted to offices, all of which were occupied. On the fourth floor were the editorial and composing rooms, all superbly fitted up.

As stated above, the building withstood the storm for several hours, and it was not until 10 o'clock on Monday forenoon, six hours after it had seemingly escaped, that it was reached from the eastward from McVicker's Theatre. The interior woodwork and combustible material was consumed at once, but the floors and walls generally remained intact, although all were so blistered, cracked and twisted as to be almost worthless for future use.

In the private office of the business manager on the ground floor was a relic of the siege of Paris, a Krupp shell, which fired by the heat, and, exploding tore a wide breach in the walls in its vicinity.

A search among the ruins reveals the gratifying fact that the two eight cyliner presses, valued at about $60,000, are not seriously damaged. It is believed that both can be restored to service at a small cost. The four turtles are also all right, including the two which were on the press when the men got scared and left. The Post Office building also stood well, its wall being intact, and its roof is not entirely gone. It can probably be repaired. At the northeast corner of State and Madison Street stands, comparatively uninjured, the unfinished brown stone front which was erecting there.

Since there was nothing in it to burn, its front shows very few traces of scorching. The derrick which stood in front of it has fallen against one of the upper windows, but has broken nothing. Of the magnificent block occupied by the Western News Company, S. C. Griggs & Co., only a fragment remains; the southwestern corner of the wall rising to the second story height.

At the corner of Washington and State stands the building which has unquestionably best stood the trial by fire—the First National Bank. Its walls seem perfectly safe, although the floors have suffered. Field, King & Co. retain their office in the basement, where Robert Law is also installed, and if the room were only swept out, and the pieces of paper removed, no one could percieve that anything had gone wrong overhead. Unquestionably the comparatively slight repairs will put it in order again, and it will serve as a nucleus for building in that quarter. Turning east into Washington street, the way is encumbered with the limestone blocks which once formed part of Field, Leiter & Co.'s store, and which were thrown there when the building was blown up. Mixed up with brick, telegraph wire, and other debris, it makes a mass of rubbish which ought to have impeded the progress of the flames, but did not do so. Down in the basement, piles of dry goods are still burning and emitting an unpleasant stench. On the opposite side of Washington, the photographers' places and the other stores have vanished, while Drake's Block is decidedly more of a ruin than it was a year ago. The question of the removal of the Second Presbyterian congregation has been eternally settled. The hard limestone walls of the church resisted very well, notwithstanding the slight amount of bitumen in them. The southern tower remains, and the walls are all upon a level with a point just above the great front windows. The experience of this fire has been rather unfavorable to the softer limestones from Lemont, and has shown that, after all, a thick wall of good brick will stand as well, and resist the action of the flames, as well as any stone that is used here, excepting granite. The effect of the fire upon the Athens marble has been remarkable. In some places the stone has disappeared altogether. In others, such as the LaSalle street front of the Court House, it has been gnawed and eaten away, or fallen off in great flakes. The sandstone and granite may not have been exposed to so intense a flame, but they certainly stood very well. The *Tribune* building was badly scorched, but the stone was not materially injured. Dearborn Park has been taken possession of by Keen & Cooke and Lord & Smith, while right across the way, on the Base Ball Ground, the fence surrounding which, has been wiped out, is a sign to the effect that parties wanting room on public grounds must go to C. B. Farwell, at the corner of Thirteenth and Michigan Avenue. The American Merchants' Union Express have obtained possession of a part of the ground, including the diamond, and Gray Brothers have hold of the north fifty feet of the base ball lot. C. T. Bolles, dealer in stoves, has also begun running up a small booth. The ground is covered with piles of lumber, and bears a more striking resemblance to Cheyenne in its incipient days, than anything else. The iron stores of J. V. Ayer, Hall, Kimbark & Co., and others, on Michigan avenue, between Lake and Randolph streets, present a curious spectacle. They are filled with iron, twisted, distorted, and bent out of all shape, while across the street the immense iron rafters and beams have been dealt with in a most extraordinary fashion. In many of these stores, and, indeed, generally in the wholesale warehouses, the fires were still burning, and, of course, no attempt was made to put them out. The sidewalks of the Union Depot, thick and strong, are still standing, but the offices in the rear have caved in, except at the northeast corner, where one tall pinnacle remains. The building occupied by the Chicago, Burlington & Quincy and Michigan Central Roads has been gutted, but the walls are still partially standing. The Michigan Central Freight Depot has also been cleaned out, though the walls are up to the spring of the roof. Quite an amount of sugar was lost here. Just south of this depot half a dozen cars were burned, the trucks yet remaining on the track. Near by was a car which had just run up from Tolono, on the Illinois Central Road, filled with provisions, generally bread and cheese, some of which were issued on the spot to hungry men who happened to be near by. The trains of the Illinois and Michigan Central stop just in front of the old depot.

At the head of the slip which lies just west of Elevator A was the Providence, one of the five Amoskeag steamers which came on from Pittsburg, and the Phœnix, of Detroit, engaged in pumping water through a long line of hose, past the ruins of the Massasoit House, to wet down the ruins beyond. Another engine was near the Central Elevator, playing upon the immense hill of wheat, which was in Elevator A, and which was bursting in little puffs of smoke all over its surface. It cannot be very easily extinguished, and all that is expected is that it will gradually smoulder away. The Marine Hospital, an old and substantial building, is in very good order, comparatively. Of course the inner walls and the roof are gone, but the outside walls have stood it very well.

It is not possible to ascertain as yet the entire amount of shipping lost along the river and the branches. The Navarino, however, a new vessel belonging to Captain Goodrich, was lying off Goodrich's docks, and tried to run out, but stuck just beyond and behind Rathbone's stove manufactory on the north side of the river and sunk there, her boilers now been just visible. Eight or nine schooners and brigs were also caught near the mouth of the river, and burned to the water's edge. From Rush street bridge east, on the north bank, the coal heaps are in a blaze. Rathbone's place, and all immediately east of that, are safe. Rush street bridge itself is a hopeless and utter wreck, as is also the state one. The great wholesale houses on River street have been completely swept away, and nothing is left to give an idea of what was once done there, except that in some places there is iron, and in another a quantity of lime which has been effectually ruined by the heat. Along here were one or two burnt safes, and as many disgusted, but uncomplaining, owners.

Water street is done for, and State street, from the bridge to the First National Bank, is in the same condition. At the northwest corner of Clark and Water streets, one corner of a building is standing, but ought to be taken down as soon as possible.

The Sherman House has totally disappeared, and the remains in that part of the city are so scanty as to make it almost impossible to identify localities. On many of these streets women and children were engaged in collecting scraps of iron and all kinds of rubbish from the still hot buildings. Some boys had found on Water street a lot of China doll heads, scorched but unbroken, and were carrying them off as relics. Three men were also moving up the river in a row boat, intent on doing a little wrecking, if they got a chance. The burnt district is now so thoroughly patrolled by regulars that there need be no apprehensions as to the perpetration of more thefts.

The old part of the Court House is gutted, but the wings have stood very well, and the first floors are safe.

The walls of the first storey of the Board of Trade building are still standing.

The effect of the fire upon the different kinds of pavement has been very curious. As a matter of course the stone stood it the best, but the large cobble stones split in many instances. The asphalt laid in the Court House square was not injured at all. The new cylindrical block pavement on Clark street stood very well, except in one place, where the tar kettle had run over and a great strip was eaten out. The tar was gone from between the blocks where the gravel had not been laid on it, but the blocks were generally uninjured. The pavements o Madison, Randolph and the other streets were in much better condition than was expected. They were badly honeycombed in many places, and sometimes twisted and upheaved, but can be generally repaired. The rails of the street cars were in many cases badly sprung, but the sills are uninjured.

The South side road will have its track all repaired in a day or two, and it will take the West Side companies but a short time to relay their's. There is considerable *debris* in many of the streets, but the work of clearing has already begun. The sidewalks, wood and stone, have gone, the large limestone blocks. Along the South Branch Lind's building stands, and the *Evening Mail* has its office there. The coal yards south to Madison street are still burning, and will do so despite the water, with the exception of the one at Randolph street bridge. The LaSalle street tunnel is in perfect order, but on account of the of the darkness there, and the fear of accidents, no carriages were allowed to go through. There are no records in there at present, and, if any were stored there, they have been destroyed.

The real headquarters of the order-preserving force of the city is now at No. 569 Wabash avenue, where General Phil Sheridan has established his headquarters, in the house formerly occupied by the Phœnix Club. Here the head of the city has planted a pine table and entertained his numerous visitors.

The force at the General's command, in addition to the city regular and special police, consists of seven companies of regulars and six of volunteers. The former are from Omaha and other western points, and are all camped upon the site of the Ball Park, on Michigan avenue. To them, as the most trustworthy and vigilant force at hand, has been entrusted the care of the South Side burnt district, reaching from Harrison street to the main river, in this space is at present the wealth and treasure of the city yet in safes, and in most cases buried in the ruins. The number of thieves now known to be in the city, and the presumption that they will make the safes their objective point render this disposition of the troops the most prudent one possible. The orders to the sentinels Tuesday were of the strictest possible kind, and it will be wonderful indeed if the ruffianly element shall triumph.

The militia are from Bloomington, Springfield and Champaign in Illinois, and number six companies in all. They arrived in the city on Tuesday morning under orders from Adjutant General Dilger, and were immediately stationed in different parts of the city to repress pillage, and generally to preserve order. Two companies were placed on the corner of Prairie avenue and Twenty-second street, and were as fine looking men as one could see. They were from the Illinois Industrial University at

Champaign, and a heartier, healthier, more intelligent set of men would be hard to find.

One other company of militia was stationed at the corner of Canal and Wilson streets, for the protection of the thoroughly affrighted residents of that portion of the city.

Another company was placed at Halstead street, with headquarters at the railroad station, on Twelfth street.

The North side did not need much military protection in its dilapidated condition, and was abundantly guarded by two militia companies stationed at Lincoln Park.

A part of the Champaign company was also at the corner of Randolph and Elizabeth streets.

General Sheridan seemed satisfied that the city was perfectly safe under the protection already at hand; but, in order to assure this, more troops will arrive shortly. Three additional companies of regulars were expected last night, and ten companies more will arrive to-day, making a force large enough to keep in order all the roughs in the United States.

WEDNESDAY, and the smoke commenced to clear away; men were braver, truer to themselves, more collected, more energetic. The Corn Exchange members had secured a large, dark-looking hall at 51 Canal street, and there the question was mooted as to the best course to be pursued with regard to business on hand—whether to repudiate or declare all transactions "off," or to await the settlement of insurances and opening of banks. Men were certainly downhearted, and yet they spoke brave words —and they meant what they said; "Chicago must rise," "Chicago is our city," and they were justly proud in being able to feel that the world's sympathy was with them in this awful hour of doubt and affliction.

Little printing offices were commencing to distribute, and these little ones now had the upper hand; neglected workers who had feared the sheriff and dodged the baliff, put on their best clothes, and in some cases sold out for satisfactory prices to those daily publishers who were short of sorts, or perhaps "sort of short." The *Post* came out—the *Tribune* came out—the *Journal* came out—the *Republican* came out, but save and except the *Tribune* and perhaps the *Journal*, it was a weakly "come." No men deserve more credit than the journalistic refugees of Canal and adjacent streets; they slept in old wagons one night, and had rented offices and secured a few hard looking "cases," and set to work; verily they were obliged to work in order to set, for matters generally were in a demoralized condition. Boys took advantage of limited issues of the paper and charged 25 cents, 50 cents and even $1.00 per copy for the *Tribune* and other papers; the proprietors grumbled, but the boys—for these city Arabs were now the pompous and wealthy classes—maintained their prices and formed a ring, so that no youth dare dispose of his newspapers at an unfair figure—or rather at a fair, honest figure.

The following, from the Governor of Michigan, was read with much pleasure by the community at large:—

"The City of Chicago, in the neighboring State of Illinois, has been visited in the providence of Almighty God with a calamity almost unequalled in the annals of history. A large portion of that beautiful and most prosperous city has been reduced to ashes and is now in ruins. Many millions of dollars in property, the accumulation of years of industry and toil, have been swept away, almost in a moment. The rich have been reduced to penury, the poor have lost the little they possessed, and many thousands of people rendered homeless and houseless, and are now without the absolute necessaries of life. I, therefore, earnestly call upon the citizens of every portion of Michigan to take immediate measures for alleviating the pressing wants of that fearfully afflicted city by collecting and forwarding to the Mayor, or proper authorities of Chicago, supplies of food as well as liberal collections of money. Let this sore calamity of our neighbors remind us of the uncertainty of earthly possessions, and that when one member suffers all the members should suffer with it. I cannot doubt that the whole people of the State will most gladly, most promptly, and most liberally respond to this urgent demand upon their sympathy, but no words of mine can plead so strongly as the calamity itself.

HENRY P. BALDWIN,
Governor of Michigan.

The Secretary of War telegraphed:—

War Department,
Washington, D. C; October 11, 1871.

To Lieutenant General Sheridan, Chicago, Ill.

I agree with you, that the fire is a National calamity. The sufferers have the sincere sympathy of the nation. Officers at the Depots at St. Louis and Jeffersonville, and elsewhere, have been ordered to forward supplies liberally and promptly.

WILLIAM W. BELKNAP,
Secretary of War.

To add to this, Robert Bonner, of the *Ledger*, telegraphed to Mr. J. Walsh of the American News Company, that he could draw upon him for $10,000 to be used in relieving members of the press—whilst the manly tone of the press sustained and fortified many through the dark shadows of the hour.

Then news arrived from London, (England,) that in response to the call of the American Minister for a meeting to express sympathy and provide relief for the people of Chicago, over 400 American and English gentlemen assembled at the Lengham Hotel. One of the speakers drew a parallel between the conflagration of Chicago and the great fire in London. Great enthusiasm was evident from the opening, and the meeting needed no stimulus. Everybody was eager to contribute, and within a short time from the opening of the list £1000 was subscribed *viva voce*. Conspicuous among the subscribers were several Confederates, who requested that their names should not appear. A few merchants of Chicago, whose establishments were destroyed by fire, also offered their contributions amid the cheers of the assemblage. Resolutions expressing the deepest sympathy for the sufferers, and pledging further aid, were adopted by acclamation. A committee was appointed, with J. S. Morgan and Gen. Schenck at the head, to produce additional subscriptions in London and throughout the kingdom, and there was every reason to expect that a large sum would be raised. Expressions of sympathy were received by telegraph and by mail from all parts of the country, and read by the chairman. Among those present were Hon. A. Curtin, Minister to Russia, General A. E. Burnside, General J. G. Barnard, Hon. Hugh McCullough, Messrs. Morgan and Woodhull, of the American Legation, Adam Badeau, Consul General at London, Wm. E. Dodge, of New York, John I. Cisco, of New York, Messrs. Munn, Storring, Habicht, of Clews, Habicht & Co., Bowles, Randolph Clay, George Wilkes, Boughton, the artist, John Healy, and Thaddeus Hyatt. Many eminent Englishmen also attended the meeting and manifested their interest in its objects liberally by word and deed. Such charity kindly expressed nerved the sufferers—who had now not only to think for themselves but also for the poor—and as the news of subscriptions—announced above—was received, proud men wept, and manly hearts yearned to prove that a world's sympathy was appreciated. Men said it was Christlike. Let us hope it will bear fruits and make a more than lasting impression on them, in the future.

We shall pass over the frightful scenes observable in visiting the morgue, where over eighty unfortunate and almost unrecognizable bodies were laid out; some had been suffocated, trampled to death; a few had fallen, others been taken from ruins, but hundreds more must still remain in the ruins.

THURSDAY DAWNED and now that telegrams were received and messengers arrived it became known that a majority of the insurance companies were anxious to settle all claims in full; such announcements as the following creating intense excitement, as thousands had anticipated advantage being taken, and an apportionment of 10 or 15 per cent being declared:—

The Liverpool and London and Globe Insurance Co's. telegraphed their agents:—

NEW YORK, Oct. 12, 1871.

"Chicago losses probably under two and a half millions. The Directors in New York are authorized to draw on London. Charge higher rates."

ALFRED PELL, Manager.

The Hanover Fire Insurance Company telegraphed:—

NEW YORK, Oct. 12, 1871.

"In view of the intense feeling existing relative to the standing of Fire Insurance Companies, we take pleasure in saying to our friends and the public, that we have telegraphed to our agents to draw at sight in settlement of all losses by the Chicago fire as fast as they are adjusted. After the payment of which we shall have our Capital intact and a surplus of over $125,000, leaving our Cash Assets over $525,000.

B. S. WALCOTT, President.

I. REMSEN LANE, Secretary.

The New York managers of the North British and Mercantile Insurance Company received the following kindly and generous cable telegram from Mr. J. W. Cater, Chairman of the London Board:—

"Subscribe $5,000 for the Chicago sufferers. Settle all losses promptly. Draw, at three days sight."

"The assets of this company in the United States, amounting to over $1,300,000, will not be touched in the payment of losses in Chicago."

WM. CONNER,
CHAS. E. WHITE, } Associate Managers.
WM. P. BLAGDEN.

The managers of the Niagara Fire Insurance Company issued the following:—

NEW YORK, Oct. 10, 1871.

"The losses of this company by the recent fires in Chicago cannot exceed a quarter of a million of dollars, which will be promptly paid as the various claims shall be adjusted.

This Company will have remaining more than a million of dollars of good assets, as a guarantee to its policy holders."

H. A. HOWE, President.

P. NOTMAN, Vice President and Secretary.

The Jefferson Insurance Company, (New York):—

TRINITY BUILDING, No. 111 Broadway,
NEW YORK, Oct. 10, 1871.

To the public: This Company having no out-of-town Agents, and doing business only at this Office, is not materially affected by the great fire in Chicago, the entire amount at risk there being only $17,500."

SAMUEL E. BELCHER, President.

The following was issued by the Andes Insurance Company

CHICAGO, October 11, 1871.

"To the Andes Insurance Co.:
Andes losses will not exceed $300,000."

E. B. RYAN, Agent.

"The Andes is solvent and very strong, and has already commenced paying the Chicago losses."

J. B. BENNETT, President.

The "Commercial" agency announced:
"The Company has only $5,000 at risk in Chicago."

M. V. B. POWLER, President.

The Columbia Fire Insurance Company announced:
"In reply to the numerous inquiries as to our losses by the disastrous fire in Chicago, we have no agency there, and but one risk of three thousand dollars."

ALFRED DOUGLAS, President.

The International Insurance Company, of New York, stated:
"In view of the general alarm created by the insurance losses consequent upon the recent fire in Chicago, it may be proper to state, on behalf of this company, that, if all our risks in the burnt district should prove total losses, they will not absorb much more than our net reserve, leaving our capital and assets $800,000.

GEO. W. SAVAGE, President.

The following dispatch was received from the office of the American Central Fire Insurance Company of St. Louis, Mo.:

ST. LOUIS, Mo., October 12, 1871.

"Messrs. Wm. H. Cheppu & Co., Managers of the New York Branch American Central Fire Insurance Company, 163 Broadway, New York:
Our loss in Chicago is $300,000, which will be paid at once without interruption to business, twenty per cent call made.

GEO. T. CRAM, Secretary.

From the Ætna of Hartford, largely interested, the following arrived:
"A telegram from E. P. Dorr, General Agent of this Company at Buffalo, says the Ætna Company pays all losses promptly at Chicago and elsewhere, and continues all branches of business at all points as heretofore."

GEO. W. WOLVERTON, Agent Marine Department.

The annexed telegram was from the underwriters' agency:

NEW YORK, October 10, 1871.

Alex. McLane, Agent, 101 Griswold street, Detroit:
"At a meeting of the Germania, Hanover, Niagara and Republic Insurance Companies of New York, composing the "Underwriters' Agency," held this day, due preparations were made to pay immediately upon adjustments, all losses incurred at the fire in Chicago; after doing which, the capitals of all the companies will remain unimpaired, and have a surplus of over half a million dollars, leaving the gross cash assets of the "Underwriters' Agency" over two and one-half millions of dollars.

ALEX. STODDART, General Agent.

The Pacific Company, of San Francisco, telegraphed their agent that the losses would be fully $1,000,000, and they had levied an assessment of seventy-five per cent, which would meet all demands and leave a surplus.

The Agents of various companies issued a notice that the following Companies represented by them can pay all losses sustained by the late fires in Chicago, after which their respective capitals will remain unimpaired:

"Detroit Fire and Marine Insurance Company; City Fire Insurance Company, Hartford; Pacific Insurance Company, San Francisco."

PELTIER & BELANGER.

The following card was published by the Agents:
"Official advices show that the losses of the Lamar Fire Inurance Company, of New York, will not consume the surplus. The Merchants Insurance Company, of Providence, had no Agency in Chicago—losses by insurance, $13,000 only."

WM. S. TALMAN & Co., Agents.

The People's Fire Insurance Company, of Worcester, Mass., said:

"The People's Fire Insurance Company, of Worcester, Massachusetts, is perfectly solvent, and all their losses at Chicago and elsewhere will be paid promptly on demand."

AUG. N. CUNIER, Secretary.

The Williamsburg City Fire Insurance Company:

"October 11, 1871.

At a meeting of the Committee on Claims and Losses, convened by the President, a resolution was passed unanimously authorising him to telegraph to Chicago that all losses sustained by the Company, as soon as adjusted, would be settled by sight drafts without deducting the sixty days' interest."

EDMUND DRIGGS, President.

The Firemen's Fund Company:

"This Company has no Agencies; will suffer loss in Chicago to the extent of two-thirds of its surplus, leaving capital unharmed. The President is now in Chicago prepared to give sight drafts for all losses as soon as adjusted."

JAMES D. SPARKMAN, President.

The Lamar Insurance Company, of New York, said:

"The Agents of the Company at Chicago telegraphed that the losses by the late fire, after a careful examination, will be less than $200,000, thus leaving the capital whole, with a handsome surplus, and the Company are prepared to pay on demand all losses as soon as adjusted."

W. R. MACDIARMID, Secretary.

The Corn Exchange Insurance Company (N. Y.) announced:

"In reply to the numerous inquiries as to our losses by the Chicago fire, and to refute the many false rumors in regard to the standing of this Company, we have to state that we have taken no risks in that city since December, 1870, and the whole amount of the unexpired risks within the burnt district is but sixty-one thousand dollars, all of which is re-insured."

E. J. LOWBER, President.

The U. S. Branch of Imperial Fire Insurance Company announced:

"Our net losses will not exceed $125,000, by the Chicago fire."

E. W. CROWELL, Resident Manager.

The Ætna, Hartford and Phœnix were largely interested, and the announcement that they would pay their losses in full, gave wide satisfaction. Further telegrams were as follows:—

HARTFORD, Conn., October 13.—The following circular was issued:

OFFICE OF THE CONNECTICUT FIRE INSURANCE COMPANY,
HARTFORD, Conn., October 13, 1871.

Definite information just received from Chicago, places our losses at so high a figure that we are obliged to suspend business until the question of reorganization shall be settled. (Signed)

JOHN B. ELDREDGE, President.

BOSTON, October 13.—It is announced that a guarantee fund has been raised by the directors of the New England Fire Insurance Company, and it will continue business.

LONDON, October 12.—The losses of the Liverpool Insurance Companies by the Chicago fire are estimated at £120,000.

The following notice to the policy-holders and stockholders of the Commerce Insurance Company, of Albany, has been issued:

I have just received (midnight, October 13) telegraphic advices from our General Agent, who is in Chicago, which convinces me that our loss will not exceed $450,000, and probably will be adjusted for less. As our assets amount to over $650,000, there remains $200,000 if not more, to protect outstanding policies.

(Signed)

G. A. VAN ALLEN, Vice President.

The banks issued cards stating their being prepared to pay 15 per cent on all deposits in a few days, and promising prompt arrangement of claims and liabilities—

one bank stating that it would pay ½ dollar for dollar after the lapse of a few weeks. Then came a statement of the position of all insurance companies—sent privately to leading men, but now published in full—it will there be seen that many companies doing a large business, by reason of lacking judgment, were straw corporations, and it is to be hoped that when the National Convention of Insurance Companies takes place, stringent State action will be advised, to prohibit the reckless and careless conduct of insurance business.

New York Companies.

Name.	Capital.	Gross Assets Jan. 1, 1871.	Losses.
Ætna, City	$ 300,000	$ 442,709	$250,000
Adriatic, City	200,000	246,120	5,000
Agricultural, Watertown	100,000	550,848	....
Albany, Albany	150,000	264,973	....
Albany City, Albany	200,000	397,646	Suspended
American, P., City	200,000	741,405	25,000
American Exchange, City	200,000	274,350	15,000
Arctic, City	250,000	290,482	Nothing
Astor, City	250,000	405,571	....
Atlantic, City	300,000	556,179	250,000
Beekman, City	200,000	261,351	Suspended
Brewers' and Maisters', City	200,000	220,000	Nothing
Broadway, City	200,000	370,004	Nothing
Brooklyn, L. I., City	153,000	204,444	Nothing
Buffalo City, Buffalo	200,000	370,934	....
Buffalo Fire and Marine	204,222	473,577	....
Buffalo German, Buffalo	200,000	270,081	5,000
Capital City, Albany	200,000	293,706	....
Citizens' P., City	300,000	684,768	25,000
City, City	210,000	466,069	Nothing
Clinton, City	250,000	392,704	2,000
Columbia, City	300,000	451,532	3,000
Commerce, Albany	400,000	692,377	10,000
Commerce Fire, City	200,000	249,372	15,000
Commercial, City	200,000	306,002	5,000
Continental, P., City	500,000	2,538,038	1,000,000
Corn Exchange, City	300,000	398,936	Nothing
Eagle, City	500,000	505,440	Nothing
Empire City, City	200,000	266,409	Nothing
Excelsior, City	200,000	325,724	Suspended
Exchange, City	170,000	183,959	....
Farmers' Joint Stock, Meridan	100,000	193,675	Nothing
Firemen's, City	204,000	350,961	15,000
Firemen's Fund, City	150,000	173,577	....
Firemen's Trust	150,000	226,369	5,000
Fulton, City (suspended)	200,000	363,002	Ad'ts 700,000
Gebhard, City	200,000	250,892	Nothing
Germania, City	500,000	1,077,849	250,000
Glens Falls, Glens Falls	200,000	571,123	10,000
Globe, City	200,000	315,738	Nothing
Greenwich, City	200,000	429,872	Nothing
Guardian, City	200,000	279,088	40,000
Hamilton, City	150,000	260,135	Nothing
Hanover, P., City	400,000	700,325	230,000
Hoffman, City	200,000	235,242	10,000
Holland, Purchase, Batavia	100,000	171,495	....
Home, City	2,500,000	4,578,008	Over 2,000,000
Hope, City	150,000	214,241	Nothing
Howard, P., City	500,000	783,351	275,000
Humboldt, City	200,000	234,186	10,000
Importers' and Traders', City	200,000	302,889	22,500
International, City	500,000	1,529,454	400,000
Irving, City	200,000	322,745	Refuses risks
Jefferson, City	200,010	411,155	47,500
Kings County, City	150,000	282,575	35,000
Knickerbocker, City	280,000	394,079	Nothing
Lafayette, L. I., City	150,000	214,757	7,500
Lamar, City	300,000	551,402	200,000
Lenox, City	150,000	240,801	30,000
Long Island, P., City	200,000	384,932	....
Lorillard, P., City	1,500,000	1,715,969	815,000
Manhattan, City	500,000	1,467,758	Suspended
Manufacturers and Builders, City	200,000	236,409	Nothing
Market, P., City	200,000	704,024	Suspended
Mechanics' L. I., City	150,000	218,047	22,500

Name.	Capital.	Gross Assets Jan. 1, 1871.	Losses.
Mechanics' and Traders' City	$200,000	$460,002	....
Mercantile, City	200,000	273,399	100,000
Merchants, City	200,000	442,090	15,000
Metropolitan, City	300,000	369,434	Nothing
Montauk, L. I., City	150,000	254,405	Nothing
Nassau, L. I., City	200,000	391,518	....
National, City	200,000	232,671	15,000
New Amsterdam, P., City	300,000	432,628	40,000
N. Y. Bowery, City	300,000	562,835	Nothing
N. Y. Central, Union Springs	100,000	201,864	....
New York Equitable	210,000	423,063	Nothing
New York Fire	200,000	392,278	15,000
Niagara, City	1,000,000	1,304,067	230,000
North American, City	500,000	770,295	250,000
North River	350,000	467,425	....
Pacific, City	200,000	443,257	12,500
Park, City	200,000	302,493	Nothing
Peoples, City	150,000	231,670	Nothing
Peter Cooper, City	150,000	295,724	....
Phœnix, L. I, City	1,000,000	1,890,010	350,000
Relief, City	200,000	310,993	10,000
Republic, City	300,000	633,478	225,000
Resolute, City	200,000	252,452	80,000
Rutgers, City	200,000	343,034	Nothing
Schenectady, Schenectady	100,000	93,737	Insolvent
Security, City	1,100,000	1,880,233 Ad'ts	1,000,000
Standard, City	200,000	372,707	Nothing
Star, City	200,000	300,441	Nothing
Sterling, City	200,000	247,927	7,500
Stuyvesant, City	200,000	308,640	Nothing
St. Nicholas, City	150,000	222,572	Nothing
Tradesmen's City	150,000	423,181	25,000
United States, City	250,000	437,250	Nothing
Washington, P., City	400,000	774,411	400,000
Watertown, Watertown	100,000	171,754	Nothing
Westchester, New Rochelle	200,000	485,314	Nothing
Western, of Buffalo	300,000	582,547	Nothing
Williamsburg City, City	250,000	539,092	70,000
Yonkers and New York, City	500,000	863,933	300,000

Massachusetts Companies.

Name	Capital	Gross Assets	Losses
American, Boston	$ 300,000	$ 344,481	....
Bay State, Worcester	104,800	196,275	....
Beverly, Beverly	30,000	41,893	....
Boston, Boston	300,000	678,740	Nothing
Boylston, Boston	300,000	933,256	....
City, Boston	200,000	389,427	....
Eliot, Boston	300,000	672,212	12,000
Equitable, Provinstown	50,000	42,129	....
Exchange, Boston	100,000	111,092	....
Firemen's, Boston	300,000	1,033,330	....
First National, Worcester	100,000	157,356	....
Franklin, Boston	300,000	541,908	....
Gloucester, Gloucester	100,000	116,751	....
Hide and Leather, Boston	300,000	419,211	700,000
Howard, Boston	200,000	358,612	....
Independent, Boston	300,000	646,048	Suspended
Lawrence, Boston	250,000	262,504	12,000
Manufacturers', Boston	400,000	1,430,464	350,000
Mercantile, Boston	300,000	704,299	....
Merchants', Boston	500,000	954,559	10,000
Mutual Benefit, Boston	100,000	254,092	....
National Boston	300,000	821,840	300,000
Neptune, Boston	300,000	852,195	....
New England Mutual M, Boston	200,000	1,030,973	700,000
North American, Boston	200,000	601,747	10,000
People's, Worcester	400,000	887,756	....
Prescott, Boston	200,000	452,699	....
Salem, Salem	100,000	197,949	....
Shoe and Leather Dealer', Boston	200,000	549,806	....
Springfield, Springfield	500,000	939,101	....
Suffolk, Boston	150,000	283,288	....
Trader's and Mechanics', Lowell	100,000	192,401	....
Tremont, Boston	200,000	234,543	....
Washington, Boston	300,000	935,875	Losses

Ohio Companies.

Name	Capital	Gross Assets	Losses
Alllemannia, Cleveland	$ 250,000	$255,545	$25,000
American, Cincinnati	100,000	125,513	....

Name.	Capital.	Gross Assets. Jan. 1, 1871.	Losses.
Andes, Cincinnati	$1,000,000	$1,203,425	$400,000
Burnet, Cincinnati	60,000	75,369	
Butler, Hamilton	14,000	22,322	
Capital City, Columbus	60,000	78,000	
Central, Columbus	40,000	55,541	
Central, Dayton	20,832	29,396	
Cincinnati, Cincinnati	150,000	209,223	
Citizens', Cincinnati	52,500	67,690	
Cleveland, Cleveland	414,400	530,208	175,000
Commercial, Cincinnati	100,000	153,987	
Cooper, Dayton	23,800	32,527	
Eagle, Cincinnati	160,000	123,694	
Eclipse, Cincinnati	27,350	46,667	
Enterprise, Cincinnati	193,400	392,922	
Eureka, Cincinnati	26,425	67,607	
Farmer', Cincinnati	23,360	24,142	
Farmers', Jellowny	100,000	131,026	
Farmers' and Merchant's, Dayton	32,000	55,770	
Farmers', Mer. and M'f's., Hamilton	100,000	123,366	
Firemen's, Cincinnati	100,000	225,600	
Firemen's, Dayton	100,000	126,893	
Franklin, Cincinnati	100,000	182,465	
Franklin, Columbus	70,000	88,071	
German, Cleveland	200,000	281,296	
German, Dayton	22,500	23,947	
German, Cincinnati	100,000	127,858	
German, Toledo	45,001	54,500	
Globe, Cincinnati	100,000	173,143	25,000
Hamilton, Hamilton	17,500	41,620	
Hibernia, Cleveland	200,000	225,000	
Home, Columbus	500,000	637,947	150,000
Home, Toledo	69,000	76,385	
Jefferson, Steubenville	43,292	60,632	
Merchants' and Manufacturers' Cincinnati	150,000	208,780	
Miami Valley, Cincinnati	100,000	141,094	
Miami Valley, Dayton	26,100	51,183	
Mutual, Toledo	90,000	90,246	
National, Cincinnati	100,000	120,514	
Ohio, Chillicothe	40,000	49,092	
Ohio, Dayton	35,282	54,318	
Ohio Valley, Cincinnati	50,760	79,921	
People's, Cincinnati	25,000	43,923	
Sun, Cleveland	200,000	391,340	75,000
Teutonia, Cleveland	200,000	237,016	
Teutonia, Dayton	26,000	46,572	
Tobacco, Cincinnati	100,000	103,343	
Toledo, Toledo	75,000	105,837	
Union, Cincinnati	100,000	130,845	
Washington, Cincinnati	125,100	143,747	
Western, Cincinnati	100,000	173,550	

Missouri Companies.

American Central, St. Louis	$231,370	$254,875	$350,000
Anchor, St. Louis	105,225	121,974	27,000
Boatmen's, St. Louis	106,550	51,786	20,000
Chouteau, St. Louis	19,319	21,808	25,000
Citizen's, st. Louis	175,000	271,373	
Commercial, St. Louis	49,669	43,896	
Excelsior, St. Louis	73,037	19,815	
Franklin, St. Louis	106,900	119,701	
German, St. Louis	55,500	79,673	
Globe Mutual, St. Louis	125,000	150,793	
Home, St. Joseph	63,850	66,061	
Jefferson, St. Louis	101,272	121,842	
Lafayette, Lexington	51,884	56,439	
Lumbermen & Mechanics, St. Louis	166,000	200,469	
Marine, St. Louis	150,000	219,525	
Merchant's, St. Joseph	69,636	79,682	
National, Hannibal	111,201	147,723	
North Missouri, Macon	133,650	154,166	
Pacific, St. Louis	25,000	36,835	
Phoenix, St. Louis	108,959	126,654	
St. Joseph, St. Joseph	64,000	105,729	
St. Louis, St. Louis	249,000	307,342	
State, Hannibal	169,000	162,099	
Union, St. Louis	100,000	107,675	
United States, St. Louis	170,060	184,279	

GREAT FIRE IN CHICAGO.

Illinois

Name.	Capital.	Gross Assets Jan. 1, 1871.	Losses.
American, Chicago	$ 150,000	$548,875	....
Aurora, Aurora	200,000	229,471	....
Chicago Fire, Chicago	101,800	151,566	....
Chicago Firemen's, Chicago	200,000	372,544	....
Commercial, Chicago	180,000	266,535	....
Equitable, Chicago	100,000	120,191	....
Farmer's, Freeport	100,000	191,505	....
German, Freeport	111,000	119,824	....
German Ins. and Sav's. Co., Quincy	132,301	153,951	....
German, Chicago	200,000	257,821	....
Great Western, Chicago	222,731	274,125	....
Home, Chicago	200,000	245,338	....
Illinois Mutual, Alton	115,000	250,016	....
Knickerbocker, Chicago	160,000	189,129	....
Merchant's, Chicago	500,000	878,252	....
Mutual Security, Chicago	118,325	145,534	....
Republic, Chicago	968,230	1,132,812	....
Rockford, Rockford	100,000	235,442	....
Winneshiek, Freeport	100,000	143,702	....

These companies cannot furnish figures—but most of them lose heavily, and many suspensions will follow.

Pennsylvania.

American, Philadelphia	$ 400,000	$1,047,612	Nothing
Franklin, Philadelphia	400,000	3,031,452	500,000
Girard, Philadelphia	200,000	413,062	Nothing
Ins. Company of North America, Phil	500,000	3,050,538	600,000
Ins. Company State of Pennsylvania, Phil	200,000	542,968	......
Lancaster, Lancaster	200,000	250,349	Nothing
Pennsylvania, Philadelphia	400,000	1,094,601	Nothing
Delaware Mutual Safety, Phila	300,000	1,821,462	......
Enterprise, Philadelphia	200,000	611,634	125,000
Lycoming, Muncy	Mutual	516,846	......
Alpa, Erie	250,000	365,624	12,000
Reading Fire, Reading	150,000	177,503	......
Williamsport Fire, Williamsport	100,000	110,500	......
Columbia, Columbia	......	250,000	......

Connecticut.

Ætna, Hartford	$ 3,000,000	$5,732,635	$2,000,000
City, Hartford	250,000	354,287	225,000
Charter Oak, Hartford	150,000	251,951	200,000
Connecticut, Hartford	200,000	405,669	Suspended
Fairfield County, Norwalk	200,000	216,378	50,000
Hartford, Hartford	1,000,000	2,737,510	1,500,000
Merchants, Hartford	200,000	340,006	150,000
North American, Hartford	200,000	456,584	......
Norwich, Norwich	300,000	581,736	......
Phœnix, Hartford	600,000	1,717,947	700,000
Putnam, Hartford	500,000	785,723	425,000

Rhode Island.

American, Providence	$ 400,000	$ 371,069	$ 400,000
Atlantic, Providence	500,000	326,013	275,000
City, Providence	50,000	72,150	......
Equitable, Providence	200,000	271,168	Nothing
Hope, Providence	150,000	211,673	110,000
Merchants', Providence	300,000	372,199	15,000
Narragansett, Providence	500,000	792,947	38,000
Providence Washington, Providence	200,000	415,149	550,000
Roger Williams, Providence	200,000	228,946	100,000

California.

California, San Francisco	$ 300,000	$ 406,324	......
Firemen's Fund, San Francisco	500,000	739,627	......
Home Mutual, San Francisco	600,000	657,243	......
Occidental, San Francisco	300,000	474,095	......
Pacific, San Francisco	1,000,000	1,717,267	$1,000,000
People's San Francisco	300,000	300,000	......
Union, San Francisco	750,000	1,115,574	......

Maine.

Eastern, Bangor	$ 150,000	$ 237,648	Nothing
National, Bangor	200,000	241,309	17,500
Union, Bangor	200,000	421,295	5,000

Michigan.

Name.	Capital.	Gross Assets Jan. 1, 1871.	Losses.
Detroit Fire and Marine, Detroit	$ 150,000	$ 273,063	$ 80,000
Michigan State, Adrian	150,000	266,123	......
State, Lansing	100,000	......	......

Wisconsin.

Brewers' Protective, Milwaukee	$ 164,175	$ 183,631	$ 75,000
North-western National, Milwaukee	150,000	191,202	90,000

Minnesota.

St. Paul Fire and Marine, St. Paul	$ 120,000	$ 280,593	$ 60,000

Kentucky.

Aurora, Covington	$ 150,000	$ 163,513	$ 35,000

New Hampshire.

New Hampshire Fire, Manchester	$ 100,000	$ 134,586	......

Foreign Companies.

The list of foreign companies doing business in the United States gives the whole assets of the companies. All of them except the Imperial do a life insurance business, and the largest portion of their assets are credited to that department.

Commercial Union	$1,250,000	$4,000,000	$ 65,000
Imperial	3,500,000	5,432,635	150,000
Liverpool & London and Globe	1,953,760	20,136,420	2,000,000
North British and Mercantile	1,350,000	4,104,593	5,000,000
Queen	953,860	2,347,495	Nothing
Royal	1,444,475	9,274,776	98,000

The Companies whose losses are designated by dots or "leaders," have not been heard from, though in the case of the Chicago companies it is feared a very large majority—if not all—are bankrupt. The "American," "Merchants'," "Republic," and a few others, however, giving promise of reasonable adjustment. However, their personal losses have been immense—papers have disappeared and been destroyed, records burned, and matters so disturbed and disarranged that it must be a long time ere satisfactory or definite evidence will be forthcoming. The other outside Companies not heard from have not been very great sufferers, though many will be hard pressed. We from inquiry and close investigation are convinced that many stated losses are from 25 to 50 per cent. more than at presented asserted.

At the Chamber of Commerce the wildest excitement was manifested; men grew desperate as they discussed the removal of the Board to Mich ave. on the South Side —the repudiation of former transactions—the losses of a few days past—and other matters of grave importance. Within a few hours between two and three thousand acres of magnificent buildings had been destroyed—within a few hours over 15,000— yes 16,000 edifices had been swept away—within a few hours 80,000 or 90,000 people were left homeless, houseless, starving—and within a few hours property to the extent of over $300,000,000 had been stricken down before the march of the destroyer; had acted a brilliant part in the Fire Fiend's Carnival—and bade the proudest head droop and coldest hearts yearn for the miseries of the Doomed City. Doomed City! It was indeed;—years of strife against misfortune, years of strife with creditors, and years of deep anxiety—this to secure prosperity—this to build up a city famed throughout the civilized world;—and now for miles around, naught save wrecked fragments of masonry, ghastly beds of ashes, and poverty's gaunt form mocking the millionaire of yesterday Fragments of masonry! let those who doubt this assertion seek the sites of the following magnificent structures:—

Academy of Design, Adams, between State and Dearborn.
A. H. Miller's building, corner State and Madison.
Andrew's building, La Salle, between Madison and Monroe.

Andrews & Otis's building, Clark, between Monroe and Adams.
Arcade buildings, Clark, between Madison and Monroe.
Berlin block, corner State and Monroe.
Blake's building, Washington, between Fifth avenue and Franklin.
Boone block, La Salle, between Washington and Madison.
Bowen's building, Randolph, between Michigan and Wabash avenue.
Bryan block, corner La Salle and Monroe.
Burch's block, Lake, between Wabash avenue and State street.
Calhoun block, Clark, between Washington and Madison.
Chamber of Commerce building, corner La Salle and Washington.
Chicago Mutual Life Insurance building, Fifth avenue, between Washington and Randolph.
The Chicago Times building, Dearborn, between Washington and Madison.
City Water Works, corner Chicago avenue and Pine.
Cobb's block, corner Lake and Wabash avenue.
Cobb's block, Washington, between Clark and Dearborn.
Cobb's building, Dearborn, between Washington and Madison.
Commercial building, corner La Salle and Lake.
Commercial Insurance Company's building, Washington, between La Salle and Fifth avenue.
Court House, Randolph and Washington, between Clark and La Salle.
Crosby's building, State, between Randolph and Washington.
Custom House, corner Dearborn and Monroe.
DeHaven block, Dearborn, between Quincy and Jackson.
Depository building, Randolph, between Clark and La Salle.
Dickey's building, corner Dearborn and Lake.
Dole's building, corner Clark and South Water.
Drake's block, corner Wabash avenue and Washington.
Eagle Work's block, corner Madison and Clinton.
Ewing block, North Clark, between North Water and Kinzie.
Exchange Bank building, corner Lake and Clark.
Flander's block, foot South Water.
Fry's building, La Salle, between Washington and Randolph.
Fullerton's block, corner Washington and Dearborn.
Gallup building, corner La Salle and Madison.
Garrett block, corner Randolph and State.
Hartford Fire Insurance building, La Salle, between Randolph and Lake.
Holt's building, Washington, between La Salle and Fifth avenue.
Honore block, Dearborn, between Monroe and Adams.
Illinois Central Land Department building, Michigan avenue, between Lake and South Water.
Keep's building, Clark, between Madison and Monroe.
Kehoe's building, corner Twelfth and Blue Island avenue.
Kent's building, No. 153 Monroe.
King's block, corner Washington and Dearborn.
Lakeside building, corner Adams and Clark.
Larmon Block, corner Clark and Washington.
Lincoln block, corner Lake and Franklin.
Lind's block, corner Randolph and Market.
Link's block, corner La Salle and Lake.
Lloyd's block, corner Randolph and Fifth avenue.
Lombard block, corner Monroe and Custom House place, between Clark and Dearborn.
Loomis Block, corner Clark and South Water.
Lumberman's Exchange, corner South Water and Franklin.
McCarthy's Building, corner Dearborn and Washington.
McCarthy's Building, corner Clark and Randolph.
McCormick's Block, corner Dearborn and Randolph.
McCormick's Building, corner Michigan ave. and Lake.
McKee's Building, corner Wabash ave. and Randolph.
Mackin's Building, State, between Madison and Monroe.
Magie's Building, corner LaSalle and Randolph.

Major Block, corner LaSalle and Madison.
Marine Bank Building, corner Lake and LaSalle.
Mechanics' Building, Washington, between LaSalle and Fifth ave.
Mercantile Building, LaSalle, between Madison and Washington.
Merchant's Insurance Building, corner LaSalle and Washington.
Methodist Church Block, corner Clark and Washington.
Metropolitan Block, corner Randolph and LaSalle.
Monroe Building, corner Clark and Monroe.
Morrison Block, Clark, between Madison and Monroe.
Morrison Building, Clark, between Madison and Washington.
Newbury Block, corner Wells and Kinzie.
Nixon Building, corner LaSalle and Monroe.
Norton Block, Nos. 136 and 138 South Water.
Old Board of Trade Buildings, South Water, between LaSalle and Fifth ave.
Open Board Building, Madison, between Clark and LaSalle.
Oriental Building, LaSalle, between Washington and Madison.
Otis Block, corner Madison and LaSalle.
Otis Building, corner State and Madison.
Pacific Hotel, corner Clark and Quincy.
Pardee's Building, corner South Water and Fifth ave.
Phœnix Building, LaSalle, between Randolph and Washington.
Pomeroy's Building, No 160 South Water.
Pope's Block, Madison, between Clark and LaSalle.
Portland Block, corner Dearborn and Washington.
Post-Office, corner Dearborn and Monroe.
Post-Office Building, Dearborn, between Madison and Monroe.
Prairie Farmer Building, Monroe, between Dearborn and Clark.
Purple's Block, corner North Clark and Ontario.
Raymond Block, corner State and Madison.
Republic Life Insurance Building, LaSalle, between Madison and Monroe.
Reynold's Block, corner Dearborn and Madison.
Rice's Building, 74 to 81 Dearborn.
Scammon's Building, corner Randolph and Michigan ave.
Shepard's Building, Dearborn, between Monroe and Adams.
Sherman House Block, corner Clark and Randolph.
Smith & Nixon's Block, corner Clark and Washington.
Speed's Building, 125 Dearborn.
Staats Zeitung Building, Madison, between Dearborn and Clark.
Stearn's Building, Washington, between LaSalle and Fifth ave.
Steel's Block, corner LaSalle and South Water.
Stone's Building, Madison, between Clark and LaSalle.
Taylor's Block, corner Franklin and South Water.
Tribune Building, corner Dearborn and Madison.
Turner's Building, corner North State and Kinzie.
Tyler Block, LaSalle between Lake and South Water.
Uhlich Block, North Clark, between Kinzie and Water.
Union Building, corner LaSalle and Washington.
Volk's Building, 197 Washington.
Walker's Block, Dearborn, between Lake and Randolph.
Warner's Block, 123 and 125 Randolph.
Washington Block, Clark, between Washington and Madison.
Wheeler's Block, corner Clark and South Water.
Wicker's Building, corner State and South Water.
Wright Brother's Building, corner North State and Kinzie.
Five Public Schools.

HOTELS.

Palmer House.
Sherman House.
Tremont House.
Pacific
Adams House.
Briggs House.
Mattison House.
Revere House.
Orient House
Everett House.
Metropolitan House.
Central House.
Howard House.
City Hotel.
Clifton House.
Clarendon House.
Bigelow House.

CHURCHES.

Episcopal	3	New England	1
Presbyterian	5	Congregational	1
Methodist	5	Catholic	5
Unitarian	2	Jewish	3
Swedenborgian	2	Lutheran	2

Besides many other places of worship, fully seventy being destroyed.

THEATRES.

Crosby's Opera House.
McVicker's.
Hooley's.
Dearborn.
Wood's Museum.
King's Opera House.
Olympic.
German.
Turner Hall.

The following buildings escaped:

BLOCKS AND PUBLIC BUILDINGS.

Barnaeur building, corner of West Lake and Clinton streets.
Cole's building, corner West Madison and Halstead streets.
Edward's Block, Milwaukee avenue, between Noble and Cleaver streets.
High School, West Monroe street, between Desplaines and Halstead streets.
Rice & Jackson Block, West Randolph street, between Jefferson and Desplaines streets.
Sherman's Block, Wabash avenue, between Twelfth and Thirteenth streets.

SAVINGS BANKS.

Prairie State Loan and Trust Company, No. 95 West Randolph street.
Savings Bank of the Mechanics' Association, No. 164 Twenty-second street.

RAILWAY STATIONS.

Pittsburgh, Fort Wayne & Chicago, corner Canal and Madison streets.
Pittsburg, Cincinnati & St. Louis. corner Canal and Kenzie streets.
Chicago, Alton & St. Louis, corner Canal and Madison streets.
Chicago & North-western (Wisconsin and Milwaukee division) corner West Water and Kenzie streets.
Chicago, Dansville and Vincennes, corner Canal and Kenzie streets.

BANKS.

Chicago Clearing House Association, 82 Dearborn street.
City National Bank, 156 Washington street.
Commercial National Bank, 55 Dearborn street.
Commercial Loan Company, 44 North Clark street.
Cook County National Bank, Honore Block, corner Dearborn and Monroe streets
Corn Exchange National Bank, room 2 Chamber of Commerce.
Fifth National Bank, north-east corner Clark and Dearborn streets.
First National Bank, south-west corner State and Washington streets.
Fourth National Bank, south-east corner Dearborn and Washington streets.
Germania Bank, 40 South Clark street.
Hibernian Banking Association, south-west corner Clark and Lake streets.
Illinois Mutual Trust Company, 147 and 149 Randolph street.
Manufacturers' National Bank, north-west corner Dearborn and Washington streets.
Marine Company of Chicago, 156 Lake, north-east corner LaSalle street.
Mechanics' National Bank, 154 Lake street.
Merchants' National Bank, 108 LaSalle street.
National Bank of Commerce, 87 Dearborn street.
National Bank of Illinois, 95 Washington street.
North-Western National Bank, 1 Chamber of Commerce.
Prairie State Loan and Trust Company, north-west corner Randolph and Jefferson streets.
Real Estate Loan and Trust Company, 105 and 107 Monroe street, Lombard Block.
Second National Bank, north-west corner Lake and Clark streets.
Traders' National Bank, 44 Clark street.

Third National Bank, corner Randolph and Dearborn streets.
Union Insurance and Trust Company, No 133 Dearborn street.
Union National Bank, south-west corner LaSalle and Washington streets.
Union Stock Yards National Bank, Union Stock Yards.
J R. Valentine & Co.

SAVINGS' BANKS.

Chicago Savings Institution and Trust Campany, basement south-west corner State and Washington streets.
Com. Loan Company. No. 60 North Clark street.
Fourth National Bank, south-east corner Washington and Dearborn streets.
German Savings Bank, Nos. 34 and 36 LaSalle street.
Hibernian Bank Association Savings Bank, south-west corner Clark and Lake streets.
International Mutual Trust Company, No. 135 LaSalle street.
Marine Company of Chicago, No 156 Lake street.
Merchants', Farmers' and Mechanics' Savings Bank, No. 13 Clark street.
Merchants' Saving Loan and Trust Company, south-west corner Lake and Dearborn streets.
National Loan and Trust Company, 92 LaSalle street.
Prairie State Loan and Trust Company, 95 West Randolph street.
Real Estate, Loan and Trust Company, next west of the Post Office.
Savings Bank of the Mechanics Asssociation, 164 Twenty-second street.
State Savings' Institution, 82 and 84 LaSalle street.
Union Insurance and Trust Company, 133 Dearborn street; Branch at 316 Milwaukee street.

RAILWAY STATIONS.

Michigan Central and Great Western of Canada, Union Depot, foot of Lake street.
Lake Shore & Michigan Southern, Van Buren street, head of LaSalle.
Illinois Central, foot of Lake street.
Chicago, Burlington & Quincy, foot of Lake street.
Chicago, Rock Island & Pacific, corner Van Buren and Sherman streets, head of LaSalle.
Chicago & North-western (Galena division) corner of North Water and Wells streets, North Side.

The following Elevators were burned: Munger & Armour's, Galena, Illinois Central A., Hiram Wheeler's, National, Vincent Nelson & Co.'s. The following Elevators were reported safe: Illinois Central B., Flint & Thompson, two of Munn & Scott, two of Armour, Dale & Co., Burlington, and Old Iowa and Illinois River. The total amount of grain remaining in the Elevators is 5,000,000 bushels. It is estimated that the loss in grain will amount to nearly 2,000,000 of bushels.

Between eighty and ninety printing offices were destroyed, including lithography and stereotyping establishments.

Friday—and the work of building up Chicago is proceeded with; various sections of the burned district are dotted with wooden structures; men are busily clearing away bricks, opening safes, making contracts, organizing their affairs. Foolish rumors were abroad that the millionaire of last week, Potter Palmer, had committed suicide. Wise men shook their heads and said, "He's not the man to go into that business—his splendid hotels and stores may have been flattened to the ground, but he has been through too much and learned too much to be afraid of the world; he has more blood, and will yet get full value for all he has lost." This was the universal verdict in favor of the moral probity of a man who has done more for Chicago than any single individual in it during the past few years. It was talked of, too, that a few of the firemen gloated over his hotel being destroyed, owing to Mr. Palmer having advised economy in the Fire Department, but we received no authentic evidence of such unmanly conduct. If Potter Palmer possesses the same nerve he did but ten years ago, he cannot be a ruined man. A story is also circulating that Gen. Sheridan, hearing that a certain hotel keeper on the South-east Side was extortionate in his prices, disguised himself and visited the individual, asking him what he " charged by the day ?"

" Ten dollars," was the response.

" Could you not run it at $2.50 ?"

" No, we charge ten dollars per day," was the reply.

" Well," answered Sheridan, " if you do not take your sign down and replace the $10 with $2.50, *we will run it for you !*

Whatever followed few knew, but $2.50 per day was the charge from that hour.

A further rumor that Mr. Ullhman, of the firm of Wren, Ullhman & Co., bankers, who was found dead near his place of business on the night of the fire, had been murdered, and not burned to death as was supposed; this story was fully credited by good authorities. Various cases of shooting, hanging, killing had occurred during the week, but excited less attention than a runaway team on an ordinary occasion; some who were special policemen took advantage of their position, and used force where gentle words would have answered. Allan Pinkerton had issued notices that anyone discovered stealing would be put to death, and as Gen. Sheridan behaved most humanely, at the same time enforcing strict discipline, there were fewer cases of crime than might have been reasonably anticipated. Some who were given water by those in a position to bestow, sold it at good prices until they were discovered.

The German population were really in great distress, and as they had ever been a liberal-minded, industrious and peaceable class, it was hoped that a fund would be provided for them; large numbers of these living in the North Division were totally ruined. The Oddfellows, Masons and members of other societies are issuing circulars to their distant brethren, calling for aid. A meeting of the Louisville, Cincinnati, Indianapolis and St. Louis relief committees took place, at which representatives from other cities were present. They unanimously resolved upon definite arrangements, so that subscriber and receiver might be protected; this was to see that the contributions hereafter should be properly disposed of. To meet this view a thorough organization was effected, consisting of the Chicago Relief and Aid Society, assisted by prominent citizens. All bills were to be audited by the Executive Committee of that Society, consisting of seven well-known citizens, the Controller and R. B. Mason, Mayor.

This organization made the following suggestions to people :

" So far as practicable, we suggest that money be remitted, as with that we can buy articles, which from time to time we most need. All funds collected elsewhere should be remitted direct to, or held subject to the order of " The Chicago Relief and Aid Society." Funds already deposited in other cities will be drawn upon by orders or drafts of ' The Chicago Relief and Aid Society,' signed by R. B. Mason. All materials should be consigned to ' The Chicago Relief and Aid Society,' at Chicago, great care being taken to mark contents on packages, and to send invoices promptly by mail. Send cooked or perishable food only upon special order from our Society.

R. B. MASON, Mayor.

HENRY W. KING, President of the Chicago Relief and Aid Society.

WIRT DEXTER, Chairman Executive Committee."

Allan Pinkerton's circular occasions considerable interest :—

OFFICE OF PINKERTON'S POLICE.

Orders are hereby given to Captains, Lieutenants, Sergeants, and men of Pinkerton's preventive police, that they are in charge of the burning district, in the South Divi-

quarter. But Chicago was built of brick and stone. Yet, once started, the flames lapped up even the buildings deemed absolutely fire-proof. Chicago had grand waterworks, and an abundant supply of water; she had the best modern appliances for fighting fire with water and steam. But when the fiend got way, and his rage was fanned by the fierce gale, he mocked all the futile attempts of man to stay his course. He laid Chicago—fresh, grand, beautiful Chicago—all in ruins!

What can we say more? We do not yet know the worst. But we know that already an area of *five square miles* is covered with blackened walls—and the flames are unquenched! We know that the Court House—twenty years in building, half the life-time of the city—was swept away in thirty minutes; that the Sherman House, and the new Pacific Hotel, the largest in the world, have perished; that those monster railroad depots, and those grain elevators, which Chicago invented, and which were just then filled to repletion with six million bushels of wheat and corn, are all destroyed; that no newspaper will this (Tuesday) morning show Chicago's houseless wanderers the callous figures that indicate its loss, for their type is all melted by the flames; that by the destruction of its telegraph stations the doomed city has once again been cut off from communication with the sympathizing world; that the gasworks and waterworks are gone, and that when the flames are extinguished the city will be in darkness, and its children will suffer for water; that, in short, the entire business part of the city and miles in extent of its residences are in ashes. The great fire in New York in 1835 destroyed 648 houses. This has leveled 12,000. The great fire in London in 1666 ravaged 436 acres. This covers over three thousand acres with ruins. That fire—which, like this, burned from a fatal Sunday through three days, consumed the infection of the plague, and in time replaced the narrow lanes and the wooden structures with solid masonry and with broad streets—destroyed by a liberal computation fifty million dollars of wealth. A like computation will count the losses of Chicago by hundreds of millions, and will, for a season, cripple the commerce of the continent; but no such incidental, lasting gain will follow from the destruction of a new city, that had been built with no stint of money and skill.

Last week a public spirited citizen of Cincinnati presented to that city the most beautiful and costly fountain ever yet set up in any plaza in the world. All day, throughout all time, was it stipulated, that its sprays and jets of water should spirt and flirt their fairy foam to delight the children and nursery-maids that shall play about it for generations after Mr. Probasco is dead. It is a purely modern device, with not a suggestion of Amphitrite, nor of her nymphs and dolphins, and yet in severely classic taste. Above its polished granite columns, its basins and its statuary, rises a majestic figure of the Genius of Water, distributing her flowing treasures for the myriad comforts and needs of man. There is nothing more striking among the bronze groups below her than the colossal figure of a man, driven to the roof of his burning house, holding an empty bucket, and supplicating the Genius above for the saving element. How soon we have its counterpart! The Mayor of Chicago telegraphs to Milwaukee, to Cincinnati, for aid to quench the devouring flames: "Send us all the steamers you can spare!" And when the mad fire has disabled those monster engines that supply the city with water, hear the despairing note which sounds across the prairies and passes down the Mississippi to her old rival, St. Louis: "The city is burned up; the *waterworks are gone;* send us food for a hundred thousand homeless people!"

Food for Chicago! Food for the granary of the West! This is the cry to-day. And for weeks to come there will be a call for all the aid that the benevolent can supply. Let the President unrebuked assume war powers

SUNDAY—The day of rest from labor! On this evening a meeting of the officers of the National Banks of Chicago took place, in order that a conference might be held to confer with Mr. Hulburd, Controller of Currency. The Chair was occupied by J. Irving Pearce, President of the Third National Bank. Henry Greenbaum, of the German National Bank, Secretary. A lengthy discussion, touching the condition of the Chicago banks as affected by the fire, was the result. It was ascertained upon comparison of liabilities and resources, that all the banks were perfectly solvent, and should resume business at once. The only delay asked by any of the banks was for sufficient time to convey their safes from the ruins to new places of business, and to arrange their books and office furniture. A resolution, heretofore passed, to pay fifteen per cent. cash immediately, was unanimously rescinded, and a resolution adopted to open for regular transaction of business at 10 A. M. on the 17th inst.

The following was issued:

To the Public:

Having ascertained from personal investigation, that the National Banks of Chicago are solvent institutions, and that, notwithstanding the late fire, they are able and ready to pay all just claims on presentation. I hereby announce that the National Banks of Chicago will open their doors for the transaction of business, as usual on Tuesday the 17th inst. at 10 A. M., and I hereby express my belief in their ability to meet all their legitimate engagements on demand.

(Signed)   H. R. HURLBURD, Controller of Currency.

Many of the edifices remaining intact were converted into Houses of Refuge. There were a few churches left, but these clergymen—of all denominations—whose sacred temples had been destroyed, preached in the open air to those who had been "through the fire." The occasion was solemn and impressive. Tears fell from eyes unused to weeping, and their Creator looked down on—and let us hope pitied—those brought to his foot-stool and subdued by adversity. At St. Patrick's Cathedral, New York, the Very Rev. Dr. Starrs, Vicar General, read the following circular:

To the Reverend Pastors of Catholic Churches in this City :

The cry for help which comes to us in such piercing tones from the thousands of our fellow beings in Chicago, seated amid the ashes of their desolated city, without food or shelter, appeals so forcibly to every human heart, that there is not one, I am sure, having it in his power to give relief, be it much or be it little, that will not promptly do so with willingness and generous hand. In order that the greater facilities may be offered to all the members of our flock for the expression of a great act of Christian Charity, I hereby recommend that a collection be made in all the churches of the city on the Sunday after next, 22d. inst., due announcement to be made on next Sunday. The sums collected should be sent immediately to the Chancery office, that they may be remitted without delay to succor the distressed.

†JOHN, Archbishop of New York.

Given at New York, this 10th day of October, 1871.

In New York and Brooklyn the Reverends **Dr. Ewer, Dr. Richardson, Dr. Thompson, Dr. Chapin, Hepworth, Dr. Bellowes, Henry Ward Beecher, Dr. Houghton, Talmage, Dr. Duncan** and others, spoke eloquently. In fact, throughout the length and breadth of the land, voices were raised and fervent prayers offered up, and the great principle vindicated, that nations—as well as individuals—must ever be knit together in one common, but God-like bond of brotherhood.

Throughout the continent the churches were doing their part, thousands of dollars being subscribed, and it was found that New York, in cash and supplies, had already raised over $2,000,000. Detroit also had raised between $30,000 and $40,000, and Mr. G. F. Bagley, in response to a request, replied that he would, as chairman of the committee, forward $10,000 worth of lumber at once, this being much needed. Major D. C. Houston of the Engineer Corps, U. S., wrote some admirable suggestions on the reconstruction of Chicago—a few extracts being interesting:—

"Where the whole city to be laid out anew the natural features of the country and the railroad communications would point to the south side as the centre. The business operations will commence here and radiate as heretofore to the southwest and north, but more to the south, owing to the fact that the communication is interrupted by natural obstacles. Into this centre hundreds of thousands of people will pour daily, coming from the residence portion of the city, the suburbs and the whole country. * * * * Two or three hours of the day are consumed in traveling to and fro, and owing to the crowds in the streets, the contracted markets, and places of exchange, the time required to transact business is doubled and trebled. Now the points which seem to me to be considered at this time and be fully provided for are, first, the laying out of certain lines for steam communication from the centre of business to the suburbs, to be so arranged as not to obstruct the street travel or be interrupted by it. * * * * Second, the arrangement of commodious and central depots for the great lines of railroads centerring in the city. Third, a commodious levee along the river for public docks, a grand market and a grand plaza where all can go without paying tribute. * * * * Fourth, the great leading lines of business should be consolidated or concentrated on certain streets running north and south. There should be a financial centre, a dry goods centre, a hardware centre, &c. Fifth, an open square for public meetings and outdoor business; The Court House Square suggests itself at once. Let the Court House go further south, and leave the present square open. Let it be surrounded by banks, brokers' offices, &c. and there will be room for everybody."

Every reader as a general thing has seen some map of what purported to be an exact and reliable description of the burned district; some of these were good, others vile and entirely inaccurate; they either destroyed the entire city or not enough of it, slashing a streak of ruin where no ruin existed, and designating portions saved which smouldered in ashes. Chicago, however, is so well known, its topography having been carefully studied for years past by business men, that it is unnecessary to enter upon a lengthy description of the favored Prairie City of the West—which occupies a level plain, the shore of Lake Michigan, at that point, running nearly north and south. From the north-west and south-west, and becoming nearly parallel to the lake shore, the north branch and the south branch of the Chicago River come at right angles to a junction, forming the main channel, three-quarters of a mile from the shore, thence flowing east to the lake. By this impediment, the city is divided into three sections, popularly known as the North Division, the South Division and the West Division. Edwards in his compilation states the population to be: North Division 75,000, West Division 125,000, South Division 100,000, making up the total of 300,000. Settlement began about old Fort Dearborn, on the lake shore, one of the log structures of which passed away in the great conflagration. Business gradually moved westward toward the fork of the river, outside the Government reservation bounded by State street. The North Side had, in 1836, its early stage of ambition which had left the Lake House and a few old-time brick structures, of a pretentious class in their day, along North Water and Kinzie streets, parallel to the river. Twenty-five years ago, however, the question was settled for all time, originally by common consent, but since solidly confirmed by the location of the railway termini, that the region from the river southward along the lake shore, constituting the upper portion of the South Division, should be the business heart of Chicago, its southern line moving southward with the progress of improvements.

And now we close this hurriedly written sketch of a great National calamity. 'SHALL THERE BE A NEW CHICAGO?" Men already ask this significant question; we believe there will be a new Chicago· new, so far as stately edifices, carefully planned residences, massive warehouses—erected upon sites now vast wildernesses of ashes—can make it new; but the men of to-day will be at the helm, and the beautiful Garden City will bloom with verdure for them during their prime and advancing age; they will look back with pride and say to those springing up—"This was once a ruin—men scoffed at us for hoping to see old landmarks of business and enterprise replaced, but we accomplished the work, we fulfilled our mission, and we thank our God." To-day the ashes may sweep over desolated districts, but the lake is not dry, the Railway lines are not as things of the past; the great Northwest is a friend and patron. Commerce acknowledges her sway, and this hour Chicago's credit and honor are unimpeachable. The men who built Chicago will build it again; but the city will be more carefully planned. When Haussman reconstructed Paris, he destroyed property of immense value; but now Chicago stands as a virgin soil ready for the designer, the architect and the builder. Let commissioners—not the old fogy description of commissioners, drawing pay and doing nothing—be appointed, let competent men be entrusted with the work, and ere the tenth annual anniversary of the awful fire rolls around, Chicago will indeed prove to all nations that their sympathies were deserved, their beneficence wisely bestowed. The hearts, the will, the energies are there, and NEW CHICAGO shall be again built up by those who planted her first great commercial corner stone, in reality not more than a quarter of a century ago; they will have learned a lesson, and hand that lesson down to their children—a bitter lesson though it be; they will emerge from the ordeal purified, and with manly zeal, endeavor to accomplish the labor before them; the sons of these men, too, will work; they will forget the club and gambling rooms, and haunt the busy marts of commerce and the counting-house; the pampered-petted—yet tender and loving—daughters of the stricken, will forsake the fashionable milliner and the fascinating watering place—one and all joining in the great struggle which assuredly precedes success—and one and all remembering that, notwithstanding worldly prosperity and goodly possessions, the words of the poet will stand true to the end:—

> "'Tis only noble to be good;
> Kind hearts are more than coronets,
> And simple faith than Norman blood."

THE GREAT FIRE OF CHICAGO.

A FULL ACCOUNT

OF

ITS ORIGIN AND PROGRESS

AS

SEEN BY EYE WITNESSES,

AND COMPILED

FROM AUTHENTIC REPORTS.

THE CITY BEFORE AND AFTER THE FIRE.

TELEGRAPHIC DISPATCHES—HANGING OF INCENDIARIES—CRUCIFIXION OF ONE OF THE WRETCHES—THRILLING INCIDENTS AND HEART-RENDING SCENES. TO WHICH IS ADDED ACCOUNTS OF THE FIRES IN MICHIGAN AND MINNESOTA.

INDIANAPOLIS:
J. G. DOUGHTY, PRINTER, 2D FLOOR, TILFORD'S BUILDING.
1871.

THE GREAT FIRE OF CHICAGO.

CHAPTER I.

Chicago Before and After the Fire—The Unestimated Dead—Hanging and Crucifixion of Incendiaries—Scenes at the Improvised Morgue.

In view of the great calamity that has befallen our sister city of Chicago, how insignificant and trivial seem all our petty ills and afflictions—they pale their ineffectual fires in the presence of a great conflagration by which one hundred and fifty thousand souls have been rendered homeless, and a great metropolitan city, the pride of the Northwest, reduced almost to ashes in two or three scores of hours. In order to fully comprehend the loss it will be necessary to resort to the history of the city of Chicago, which so suddenly rose to grandeur and greatness, until it rivaled far older cities and was looked up to as a marvel of enterprise, and in many respects the wonder of the world. There was probably no greater grain market ever known—certainly none that ever commanded more attention throughout this and other civilized countries. The citizens of Chicago were always noted for their enterprise and energy—insomuch, indeed, was this the case that many supposed Chicago's growth was of that mushroom character that would not stand the test of time, but was of an evanescent and transitory quality. The reverse of this was proven before the fire fiend laid its beautiful temples in ruins, and scattered the ashes of the once palatial edifices of its merchant princes to the four winds of heaven. In no city of the Union were as substantial buildings erected with greater celerity, and no city outside of the great metropolis could boast of a greater number of magnificent and costly piles of architectural beauty and finish. Chicago was indeed going on prospering and to prosper, when this great fire —like a besom of destruction—swept over the plain and left ruin and desolation in its wake.

The question of the recovery of Chicago is no uncerain problem. It is only one of time, and very little time at that. Those who are willing to help themselves will always be helped. Chicago's set back is only one of days—certainly not of years. It will only be a little time and she will again blossom as the rose. She is endeavoring to help herself, and her sister cities are coming up nobly to her relief. Not only this, but way across the ocean they have heard the cry of distress, and the great cities of Europe give of their plenty in this the great time of her need. All jealousy is cast aside, and those who looked upon Chicago as a possible rival are now the first to extend to her the helping hand.

It is as yet uncertain how many lives were destroyed in this great calamity. The true number will perhaps never be known. It can only be guessed at by the remains recovered that bear the least resemblance to humanity. Some eighty odd were displayed at the Morgue the following Thursday, and it is probable that the half was not told.

The heart of man would hardly conceive that amid such general devastation and ruin there would be those who could wilfully add by dastardly acts to the universal woe; yet such was known to be the case. Fiends in the shape of men were discovered setting fire to buildings and thus adding to the flames. They were immediately hung when discovered by the excited populace, or a speedy termination otherwise put to their miserable existence. One wretch, it is stated, being caught in the act of firing a building, was actually crucified to the blocks of the wooden pavement, by having his hands and feet pinioned thereto.

The following is a graphic description of the improvised Morgue, by a correspondent of the *Cincinnati Commercial*:

The sickening sensation of the day is the establishment of a Morgue for the exhumed remains of the victims of the mighty fire.

This shocking repository is the hearse and carriage-room of a lower class undertaker on Hubbard street, near Halstead, three or four squares from the freight depot of the Pittsburg, Cincinnati and St. Louis Railway. It is little better than a barn, and yet is incorporated with the dwelling of the proprietor and the stable for his horses. The place to-day was strongly guarded by armed policemen, who found it difficult to keep off a constantly renewed crowd of people, with horror and anxiety strongly depicted in every pale and pitiful face.

At the far end of the room was a partitioned space lighted by dirty cobwebbed windows, and on the floor, arranged in rows, first all around three sides and then down the middle, were the charred remains of seventy human beings.

The first noticeable object in this dreadful company was the form of a Sister of some Roman Catholic Order, completely shrouded in her brown habit, with the cross and I. H. S. in white letters stitched on the bosom. The face was thickly veiled and even the feet carefully covered up. "She was smothered, but not burned," observed the grim master of ceremonies.

The next was the body of a young man partially clad in common workingmen's attire. The hair was completely burned off his head and body. The features were blackened and distorted with pain; the swollen lips were wide apart, disclosing the glistening teeth and imparting a horrid grin, such only as agonizing death can stamp upon the face. The flesh was bloated to an astonishing size. The poor wretch was roasted alive. What is the use now of giving utterance to the passing thought as these two corpses—the only two whose faces could be recognized—met the gaze? Let it pass.

There was one charred form in the attitude of prayer —the form of a woman, but every feature of the face, every graceful line of the body, was gone. The head was nothing but a black lump; the body a blackened, hideous mass.

Some bodies of men could be distinguished by the remnants of clothing and boots, but nearly all traces of humanity were gone. Then there were remains of children and young people, but they, with the majority, were nothing more than mere blackened, charred torsos. Those whose limbs or arms remained exhibited a supplicatory attitude as if begging mercy of the Destroyer.

To this ghastly, hideous and melancholy spectacle were admitted in little parties of four or five at a time, those who had friends or relatives missing, but no language can describe the scenes of heart-rending agony which these grim visits elicited.

A family of little ones led by an elder sister, comes, and after the first sickening shock tries to distinguish the lost mother. A frantic wife, attended by a friend, comes in search of her unreturning husband. Brothers seek sisters lost, and sisters their brothers gone, but who can tell in that undistinguishable charnel what home the living being made happy. All personal identification is gone with the obliterating fire, and nothing is left but ashes. But perhaps the bitter disappointment at not finding, or rather recognizing the lost one, is worse than if there and then had ended the fearful search. Heart-bursting sobs, hysterical exclamations and unutterable wailings rent the air as the disappointed sad ones turned away from the sickening scene.

But besides the bodies burned to a crisp, the improvised Morgue had other horrors to reveal. On the near side of the partitioned space lay half a dozen tenanted coffins—paupers' coffins—of painted pine, with the bodies laid in without any preparatory equipment for the grave, not even the common composure of the arms and limbs, the closing of the eyes and the washing of the features.

In one the visitor was shown the corpse of the man shot through the head and hung to the lamp post—a dreadful warning to incendiaries. In another lay the body of a man with a bayonet stab through the body; by whom stabbed no one knew. In another was squeezed the body of a German tailor, well known in the neighborhood, who had lost his all by the fire, and acting on the cowardly principle sentimentally inculcated by Goethe in The Sorrows of Werther, committed suicide rather than bravely live out his allotted time. He had first opened a vein in his arm and then cut his throat from ear to ear with a razor. His hands, face and clothes were smeared with gore, and a more ghastly and sickening spectacle than that coffin presented could hardly be found. There, shut it up forever and shut out the sight from our eyes—if we can, and leave the horrid place, never, never to return.

But where did these sad remnants of mortality come from? Who brought them and why were they brought? Away over there in the burned district they were gathered among the ruins and ashes of happy homes, and hither brought for recognition and decent burial. And over there the fearful search is prosecuted on private and public account by squads of men whose calling it is to prepare corpses for the grave and close it up with burial clods.

CHAPTER II.

Origin of the Fire—It Crosses the River—A Roaring, Raging Hell of Fire—The Burnt District—The Homeless.

ORIGIN OF THE FIRE.

On Saturday night, the 7th of October, 1871, a fire broke out in Chicago, Illinois, consuming four blocks before it was arrested and the flames subdued. On Sunday night, between eight and nine o'clock, the dread alarm of fire was again given, which may be said to have been the real commencement of the Great Fire of Chicago, before which most every other fire, of which the present world knows aught, sinks into comparative insignificance.

The following we believe is conceded to be the true story of the origin of the fire which commenced on Sunday night:

About eight o'clock on Sunday evening, a German woman who resided on the northeast corner of Jefferson and De Koven streets, on the "West Side," went to the stable in the rear of her house to milk a cow. It being dark she carried with her a lighted kerosene lamp, which she placed on a stool. The cow became frightened at something, and being blinded by the light ran over the stool and broke the lamp. The fire at once caught in straw and hay in the stable, and in five minutes the stable was a sheet of flame. The houses surrounding the stable were all frame, as were nearly all between that place and the river in the direction which the flames went. The alarm of fire was promptly given, but the firemen being exhausted by their work during the previous night and day, at the "Saturday Night Fire," did not get on the ground until the flames had broken out in nearly a dozen buildings. The wind was blowing almost a gale from the southwest directly toward the heart of the city. By the time the engines were in operation there were three houses in flames for every stream of water which could be thrown upon them. The Fire Marshal, finding that it was beyond the power of the department to put out the fire, and that it was going before the wind, but making a wider track as it progressed, placed several engines on the west bank of the south branch of the river, below Madison street bridge, to prevent the flames crossing by the bridges or being carried over by the wind, in catching in the lumber yards on the South Side. All their efforts, however, went for naught. The wind drove the fire faster, as it spread. The fire surrounded two of the engines, and cut off their retreat, and the firemen only saved their lives by crossing the river, leaving the engines in operation, and like faithful servants, they worked until they were burned out. The wind blew the cinders and sparks two squares, and often more, consequently the fire could cross the river at any point.

Farther and farther the cinders blew, setting fire to new blocks, and increasing the heat and fury of the flames at every fresh addition. At one o'clock A. M. the fire had already swept over twenty blocks, and was increasing at every step, the engines, though doing their utmost, appearing almost powerless. The Fire Marshal, Williams, telegraphed to Milwaukee for all the steamers they could spare, but it appeared as if no power short of the Almighty's could prevent the city from total destruction. The brands and sparks kept showering over the city, and additional alarms were constantly being struck. The tower of the Court House caught, but was extinguished by the watchman. At 1:15 A. M. the fire had traveled a mile and was a half-mile in width, reaching from the river to Jefferson street. Within this area were some of the most extensive lumber yards, and also the frieght depots of the Chicago and St. Louis, and

Pittsburgh, Fort Wayne and Chicago Railroads, which melted away in an incredibly short space of time.

IT CROSSES THE RIVER.

And now those who had hopes that the river would stay the flames abandoned them, for brands flying fully two hundred feet lodged on the east side of the stream, and set fire to some wooden buildings adjoining the gas house. With fresh vigor the flames swept on, devouring everything in their course. Hopes of saving the city seemed almost to be given up. The flames swept through the wooden houses as though they were of paper; vast crowds of people surged through the streets fleeing for safety. It was almost useless to attempt to save property, for so suddenly would the flames come upon them, that the inmates of dwellings had barely time to save their lives.

The Gas-works were soon destroyed, and still on swept the devouring element,

A ROARING, RAGING HELL OF FIRE,

Utterly beyond the power of pen to describe. It was now in the part of the city where the most wealth and finest buildings were located—the South Side. Here was to be found the heaviest business houses, wholesale and retail, all the banks and insurance offices, and all the best hotels—Lake street with its heavy wholesale houses, and State street with its equally large general business establishments, while the Court House, Post office, and Union Depot, went to fill up the list of costly buildings. In this quarter were the, so-called, *fire-proof* buildings. But in such a fire as was this, no known material could be called fire-proof. The heaviest stone walls chipped off and melted down like cheese, while iron beams, etc., writhed and twisted like wire. The *Tribune* building—a noble structure—withstood the flames so long, that hopes were entertained of its being saved; but it succumbed, at last, and was soon a mass of ruins. By morning all this space on the South Side, from Harrison street to the river, was burned, and the main part of Chicago's wealth lay in ashes. At Harrison street the flames were stayed from sweeping further south, by the vigorous exertions of the people led by gallant Phil Sheridan, who blew up several buildings on Wabash avenue and Congress street. But northward no power on earth could stay the fire from spreading. In an instant they had leaped the river and rushed on, carrying death and destruction in their path, sparing neither the rich nor the poor. They soon reached and

DESTROYED THE WATER-WORKS,

Over a mile from the river, thus shutting off all hope of aid from the engines, as no water could be obtained. Still northward the fire fiend flew, to Lincoln Park, and on, and on, until it reached the very outer limits of the city, and finally stopped when there were no more buildings to destroy. Thus, in less than forty-eight hours, an area of two thousand acres of closely built ground was consumed, and the proud city of the west mourned for her most beautiful and costly structures, and her great wealth had mostly disappeared in smoke. Millionaires of the day before were now penniless and desolation stared all in the face.

THE BURNT DISTRICT.

To describe the appearance of the ruins so that the reader might fully comprehend the full extent of the devastation, is simply impossible. The reader may try to imagine himself on top of the Court House, which would give a view of the whole scene. To the south for nearly a mile, he would see nothing but the blackened and smoking ruins of what was once the finest portion of one of the most beautiful built cities in the world. Looking south and west for more than a mile, he will see the horrible scar upon the ground, reaching back, wedge shaped, to the corner of DeKoven and Jefferson streets. To the west on the west side of the river, he will see a few acres of houses still standing, what is left of the "West Side." To the north as far as he can see for Lincoln Park and the intervening burnt and blackened trees, the sight will take in nothing but the ruins of hundreds of palatial residences, and interspersed throughout, here and there, parts of walls of stately churches, convents and school houses. In this north outlook the eye takes in the greater part of the city in which the finest private residences were located. And over all of this vast space is scattered thousands of men, women and children, looking among the ruins and debris of their late homes and business places for some article which might have escaped the devouring element.

The business portion of the burnt district was guarded by extra and regular policemen under the charge of Allen Pinkerton, who issued a proclamation setting forth that the officers, special and regular, were patroling the district under his orders, and that no time would be wasted in taking any violator of the law to any place of arrest, but that they would be shot down whenever detected.

THE HOMELESS.

In the portions of the city which are burned, were the residences of about one hundred and fifty thousand people. As the fire progressed they fled from their houses toward the Lake, the parks and the open lots of prairie around the city. Hundreds of men became separated from their wives and children, children from their parents, and thus made the confusion greater. People who owned carriages and horses, or could hire a vehicle of any kind, put what few articles they could carry, upon it, and fled to some place where they thought they would be safe. Thousands of people fled to Lincoln Park, expecting to be safe there, with what little furniture they had, but the sparks soon set fire to the dried grass, and burned what was there. The Park buildings, save one or two at the extreme north end, were destroyed. Being thus scattered, over fifty thousands people spent Monday night out in the open prairie, in Lincoln Park, and along the sandy beach of the lake. Some of them had a few pieces of bed clothing, and some a piece or two of carpet for shelter, but the great majority of them spent the night exposed to the bitter wind and the driving rain which began to fall about two o'clock in the morning. Many outrages too horrible to be written were committed by the fiends who fattened on the miseries of their fellow-creatures. Old men and women, the sick and tender women with still tenderer babes, sat in these exposed places all that long, long night. Undoubtedly hundreds of little children and babes will die from the dreadful exposure. On Tuesday night the authorities sated that there would still be from twenty-five to thirty thousand out of doors.

CHAPTER III.

Progress of the Fire—A Graphic and Heartrending Account—Further Details—How the Fire in the South Division was stopped.

In order that the reader may fully comprehend the extent and progress of the fire, it will be as well to reproduce the following graphic account condensed from the *Cincinnati Enquirer* of October 10:

On Sunday night, October 8th, at nine o'clock, a second fire broke out in the First Division (western) of Chicago, which has since proved one of the most disastrous calamities that ever visited a city upon this hemisphere. Our edition of yesterday contained dispatches up to 1:45 A. M. At that time twenty blocks were enveloped in flames, the shipping in the river on fire, and the fiend was rapidly eating its way into the business heart of the city. We continue the history of the heartrending catastrophe in as succinct a manner as the nature of the dispatches will permit.

2 10 A. M.—The block immediately across the street from the telegraph office, one of the finest—

At this point communication was broken, the fire having reached the telegraph office. An office was opened at Calumet, ten miles from the city, and the dispatches of the Associated Press were forwarded by Pony Express. The next advices were as follows:

Chicago, October 9–9:45 A. M.—The Court-house, Sherman House, Michigan Central and Illinois Central Railroad Depots, the Chamber of Commerce, Western Union Telegraph office, and all the intervening blocks are burned. In order to stop the progress of the fire southward from this line, powder was brought from the Arsenal and a number of whole blocks blown up.

The following dispatch was received at ten o'clock A. M., at St. Louis, from Mayor Mason, of Chicago:

"Send us food for the suffering. Our city is in ashes, our water-works are burnt."

Chicago, October 9–10 A. M.—The entire business portion of the city is destroyed. All the banks, express and telegraph offices; all the newspaper offices, except the *Tribune*, six elevators and the water-works are gone. There is no water in the city. Not less than ten thousand buildings have already been destroyed. The fire has burned a distance of five miles, and is still raging. The wind is blowing a gale.

New York, October 9.—The following dispatch has just been received here by the officers of the Western Union Telegraph Company:

Chicago, October 9.

" Hon. Wm. Orton, New York:

" We are trying to establish a Supply Department, but as the fire is now coming up this way, on Wabash avenue, will probably be driven out of here before night. The Water-works are burned, as is also every banking house and railroad depot in the city.

J. J. S. WILSON, Superintendent."

Cincinnati, October 9.—The following is from J. J. S. Wilson:

"*Chicago*, 10 A. M.—There is no water. The fire is now coming south on Wabash avenue, and will probably reach us before night."

One third of the city is in ruins. All the banks, insurance offices, warehouses and elevators are destroyed. There have been fully ten thousand buildings burned, and the fire is still raging.

Chicago, October 9–Noon.—The whole business portion of the city is in ashes from Harrison street north to Chicago and east of the river to the lake. The burnt district is three miles in length, and from a mile to a mile and a half in width. Every hotel, bank, express office, telegraph office, theater and newspaper office, with all the wholesale houses in the city, are totally destroyed, with many thousand dwellings. The Water-works were destroyed early this morning. The wind is blowing a perfect gale from the south-west, with a sky of brass.

No one can tell what the end will be. The only salvation for the remainder of the city is in the wind keeping its present direction. Fifty thousand people are homeless, the most of them in a destitute condition. The unburned streets for miles are lined with household goods. No one dares to think what the loss of life may be. The flames swept through the city with the rapidity of a prairie-fire, and many must have perished. The Western Union Telegraph Company has succeeded in getting up a few wires from a hastily improvised office in the southern part of the city, and establishing communication in nearly all directions. Munificent offers of assistance are coming from every quarter.

Englewood, Ten Miles from Chicago, October 9–11 A. M.— The work of destruction continues. More than one-half of the city is already destroyed, and the flames continue their ravages almost unopposed. At about one o'clock this morning the fire crossed the river at Adams street bridge, and soon destroyed the Gas-works, and then spread itself in every direction, and at this hour almost every building from Harrison street north to Chicago River is destroyed, including all the insurance offices, banks, hotels, telegraph offices and newspaper establishments, with the single exception of the *Tribune* office, which is fire-proof.

The Court-house, Sherman House, Tremont House, Palmer House, new Pacific Hotel, new Bigelow House, in fact every hotel, and everything else is swept clean. This district embraces all the heavy business houses in the city. The reign of fire and brimstone on Sodom and Gomorrah can hardly be compared to the devastating reign of the fire fiend in Chicago. More than one-half the population are rushing through the streets in vehicles which are obtained at enormous prices, on foot and in every other way, with the choicest household treasures in their arms and on their backs, in utter confusion, not knowing whither to go. Fearful suffering must follow, and almost immediately. Fully one hundred and fifty thousand people are at this moment homeless and houseless, not knowing where to lay their heads or get anything to satisfy the cravings of hunger.

Over ten thousand buildings are burned, and the fire still raging, and coming south on Wabash avenue. City Water-works burned. Wind blowing a gale.

The awful work of destruction goes on with relentless fury. From Harrison south, to Division street north, and from the river to Lake, an area of four miles long by one wide, the flames have swept everything before them. It is estimated that at least one hundred thousand persons are homeless and in a suffering condition. The streets in districts still unburned are lined for miles with such household goods as have been saved from destruction. Most generous offers of assistance in money, food or anything wanted are coming from every city and town possible by telegraph. The Mayor has responded to several offers, asking that cooked food be forwarded as soon as possible. Firemen are on their way here from Cincinnati, St. Louis and other cities. The Water-works is entirely destroyed. They are now blowing up buildings on the line of the fire, with an attempt to arrest its progress.

A GRAPHIC AND HEART-RENDING ACCOUNT.

Later.—Now it is believed the spread of the fire southward has been stayed at Harrison street, but on the north side there is no diminution in its fury, and that entire division of the city is certainly doomed to utter destruction, and there are grave fears that the flames may spread to the west side of North Branch River, and the inhabitants of the streets nearest the river are already moving to places of greater safety.

The Western Union Telegraph have now six wires working east and south, and are moving into a temporary office on the corner of State and Sixteenth streets.

The North-western Railroad is running trains on both its branches, which are crowded with fleeing citizens.

It is now positively asserted by some that the Waterworks are still intact, but that the water has been shut off from the south and west divisions on account of the quantity being used on the north side.

A reliable gentleman, just returned from the north division, brings the joyful intelligence that the Waterworks are uninjured. God grant it may prove true. It is impossible now to give even an approximately correct statement of the losses, but a faint idea may be formed when it is stated that every bank in the city, except two small savings institutions, one on Twenty-second street, in the South Division, and one on Randolph street, on the West, are destroyed. All the wholesale stores and all the large retail establishments, the Post-office, Court-house, Chamber of Commerce, and every hotel in the South Division, except the Michigan Avenue Hotel, (which, standing on the extreme southern limit of the fire, escaped, though badly scorched); every newspaper office, the *Tribune* having finally succumbed; every theater, six of the largest elevators, the immense depots of the Michigan Southern and Illinois Central Railroads, both passenger and freight depots of the latter, and more than a score of churches, and much of the shipping in the river. Men who were millionaires yesterday morning are nearly penniless to-day. But more terrible than all is the awful certainty that many human beings have found a fiery grave; how many, no one can now tell. Perhaps no one can ever tell; but some are known to have perished, and there is the most sickening fear that

the victims of the fiery monster may be counted by
scores. Hundreds of horses and cows have been burned
in stables, and on the North Side numbers, though released from confinement, were so bewildered and confused by the sea of fire which surrounded them that they
rushed wildly to and fro, uttering cries of fright and
pain until scorched and killed. Any attempt at a description of the scenes of this appalling calamity would
be idle. The simple facts that the once great city of
Chicago is destroyed, that hundreds of millions of her
active capital has vanished, and that nearly one-third of
her inhabitants are homeless dependents, are enough.
Any attempt to embellish would be but mockery. As
this awful day draws to a close, thousands of anxious
eyes watch the dense clouds of smoke which still roll
over the burnt district, with evident dread that a sudden
change of the wind may change the flames upon the
portion of the city yet spared. There seems, however,
little cause for apprehension, as reinforcements of firemen from other cities are constantly arriving. Colonel
J. J. S. Wilson, Superintendent of the Telegraph, is in
receipt of dispatches from leading cities, announcing
that aid is being provided for the sufferers. Colonel
Clowry, of St. Louis, telegraphs that seventy thousand
dollars has been subscribed by the merchants. Cincinnati promises one hundred thousand dollars, and Cleveland is proportionately generous. All this and a great
deal more will be needed to relieve the immediate pressing wants, and everything is being done by General
Stager and his assistants to keep up communication for
the citizens and press with the world outside. Colonel
George T. Williams, Superintendent of Cincinnati, reported promptly for duty this morning. About three
fourths of the United States mail was saved and taken
possession of by Colonel Wood of the Post-office service.

HOW THE FIRE IN SOUTH DIVISION WAS STOPPED.

Chicago, October 9-6 P. M.—The progress of the flames

in South Division was finally arrested about one o'clock P. M. This was accomplished by the blowing up and demolishing of several buildings on Wabash avenue and Congress street, by Lieutenant-General Sheridan. The district burnt over in South Division embraces everything from the main branch of the Chicago river to the lake, embracing about one hundred blocks, and this district contained all the leading business houses, the banks, insurance offices, hotels, etc., and a large number of churches, including St. Mary's (Catholic), St. Trinity, First Presbyterian, Second Presbyterian, St. Paul's, Swedenborgian, etc. The Methodist Church on the corner of Wabash avenue and Congress street is saved. The Michigan Avenue Hotel, on the corner of Michgan and Congress street, and Congress Hall, directly adjoining on Congress street, are saved. Michigan Terrace, on Michigan avenue, embracing the residences of Lieutenant-Governor Bross, Hon. John Scammor, S. C. Griggs, Peter L. Ross and other leading citizens, is completly destroyed, with the furniture and nearly all the other contents. All the newspaper establishments are totally wiped out. The *Tribune* building resisted the fire for several hours, but finally yielded; when McVicker's Theater, immediately adjoining, also withstood the raging elements, but finally succumbed. In fact, all the buildings in the District which claimed to be fire-proof shared the fate of those which could make no such claim. The great Central Depot, at the foot of Lake street, became a heap of ruins about nine o'clock. Most of the passenger cars of the Michigan Central, Burlington and Quincy, and Illinois Central Railroad were moved on the breakwater and saved. West of Clark street, in the South Division, the fire extended south as far as Polk street, sweeping everything before it. The distance burned over here is some three blocks wide and over half a mile in length, numbering about twenty blocks. The buildings were generally of the cheaper character—

embracing saloons, small shops, poor residences, etc. The district burned over on the west side commences at Taylor street, running from DeKoven to Jefferson, ran thence four or five blocks north and then moved diagonally toward the river, and finally the west line was established on Clinton street, and reaching thence to the river. It moved in this line northward until it reached North-western West Side depots, where it stopped. A distance of nearly two miles from where it started. The P., Ft. W, and C. and C. and St. Louis depots were in this territory. Both passenger and freight were in this district, and are wiped out. Almost the entire northern division, from the main branch of Chicago River to Lincoln Park, nearly two miles in length and one mile wide, is completely destroyed, including the Waterworks, a large number of elegant churches, etc. This statement embraces the district devastated, and comprises almost the entire business portion of the city. South of Harmon street, in South Division street, and reaching out many miles, and covered almost entirely with dwellings composed largely of the more elegant class, is untouched, and may now be regarded as safe from injury. For miles and miles in every direction the sidewalks, lawns, vacant lots and front yards of dwellings are filled with people who have escaped from these burning dwellings, taking with them only a scanty amount of furniture and clothing. The sight is truly pitiful and harrowing. Unless they receive immediate relief, many, from exposure and starvation, will perish, of course. As stated in my previous dispatch, it is utterly impossible to make an approximate estimate of the entire loss, but it can scarcely fall below one hundred and fifty millions of dollars. Of course but a fraction of this amount can be realized from the insurance.

General Sheridan has to-day telegraphed to St. Louis, to the Missouri Department there, to send at once to Chicago one hundred thousand rations. He has telegraphed to Omaha for two companies of soldiers and one hundred tents. They will be all here as soon as they can reach us by rail. He will also order another one hundred thousand rations. Mayor Mason has issued a proclamation calling a meeting to-night in the West Division to see what the citizens can do for the relief of the sufferers. There are at least 100,000 people who know not where they can get enough provisions to satisfy the cravings of hunger. A later rumor from the North Division says the devastation is less widespread than heretofore reported. I hear of no deaths reported by the disaster yet, but, undoubtedly, many have perished.

Chicago, October 10, 3–10 P. M.—Word is just brought that a fierce fire is raging on Thirty-first street. This street is two miles south of the southern fire limit on the South Side, and a little less than that from the limit on the West Side. This has been set on fire for the purpose evidently of destroying the remaining part of the city, largely occupied by wealthy residents. It is also known that two men, caught in the act of firing buildings, have been shot, and two others led off with ropes round their necks. As the wind is blowing a perfect gale the end can not be foretold.

Chicago, 4 P. M., October 10.—Another fire has broken out on the south side of Thirty-first street, which it is feared will take the ballance of the southern part of the city.

STILL LATER.—A dispatch from Chicago dated at 3 P. M., says the reported new attack of fire was greatly overdrawn. Only two or three houses had caught when the flames were promptly suppressed.

It will be seen from the above that during the process of the fire all sorts of sensational rumors were spread abroad, some of them having little if any foundation in truth. There were those in one city at least, who taking advantage of the distress of others, sought to make money by the issuing of sensational extras, por-

porting to give an account of the demolition of the entire city, and of the shooting of citizens by Government troops. It is almost needless to add that these dispatches were manufactured pretty much out of whole cloth, and when this fact became fully known, the perpetrators were visited by the bitter condemnation of all good men.

A VIVID PICTURE.

The following graphic account of the terrible work of the fire fiend, as it raged in its irresistible fury, is given by an eye witness in the Chicago *Tribune:*

At times it seemed but the work of a moment for the fire to enter the south end of buildings fronting on Randolph, Lake and Water streets, and reappear at the north doors and windows, belching forth in fierce flames, which often licked the opposite buildings, and then the flames belching from buildings on both sides of the street, would unite and present a solid mass of fire, completely filling the street from side to side, and shooting up an hundred feet into the air above the housetops in their mad career. Thus was street after street filled with flame and fire, and the exultation of the fire fiend was given vent to in a roar which can only be equaled by combining the noise of the ocean when its waters are driven during a tempest upon a rocky beach with the howl of the blast. Huge walls would topple and fall into the sea of fire, without apparently giving a sound, as the roar of the fierce element was so great that all the minor sounds were swallowed up, and the fall of walls was only perceptible to the eye and not to ear. If our readers will call to their mind the fiercest snow storm in their experience, and imagine the snow to be fire, as it surged hither and thither before the fury of the wind, they will be able to form a faint conception of the flames, as they raged through the streets of our doomed city. Many of the buildings situated along South Water street buried their red-hot rear walls in the water of the river, into which they plunged with a hiss like unto nothing earthly, throwing up a billow of water, which would gradually subside, until other walls would follow. The heat was so intense at times from some of the burning buildings, that they could not be approached within one hundred and fifty feet, which accounts for the manner in which the fire worked back, and often agaiust the wind. The fire, after reaching the business portion of Randolph and South Water street, leaped the river on to the North side in an incredibly short space of time, and thence among the wooden buildings on that side, reached the lake shore after touching block after block, happy dwelling after happy dwelling, with its fierce blast. A scene of more powerless efforts to fight an enemy was never presented than that of this, the people trying to baffle the fire fiend; and the combat was not of long duration, for the people bowed their heads in anguish of spirit, and suffered the fiend to have untrammeled sway; and well and thoroughly has he done his work, and nothing of the past history of civilized nations chronicles any efforts of his to which this present can be compared; so in all future time "The great Chicago fire" when mentioned will bring to the heart of its participants a pang of anguish, to future generations a simile of everything that is frightful and terrible. While there are a great many instances of generous devotion on the part of rich and poor individuals to the destitute, there are painful instances of meanness and selfishness. One was trying to remove valuable papers from an office, and asked two firemen to help him, which they refused to do unless he paid them fifty dollars. The papers were destroyed. Drivers of express-wagons have taken one hundred, and even five hundred dollars, for an hour's use of their vehicles in getting distressed people away.

Among the sad accompaniments of the calamity was to see hundreds of men and boys beastly intoxicated around the streets of the North Division, where the saloon-keepers' stock, turned into the street, furnished a convenient opportunity for the gratification of slavish propensities, and there can hardly be a doubt that many of these poor wretches found their death in the flames, from which they were too helpless to escape.

One poor man had crawled for refuge into a water main lying in the street near the Water-works, but the fire fiend found him even there before he could get his body wholly in safety, and robbed him of his life.

The *Herald* reporter furnishes the following: Women and children are going around the burnt districts vainly seeking something to satisfy their hunger. They ask for relief, but there is none to give them. No one has provisions or money. What provisions there were in the city is burned or eaten, and some few people have enough to last them a day and not longer. Provisions have arrived from Detroit, Cincinnati, Milwaukee and St. Louis, and are being distributed as fast as possible. Twenty-three dead bodies have been taken to a station on the North Side. At the present time it is impossible to know where they are. As night comes on, the want of gas is keenly felt, as there are but few candles in the city. No water, except what is gotten from the lake. Very grave fears of outrages by thieves on the West Side are felt on every hand.

Gen. Sheridan who has been a hard worker all through the fire is still calling for troops from different points to keep order. All business and work is suspended, and every one is intent on securing first something to eat, and next shelter. The suffering on the North Side is heartrending. Men, women and children—50,000 of them—are huddled together like so many wild animals, and in another place 17,000 Germans and Irish are praying for relief; helpless children asking for bread; heartbroken parents who do not know which way to turn or what to say, have nothing to do but to await the distribution of supplies, which at best must be a slow proceeding, as there are parts of the burnt districts over which it is almost impossible to travel. Women in the pains of child-birth, and patients who have been moved from beds of sickness to save their lives that at best were nearly spent, were all exposed to the rains of last night and the cold, raw winds of to-day. Several deaths have occurred in Lincoln Park, and three women have brought children into the world only to die. There are people who, in the bitterness of their souls, ascribe the calamity to God's judgment. A German said to me: "This is a second Sodom and Gomorrah, and the curse is on it." Another night must be spent in Lincoln Park and the brick-fields at Division street, and yet another and another. Each train, and extras, are loaded to their fullest capacity, taking people away who, in many instances, have no place to go, yet can't stay here, and every train is obliged to leave five times as many as they take. Every precaution is being taken by the authorities to guard the people to-night, and if morning comes without robberies, murders or a renewal of fires, then all will thank God and go forward with courage.

The Indianapolis Fire Department are here, and doing good service. Springfield and Peoria have done nobly, contributing liberally. The expression of sympathy on all hands is most gratifying, but help must come. The *Evening Journal* got out a half sheet to-night. Other papers will follow to-morrow, some of the presses having been found.

The private residence of Horace White and Wm. Brown, of the *Tribune*, were consumed.

Messrs. Medill and Cowles, of the *Times*, and Mr. Wilson, of the *Journal*, and also Mr. Storey, were more fortunate.

CHAPTER IV.

The Fire Compared with Those of Other Cities— What is Left —South Side—The Prominent Buildings Destroyed—In the North Division—Real Estate Titles Destroyed—Banks —In the Suburbs.

The following pen-pictures are taken from the *Chicago Evening Journal* of the 10th, that paper having been able to issue an extra upon the morning of the day named:

THE FIRE COMPARED WITH THOSE OF OTHER CITIES.

The awful intelligence of the destruction by fire of the noble, magnificent, wonderful city of Chicago, will be received all over the world with dismay and feelings of the deepest sorrow. Never before in the annals of history can such a parallel of destruction be found. The burning of Rome, London, Moscow, New York, Portland and Paris were undoubtedly appalling, disastrous events; but pale into insignificance before the awful work of devastation which has resulted in the reduction to ashes of Chicago, the city of the world—the spot on which the eyes of all nations of the earth have been fixed with mixed envy and admiration ever since she started into existence. That the great works of destruction alluded to were attended with dire loss there is no question, but neither of them spread over such a vast territory and destroyed so much valuable property, and in so awfully short a time as has that which has just laid waste the pride not only of America but of the world. No one but those who witnessed the scene can realize the sad, appalling character of the conflagration. Fancy one vast ocean of flame, five to seven miles in length and over an average of a mile in width, those huge billows swept onward, upward, forward, roaring, hissing, cracking, dashing a spray of lurid, livid sparks and flashes of fire in every direction, aided by a terrific gale which had enlisted itself under the flaming banner of the merciless and cruel Fire Fiend, to assist in the work of demolition. Steadily and relentlessly did the fearful scourge sweep forward, causing thousands of suddenly impoverished, terror-stricken human beings to flee before it for safety. The four elements all combined in the work of havoc— in the leveling to the ground, and reducing to humility the proudest, wealthiest city of the universe. The wind aided and encouraged the fire, the latter kept the water under control while the wind again, as if to add torture to the thousands of fleeing, weeping men, women and children, and to baffle the efforts of citizens, firemen and policemen in the encounter, hurled almost impenetrable clouds of stinging, blinding sand and dust in their eyes, ears and nostrils. The spectacle was appallingly grand, yet such as to make great strong men weep like children —not altogether at the losses they had and were sustaining, the dark prospects which shrouded their future, but at witnessing the ruin and demolishing of the city which they had regarded with pride, and over whose progress and welfare they had watched with the tender care, similar to that with which anxious, loving parents regard the career of their offspring. Hundreds of millions of dollars' worth of property have been laid in ashes. Thousands of magnificent buildings which reared their proud heads above their more humble frame neighbors, have been laid low, all suffering the same fate, in the crushing embrace of the great leveller—fire. Thousands of families have lost—some part of their goods and homes—more, homes and everything they possessed in the world; many even their friends and relatives, who were crushed, burned or suffocated during the awful visitation. It is feared that a great number of lives have been lost. Thus, even dread Death lent a helping hand in the work of havoc.

The glare on the sky occasioned by the flames could

be seen at nights at a distance of many miles, and the heavens appeared in many directions to be in a state of calidity, and seemed as if they would melt and pour down on each in a great mass of liquid fire. The dense, black clouds of suffocating smoke, which, under the influence of the gale which swept lakeward, rendered navigation on that "sheet" of water almost impossible numbers of miles distant from shore, day and night; while on the shore, miles from the scene of devastation, the night was so far turned into day by the brightness of the flames, that the reading of the smallest print was an easy matter of accomplishment. All these attending circumstances of what in history will be handed down to future generations as the " Great Fire of Chicago," will remain vividly in the memory of all who were present in Chicago on the 7th, 8th and 9th of October, A. D. 1871.

Some idea of the fearful ravages during the Great Fire of Chicago, may be entertained by comparing it with the other two greatest of fiery visitations in the history of the world—those of London and Moscow. The Great Fire of London covered 500 acres of ground, rendered homeless 200,000 inhabitants, and destroyed 13,-000 houses. That of Moscow burned over a space of 400 acres, and destroyed 12,000 houses. The Great Fire of Chicago laid waste over 1,800 acres, upward of 18,-000 buildings, and rendered about 185,000 persons homeless.

As to pecuniary loss, no fire which ever occurred in the world has been attended with that suffered by Chicago, as in no city was there such an amount of valuable merchandize or so many expensive buildings destroyed. Most of our merchants had received their winter stocks of goods, none of which they were able to save. The loss in merchandize alone at this last great conflagration will be double that suffered by London and Moscow combined.

The great calamity which has fallen upon our city, as overwhelming as it is, has not broken the spirit of our citizens. She will arise from her ashes, with an energy that will eclipse all her former efforts, and speedily regain her former position.

One thing particularly strikes the passengers through the streets—the absence of everything of a combustible nature. Brick, stone and iron abound, and make up whatever is left of the most magnificent and costly structures. Dirt, in the ordinary sense of the term, has vanished; all is clean, but oh, how desolate. Another thing is the uniformity of the destruction. The marble palace and the cheaper brick and mortar blocks lie in common disorder. There is no distinction, except in the presence of iron pillars and marble door and window ornaments.

WHAT IS LEFT.

The only buildings left intact between the river and the lake and the river and Madison street are Hathaway's coal office, one of the Buckingham elevators, on the lake shore, and the Lind block, at the corner of Randolph and Market. Not a vestige of any wooden structure is left in sight, and the walls in the majority of the buildings described are leveled with the ground. In some instances, partition walls have not altogether fallen, but rear their pointed heads high above the surrounding ruins.

The pavements are burnt, broken and strewn with debris—not impassable, but dusty and smoky.

Crowds of people, men, women and children, rich and poor, thronged the streets this forenoon, satisfying the general curiosity, and wondering at the fearful power which had wrought so great and sudden a calamity. Here and there parties were examining and breaking portions of such articles as lay near the surface in search of valuables. The general expression is one of sadness, but nowhere was despair visible.

The building recently erected at the corner of Madison street, and not finished, is a pile of brick and mortar. The old Transportation Company's wooden shed no longer distresses the sight on the dock—it is all burned up.

On the opposite corner lies in ruins the old Garden City House, which the writer saw erected twenty years ago. Thousands will remember the old hotel with pleasure, mingled with regret at its loss.

From Madison to Washington street all buildings are leveled on both sides of Market. Between Washington and Randolph streets, Hathaway's coal pile is still burning bright. All the business blocks north to the river, on the east side of Market, are destroyed. Among these were the new buildings owned by the Garrett Biblical Institute, the walls of which are nearly all down.

Eddy's horse market, near Market street, is leveled, and the debris emits the smell of burning horseflesh. Farther east the great six-story wagon manufactory of Peter Schuttler, extending along Franklin street, was brought to the ground. Not a vestige of Peacock's jewelry store remains.

The great iron block of the northwest corner of Wells and Randolph is a mass of broken columns, brick and mortar. This building made a wreck of the man who erected it, and is now itself a dismal wreck.

Opposite lays that which was once the Metropolitan Hotel, around the memory of which lingers a history of unusual interest—the means which built it having been stolen from the jewelry store of Isaac Speer some eighteen years ago.

On the other corner, where stood the favorite old Briggs House, is an unshaped mass of material, little consonant with the comfort, hospitality and mirth for which that old hostelry was ever famous.

Again, on the southeast corner, lie the remains of Schick & Ibach's Hotel Garni, a stately block.

Farther down, bricks and mortar point to the location of many well-known business houses; John Alston's, Heath & Milligan's, Ducat's Insurance Agency, the Northwestern Engraving Company's rooms, etc., and on the other corner, low in the dust, what was once Metropolitan Hall, redolent of its charitable dinners and the gas of George Francis Train.

Bleak, smoked, hollow and desolate, upon the scene, rear the walls of the Court House—scene of so many a distressing and exciting trial, of local legislation and public business. Not only have the roofs "buckled," but the entire structure looms up from where we write, a ruined monument of departed greatness. The old fence remains, with the tessellated pavements, but the glory of the tribunals and the Council Chamber are things of the past.

Across the street, a heap of brick, iron rods and shattered ornaments of stone, mark the grave of the Fidelity Safe Company's magnificent structure and the stately Sherman House. Words are weak to express the air of desolation that hovers around this corner, so recently brilliant with business and pleasure. The skull on the banquet table could scarcely be more saddening to a reflective mind.

Last week, high in air, on the southeast corner, stood Miller's jewelry store. Wood's Museum, with its half a million curiosities, and nights of tragedy and comedy, graced the vicinity with its fair front, beneath the Colonel's benign portrait; clothing for the million enticed the wayfarer to stop and buy, and whisky and stationery, printing and engraving, made this section of Randolph street a popular resort. This morning it is a desert.

And so we could go on, down to the lake, calling up a hundred reminiscences of old and cherished times and places. What memories cluster around the Matteson House, the old Garrett block, the auction house of shrill-voiced Butters, etc. Now the heart sickens as it sees the bitter end of all these things.

From the bridge to La Salle street, Lake street was built up on both sides with business blocks of brick and stone, remarkable more for their commodiousness and convenience than beauty. All are gone.

The Board of Education rooms; brokers' offices; the Northwestern railway ticket offices; the United States and American Express offices; the jewelry stores of Rodin & Hamlin, A. Van Cott & Co., and others, and the dry goods stores of J. B. Shay & Co., all well known places of business, are as unsightly as a neglected grave.

No building in Chicago claims a kinder remembrance than the old Tremont House. Its broken walls and towering chimney-stack speak nothing of the elegance, sociability and comfort that always met the traveler at the threshold, and made him a friend for life.

From the Tremont to the great Union Depot is not far, but its wealth of merchandise and stately edifices were known far and near throughout the West, but the eye dims and the pulse goes slow when the ruin of this noble mart meets the sight. Names of firms who did business here might be given, but they stand engraven in the heart of many a country merchant, who has profited by the courtesies of the Lake street jobbers.

SOUTH SIDE.

The scene in this section of the city is too appalling to be dwelt upon with other words than those which will in the most adequate manner convey an idea of the reality, which seems beyond the power of tongue or pen to relate. The streets that are burned over are Madison, Monroe, Adams, Jackson, Van Buren, Congress and Michigan avenue, where it was checked, the Michigan avenue hotel being saved. On Wabash it burned through to Harrison street. The last house burned on the east side of Wabash avenue. On the west side, Dr. McChesney's (the Wabash Avenue Methodist)

Church was not burned, at the northeast corner of Harrison and Wabash avenue. On State street, 356 was the last number burned. This was the south limit so far west as the line of the Michigan Southern Railroad track. The long freight houses (in and out freight) were burned with all their contents; cars and everything as far south as Taylor, and west of the east track. Taylor street, the north limit of a great lumber district, was not crossed to the south. Thus, in short, there is only one building within the limits above described which is not burned to ashes, and this seems to have escaped through a miracle—it is numbered 91 to 99 Harrison street, corner of North avenue. The streets which run north and south are Michigan avenue, Wabash avenue, State, Dearborn, Clark, La Salle, Wells, Sherman, Griswold and Market. This section of the city contained the glory of our architecture, and the palatial residences of some of our most wealthy citizens. The names of individual owners can not be given, but the prominent business structures were the depot of the Lake Shore, and Chicago and Rock Island and Pacific Railroad, on Van Buren, from Sherman to Griswold, and south to Harrison; the Pacific Hotel, which was ready for the roof, and occupied a block. The Custom House, which is gutted, the whitened walls alone standing, Honore's blocks, finished and unfinished, on Dearborn, from Monroe to Adams, the *Tribune* building, the *Times* office, the *Post* building, the office of the *Staats Zeitung*, and numerous publications. The elegant structure known as the Lake Side Press building, on Clark, the Young Men's Christian Association library, the Republic Insurance building, Farwell Hall, McVicker's Theater, the Clifton House, the Academy of Design, Coan & Ten Broeck's Manufacturing Company's building on Adams street, the Palmer House, St. Mary's St. Paul's Catholic Church, Universalist, Second Presbyterian, Trinity Episcopal Church, First Presbyterian

Church, Michigan avenue, Terrace Row, the Chicago Club, Potter Palmer's new hotel, (unfinished) Robert Law's coal yard, Rogers & Co.'s coal yard, the largest firms in the city, the Jewish Synagogue, northeast corner of Fourth avenue and Harrison street, the New Club on Harrison and State, the Bigelow House on Dearborn and Adams, which would have been opened this week. All the bridges over the river, from Madison to Twelfth street, are burned. On the West Side the ravages were dire, sweeping away the great manufactories, and mills, and the elevators of that section were burned, together with two large ice houses, section "C" of the warehouses alone being saved. The apex of the field of desolation, which is an horizontal cone, is at the corner of De Koven and Jefferson streets, and from there the burnt track sweeps northeast, widening and widening for the distance of some five miles, while the distance to the lake is almost between Jefferson and the river east and west, and Van Buren and De Koven, the first street north of Twelfth, north and south, and from any point can be seen a dozen or more tall chimneys marking the sites of as many enormous manufacturing buildings. None of them can be named accurately. The Chicago Dock Company's warehouse, on Taylor street, and the Pittsburgh and Fort Wayne Railroad.

The thoroughfares are crowded with a constantly flowing stream of people which seems to take its rise at Madison street bridge and move sluggishly along through the streets and avenues, gazing at the burnt and burning ruins.

With but one or two exceptions, the walls of buildings on Lake street have fallen in.

The ruins of the jewelry, grocery and other stores on Lake and South Water streets, are being ransacked by hundreds of people.

The Eastern Illinois Elevator stands uninjured.

The walls of the Marine Hospital are mostly standing.

All the bridges over the river, from the South to the North Divisions are gone.

A gentleman we saw this morning, who had been in Paris during the past year, says the devastation there did not compare with Chicago this morning.

Among the hundreds of buildings on Lake street that in themselves would have made an extensive conflagration, not even the walls of one is standing.

IN THE NORTH DIVISION.

The scene in the North Division, from the time the flames showed their terrible presence there, beggars description approaching anything like what really occurred. Those who had time caused their furniture and other effects to be placed on the sidewalk in front of the various buildings in which they resided, ready to be carted off. Before, however, vehicles of any kind could be procured, the flames had devoured the interposing structures, and in less time than it takes to write it had seized upon the piles of furniture and driven the owners away to seek security. This occurred in thousands of instances. Many succeeded in reaching what they considered a safe distance from the fire, but in half an hour were forced to flee again and again, many families moving half a dozen times, in face of the fearful element each time, leaving behind the portion of goods they had saved, until finally they found that they had lost all. Toward the lake, northward, northeastward, flocked the thousands of pallid featured citizens, in all conditions of health and distress. It would take too much time and space to-day to describe the heart-rending spectacles which were presented and witnessed. All means of communication were cut off, which fact tended to render the general horror, dismay and confusion the more general as the flames pressed onward, and no one knew where to go or where the dreadful conflagration would end. Expressmen and others demanded from $25 to $100 a load, to even take sufferers and their baggage out of reach of the flames, and in many instances such sums were paid by persons who soon found the flames close at hand and then being unable to obtain more aid had to leave all their goods to the fury of the greedy element.

All that portion of the city lying between the river, east of Clark street and west of the lake, and as far north as Fullerton avenue, is entirely destroyed, except the residence of W. B. Ogden, corner Clark and Oak streets, and nearly all the glass observatory, and also three or four buildings west of Lincoln Park. These few land-marks are all that remain of that once beautiful part of the city. Even the "City of the Dead,"—the old burying-ground—was not exempt from the ravages of the fire, it being burned over, leaving tomb-stones looking most sad.

There are only four buildings left standing on the South Side below Van Buren street. Those four are the Custom House, the Court House, the First National Bank building, and the *Tribune* building. They were all completely burned out, nothing remaining except the walls and parts of partitions. We doubt if any of them can ever be used again except the Custom House. Those immense walls seem to have stood the fire test without flinching. The masonry of the other three has been very seriously impaired.

REAL ESTATE TITLES DESTROYED.

All the records of deeds and mortgages are destroyed. This includes all the real estate not only in Chicago, but in Cook county, with its numerous suburban towns. Fortunately the abstracts of titles in the office of Shortall & Hoard, conveyancers, are known to be safe. There is great hope that when the vaults are opened at the other abstract offices, the record books which are intended to be perfect copies of every real estate transfer in the county, are safe. There are several of them, and it would be strange if some of them besides the one already examined are not safe. A leading member of the Chicago bar gives it as his opinion that the title to all the property in the county can be re-established by means of these abstracts. The Legislature will probably pass some enabling act to cover the case. As to the value of real estate, it is now entirely indeterminate, because it is impossible to divine where the future business center will be. The latter will depend upon the location selected by the leading business houses, which are already in consultation.

BANKS.

There is not a bank left in all Chicago, unless it be some little house remote from what was the center of business. The actual losses of the bankers can not be computed, even approximately, in any one case. One thing we are authorized to state positively. The banks will resume regular business in a few days. It should be added that the Union Stock Yards National Bank is the only National Bank now in working order in Cook county. The Cook County National Bank suffered less than any other, because the farthest south of any. It was located in the northern corner of the Honore block. The Union National was the first to go, although the Northwestern and Corn Exchange, located in the Chamber of Commerce, went about the same time. Indeed, it was not an hour after those on the ground thought any bank in danger, before all, unless it were the First National and the Cook County National, were in flames.

The Directors of the Chamber of Commerce held a meeting this morning, and resolved to commence the erection of a new building to-morrow.

The building now occupied by the Chamber of Commerce is already furnished with a telegraph office, making communication with the principal points East and West.

The burned district embraces all of the South Division of the city lying north of Harrison street—more than a square mile of the business heart of the city. In all that area, covered two days ago with marble business places filled with merchandize and the fabrics of all the world, there remains standing but a single building untouched by fire. Elevator A, with its hundreds of thousands of bushels of grain, escaped even a touch of the demon of destruction. Perched upon the extreme northwest point of the South Division where the river and the lake mingle their waters, this great granary, partly because of its somewhat isolated position, and more because of its rare good fortune, escaped destruction.

The North Division has been terribly scourged. Stretching from the Lake to the North Branch, and from the main river to beyond Lincoln Park, everything is swept away except a little group of dwellings near Division street. Fully three square miles of buildings, business houses and residences, including many of the costliest dwellings in Chicago, were devastated over there.

In the West Division the fire started between Twelfth and DeKoven, running northeasterly to Van Buren and Jefferson streets, burning a narrow strip through the entire distance, it at once laid out its plans for a big job. In a few hours nothing was left standing between Van Buren and Adams to the South Branch. More than half a mile square of densely built-up territory was converted into a mass of smouldering ruins. Founderies, machine shops, manufactories of various kinds, elevators filled with grain, coal yards filled with coal, railroad freight houses, etc., were carried down in common ruin.

IN THE SUBURBS.

Around about Hyde Park, south of the city, the excitement and anxiety was intense. The straggling and unconnected accounts of the fire and its progress, the different buildings which were already reported in flames, and those the hungry element was commencing to devour; the bridges all gone; the railroad depots gone and going—were rehearsed to eager listeners, and by them told again to others. The early train brought out the news as far south as the crossing, but the stories told were apparently so incredible, and seemingly so impossible, that even the most credulous believed they were exaggerated.

The major portion of the people in Hyde Park township do, or rather did, business in Chicago, and as is the case in all country villages, everybody knew everybody else, and as one familiar name after another was announced as overwhelmed in the general ruin, the strong feeling of sympathy was manifested in the most pathetic and condoling ejaculations.

At Woodlawn, Messrs. T. S. and John Fitch, extensive real estate men, and owning the Post Office Block; James Wadsworth, on Lake street; J. M. Harvey, clothier on Lake near Dearborn; Dr. Trine and others of that suburb; Farrington, Nelson, Cady, Waters, Barrett, Root, Favor, Van Higgins, Jameson, Bogues, and a host of others, all suffered to a greater or lesser degree.

The train that bore the victims to the scene of their great loss was delayed by the passing out of freight and passenger cars from the sweep of the fire, and the feeling was heightened and intensified as the waiting continued, for the air was filled with the wildest rumors, and the knowledge of the worst would be far preferable and less painful than the state of uncertainty which seemed to shroud the minds of all. So eager were the people to get to the city that at every stoppage many jumped off, and either walked or procured other conveyance to the place upon which all thought centered. But the half had not been told, and the most fearful accounts of the wreck and ruin were but a faint glimmer of the fearful and wide-spread desolation. Seemingly their cup of misery was not yet full, for as darkness began to gather over the city, the rumor gained ground that the woods around Woodlawn were afire, and that the residences were in great danger. Horror pervaded the minds of all—their places of business had been swept away, and now their homes were to be sacrificed. Happily the rumor was found to be false, and a weight was lifted from many a despondent heart. The foundation for the report was the fact that the prairie round about was on fire, but it was controlled, and although it was reported that the glue factory and the Casgrain Hotel, at Ainsworth were burned, the report could not be traced to a reliable source.

CHAPTER V.

A Graphic Story—Statement of Ex-Lieutenant Governor Bross, of The Chicago Tribune—Scenes During and After the Fire—Theodore Tilton on the Fire—George Alfred Townsend's Poem.

From the New York Tribune of October 16th.

Ex-Lieutenant Governor Bross, of Illinois, arrived in this city from Chicago yesterday morning. A *Tribune* reporter called upon him at the St. Nicholas Hotel, immediately after his arrival, and, although Governor Bross was suffering greatly from fatigue and the reaction consequent on the excitement of the last few days, he kindly and cheerfully dictated the following statement of his experiences during the conflagration. Governor Bross is well known as one of the principal proprietors of the Chicago *Tribune*, and his statement will be read with the greatest interest.

As to what I saw of the fire. About two o'clock on Monday morning my family and I were aroused by Mrs. Samuel Bowles, the wife of the proprietor of the *Springfield Republican*, who happened to be a guest in our house. We had all gone to bed very tired the night before, and had slept so soundly that we were unaware of the conflagration till it had assumed terrible force.

My family were all very much alarmed at the glare which illuminated the sky and lake. I saw at once that a fearful disaster was impending over Chicago, and immediately left the house to determine the locality and extent of the fire. I found that it was then a good deal south of my house and west of the Michigan Southern and Rock Island Railroad depots. I went home considerably reassured in half an hour, and, finding my family packing things up, told them that I did not anticipate danger and requested them to leave off packing. But, I said: "The result of this night's work will be awful. At least ten thousand people will want breakfast in the morning; you prepare breakfast for one hundred?" This they proceeded to do, but soon became again alarmed and recommenced packing. Soon after half-past two o'clock I started for the *Tribune* office to see if it was in any danger. By this time the fire had crossed the river, and that portion of the city south of Harrison street, and between Third avenue and the river, seemed in a blaze of fire, as well as on the west side. I reached the *Tribune* office, and, seeing no cause for any apprehension as to its safety, I did not remain there more than twenty minutes. On leaving the office I proceeded to the Nevada Hotel (which is my property,) at Washington and Franklin streets. I remained there for an hour watching the progress of the flames and contemplating the ruinous destruction of property going on around. The fire had passed east of the hotel, and I hoped that the building was safe; but it soon began to extend in a westerly direction, and the hotel was quickly enveloped in flames. I became seriously alarmed, and ran round North street to Randolph street, so as to head off the flames and get back to my house, which was on Michigan avenue, on the shore of the Lake. My house was a part of almost the last block burned.

MAGNIFICENT APPEARANCE OF THE FIRE WHEN AT ITS HEIGHT.

At this time the fire was the most grandly-magnificent scene that one can conceive. The Court House, Post office, Farwell Hall, the Tremont House, Sherman House, and all the splendid buildings on La Salle and Wells streets, were burning with a sublimity of effect which astounded me. All the adjectives in the language would fail to convey the intensity of its wonders. Crowds of men, women and children, were huddling away, running first in one direction, then in another, shouting and crying in their terror, and trying to save anything they could lay their hands on, no matter how trivial in value; while every now and then explosions, which seemed to shake the solid earth, reverberated through the air and added to the terrors of the poor people. I crossed Lake street bridge to the west, ran north to Kinsey street bridge, and crossed over east to the north side, hoping to head off the fire. It had, however, already swept north of me, and was traveling faster than I could go, and I soon came to the conclusion that it would be impossible for me to get east in that direction. I accordingly recrossed Kinsey street bridge, and went west as far as Desplaines street, where I fortunately met a gentleman in a buggy, who very kindly drove me over Twelfth street bridge to my house on Michigan avenue. It was by this time getting on toward 5 o'clock, and the day was beginning to break. On my arrival home I found my horses already harnessed and my riding-horse saddled for me. My family and some friends were all busily engaged in packing up and in distributing sandwiches and coffee to all who wanted them or could spare a minute to partake of them.

BURNING OF THE TRIBUNE BUILDING, AND THE DWELLINGS ON MICHIGAN AVENUE.

I immediately jumped on my horse, and rode as fast as I could to the Tribune office. I found everything safe; the men were all there, and we fondly hoped that all danger was passed as far as we were concerned, and for this reason: the blocks in front of the Tribune building on Dearborn street, and north on Madison street, had both been burned; the only damage accruing to us being confined to a cracking of some of the plate glass windows from the heat. But a somewhat curious incident soon set us all in a state of excitement. The fire had unknown to us crawled under the sidewalk from the wooden pavement, and had caught the wood-work of the barber's shop which comprises a portion of our basement. As soon as we ascertained the extent of the mischief we no longer apprehended any special danger, believing, as we did, that the building was fire-proof. My associates, Mr. Medill and Mr. White, were present; and with the help of some of our employes, we went to work with water and one of Babcock's Fire Extinguishers. The fire was soon put out, and we once more returned to business. The forms had been sent down stairs, and I ordered our foreman, Mr. Keller, to get all the pressmen together, in order to issue the papers as soon as a paragraph showing how far the fire had then extended could be prepared and inserted. Many kind friends gathered around the office and warmly expressed their gratification at the preservation of our building. Believing all things safe, I again mounted my horse and rode south on State street, to see what progress the fire was making, and if it was moving eastward on Dearborn street. To my great surprise and horror, I found that its current had taken an easterly direction, nearly as far as State street, and that it was also advancing in a northerly direction with terrible swiftness and power. I at once saw the danger so imminently threatening us, and with some friends endeavored to obtain some powder for the purpose of blowing up some buildings south of the Palmer House. Failing in finding any powder, I proposed to tear them down. I proceeded to Church's hardware store and succeeded in procuring a dozen heavy axes, and, handing them to my friends, requested them to mount the buildings with me and literally " chop them down." All but two or three seemed utterly paralyzed at this unexpected change in the course of the fire; and even these, seeing the others stand back, were unwilling to make the effort alone. At this moment I saw that some wooden buildings and a new brick house, west of the Palmer House, had already caught fire. I saw at a glance that the Tribune building was doomed, and I rode back to the office and told them that nothing more could be done to save the building, McVicker's Theater, or anything else in that vicinity.

In this hopeless frame of mind I rode home to look after my residence and family, intently watching the ominous eastward movement of the flames. I at once set to work with my family and friends to move as much of my furniture as possible across the narrow park east of Michigan avenue, on to the shore of the lake, a distance of about three hundred feet. At the same time I sent my family to the house of some friends in the south part of the city for safety; My daughter, Miss Jessie Bross, was the last to leave us. The work of carrying our furniture across the avenue to the shore was most difficult and even dangerous. For six or eight hours Michigan avenue was jammed with every description of vehicles containing families escaping from the city, or baggage wagons laden with goods or furniture. The sidewalks were crowded with men, women and children, all carrying something. Some of the things saved and carried away were valueless. One woman carried an empty bird-cage; another an old work-box; another some dirty, empty baskets, old, useless bedding, anything that could be hurriedly snatched up, seemed to have been carried away without judgment or forethought. In the meantime the fire had lapped up the Palmer House, the theaters, and the *Tribune* building; and, contrary to our expectations, for we thought the current of the fire would pass my residence, judging by the direction of the wind, we saw by the advancing clouds of smoke and the rapidly approaching flames that we were in imminent peril. The fire had already worked so far south and east as to attack the stables in the rear of Terrace Block, between Van Buren and Congress streets. Many friends rushed into the houses in the block and helped to carry out heavy furniture, such as pianos and bookcases. We succeeded in carrying the bulk of it to the shore, where it now lies stored; much of it, however, is seriously damaged. There I and a few others sat by our household goods, calmly awaiting the contemplated coming destruction of our property—one of the most splendid blocks in Chicago. The eleven fine houses which composed the block were occupied by Denton Gurney, Peter L. Yeo, Mrs. Humphreys, (owned by Mrs. Walker,) William Bross, P. F. W. Peck, S. C. Griggs, Tutnill King, Judge U. T. Dickey, General Cook, John L. Clarke, and the Hon. J. Y. Scammon.

THE APPEARANCE OF THE CITY AFTER THE FIRE—ENTERPRISE OF THE TRIBUNE.

The next morning I was, of course, out early, and found the streets thronged with crowds of people moving in all directions. To me the sight of the ruin, though so sad, was wonderful to a degree, and especially being wrought in so short a time. It was the destruction of the entire business portion of one of the greatest cities in the world! Every bank and insurance office, law offices, hotels, theaters, railroad depots, most of the churches, and many of the principal residences of the city a charred mass, and property without estimate gone!

Mr. White, my associate, like myself, had been burned out of house and home. He had removed his family to a place of safety, and I had no idea where he or any one else connected with the *Tribune* office might be found. My first point to make was naturally the site of our late office; but before I reached it I met two former tenants of our building who told me that there was a job printing office on Randolph street that could probably be bought.

I immediately started for Randolph street. While making my way west through the crowds of people, over the Madison street bridge, desolation stared me in the face at every step. And yet I was much struck with the tone and temper of the people. On all sides men said to one another: "Cheer up; we'll be all right again before long;" and many other plucky things. Their pluck and courage was wonderful. Every one was bright, cheerful, pleasant, hopeful, and even inclined to be jolly in spite of the misery and destitution which surrounded them and which they shared. One and all said Chicago must and should be rebuilt at once. On reaching Canal street, on my way to purchase the printing office I had heard of, I was informed that while Mr. White and I were saving our families and as much of our furniture as we could on Monday afternoon, Mr. Medill, seeing that the Tribune office must inevitably be burned, sought for and purchased Edwards' job printing office, No. 15 Canal street, had got out a small paper in the morning, and was then busy organizing things. One after another, all hands turned up, and by the afternoon we had improvised the back part of the room into our editorial department, while an old wooden box did duty as a business counter in the front window. We were soon as busy as bees, writing editorials and paragraphs, and taking in any number of advertisements. By evening several orders for type and fixtures were made out, and things were generally so far advanced that I left for the depot at Twenty-second street, with the intention of coming on to New York. Unfortunately I missed the train, and had to wait till Wednesday morning. We shall get along as best we can till the rebuilding of our office is finished. Going down to the ruins I found a large section thrown out of the north wall on Madison street. The other three walls are standing; but the east and west walls are so seriously injured that they must be pulled down. The south wall is in good condition. More of our office and the Post office remains standing than any other buildings that I saw. Our building was put up to stand a thousand years, and it would have done so but for that awful furnace of fire, fanned by an intense gale on the windward side, literally melting it up where it stood.

THE LOSS $300,000,000—GRATITUDE OF THE CHICAGO PEOPLE.

With regard to the probable loss from the fire it is impossible to say anything certain. I saw an estimate the other day which was based on the tax list of the city, which is over $500,000,000; and the writer inferred from that list that the loss can not exceed $125,000,000. Now, according to our system of taxation in Illinois, this city tax list never shows anything like the proper amount of property in the city. To my knowledge, houses having from $20,000 to $30,000 worth of furniture in them are not rated at more than $2,000 to $4,000. Stocks of goods were never valued among us at more than one-fifth or one-tenth of their real value on the tax list. All our merchants had just filled up their stores with fall and winter trade stocks. From these and other facts I estimate the loss by the fire at considerably over $200,000,000, and, if damage, depreciation of real estate and property, and loss of business are considered, the loss would, in my judgment, exceed $300,000,000.

From the Independent.

Chicago—incomparable in her magic industry, enterprise, and growth; unapproachable in her calamity!

Pen cannot express the horror of that fearful Sunday night, that more fearful Monday; and even as we write on Tuesday the destruction is unstayed. Sunday morning Chicago was the fairest, as she was the most audacious city on the continent. Built up from creamy quarries, lifted like a sudden exhalation, as if from the magic nest of some mighty Mulciber, and solid, it seemed, and secure, except from the visitation of God, it has sunk down into the earth—wood, brick, stone and iron—under His visitation in the most terrible fiery ruin that history recounts!

It had not seemed possible. Human skill, we had thought, in years of conflict against the demon of flame, had secured the advantage. The fire started in a wooden quarter. But Chicago was built of brick and stone. Yet, once started, the flames lapped up even the buildings deemed absolutely fire-proof. Chicago had grand waterworks, and an abundant supply of water; she had the best modern appliances for fighting fire with water and steam. But when the fiend got way, and his rage was fanned by the fierce gale, he mocked all the futile attempts of man to stay his course. He laid Chicago—fresh, grand, beautiful Chicago—all in ruins!

What can we say more? We do not yet know the worst. But we know that already an area of *five square miles* is covered with blackened walls—and the flames are unquenched! We know that the Court House—twenty years in building, half the life-time of the city—was swept away in thirty minutes; that the Sherman House, and the new Pacific Hotel, the largest in the world, have perished; that those monster railroad depots, and those grain elevators, which Chicago invented, and which were just then filled to repletion with six million bushels of wheat and corn, are all destroyed; that no newspaper will this (Tuesday) morning show Chicago's houseless wanderers the callous figures that indicate its loss, for their type is all melted by the flames; that by the destruction of its telegraph stations the doomed city has once again been cut off from communication with the sympathizing world; that the gasworks and waterworks are gone, and that when the flames are extinguished the city will be in darkness, and its children will suffer for water; that, in short, the entire business part of the city and miles in extent of its residences are in ashes. The great fire in New York in 1835 destroyed 648 houses. This has leveled 12,000. The great fire in London in 1666 ravaged 436 acres. This covers over three thousand acres with ruins. That fire—which, like this, burned from a fatal Sunday through three days, consumed the infection of the plague, and in time replaced the narrow lanes and the wooden structures with solid masonry and with broad streets—destroyed by a liberal computation fifty million dollars of wealth. A like computation will count the losses of Chicago by hundreds of millions, and will, for a season, cripple the commerce of the continent; but no such incidental, lasting gain will follow from the destruction of a new city, that had been built with no stint of money and skill.

Last week a public spirited citizen of Cincinnati presented to that city the most beautiful and costly fountain ever yet set up in any plaza in the world. All day, throughout all time, was it stipulated, that its sprays and jets of water should spirt and flirt their fairy foam to delight the children and nursery-maids that shall play about it for generations after Mr. Probasco is dead. It is a purely modern device, with not a suggestion of Amphitrite, nor of her nymphs and dolphins, and yet in severely classic taste. Above its polished granite columns, its basins and its statuary, rises a majestic figure of the Genius of Water, distributing her flowing treasures for the myriad comforts and needs of man. There is nothing more striking among the bronze groups below her than the colossal figure of a man, driven to the roof of his burning house, holding an empty bucket, and supplicating the Genius above for the saving element. How soon we have its counterpart! The Mayor of Chicago telegraphs to Milwaukee, to Cincinnati, for aid to quench the devouring flames: "Send us all the steamers you can spare!" And when the mad fire has disabled those monster engines that supply the city with water, hear the despairing note which sounds across the prairies and passes down the Mississippi to her old rival, St. Louis: "The city is burned up; the *waterworks are gone;* send us food for a hundred thousand homeless people!"

Food for Chicago! Food for the granary of the West! This is the cry to-day. And for weeks to come there will be a call for all the aid that the benevolent can supply. Let the President unrebuked assume war powers to answer the call. Let Cincinnati rival St. Louis in the labor of mercy. Let plundered New York pour forth her yet unsquandered wealth. Let church vie with church, and man with man; and let no Christian and no citizen withhold his bounty.

And to the God of mercy—whose overmastering powers of fire or of flood man thus learns that he can not curb—let the prayer go up for the homeless and the suffering.

[From the Cincinnati Commercial.

THE SMITTEN CITY.

BY GEORGE ALFRED TOWNSEND.

I heard a parson of the school of Baalam
    Lift up the lesson of the flaming town,
And, like a peddler in the will of Heaven,
    Show how its sins invoked the Sovereign frown.

Thus the dead lion ever is insulted
    By asses' colts, whose pity is a blow,
And fallen empires find their last misfortune
    In shallow platitudes from fool and foe.

Bright, Christian capital of lakes and prairie,
    Heaven had no interest in thy scourge and scath
Thou wert the newest shrine of our religion,
    The youngest witness of our hope and faith.

Not in thy embers do we rake for folly,
    But like a martyr's ashes gather thee,
With chastened pride and tender melancholy,—
    The miracle thou wast, and yet will be!

Not merely in the homages of churches,
    Or bells of praise tolled o'er the inland seas,—
Thou glorified our God and human nature
    With meeter works and grander melodies.

Of cheerful toil and willing eterprises,
    Of hearty faith in freedom and in man;
The hoar old capitals looked on in wonder
    To see the swift, strong race this stripling ran.

The Smitten City.

How like the sun he rose above the marshes,
   And built the world beneath his airy feet,
And changed the course of immemorial rivers,
   And tapped the lakes for water cool and sweet.

How skillfully the golden grain transmuted
   To birds of sail and meteors of spark,
And, like another Noah, bade creation
   March in the teeming mazes of his ark.

Yet in his power, most frank and democratic,
   He roused no envious witness of his joy;
And in the stature of the Prince and hero,
   We saw the laughing dimples of a boy.

Still wise and apt among the oldest merchants,
   His young example steered the wary mart,
And amplest credit poured its gold around him
   And trade imperial gave scope for art.

His architectures passed all heathen splendor,
   The immigrating Goth drew wondering near;
To see his shafts and arches tall and slender
   Branch o'er the new homes of this pioneer.

The Greek and Roman there might see rebuilded,
   In vastness equal and in style as pure,
The merchants' markets like a palace gilded,
   With marble walls and deep entablature.

His two score bridges swinging on their pivots,
   The long and laden line of vessels speed,
While he, impatient, marched beneath the sluices
   His hosts, like Cyrus, in the river's bed.

Then, when all weak predictions proved but scandal,
   And the wild marshes grew a sovereign's home,
A dozing cow o'erset an urchin's candle,—
   Once more a fool fired the Ephesian dome.

The artless winds that blew o'er plains of cattle,
   And cooled the corn through all the summer days,
Plunged like wild steeds in pastime or in battle,
   Straight in the blinding brightness of the blaze.

And down fell bridge, and parapet, and lintle,
   The blazing barques went drifting, one by one,
The mighty city wrapped its head in splendor,
   And sank into the waters like a sun!

Oh! thou, my master, champion of the people,
   Tribune august, who e'er kept righteous court,
Long after fire had toppled church and steeple,
   Thou stoodst amid the ruins like a fort.

High and serene thy cornices extended,
   Though scorched by smoke and of the flame the prey,
Above the vault where, grim, and calm, and splendid,
   The sleeping lions of thy presses lay.

Till looking round thee on the wondrous pity,
   Thyself alone erect, intact, upreared,
Disdaining to outlive the glorious city,
   With innate heat transfigured, disappeared.

Yet, from the grave Chicago's wonderous spirit
   Comes forth all brightness, o'er the darkened town
To say again: "Lo! I am with yon brethren:
   With all my thorns, I wear my civic crown.

"To die is sweet embalmed in your compassion
   Your oil and wine make life in every rent,
Oh! let me lean a little while upon you,
   And walk to strength in your encouragemen

CINCINNATI, October 13, 1871.

CHAPTER VI.

The Rebuilding of Chicago—Energetic Action Looking Thereto—The Great Fires of Other Cities—A Hopeful Picture—Chicago Must Rise Again.

The following telegraphic dispatch passed over the wires from Chicago on the 13th of October, but two or three days after the conflagration had laid the business portion of the city in ruins. This will serve to show the indomitable character of the merchants and others of the Lake city:

THE REBUILDING OF CHICAGO.

CHICAGO, October 13.—The dawn of each succeding day brings brighter prospects for the smitten city, and the feeling of hope and faith which springs up within the breasts of the energetic men who have made Chicago what it was, is strengthened and extended every hour. Twenty-one of the twenty-four columns of this morning's Tribune are filled with advertisements of business firms who have already secured new locations, and are either now ready, or will be in a few days, for business. Stocks of new goods are already on the way here. Builders are overwhelmed with applications to put up new buildings for business purposes. One contractor had, last night, sixteen contracts for substantial structures, to be erected at once. The Tribune's commercial article says there is still but little doing in produce circles, but our commission merchants and grain dealers are hard at work preparing to open out again on a full scale, just as soon as the pecuniary arrangements will permit, which will be in a day or two, probably by the first of next week. Many of them are busy helping distribute food and clothing to the destitute. The remainder are fitting up offices in the vicinity of the temporary Trade Rooms, at Nos. 51 and 53 Canal street, where the Board will do business till the Chamber of Commerce can be rebuilt.

Some grain is moving out. Four charters were reported to-day. It is expected the grain will be moved out much more rapidly towards Monday, as the banks will be able to make advances by that time.

BANK VAULTS ALL SAFE.

So far none of the bank vaults have been found at all injured. The Union Nationals, which were at first reported blown up, are in a correct condition so far as the contents are concerned. The safes of the Fidelity were found, when opened, to have no hurt, and every dollar of the millions on deposit there was safe. C. Wilson took out $30,000 in fresh, clean greenbacks. The Company have established an office in the ruins, and invite all to bring their money and other valuables there, and deposit them, free of charge, until they can get better accommodations. The savings banks of the city announce that they will at once pay in full all depositors whose deposits do not exceed $20, and not less than $20, and $20 to every depositor whose balance is more than that sum.

The agents of the Ætna Insurance Company commenced at once to adjust and pay their losses, which they say will not exceed two and a half or three million dollars.

CONDITION OF THE WOODEN PAVEMENT.

It was at first thought that most all the Nicholson pavements of the city had been consumed, but this is found not to be the case. In this connection a dispatch says:

A noticeable fact, and one of immense importance in the rebuilding of the city is the almost perfect condition in which the fire has left the Nicholson pavement. The damage is so trifling as not to be worthy of mention. Miles of pavement on the North Side are almost unscorched, and perfectly free of debris; and even in the South Division, where both sides of the streets were lined with lofty brick and stone buildings, there is scarcely a point where a carriage may not be safely driven through the streets. Indeed, except where buildings were blown up, or partially blown up, in the endeavor to stop the progress of the flames, the ruins have almost invariably fallen upon their own sites. At points where the pavements were burned at all, the fire only charred the outside; and it is a question whether the process to which they were subjected will not add to their durability.

PREPARATIONS FOR REBUILDING.

The Commercial and National Banks will recommence building on their old sites at once. Meanwhile, they reopened for business on West Washington street. They opened their vaults and found all their books, papers and securities in perfect order. There is a rumor that in a burnt blacksmith shop on Rush street the bodies of fifteen men were found burned to a crisp, they having rushed into the shop to escape from the flames, which had surrounded them before they discovered their peril. Immense numbers of people were missing, and for the purpose of aiding in the discovery of the missing ones, a Central Intelligence Office was established where the names of all missing could be left and given to the police.

The large hotel in the West Division, just completed, has been taken by Gage Bros. & Rice, late of the Sherman House, and they will open it in ten days. It will be known as the Sherman House. The entire North Division is swept clear from the Chicago River to Wright's Grove, a distance of more than three miles. But one house, that of Mahlon D. Ogden, formerly Hon. William B. Ogden's, remains standing in the entire district. A large portion of the population driven from this desolated ground are encamped on the prairie to the north, where they have nothing but the canopy of Heaven to cover them, and scarcely sufficient food to satisfy their hunger.

A meeting of citizens of this State was held, at which resolutions were passed recommending Governor Palmer to call an extra session of the Legislature at once. Ex-Governor Oglesby was appointed to proceed to Springfield to lay the matter before Governor Palmer

All the packing houses in Chicago, and many of the elevators remain uninjured, and these two branches of Chicago's best property will be but slightly interrupted. The Director's of the Chamber of Commerce met and resolved to proceed at once to the re-erection of their elegant edifice. Two companies of United States Infantry arrived and was at once put on patrol duty.

THE GREAT FIRES OF OTHER CITIES.

The Chicago Tribune draws the following comparison between this and the great fires of other cities, hopefully closing with the assertion that Chicago must rise again.

And will Chicago recover from this terrible blow? The energy, the enterprise, the progress of Chicago has been a marvel, and we expect that wonderful energy will be still further exhibited in the rapid rebuilding of the waste places and on more durable foundations. The tinder-boxes that have been food for the flames should not be replaced to make fuel for another conflagration. The calamity at Chicago should be a lesson to all cities, and our own should profit by it, and to this point the attention of the authorities can not be too urgently directed. The waste places that conflagrations have made in other cities, have been speedily rebuilt, and why not those of Chicago, the gate to the Western World?

The conflagration in Chicago, if the reports are not greatly exaggerated, is the most extensive not only in area, but in the value of property destroyed, that has ever occurred. Other cities have suffered similar calamities, and from the effects of which it was thought at the time that they could not recover, or that the restoration would require many years. But in nearly every instance the recovery from the terrible devastations occasioned by the devouring element has been so rapid as to appear more like the work of genii than of energy and the toil of patient industry. A brief recital of some of the great fires that have occurred in other cities will not be uninteresting in connection with the ruin occasioned by the Fire King in devoted Chicago.

A terrible conflagration took place in London over two centuries ago. The summer had been the hottest and driest that had been known for many years, and London, being then for the most part built of timber, filled up with plaster, was as dry and combustible as firewood; and in the middle of the night, between the 2d and 3d of September, 1666, a fire broke out "that raged for three days as if it had a commission to devour everything that was in its way. It began at a baker's house, near London Bridge, on the spot where the obelisk called the monument now stands, and it was not stopped until it had reduced nearly the whole of the city, from the Tower to Temple Bar, to a sightless heap of cinders and ashes."

For days and nights did the fire advance, and it was only by the blowing up of houses that it was at last extinguished. About four hundred streets and thirteen thousand houses were reduced to ashes. A violent east wind blew throughout the conflagration. Clarendon says: "The fire and the wind continued in the same excess all Monday, Tuesday and Wednesday, till afternoon, and flung and scattered brands burning into all quarters; the nights more terrible than the days, and the light the same, the light of the fire supplying that of the sun. Let the cause be what it would the effect was terrible; for above two parts of three of that great city were burned to ashes, and those the most rich and wealthy parts of the city, where the greatest warehouses and the best shops stood. The Royal Exchange, with all the streets about it—Lombard street, Cheapside, Paternostre—now St. Paul's Church, and almost all the churches in the city, with the old Bailey, Ludgate, and all Paul's churchyard, even to the Thames, and the greatest part of Fleet street, all of which were places the best inhabited, were all burned without one house remaining. The value, or estimate of what that devouring fire consumed, could never be computed in any degree. The city was rebuilt in four years, the streets being much wider and the buildings being of a superior character to those which were burnt.

Moscow was nearly consumed by fire 1536, in 1547, and again in 1571, when the Tartars set fire to the suburbs, a large part of the population perishing on that occasion. During the insurrection caused by the pseudo Demetrius (1605-'12,) when the Poles and Cossacks took the city, it was again partly destroyed. In 1812 it was entered by the French under Murat, on September 14th, and on the 25th by Napoleon, who took up his residence in the Terema palace, in the Kremlin. The city, deserted by its inhabitants, was set on fire by order of the Governor, Count Rostopschin, compelling Napoleon to leave October 19th, and to take his final departure on the 23d, and resulting in the disatrous defeat of the French army The greater part of the city was then destroyed, notwithstanding the efforts of the French to stay the progress of the flames It was rebuilt within a few years, and has long since recovered from the calamity.

New York has suffered greatly from fires. The most disastrous occurred on December 16th, 1835, which swept the First Ward east of Broadway, and below Wall street, destroying six hundred and forty-eight of the most valuable stores, the Merchants' Exchange, and the South Dutch Church and property, valued at more than $18,000,000. On July 19th, 1845, another great fire occurred between Broadway, Exchange Place, Broad and Stone streets, destroying over $5,000,000 worth of property. The damage done by both these fires was speedily repaired.

Pittsburgh has also suffered severely from fire. On the 10th of April, 1845, a conflagration destroyed the entire business portion of the city, consuming $5,000,000 worth of property. The fire raged about twelve hours. To illustrate how rapidly the burnt district was rebuilt, it is only necessary to state that while buildings were burning the owners were making contracts for rebuilding.

Large fires have not been an uncommon occurrence in Constantinople. In 1831 it suffered severely from a conflagration which destroyed ten thousand houses, among which were the palaces of nearly all the ambassadors, and property estimated at $8,000,000.

In the recent conflict between the Commune and the Thiers Government, Paris suffered terribly from fires ignited by the incendiaries, which at one time threatened the existence of the city; but she will overcome the calamity, and, perhaps, phœnix-like, rise from the ashes more beautiful than ever, maintaining the position of the most attractive city in the world.

A HOPEFUL PICTURE.

And with all her commanding advantages of location, what is to prevent the restoration.

Already contracts have been made for rebuilding some of the burned blocks, and the clearing away of the debris will begin to-day, if the heat is so far subdued that the charred material can be handled. Field, Leiter & Co., and John V. Farwell & Co., and many other of our leading firms, will recommence business to-day. The money and the securities in all the banks are safe. The railroads are working with all their energies to bring us out of our affliction. The three hundred millions of capital invested in these roads, is bound to see us through. They have been built with special reference to a great commercial mart at this place, and they can not fail to sustain us. CHICAGO MUST RISE AGAIN.

We do not underrate the calamity that has befallen us. The world has probably never seen the like of it. But the forces of nature, no less than the forces of reason, require that the exchanges of a great region should be conducted here. Ten, twenty years may be required to reconstruct our fair city, but the capital to rebuild it fire-proof will be forthcoming. The losses we have suffered must be borne; but the place, the time and the men are here, to commence at the bottom and work up again; not at the bottom neither, for we have credit in every land, and the experience of one upbuilding of Chicago to help us. Let us all cheer up, save what is left, and we shall come out right. The Christian world is coming to our relief. The worst is already over. In a few days more all the dangers will be past, and we can resume the battle of life with Christian faith and Western grit. Let us all cheer up?

CHAPTER VII.

Incendiaries at their Hellish Work—They Meet a Speedy and Deserved Punishment—Many are Shot and Hung to Lampposts—A short Shrift and Swift Retribution—Interesting Incidents during and subsequent to the Fire.

There can be no doubt that incendiaries helped on the fearful destruction to both life and property, by setting fire to houses, stables, etc., thus adding to the flames that might possibly have sooner been stayed. In many cases their own lives paid the forfeit of their dastardly work—the people in these cases being the judges and jurors. The engraving on the cover represents a scene which is said to have transpired. A man was caught in the act of setting a house on fire, was seized after a desperate struggle, crucified to the wooden pavements of one of the thoroughfares by the excited multitude. Crucifixion was certainly not too terrible a death for the wretch who would thus add to the general destruction of life and property.

The citizens had a terrible seige of watching, terror and excitement during the fire, as many attempts had been made to burn the remainder of the town. The law was a "short shrift and a strong rope." The authorities had instructions to shoot down every one found using the incendiary's torch, and, this, as will be seen from the following, was done in a number of instances. The ruffians and thieves from other cities poured in to secure their share of plunder, and did not scruple by the torch to gain new ground for their nefarious purposes. Some of them paid a sure and speedy penalty; and none condemn the citizen-patrols who, when a villain was taken red-handed in such a crime, "sped him to a land where his taste for fire might be indulged solely at his own cost."

A boy attempted to help on the conflagration by igniting a clothes line saturated with kerosene, and throwing it into a building on Thirty-second street. He received his deserts at the hands of the firemen who saw the act.

A man, name unknown, was shot by a negro at the corner of State and Thirty-second streets. His offense was that he set fire to a building to obtain better opportunities for pillage.

Bridget Hicky was arrested for setting fire to a barn in the rear of a house on Burnside street. By some mistaken idea of clemency, she was not hanged.

Two men, who were caught trying to set fire to a Jesuit Church, on the West Side, were disposed of without ceremony, and the lookers-on were pleased to say, Served 'em right.

A barn on the corner of Burnside and Twentieth streets was observed to be on fire. Knowing that it must have been the work of an incendiary, the neighbors united to extinguish it, filling their coats and hats and everything they could get hold of with sand. The fire was extinguished in good time, and a man found in there captured. It is stated that he was shot. Whether the report is or is not correct is not known.

A man also residing on Fourth avenue, caught a man in the basement of his house, number unknown, armed with hay and matches. He gave the alarm, and the incendiary was caught and stoned and battered to death. This was on the avenue, near Fourteenth street.

A colored man, name unknown, observed a white man sneaking round his house on Fourth avenue. He fired the barn in the rear of his house, and was instantly shot dead.

Among the special policemen sworn in on the South Side was a negro named "Dick" Costello, who was assigned to a beat on Wabash avenue, near Hubbard court. About four o'clock in the afternoon, a white man, whose name is unknown, was looking upon the ruins, when Costello warned him off. He answered that he was only a spectator and was doing no harm, when the negro raised a piece of lead pipe, with which he was armed, and smashed in the man's skull, killing him on the spot. The crowd followed the negro and would have hanged him, but for the intervention of a couple of policemen who rescued him and locked him up in the Cottage Grove Station.

Residents on the South Side were alarmed by the cry of fire, which increased when they saw smoke ascending from

Mr. Schaffer's store, corner State and Thirty-first streets. It was evidently the work of an incendiary, and, owing to the devilish ingenuity used by the scoundrel who did the work, much difficulty was found in extinguishing the fire. Commissioner Sheridan happened near the place, and assisted to put out the blaze. A meeting of over 200 citizens was held immediately, and Sheridan empowered the Chairman to swear in all he thought fit as special policemen. There was indignation enough to have put a summary end to the devil had he been caught, and a determination to treat all such as dogs unworthy of life.

A man was shot by a police officer, who detected him in the act of attempting to fire the Jesuit Church on Twelfth street.

An excited crowd gathered round the West Division Police Station, intent upon making an application of lynch law to a man who was alleged to have tried to set fire to a house on Milwaukee avenue. Three or four ropes were flourished vigorously in the crowd, and several speeches were made by parties, urging them to rescue the incendiary from the hands of the police, but the latter were firm, and at the last accounts the man was still a prisoner, in the cell.

A white man detected a negro attempting to set fire to the rear of a stable between State street and Third avenue, near Harrison street. He gave the alarm and attempted to arrest the negro, when the scoundrel stabbed him, inflicting a wound from which he died in a few minutes. The negro was arrested.

The body of a man, apparently only about twenty years old, was hanging on Belden avenue. He had been lynched, and a placard warned all persons from touching him, as he would be "taken down at the proper time by the committee of safety."

A man was seen hanging to a lamp post on one of the avenues, dead but not cold.

In the alley between Taylor and Twelfth streets, running from Halstead to Newberry street, a man attired in a black cloak was found crouching at the rear of a barn, and in the act of applying a lighted match to dry combustible material.

The party who saw the attempt, in the impulse of the moment, raised an alarm, instead of firing at the incendiary, and the wretch escaped.

At 11 o'clock on Tuesday forenoon, Charles Coy, employed at the city elevator, was on Mitchell street, near Canal street, when he heard the cry of fire raised by some women. Rushing into a shed he discovered a quantity of brimstone on the floor, burning. In this instance, too, the incendiary escaped.

At the drug store of Mead Brothers, on Canal street, between Judd and Wilson streets, there was found under the barn, on Tuesday afternoon, a piece of Manilla rope, six feet long, saturated with tar and other combustible substances. The ends were frayed, so that it would readily ignite, and on one end a loose knot was tied and soaked in tar. An experiment was subsequently tried with the rope, and it was found to burn slow. The guilty man in this case was unseen.

Hannah, Lay & Co., who own a lumber pile near the City Elevator, found a bundle of hay and straw deposited in a risky place, and saturated with kerosene. This was also on Tuesday.

A silk dress saturated with kerosene was flung over a garden fence on Wabash avenue, into a back yard, and was picked up dripping with oil.

Three women detected a man setting fire to a house, and without other aid, seized him, and with a piece of thick wire, strung him up to the nearest thing they could extemporize into a gallows.

The following scenes and incidents are among the many which, no doubt, actually transpired during and subsequent to the great fire. Some have seen the light through the columns of the daily papers, others first make their appearance here:

When fire was rushing southward along Michigan and Wabash avenues like a race horse, and firemen and people were paralyzed, a new leader suddenly appeared upon the scene. General Sheridan, "fighting Phil." who can fight rebels or flames, sprang upon a fire engine and made one of those sharp, stirring speeches for which he is noted. He told the people that if they would save the city the fire line must be broken by gunpowder; the buildings must be blown up, and if they would go to work systematically he would assist them. The effect was electrical. The crowd recognizing the hero of so many battle fields, and having faith in his leadership, replied with long hurrahs, and acting under the General's orders, in a few minutes so many buildings had been blown up that the fire line was broken and the southern portion of the city was saved from destruction.

Eight miles and a quarter from the Court House, twenty-four hours after the fire, such was the lurid brightness, that "a quarter to nine" was read on the dial face of a watch in the open street, and not a star shining in the heavens.

A gentleman well known, who has been afflicted for a long time with a cancer, resided in rooms in Lombard Block, attended by two lady relatives, a sister and niece. In the dire extremity in which the party were placed, and notwithstanding the invalid pleaded that the ladies would save themselves and what valuables they could, and leave him to be burned, and thus an end be put to his misery, they seized and carried him bodily down three flights of stairs, and finally placed him in a position of safety. And here it may be mentioned as an instance of the extortion practiced on suffering humanity, that an expressman was offered $50 to take them to Twelfth street, but refused, asking $100. Other instances of heroic self-sacrifice and abnegation, on the part of women, could be mentioned, the above being only one of many.

When the destruction of the contents of some stores was inevitable, the people were told to help themselves. In a boot and shoe establishment, a man was noted leisurely trying on a pair of boots to get a perfect fit while the rear of the store was in flames.

The only leading editors in the city whose residences were not destroyed, were Messrs. C. L. Wilson, of the Journal, J. Medill, of the Tribune, and W. F. Storey, of the Times.

Rothermel's great historical painting, "The Battle of Gettysburg," was destroyed in the Academy of Design, together with other valuable paintings and works of sculpture.

Bierstadt's great painting, the Yosemite Valley, was in the

Art Gallery, Crosby's Opera House, and was, so far as we can learn, saved in a romantic condition.

As a specimen of what the legal profession of Chicago has lost, we may state that General H. N. Eldridge, of the firm of Eldridge & Tourtelotte, the attorneys of Field, Leiter & Co., lost all his papers, not a scrap left, after having practiced for fourteen years in Chicago, and in the same office. There is not a law office, nor a library left in Chicago, except the few small duplicate libraries at the residences of the leading lawyers. There is not a paper showing that there is a suit pending in any of the six courts of record in Cook county, including the Federal Court. There is not an indictment in existence in the county against any one, not a judgment, not a petition in bankruptcy in the Federal Courts. Even the duplicate files that the lawyers kept in their offices of important cases are all gone. A few may have escaped by being taken to the houses for Sunday or night work. We may add that there are in Chicago about five hundred lawyers.

Mr. Ferd S. Winslow, the well-known banker, owns a beautiful residence and grounds nearly opposite to Wright's grove—a little paradise, in which he had taken peculiar pride. At the near approach of the fire one of the neighbors urged Mr. Winslow's family to betake themselves to their carriage and flee. They fled for their lives, and, along with thousands of others, sought the bleak prairies, where they camped out for the night. Yesterday morning Mr. Winslow wandered back to gaze upon the ruins of his happy home, when lo! there burst upon his astonished vision, a green oasis in the desert. It was his own home, unscathed. The fire had swept clean round it, missing it miraculously. The happy family returned, taking many sufferers along with them.

The little one-story frame shanty, in the rear of which was the barn in which the fire originated, on De Koven street, stands to-day alone and uninjured. The flames swept round it on every side, igniting everything else, while that miserable structure stands—a monument of the place where the fire commenced. Will some enterprising museum please purchase it at a fictitious price, and so relieve the disaster with a round sum?

John R. Walsh, President of the Western News Company, received the following dispatch from Robert Bonner, Esq., the proprietor of the New York Ledger:

New York, October 11.

To John R. Walsh, Esq., President Western News Company: All New York sympathizes with Chicago. Millions will be collected in this city alone for the general relief fund. Draw on me at sight for ten thousand dollars towards relieving sufferers who are in any way connected with the newspaper or news business.   ROBERT BONNER.

The Tribune was, by several hours, the last paper in Chicago to survive the general destruction, and its magnificent fire-proof building was the last to succumb, although it had been surrounded by fire on two sides for about four hours. The building was a perfect model of architectural elegance, and had been constructed throughout with reference to safety and durability in case of fire. The ceilings were of corrugated iron, resting on wrought iron "I" beams, while every partition in the structure was of brick. It was, in all respects, one of the most absolutely "fire-proof" buildings ever erected. That is, was fire-proof up to the date of its destruction. It was completed in April, 1869, at a cost of about $225,000, and its contents were fully $100,000 more. Relying upon the integrity of their edifice, the Tribune Company had taken no insurance, although they have little cause to regret this neglect.

The Navarino, a new vessel belonging to Capt. Goodrich, was lying off Goodrich's docks, and tried to run out, but stuck just beyond and behind Rathbone's stove manufactory on the north side of the river, and sunk there, her boilers now being just visible. Eight or nine schooners and brigs were also caught near the mouth of the river and burned to the water's edge. From Rush street bridge east, on the north branch, the coal heaps are in a blaze. Rathbone's place, and all immediately east of that are safe. Rush street bridge itself is a hopeless and utter wreck, as also is the State street one.

In front of each ruin is to be found a board placard, usually giving the place where each concern is to be found, but some of which are amusing and characteristic of Chicago.

For instance, "Moore & Son, house and sign painters, removed to 115 West Randolph street. Capital, $000 00." "This store to be rebuilt immediately; we still live: Hurlbut & Edsall." Another: "Slightly scorched; Van Schaack, Stevenson & Reid; ready for business in two days."

A German grocer of Clark street left his store with goods in a wagon on Monday morning, directing his wife and hired man to remain til he came back. He never saw his wife after, but found her bones and a portion of her hoop skirt in the ruins on Thursday. The hired man's bones were also found.

The vault of the Custom House was opened. It contained one million dollars gold and two millions greenbacks. The gold was melted into an almost solid mass and of course is safe in the shape of bullion. The greenbacks were entirely consumed beyond recognition. Of course the greenbacks belonged to the Government and there is no loss.

A man named Patrick Foley, who lived at 250 Burnside street, while passing along Purple near Grove, was shot down and killed, having refused to halt when commanded to do so by two citizens. A man named Joseph Reardon, residing on Fourteenth street, appeared at the Twenty-second Street Police Court, and stated that the deceased, just prior to being shot, fired a shot gun at him which he had seized from another man.

Henry J. Ullman, of the firm of Wrenn, Ullman & Co., perished in the flames. His body was found on the corner of Madison and Clark streets.

Dead bodies not identified were taken to 64 Milwaukee avenue. Forty corpses were displayed at one time. With one or two exceptions, the deaths occurred from burning—nothing but a skull and a blackened mass remaining of some of them, while a few were suffocated. The large proportion, however, were disfigured, and their limbs nearly burned from their bodies. The scene of forty corpses, all but two without a vestige of clothing,, with the exception of an occasional boot, was sickening beyond description, and one never to be forgotten by those who beheld it.

Six men were working on the corner of Clark and Madison streets, top of J. B. Chambers' store, and when the fire caught the lower part of the building were unable to get down, and equally unable to escape to adjoining buildings.

Chet Morehead was last seen struggling manfully with a large box containing the books of Reyburn, Hunter & Co. The flames and smoke overpowered him, and he is certainly lost.

A drunken man tried to run south from the base ball grounds on Michigan avenue, and was caught and killed by the flames.

Jacob Wolf was roasted to death in his house, No. 95 West Harrison street.

A Tribune reporter, wandering among the ruins on Ontario street, discovered, in the rear cellar of the dwelling next east of the Historical Society's building, the charred trunk of a human body, lying amid the ruins of many wine bottles and the apparatus of a water-closet.

A man jumped from a fourth story window of Speed's block, during the progress of the fire, and was instantly killed.

So little idea had the people living near the Historical Society building on Ontario street, between Dearborn and Clark, of the terrible and utter ruin which the fire would work, that, snatching up what valuables they could, they sought shelter in its cellar, which was unfortunately filled to a great extent with inflammable material. According to the statement of the librarian of the Historical Society, William Corkran, who was there at the time, the following persons certainly sought refuge there: Old Col Stone and his wife, Mr. and Mrs. Able and their daughters, Mrs. De Pelgrom, teacher of French, Mr. and Mrs. Carpenter, musical people, Dr. Freer and family, the former having with him $4,000 worth of personal property belonging to Rush Medical College, two patients from the hospital in Mr. Richards' place, and John B. Girard and family. Mr. Corkran had hold of one end of a trunk and Mrs. Gebler of the other. Her dress took fire, and he left her and ran for the stairs leading from the cellar up stairs. He is certain that old Col. Stone suffocated, and, from the sudden inrush of dense smoke, there is cause to fear that nearly all the others who were in there shared the same fate, bewildered by the fumes, and unable to find their way out of a building with which they were unacquainted.

As early as three o'clock Monday morning, the people on the North Side, or many of them, began to get a little nervous. Still they did not, at that early hour, entertain any serious apprehensions, feeling confident that the river would be an impassible barrier, amply sufficient to prevent any spreading of the conflagration. By daylight, however, things were in a somewhat different position. The fire, moving northeastward, had gotten to Rush street bridge, which was crowded with people. In order to prevent this aiding the fire in crossing, it was turned, but the only result was the destruction of the people who were upon it.

Encouraged by the absence of policemen, the roughs along on Kinzie street broke into the saloons there, and began seizing and drinking the liquor. Many others, at the very moment they most needed all the self-possession they had, fuddled themselves, and in many cases were surrounded by the flames and stifled by the smoke. Some were found lying on the sidewalk, and, since no one paid any attention to them, they met there fate there. Some women and their children who lingered too long, were either lost in the houses or compelled to jump out of the windows, and received injuries and remained where they fell.

It is reported, but not on the best authority, that fifteen men were lost at a blacksmith-shop on Rush street.

One of the most pitiful sights was that of a middle-aged woman, on State street, loaded with bundles, struggling through the crowd, singing the Mother Goose melody—

"Chickery, chickery, craney crow,
I went to the well to wash my toe." etc.

There were hundreds of others likewise distracted, and many rendered desperate by whisky or beer, which, from the excess of thirst, in the absence of water, they drank in great quantities; and spread themselves in every direction—a terror to all they met.

It is feared that a large number of children, inmates of the Catholic Orphan School, on State street, were also burned, as many of them are missing. On Chicago avenue a father rushed up stairs to carry three children away, when he was overtaken by the flames, and perished with them. The mother was afterward seen on the street, on the North Side, a raving maniac. In the same neighborhood a family of five persons perished. The list of such fatalities is very long, and can only be fully verified after the smoke shall have cleared away. There are hundreds of families on that side who saved no clothing, but barely their lives. Among these is the family of Perry Smith, formerly President of the Northwestern Railroad Company.

After the flames had consumed the store of J. H. Ross, State, near the corner of Washington, the walls were left partially standing. An express wagon was passing a short time after the conflagration, and reached the front of the building just in time to receive the falling wall. Five men were in the wagon at the time, and all were crushed and killed.

A couple of families, the heads of which were teamsters, living near the lake shore, not far from the Water Works, stuck to their homes till the last moment, in the hope of saving a portion of their effects. They were cut off by the flames, however, and compelled to flee as they could; but the only direction in which they could go was into the lake. The men succeeded in getting their teams hitched up, and hastily putting themselves and families on the truck wagons, they drove into the lake as far as possible without drowning. This was at 7 o'clock on Monday morning. There they were obliged to remain through the live-long day, scorched by the heat almost beyond the power of endurance, and obliged to dive into the water at frequent intervals, to keep from being consumed. At 6 o'clock in the evening, a small tug approached the group of sufferers and took away the women and children, but could not take the men. The husbands and fathers were left there for twelve hours longer, and finally, on Tuesday morning, were rescued by another boat. All of the party found each other at last at the houses of friends on the West Side, but the suffering and exposure of the weaker ones may yet terminate fatally.

THE FIRES IN
MICHIGAN AND WISCONSIN.

CHAPTER VIII.

Burning of Peshtigo, Menimonee, Manistee, and Saginaw City.

While the Fire Fiend was raging in Chicago, on the night of the day consecrated to rest, Sunday, October the 8th, it was also supping full of horrors in several of the towns of Michigan and Wisconsin. The result was a far greater loss of life than occurred in Chicago, the number of men, women and children burned to death, and otherwise killed outright being estimated at from twelve to fifteen hundred. We believe no account places it below one thousand.

Fires had been raging in the woods around the towns for some days, without creating any very serious apprehension —great endeavors being made, however, to stay the flames. The extreme drouth had paved the way for the pitiless fire fiend. We have endeavored to secure as correct an account from eye witnesses, telegraphic dispatches, and the papers, as possible, of the great fires in the north, which we have deemed proper should accompany the more complete recital of the Chicago horror.

From the Marinette and Menominee Eagle Extra.

Marinette, Wis., October 9.—The fires which have been lurking in this vicinity for weeks have at last culminated in the holocaust of destruction. Last night the wind raised and blew fearfully from the south. The Swamp lying back of Dr. Hall's became ignited, and the flames spread through it with an inconceivable rapidity.

The fire was about three-fourths of a mile distant from Marinette, and shooting above the tallest tree-tops, lit up the whole country, with a fierce, lurid glare. The fire fiend was holding high carnival, having selected the towns of Peshtigo, Marinette and Menekaune as its prey. Every available force that could be brought to bear to stay the force of the fire was brought into requisition.

Standing out on the Peshtigo road, we were a witness to the awful scene. The fire swept through the swamp, and destroyed several outbuildings in the rear of the Boom Company's place, and Dr. Hall's, together with a large barn, containing nearly one hundred tons of hay. The hay was the property of Mr. Bentley, of Marinette. At this time the direction of the wind changed rapidly, blowing from several points of the compass alternately; first from the southwest, then from the west, then from the northwest, then back again to the south, during which time we were visited by a series of whirlwinds, which showered cinders and sparks in every conceivable direction. The fire having partly spent its fury here, cries of distress were heard down the river in the direction of the mouth. Steam whistles of the mills and tugs in the harbor blew the first alarm, and every man that could be spared went to the scene of disaster. From the rear of J. S. Dickey's store, in the direction of the bay, all was a broad lurid sheet of flame as far as the eye could reach.

At this time no hopes was entertained of saving anything. Men worked with the energy of despair.

Sickening rumors came up from the scene of the devastations of the fire fiend. Rumors that Menekaune was destroyed—the Catholic Church, Union School House, McCartney & Hamilton's mill, Bagley & Curry's sash, door and blind factory, a new and splendid building just completed and in operation, and the whole lower part of Marinette were in flames. In company with A. M. Fairchild, we were driven to the forks of the road leading to Menekaune.

Just below the Marinette Iron Works the fire was raging so fearfully that it was impossible to go any farther. It was evident that the rumors which we had heard were, alas, too true, with the exception that the buildings in the lower portion of Marinette were not yet in flames. The fire had burned clear up to the fences, and here, by the hardest work, its progress was stayed.

The streets were lined with men, women and children, fleeing for their lives. Many of the families were engaged in making excavations in the sand and burying their household goods. Any quantity of goods was hauled over on to the island. The sick were being removed to places of safety, and thus, with alternate hope and despair, the long, weary hours of the night wore away.

The wind had at last settled to blowing steadily from the southwest, but still it blew with tremendous fury, and the flames in the swamp immediately in the rear of the town, raged with corresponding fearfulness.

MENEKAUNE DESTROYED.

At day-light we received more definite information from the scene of devastation at the mouth of the river. Everything of any particular value was destroyed. Spalding, Houghtelling & Johnson's mill, valued at $80,000 (known as the New York mill,) the Exchange House, Mill Company's store and boarding house, Dr. Sherman's drug store, John Lindquist's store, Doyle's shoe shop, and many other places of business we are not now able to call to memory, together with all the dwellings of any note, were in ashes. The luckless inhabitants are houseless and homeless.

PESHTIGO.

From Mr. Place, who has just returned from the scene of the disaster, we learn that the town is destroyed; the Peshtigo Company's wooden ware factory, valued at several hundred thousand dollars; their water saw-mill, grist mill, machine shop, sash factory, stave and boarding-house, warehouses—everything is gone. Stores, houses, churches, school-houses, dwellings, and everything were destroyed. The fire came upon them so suddenly that it was not in the reach of mortal power to stay its fury.

THE DESTRUCTION OF LIFE

was awful—awful to contemplate. Mr. Place informs us that he counted ten bodies in the streets as he passed. The loss of life at the present time is unknown, but it is estimated that over 100 have either perished or were rendered cripples for life. We have not yet been able to ascertain the names of the dead.

DREADFUL DESTRUCTION OF LIFE AND PROPERTY.

Milwaukee, October 15.—Later accounts from northern Wisconsin confirm all previous reports and rumors. The loss of life in the neighborhood of the burned village of Peshtigo, will reach over twelve hundred, or fifteen per cent. of those injured can not recover. The fire tornado was heard at a distance like the roaring of the sea. Balls of fire were observed to fall like meteors in different parts of the town, igniting whatever they touched.

People rushed with their children in their arms for a place of safety, but the storm of fire was upon them and enveloped them in the flames, smoke, burning sand and cinders, and those that were not able to reach the river were suffocated, and roasted alive. This terrible scene happened on Sunday night, the 8th of October, already made famous by the Chicago horror. A member of the Relief Committee sent from Milwaukee with supplies, says the only survivors were those who were fortunate enough to reach water, many throwing themselvs into mill ponds and clinging to floating logs. A number of these were drowned by being thrown from the logs by maddened horses and cattle that rushed into the water. The firey cyclone swept over a tract of country eight or ten miles wide. Every building, fence and all the timber were licked up clean by the tongue of fire. The town of Peshtigo, numbered two thousand inhabitants, one-third of whom perished on that fearful night.

Reports from the east shore of Green Bay placed the loss of life full as high as at Peshtigo.

The same account states that the immediate wants of the people are supplied, but large amounts of provisions and clothing will be required for the winter.

Mayor Ludington, of Milwaukee, publishes the following appeal for aid:

"*Milwaukee*, October 14.—The calamities that have befallen our State and some of our neighboring States is truly appalling. Over fifteen hundred men, women and children have been burned to death in Wisconsin alone, their business houses and farms to a large extent entirely destroyed, the very soil having been burned, and destroyed all their autumn and root crops. They are utterly destitute, and will require full support at least another season. Seven counties in our own State are thus in great part utterly desolated. Whole regions of country in Western Michigan are in the same condition, and these fires are still raging and destroying. Milwaukee is doing all she can, as by her close neighborhood to Chicago she was enabled to send large quantities of supplies into that city during the progress of the fire, feeding her exhausted citizens. Vast numbers of Chicago sufferers are now filling our houses and public buildings, and we have ministered to their necessities. We have supplied hundreds of tons of provisions, and clothing, stoves, and other useful articles, to Chicago, to Northern Wisconsin and Western Michigan. We are doing our best, but the amount of suffering in our own State is beyond our power alone to assuage, we appeal to the public for aid. We will be the dispensers of supplies in Wisconsin and Western Michigan. We have made every kind of necessary arrangement to accomplish these purposes with economy and effect. All contributions in money may be sent to Alexander Mitchell, banker. All contributions in clothing, bedding and other necessary supplies may be directed to Harrison Ludington, Mayor.

[Signed,]   HARRISON LUDINGTON, Mayor.

MENOMINEE

Has suffered to some extent, how much we are unable to tell. It is conceded some of the mills and many of the dwellings have been burned. The mill on the Point, known as the Gilmore mill, the property of R. Stephenson & Co., has been destroyed. We will try and give the public the particulars from all these points as soon as we can ascertain them. Some errors, both in expression and fact, may have crept into the foregoing, for we write this with our eyes nearly blinded from the smoke and flames of last night.

Four children were burned up the river State road, on the Menominee side.

McCartney has $8,000 insurance; loss, at least $20,000. Bagley & Curry have no insurance; loss, $1,000.

The mill and buildings at Menominee known as the Spafford & Gilmore mill, are all burned. Loss, $50,000; supposed to be insured for $25,000. It was sold last week by R. Stephenson & Co. to a company, of which Andrew Kirby, of Menominee, owns a third interest.

LATER.

Peshtigo is burnt clean as a prairie. The survivors are flocking into Marinette. The Dunlap House and several private families are already well filled up with the victims, many of them terribly burned. The people here, and the resident physicians both here and at Menominee, are nobly rendering all the aid in their power.

MANISTEE.

The following is another account of the burning of Manistee, dated October 11th:

The fire which broke out in the pineries northeast of here last week was almost subdued, when a heavy gale sprung up from the southward, driving the flames and cinders toward Gifford & Ruddock's mills. This the fire company checked; but on Sunday evening a fire broke out near Canfield's mill, which is situated at the mouth of the river, and so intense was the heat that men could not get within a thousand yards of it. In less than half an hour the mill, together with about twenty dwelling houses and boarding houses, were totally consumed. A hill intervening between this and the town, the fire could run no further, and people were already congratulating themselves upon the narrow escape of Manistee, when a bright light was noticed northeast from the scene, and, repairing to the spot, we found a number of dwellings wrapped in flames, and a regular equinoctial gale blowing—thus making it beyond human control to stay the conflagration. The damage at present is inestimable, but the largest part of the town, which is on the South Side, is destroyed, while so far twenty-seven buildings are totally gone on the North Side.

The loss, as near as I can learn, amounts to one million three hundred thousand dollars, with only about one-fifth insurance.

The swing bridge is entirely destroyed; the schooner Seneca Chief is burned to the water's edge. Every building on the North Side (excepting the Fourth Ward School house, the residence of George Thorp and the Catholic Church) is completely consumed.

Several serious accidents occurred and some lives have been lost, but there is such tumult and excitement that no one can give a fair answer to a question.

Where six mills stood yesterday, not a vestige remains except bungled-up machinery—the woodwork and logs having burned out entirely. Blackbird Island is no more. The distress is great, and if food does not come forthwith there will be starvation.

Nothing can be heard from the north or northeastern villages, as the heat prevents communication. The roads are so dry that sawdust burns like powder. The Manistee is leaving, and I cannot give further particulars.

The following is also additional in regard to Pesthigo:

Direct accounts from Pesthigo inform us that the great number of lives lost there, occurred thus: Fire had been raging around the village some days before; had become subdued, and the people felt secure; when on Sunday night, all of sudden, when the wind was blowing a tornado, it again broke out from the fires of the camps of the hands at work on the railroad, and immediately overwhelmed the village, inmates of houses having only time to escape as they arose from their beds. The village could not have contained more than five or six hundred, or a thousand at the most, of residents; but it is estimated that one thousand transient men were in the place—lumbermen mainly. The river runs directly through the village and there was but one bridge. The people living in the main portion of the village were driven by the rushing flames directly towards the river, and, horrible to contemplate, cattle had preceded them and blockaded the passage to the bridge; consequently human beings had to take to the water, when a large portion were either burned to death or drowned.

One man who escaped reports that he sank his entire body into the water, occasionally raising his head to get breath, and that he saw several women perish right alongside of him. When rescued his eyes were completely blinded, but are now partially restored.

He, as well as a boat load who escaped, came down to Green Bay on the steamer yesterday, while there was another boat load left behind awaiting a coming boat.

Some one hundred and fifty men, finding escape cut off, took to a large barn belonging to the Pesthigo Company, and they were burned up in it.

A lady who came through here has her hair and one side of her face burnt to a crisp. She says there was no smoke from the burning buildings, but it was one complete glare of glowing blaze, awful to behold. Not a vestige of anything wooden is left of the place. Those that came through have scattered throughout the State wherever they have friends. The wounded have been moved to Oconto mainly as being the nearest village, which is south of Peshtigo. The villages of Marinette and Menominee, six miles north, being themselves partly on fire, offered no chance for help or protection to the sufferers from that quarter.

FIRES IN EAST SAGINAW AND SAGINAW CITY.

On Sunday, the 8th, Saginaw City also suffered from the ravages of the Fire Fiend. The Saginaw Enterprise of the 9th reported as follows:

The whole of yesterday the city was enveloped in a dense smoke. On all sides of Saginaw—indeed, throughout the whole valley—the woods were burning fiercely, and the flames were continually sweeping onward, carrying destruction to all kinds of property. A heavy wind prevailed throughout the entire day, which added to the fury of the flames, and people were greatly alarmed for the safety of the city. About 12 o'clock last night the bell sounded the alarm. An immense column of flame was seen bursting from a house on Washington street. As our reporter reached the spot a cry arose that the occupants of the house had not escaped. A desperate effort was made to rescue them, and sleeping children were torn from their beds and carried safely out, while men and women jumped from the windows, burned and bleeding, just in time to save their lives. The flames spread to three other buildings, which were destroyed.

While this fire was in progress, property to the amount of over $75,000 was destroyed by fire in Saginaw City.

We have thus, in as brief a manner as possible, consistent with the awful incidents with which we have had to deal, told the story of the Great Fire of Chicago and the simultaneous horrors of Michigan and Wisconsin, which will be remembered long after those of the present age shall have passed away to the land of the hereafter.

Chicago's Holocaust.

THE GREAT FIRE

Its History and Incidents,

LOSSES AND SUFFERINGS,

BENEVOLENCE OF THE NATIONS, &c

BY A CHICAGO CLERGYMAN

WITH MAPS AND ILLUSTRATIONS.

PUBLISHED BY

J. W. GOODSPEED, Chicago, St. Louis, Cincinnati, and New Orleans.
H. S. GOODSPEED & CO., New York.

Entered according to Act of Congress, in the year 1871,
BY H. S. GOODSPEED,
In the Office of the Librarian of Congress, at Washington.

THE NEW YORK PRINTING COMPANY,
81, 83 and 85 Centre St.

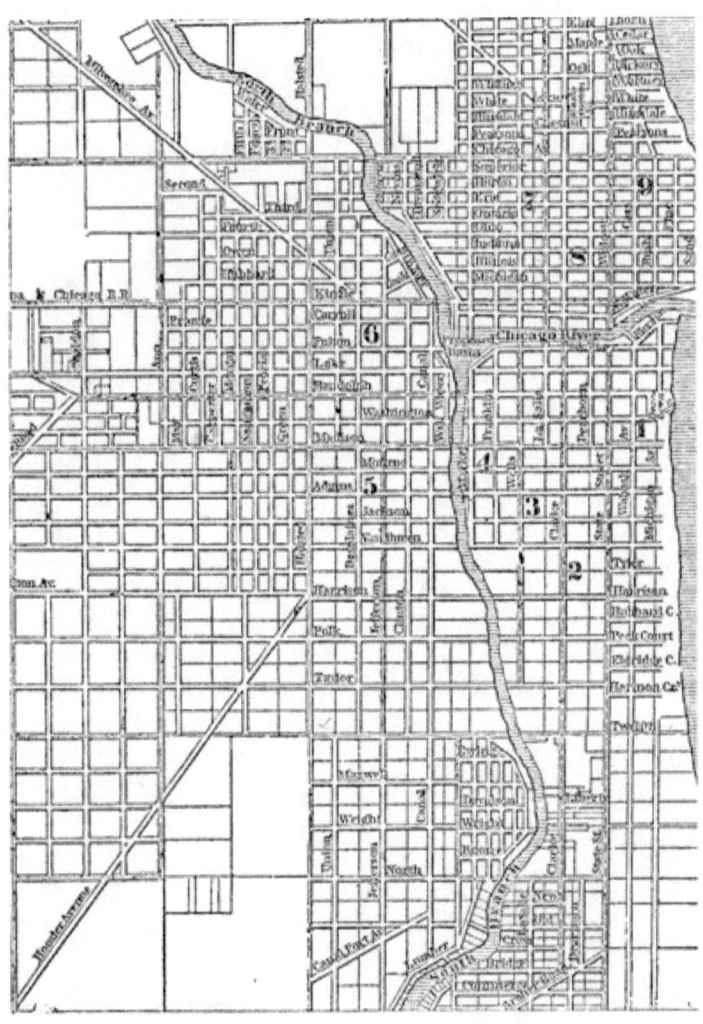

"Hear the loud alarum bells—
    Brazen bells!
What a tale of terror, now, their turbulency tells!
  In the startled ear of night
   How they scream out their affright!
    Too much horrified to speak,
    They can only shriek, shriek,
     Out of tune,
In a clamorous appealing to the mercy of the fire,
In a mad expostulation with the deaf and frantic fire,
   Leaping higher, higher, higher,
   With a desperate desire
   And a resolute endeavor,
   Now—now to sit or never,
By the side of the pale-faced moon.
   Oh, the bells, bells, bells,
   What a tale their terror tells
    Of despair!
  How they clang, and clash, and roar,
  What a horror they outpour
On the bosom of the palpitating air!"

BURNING OF THE CHAMBER OF COMMERCE.

HISTORY

OF THE

GREAT FIRE IN CHICAGO.

AMONG the saddest events of history will rank the conflagration which began in Chicago on the night of October 7th, 1871, was renewed on the night of the 8th, and raged with unchecked violence, consuming more than one-half of the area of the city, destroying several hundred millions of property, occasioning large loss of life, and making homeless nearly one hundred thousand persons.

The whole business portion of the South and North sides of the city were laid in ruins, and nothing resisted the appalling fury of the wasting element. The engines were totally helpless, and many of them scarcely escaped burning; fire-proofs were consumed as in a moment the flames lapped over whole blocks and across the river; the miracle of Mount Carmel was reproduced. When everything was licked up and devoured by the fire-fiend, people were caught in their dwellings and burned, or were overtaken on the streets and destroyed; and only when the city was consumed in the track of the hurricane did the elemental war cease, and the assaulting foe rest from his deadly work. For days the fire smouldered, and night after night the heavens glowed like the canopy of hell, and threatened universal ruin. But, thanks to a merciful Providence, the track of desolation covered not the whole of the great city, and a portion was left to furnish shelter for the homeless, and as a nucleus for rebuilding the Metropolis of the North-west.

Here we may briefly notice the origin and growth of Chicago, to enable the reader to form some idea of the nature and magnitude of the calamity which has befallen a lately prosperous community. Such a sketch may also serve to exhibit the causes of the almost world-wide and unexampled sympathy manifested toward her suffering people. The original prairie bordering Lake Michigan was intersected by a lagoon or bayou extending half a mile west, and then forking north and south for a long distance. This gave room for a harbor, and was the suggestion of a city. Here, at the shore and near the mouth of the river, in 1804 a fort was built to cover a trading post with Indians and the incoming emigrants. It was rebuilt in 1816, and abandoned in 1837, when the entire population was 4,470. In twenty years the city had multiplied its numbers so that in 1857 there were gathered on this level plain 130,000 persons. In 1871 there were, by census returns, carefully made out, 334,000 people in Chicago. When was there such a growth in so short a time, and a progress so real and substantial? Evidently Nature designed the location to be the site of a great city, and a gathering-place of the nations. Here is one of the best harbors, and thirty miles of wharves and docks; here centre several thousand miles of railways; here are accommodations for receiving and shipping grain unsurpassed in the world; here is the natural commercial depot of the immense mineral resources of the vast northwestern regions, and the fruit-market is unequalled anywhere. To many all this seems exaggeration. But hear the words of Hon. Benjamin F. Wade:—

"Again I say to you that the importance of this location transcends what most now think of it. It will never have but two rivals. San Francisco, on the Pacific, may contest the palm of greatness with it, and New York has got to run fast to get out of its way. You may deem that an extravagant expression, but recollect that New York had to struggle for one hundred and fifty years before she had the population and wealth Chicago has to-day. No people of this country have more of intelligence, more of enterprise, more of the American Yankee go-aheadativeness than the people of Chicago. I say again, that there are but two cities on this continent that can compete with it for the palm of greatness. Thirty-two years ago it had a few rude buildings, and I have been amazed to-day, as I passed through and viewed the wonderful progress that has been made; I am sure I have had no conception of the importance of this point, and, what is still more important, of the vastness and richness of the great country that lies west, and which is bound to contribute in the future so much to build up the second, if not the first city on this continent." Such was the language of the great statesman of Ohio in 1866. Five years succeeding this, and the horrible conflagration finds the city almost transformed, so that the orator would scarcely have recognized many of the principal localities in the heart of the city, where magnificent edifices had risen upon the sites of former buildings, or sprung up on vacant land. Potter Palmer, a merchant prince, had expended immense sums upon buildings for stores and hotels which hardly had any rivals in expensiveness and beauty in the old world. He had also commenced a new hotel, which was to have cost upwards of a million dollars, for which he had arranged in Europe at a low rate of interest. The Pacific Hotel was also about completed by a company having a capital of one million. In giving their grounds of confidence in entering upon their gigantic enterprise, they said, there are 426 trains moving daily each way on our railways, and some of our solid statistics are as follows:—

Wheat received, bushels............................	17,394,409
Corn " "	20,189,775
Total all grain received, bushels................	61,315,593
Flour manufactured, bbls........................	443,976
Grain shipments (equal to), bushels.............	54,745,903
High-wines manufactured, gallons..............	7,063,364
Hogs packed....................................	900,000
" received................................	1,693,158
Cattle received.................................	532,964
Lumber received, feet...........................	1,019,000,000
Value of manufactures..........................	$88,848,120
Incomes (estimated)............................	$74,000,000
Internal Revenue collected......................	$7,984,000
Clearing House returns.........................	$10,676,036
National Banks.................................	17
Private Banks..................................	10
National Banks' capital.........................	$6,800,000
" undivided surplus..................	$2,715,000
Total bank capital..............................	$12,250,000
Sales of Real Estate (transfers)..................	8,418
Value of Real Estate, total......................	$37,558,455
Chicago Post-Office, letters and papers delivered..	22,928,343

Right upon the heels of these grand enterprises followed others of equal extent and boldness, projected and sustained by men of brains and energy, integrity and courage, all of which exhibited the importance of this harbor and centre of commerce, and serve to help us to realize what devastation the enemy has wrought in sweeping all these monuments level with the ground. Not that all Chicago's buildings are down, but the central portion of business blocks is entirely gone, and what remains constitutes but a specimen of the splendor and glory reduced to ashes. Some 3,000 acres are wasted by fire, and so utterly ruined that almost nothing but débris remains. The city and county had built and just entered two wings, each owning one, to the court house in a great square, and these stand partly erect, with the old building in the middle, gloomy and desolate in their destruction. The Honore block, probably as beautiful a structure as can be found for business purposes on the globe, built of Athens stone highly wrought, having six stories with mansard roofs extending 190 feet on Dearborn street, and 114 on Adams, was in the heat of the battle and is a heap of dust. Farwell Hall, one of the great halls for concerts and lectures, and the seat of operations for the Young Men's Christian Association, the home of the Daily Prayer Meeting, is ashes and rubbish. And so the Board of Trade building perished, along with factories, distilleries, breweries, bridges, churches, colleges, theatres, depots, water-works, warehouses, and private dwellings, all involved in one total wreck. When a glance is thus taken at the ruin accomplished, one can be prepared in some measure to estimate the appalling nature of this calamity. But the effect becomes greatly intensified when it is remembered that many lost their lives in the flames, and tens of thousands lost all—homes, property, and hopes of success, and were driven out destitute, to become objects of charity. A particular account of the origin and progress of the fire, with reminiscences and actual incidents, will give the reader a better idea of the horrors and marvels of what must be pronounced one of the memorable catastrophes of Time.

It was a period of peculiar drought in the whole western country, and the dryness of the atmosphere was so remarkable that an intelligent physician, observing that his plants became desiccated in a few hours after the most profuse watering from the hydrant, trembled all day Sunday lest a spark of fire should drop near his dwelling. There was a strange lack of moisture in the air, which condition did not change until Monday afternoon. On Saturday evening, October 8, about 11 o'clock, a fire caught in a planing mill, west of the river, and within a block of it, in the neighborhood of a wooden district full of frame houses, lumber and coal-yards, and every kind of combustible material. Some contend that it originated in a beer saloon, and thence was communicated to the planing-mill.

In the almost inflammable state of the atmosphere, and under the propulsion of a strong wind, the tinder-boxes on every side ignited, and ruin rioted for hours over a space of twenty acres, and destroyed a million dollars worth of property. Grand and awful as this conflagration seemed to the thronging thousands, who crowded every approach and standpoint where a view could be obtained, it paled and faded away in comparison with that of the following night; but, as the event proved, this first fire saved the remainder of the west division of the city, for when the raging element came leaping and roaring onward it found nothing to burn, and then paused, and was stayed, while it rushed across the river, and satiated itself upon the noblest and best portion of the town, east and north.

This renewal of the fire, or, as it really was an independent conflagration, began at 9 on Sunday night in a barn, where an old woman was milking by the light of a kerosene lamp, which was thrown over and emptied upon the combustible stuff that lay around.

The starting-point was southwest of that of Saturday night. The wind was blowing a gale from the southwest, and hurled the blazing brands and showers of glittering sparks aloft and plunged them down upon the dry masses beyond. There was a hope that the river running north and south would interpose a barrier to the foe.

The fire still lapped along the edge of the river, and still, as in a savage hate of man, over whom it had for once triumphed, flung its sparks and brands further, further into the water, trying to plant some messenger of destruction where it longed to be itself. By the glare of its burning the night became a mockery of day in its abnormal, shifting light. Was there no foothold on which it could cross? This was the question asked by the fire. "The bridges! the bridges!" shouted the multitude, and one by one their ponderous ligneous lengths were swung around and left heading up and down the stream. At length the fire answered its question by flinging a shower of burning brands upon the Adams street bridge, and the wind, the friend of the fire, fanned them until the bridge was all aflame. Now it had a shorter distance to leap, and with a savage bound the fire was in the heart of the city—in its fat, rich heart, where active wealth had piled its palaces of commerce and housed its treasures in with iron and stone, and thought it was free from the sweep of flood or flame. Eastward the fire journeyed with its fevered stride, eating like a withering canker through the vitals of the city. It was not long before the Michigan Southern depot had risen up in smoke and blaze and fell in ruins, scattering a deeper volume of destruction around than ever before. Now northward the hell angel strode to the emporium of rich produce it was longing for. Now it hung around a bank, burst open its doors, shivered its windows, scorched through its roof and toiled and burned its fiercest till the great safe—ah, the safe! had succumbed to its blasting, melting breath. The fire-bells all over the city were ringing continually—a terrible tocsin, with the one word fire in its scorching throat. The people had but to wake to know what was the matter. The danger seemed everywhere. Out in the street, half clad, dragging what could be snatched in the hurry of flight, the strong man, the half-fainting women, the children with terror pictured in their wide-open eyes, all hurrying, with "nowhere to go." All the fire force in the city was combating the flames as fearlessly as brave men with their hearths and homes at stake well might. Without regard to whom it reached the panting fire licked and consumed hotels and stores. Now the Court House, now the Sherman House, anon the Western Union Telegraph Company's office, then the Tremont House, next the Chamber of Commerce, far-famed Farwell Hall—whatever lay in its fated path—until it flung itself upon the great Union depot with its spread of buildings, and had sacked with its cremating arms the corn-stored grain elevators by the lake and river side. Again it met the waters, and again it leaped them, landing on the north side of the town. Here it had nothing to stay its steps. Wooden houses were but fuel in its way, and greedily it enveloped and devoured them. Onward for a mile it stretched as the day broke, fear before and ruin and ashes behind. Animals burst forth from keeping and rushed blind among the flames, adding to the terror of the scene as they gave forth their cries of dread. The homeless began to multiply in number through the blackened light of morning that paled but did not subdue the flames. A horrid thought flashed to the mind of all. "The water-works are in danger if the wind lives."

Up to Chicago avenue the fire raged unabated in its fury. The rumor that human beings were perishing in the flames became a certainty, and what made the agony deeper was that none could tell how many. Can it ever be told? Eastward from Chicago avenue, with the whole portion of the city to the south, one seething, reeking sea of fire, it went and suddenly the water supply failed. It was said that the water works were burned. It was denied, reaffirmed, and again denied. The men in power, with the Mayor at their head, were acting with the greatest energy. To the other cities of the West went forth a cry for firemen, and one and all the cities responded. To the world went out the simple tragic demand, which, in its brevity and pith alone tells its harrowing story :—"Send us food for the suffering. Our city is in ashes." Houses were blown down that the fire might be arrested, but it seized on the débris and burned that too. Would the wilting wind never die? It did not fall, it only changed, as if it had exhausted all the demons whence it came, and then had called upon the North to send out its vandal breeze.

And yet it was salvation to the West and South Divisions, so much of which survived, that the wind blew from the same quarter Sunday, Monday, Tuesday, and continually until the fire had burned itself out. On Monday night there was a gentle rain, which seemed to many a God-send, and yet added to the forlorn condition of thousands who crowded out to the prairies and the groves north and west of the fire. Here many died from terror and exposure, and it is estimated that five hundred births occurred during these two days and nights. Some were confined in the streets and vehicles, and others found a temporary shelter until more permanent means were devised for their comfort.

The greater part of the fire in the North Division occurred after daylight on Monday, and the spectacle presented in that quarter was such as would be presented by a community fleeing before an invading army. Every vehicle that could be got was hurrying from the burning district loaded with people and their goods. Light buggies, barouches, carts, and express-wagons were mingled indiscriminately, and laden with an indescribable variety of articles. Others were hurrying to the scene from curiosity, or to complete the work of rescuing friends and property before the monster could destroy them.

People crowded the walks, leading children or pet dogs, carrying plants in pots, iron-kettles not worth ten cents, or some valueless article seized in the excitement; many looked dolefully upon the lurid clouds, still far away, and wondered whether they and their homes were in danger; and others looked as though they had spent the night in a coal-pit or a fiery furnace. There was such "hurrying to and fro" as the world seldom see, with universal agony and distress.

Families became separated and were looking for one another

and often in vain was the search—they would meet only at the great Judgment Day, which seemed to some almost at hand.

A locomotive engineer was on his freight-train, forty miles from the city, when he heard the fire was raging on Michigan Avenue. He said, "I asked permission to go on with my train and was forbidden; I put on steam, and they put down the brakes, but I pulled my train as near to the depot as I could, and left it in charge of the fireman. I hurt nobody and did no harm to anything; I went straight to the place where I left my family, and dragged out their bones. When I came back to my situation they told me I was discharged, and I am now homeless and helpless."

Men were desperate, and deemed almost anything justifiable. One who saw that he could not escape, opened his veins that he might not know the horrors of death by fire. Another, probably rendered insane by losses and terror, was found with his throat cut from ear to ear. Men who were laboring to rescue their books and papers from the peril, were so involved in the mazes of the fire, that they tried several streets before they were able to escape, and then suffered serious inconveniences or injury in the final struggle that saved them. One, in trying to gather a few things from his room, fell suffocated, and, recovering presence of mind, crawled to the window, and calling on men to catch him, leaped from the second story, and was able to rejoin his family. A fireman brought a two-year old child to a lady, which was snatched out of the upper story of a lofty building in the heart of the fire. The little thing was scorched and singed, and when asked, "Where is papa?" he answered, "Gone to church." "Where is mamma?" "Gone to church." So unexpected was the fire, that the parents had not time to find their darling after church. Some 300 were caged up near the river, and taken off by the steamer that lay close at hand. Others, hurried out of their home and cut off from egress by any street, fled to the lake shore, and as the furious element closed around them they were pressed into the water, and kept themselves for hours by dipping their heads into the cool element. Children were immersed repeatedly, in order to keep them from being scorched, and many came from their wet refuges more dead than alive. A family who had spent several years abroad, and collected many valuable works of art and souvenirs of their journeys, were driven from one place to another, and finally took refuge in a stable. The proprietor begged them to take his carriage and drive it off to save it. In this they escaped several miles to a place of safety, having nothing left but what they wore upon their persons.

A man at the corner of Division and Brandt streets had apparently secured his household goods in an open lot; but the flames mercilessly attacked his effects, and seeing there was no further chance of saving them, he knelt down and offered a brief prayer, after which he arose, clasped his hands in wild despair, and looking to heaven exclaimed, "God help me now," and was soon lost to view in the dense smoke through which he endeavored to make his escape.

Mr. Kerfoot gives the following graphic account of his escape from the fire with his wife and children: "Being the owner of a horse and carriage which I used to go to and fro from my business, when I became satisfied that my house would soon be enveloped, I brought my horse and carriage before the house, and placed my wife and children in it. There was then no room for me, so I mounted the back of the animal and acted as postilion. While driving through the flame and smoke which enveloped us on all hands, I came across a gentleman who had his wife in a buggy, and was between the thills hauling it himself. I shouted to him to hitch his carriage on behind mine, which he did, and then got in beside his wife. I then drove forward as fast as I could, for the flames were raging around us. After proceeding a short distance, another gentleman was found standing beside the street, with a carriage, waiting for a horse, which was not likely to come. I directed him to fasten on behind the second carriage, which he did, and in this way we whipped up and got out of the way of the flames with our wives and children, thank God."

A remarkable instance of courage and presence of mind is told of Mr. E. I. Tinkham, of the Second National Bank. On Monday morning, before the fire had reached that building, Mr. Tinkham went to the safe and succeeded in getting out $600,000. This pile of greenbacks he packed into a common trunk, and hired a colored man for $1,000 to convey it to the Milwaukee depot. Fearing to be recognized in connection with the precious load, Mr. Tinkham followed the man for a time at some distance, but soon lost sight of him. He was then overtaken by the firestorm, and was driven toward the lake on the south side. Here, after passing through several narrow escapes from suffocation, he succeeded in working his way, by some means, to a tug-boat, and got round to the Milwaukee depot, where he found the colored man waiting for him, with the trunk, according to promise. Mr. Tinkham paid the man the $1,000, and started with the trunk for Milwaukee. The money was safely deposited in Marshall & Illsley's bank, of that city.

Mr. Nathaniel Bacon, of Niles, Michigan, student-at-law with Messrs. Tenney, McClellan & Tenney, at No. 120 Washington street, slept in their office. On waking, at about 1 o'clock, and seeing the Court-House on fire, he saw that the office, which was immediately opposite, would surely go. Judging that one of the safes in the office would not prove fire-proof, he promptly emptied the contents of his trunk on the floor of the doomed building, and, filling it with the interior contents of the safe—books, valuable papers, money, &c.—shouldered the trunk and carried it to a place of safety on Twenty-Second street, losing thereby all his own clothing and effects except what he had on. That young man is a hero.

In the midst of all that was sad and terrible there was an occasional gleam of the humorous.

—One merchant, who found his safe and its contents destroyed, quietly remarked that there was no blame attached to the safe; that it was of chilled iron, and would have stood, but that the fire had taken the *chill all out.*

—A firm of painters on Madison street bulletin their removal as follows, on a sign-board erected like a guide-board upon the ruins of their old establishment :—

> MOORE & GOE,
> HOUSE AND SIGN PAINTERS,
> Removed to 111 Desplaines st.,
> Capital, $000,000.30.

—An editor of a daily paper has received several poetical effusions suggested by the late disaster; but he declines them all, on the ground that it is wasteful to print anything which requires every line with a capital, when capital is as scarce as it is now in Chicago.

—A bride who entered the holy married state on Tuesday evening, determined to do so in a calico dress, in deference both to the proprieties and the necessities of the occasion. But she desired that her *toilette de chambre* should be, if possible, on a more gorgeous scale. Being destitute of a *robe de nuit* of suitable elegance, she sent out to several neighbors of her temporary hostess to borrow such a garment, stipulating that it must be a *fine one.* So peculiar is the feminine nature, however, that her modest request excited no enthusiasm in her behalf among the ladies to whom it came. This is not a joke.

—A sign-board, stuck in the ruins of a building on Madison street, reads: "Owing to circumstances over which we had no control, we have removed," etc.

CHICAGO, October 12, 1871.

To the Editor of the *Chicago Evening Journal:*—

The attention of Chicagoans is called to the 8th chapter of Deuteronomy, and the clergy of the city are respectfully requested to take the same for a text on Sunday morning next.

MERCHANT.

—One of our merchants, reported insane, was heard from at New York—where he had gone to bury a sister—in the following noble manner:—

Mrs. Potter Palmer:

I have particulars of fire. Am perfectly reconciled to our losses. We shall not be embarrassed. Have an abundance left. Be cheerful and do all possible for sufferers. Will return by first train after funeral. POTTER PALMER.

The scene presented on Wabash avenue on Monday, for a period extending from 4 o'clock A.M. till late in the day, was a most extraordinary one, calling to mind most vividly the retreat of a routed army. The lower part of the avenue had, at an early hour, been occupied by residents of burning quarters, who sought safety for themselves and their chattels by depositing them on the grass-plats skirting the sidewalks. For a long distance these plats were occupied by families, mostly of the lower classes, with their household goods. They supposed that they had discovered a place of security, but their confidence in this regard proved unfounded. As the fire commenced spreading up the avenue a wild scene of confusion ensued. The street was crowded with vehicles of all descriptions, many drawn by men, who found it impossible to procure draught animals. The sidewalks were filled with a hurrying crowd, bearing in their arms and upon their backs and heads clothing, furniture, etc. Ladies dressed in elegant costumes, put on with the view of preserving them, and with costly apparel of all kinds thrown over their arms and shoulders, staggered along under the unwonted burden. Poor women, with mattresses upon their heads, or weighted down with furniture, tottered with weary steps up the crowded street. Nearly every one wore a stern expression, and moved on without a word, as if they had braced up their minds to endure the worst without manifesting any emotion. Occasionally, however, the wail of women and children rent the air, bringing tears to the eyes of those who witnessed the manifestations. Poor little children shivered in the cold night air, and looked with wildly opened eyes upon the scenes they could not comprehend. Ludicrous incidents were of occasional occurrence, lighting up with a sort of horrible humor the terrible realities of the situation. Women would go by with dogs in their arms—their pets being all they had saved from the ruins of their homes. An octogenarian ran into a yard with a large cat enfolded in his feeble embrace. Men dragging wagons wore green veils over their faces to protect their eyes from the blinding dust. Drunken men staggered among the crowds, apparently possessed of the idea that the whole affair was a grand municipal spree, in which they were taking part as a duty that should be discharged by all good citizens. Trucks passed up street loaded with trunks, on which sat ladies in costly garb, and with diamonds in their ears and on their fingers. But one day before they would have scorned the idea of riding in anything less imposing than a luxurious landau or coupé; but their pride was levelled in the presence of the universally imminent danger, and they were thoroughly glad to get the humblest cart in which to place themselves and their valuables.

The greater portion of the people knew not whither they were going. All they knew was that the horrible fire was behind them and they must move on. The stream poured southward for hours, the broad avenue being filled from house to house with men, women, children, horses, mules, vehicles, wheelbarrows—everything that could move or be moved. Truckmen and express drivers were hailed from the steps of houses, or eagerly pursued by the occupants, with the view of securing their aid in removing household goods to places of safety. In many instances the appeals were unsuccessful, their services having been previously engaged by other parties; but when they were disengaged they charged the most exorbitant prices, ranging from $5 to $100 for a load, and turning up their noses at offers of amounts less than they asked. This class of people made great profit out of the calamities of their fellow-citizens. Their pockets may be heavy to-day, but their consciences, if they have any, should be still heavier. The instances of generosity were, however, far in excess of those of greed and selfishness. People from districts which had not already been burned, or who had secured their own goods, turned in with a will and worked to assist their friends, and frequently rendered aid to persons whom they did not know. Good angels, in the shape of women, distributed food among the sufferers, and spoke kind words to those who seemed to labor under the severest affliction. Human nature, God be thanked, has its bright as well as its dark side.

Some of the scenes that transpired about and in the fire were disgraceful beyond measure. The saloons were, many of them thrown open, and men exhorted to free drinking needed but one invitation. Hundreds were soon dead drunk, or fighting and screaming; many thus fell victims to the flames, and some were dragged away by main force and rescued from roasting. Even respectable men, seeing that all was lost, sought to drown their misery by intoxication.

But worse than this were the instances of theft and cold-blooded avarice which occurred and have come to light. A book-keeper engaged in conveying away the firm's records fell fainting in the alley behind the store, overcome by exertion and suffocated by the smoke and dust. The shock restored him to consciousness, and upon attempting to rise he found himself unable to stand. Just then a man was passing, and he hailed him with a request for help. The wretch offered to assist for a hundred dollars. The fallen man said, "I have but ten, and I will give you that." For this amount he gave his arm to the poor sufferer, and saved his life. A girl carried her sewing-machine to four different points, and was forced from each by the advancing fiend. At last an expressman seized her treasure, and in spite of all her efforts drove away with it. Said the impoverished girl, "Do you wonder Chicago burned?" In front of a wholesale house the sidewalk was bloody from the punishment inflicted by the police upon sneak-thieves. Trunks were rifled after their owners had placed them out of reach of fire. They were broken open by dozens on the lake shore, and the empty trunks tossed into the water. Pieces of broadcloth were torn into strips three yards long and distributed among a party who said, "These will make us each a good suit." Persons who saw and heard these things were powerless, and the confusion was so terrible that no one could look out for any one but himself, or interfere for the protection of others' property. It was a time when the worst forces of society were jubilant, and all the villains had free course. The Court-House jail had one hundred and sixty prisoners, and these were let loose to prey upon the people in the time of their helplessness and extremity. Such an event was a public calamity; but humanity would not permit the poor wretches to perish there, and no means were at hand to convey them to any other place of confinement.

Speedily upon the appearance of daylight and the resumption of courage, the Mayor and a few citizens, like Hon. C. C. P. Holden, Alonzo Snider, and others, began to organize measures for public safety and order. The following proclamation was issued, and gave confidence:—

"WHEREAS, in the Providence of God, to whose will we humbly submit, a terrible calamity has befallen our city, which demands of us our best efforts for the preservation of order and the relief of the suffering.

"BE IT KNOWN that the faith and credit of the city of Chicago is hereby pledged for the necessary expenses for the relief of the suffering. Public order will be preserved. The Police, and Special Police now being appointed, will be responsible for the maintenance of the peace and the protection of property. All officers and men of the Fire Department and Health Department will act as Special Policemen without further notice. The Mayor and Comptroller will give vouchers for all supplies furnished by the different Relief Committees. The head-quarters of the City Government will be at the Congregational Church, corner of West Washington and Ann streets. All persons are warned against any acts tending to endanger property. All persons caught in any depredation will be immediately arrested.

"With the help of God, order and peace and private property shall be preserved. The City Government and committees of citizens pledge themselves to the community to protect them, and prepare the way for a restoration of public and private welfare.

"It is believed the fire has spent its force, and all will soon be well.

      R. B. MASON, *Mayor.*
      GEORGE TAYLOR, *Comptroller.*
       (By R. B. MASON.)
      CHARLES C. P. HOLDEN,
       President Common Council.
      T. B. BROWN,
       President Board of Police.

"CHICAGO, *October* 9, 1871."

The citizens were organized into a police force, and thousands patrolled the city with a desperate determination to preserve their property and to punish with sudden vengeance the incendiaries who were prowling about the city. The demoniac purposes of these villains who were attempting incendiarism were favored by the high winds and the dryness of everything combustible. The people were dreadfully excited in all parts of the city, and every rumor was caught up and magnified. But additional assurance was given by the presence of Gen. Phil. Sheridan, with the regulars and militia, to whom the burnt district was given up for protection. There lay hundreds of safes, either exposed or buried in the débris. When these were opened, ruffians would be on the watch to see whither the contents were conveyed. Cracksmen came in from other cities to take advantage of the disaster. But the gallant General was able to announce as follows:—

"HEAD-QUARTERS MILITARY DIVISION OF THE MISSOURI,
CHICAGO, *Oct.* 12.

"*To His Honor the Mayor:*—

"The preservation of peace and good order of the city having been entrusted to me by your Honor, I am happy to state that no case of outbreak or disorder has been reported. No authenticated attempt at incendiarism has reached me, and the people of the city are calm, quiet, and well-disposed.

"The force at my disposal is ample to maintain order, should it be necessary, and protect the district devastated by fire. Still, I would suggest to citizens not to relax in their watchfulness until the smouldering fires of the burnt buildings are entirely extinguished. "P. H. SHERIDAN,
"Lieutenant-General."

There were hideous instances of cruelty and wickedness during the conflagration, which no provision could have prevented. The inmates of the jail were only released after the cupola of the building fell in, and while they were howling, praying, and fighting for escape. Immense battering-rams had no effect on the fastenings from without, and only at the last moment did the turnkey let them loose into the heart of the burning city. That which greatly facilitated the progress of the fire, and kept all the people in terror, was the burning of the famous water-works on the north side at an early hour on the morning of Monday. The query may arise, Why any lack of this fluid when a mighty lake rolled at the city's feet and a river flowed through its heart? "Water, water everywhere!" Probably no city has better supplies of water, now that from the bosom of an inland sea we draw fresh draughts in boundless abundance. The tunnel that connects the lake-shaft with the shore is far below the bottom and is safe, but the engines which lift the water and force it into reservoirs for distribution were exposed to the irresistible element, and by some strange fatality, whether accidental or otherwise, they early fell a prey to destruction. The grand tower stands unharmed, and all the connections underground remain intact.

But massive stone walls and slate roof afforded no protection, for the city was doomed. And now, when all was dust and smoke and fire, suddenly the hydrants ceased to flow, and a pang of alarm and consternation shot through the breasts of the population.

The public parks had water in their fountains and pools, and to these the multitudes resorted day and night, with every sort of vessel that could hold water. It was almost a ludicrous, but particularly a pitiable sight. The Artesian wells also sent out their supplies, in carts and wagons, all through the west division, and the horrors of thirst were averted. The first copious rain which fell was on Saturday, October 14th, and every householder made the most of this heavenly bounty. But the next question after water was food. Our resources are all cut off; there is no business, and our hundred thousand people must have bread, and not for one day, but for many days.

The lurid flames shot up in masses that overwhelmed the city, and no one could tell when there would be a cessation of the work of ruin, or how sustenance could be provided. Fears of a bread-riot arose in many minds, because of the imminent approach of deadly want.

At this hour of our extremity, when all seemed toppling to destruction, a cry was heard like that of which we read in tales of shipwreck, when the lost discern a sail upon the waters. The tidings reached other towns and cities, and were flashed across the Atlantic, and instantly, spontaneously, nobly, munificently the responses came back, not only in words of cheer, but in substantial forms—car-loads of cooked food and provisions of every kind, good wholesome supplies, better than many of the poor had been wont to enjoy—clothing in bountiful abundance, and money to be used at the discretion of the authorities. Men who had not shed a tear till then, shook with uncontrollable emotion and wept for joy. The gratitude was equal to the charity, if such an equalization were possible.

We began to realize how intimately the interests of Chicago were bound up with those of the whole country and the world. Its losses were not local, but almost universal, so that the words of Schiller scarcely seemed inapplicable here:—

> " This kingly Wallenstein, whene'er he falls
> Will drag a world to ruin down with him;
> And as a ship that in the midst of ocean
> Catches fire, and shivering springs into the air,
> And in a moment scatters between sea and sky
> The crew it bore, so will he hurry to destruction
> Ev'ry one whose fate was joined with his."

The representatives of all nations were here, and of all States, and communities in North America—the business world were here by their money or agencies, and the fall of Chicago sent a tremor throughout the whole fabric of society. This may account, in part, for the uprising of all Christendom to assist in the terrific exigency, and roll away the burden that was crushing her into the dust.

We give several proclamations by the Governors of the States adjacent, whose people were fully roused to comprehend the calamity and meet the extreme demands of the suffering multitude:—

BY THE GOVERNOR OF ILLINOIS.

STATE OF ILLINOIS, }
EXECUTIVE DEPARTMENT. }

John M. Palmer, Governor of Illinois, To all whom these presents shall come, greeting:

Whereas, in my judgment, the great calamity that has overtaken Chicago, the largest city of the State; that has deprived many thousands of our citizens of homes and rendered them destitute; that has destroyed many millions in value of property, and thereby disturbing the business of the people and deranging the finances of the State, and interrupting the execution of the laws, is and constitutes "an extraordinary occasion" within the true intent and meaning of the eighth section of the fifth article of the Constitution.

Now, therefore, I, John M. Palmer, Governor of the State of Illinois, do by this, my proclamation, convene and invite the two Houses of the General Assembly in session in the city of Springfield, on Friday, the 13th day of the month of October, in the year of our Lord 1871, at 12 o'clock noon of said day, to take into consideration the following subjects:—

1. To appropriate such sum or sums of money, or adopt such other legislative measures as may be thought judicious, neces-

sary, or proper, for the relief of the people of the city of Chicago.

2. To make provision, by amending the revenue laws or otherwise, for the proper and just assessment and collection of taxes within the city of Chicago.

3. To enact such other laws and to adopt such other measures as may be necessary for the relief of the city of Chicago and the people of said city, and for the execution and enforcement of the laws of the State.

4. To make appropriations for the expenses of the General Assembly, and such other appropriations as may be necessary to carry on the State Government.

> In testimony whereof I have hereunto set my hand and caused the great seal of State to be affixed.
>
> [SEAL.]   Done at the city of Springfield, this 10th day of October, A.D. 1871.
>
> JOHN M. PALMER.

By the Governor,
  EDWARD RUMMELL, *Secretary of State.*

BY THE GOVERNOR OF WISCONSIN.

To the People of Wisconsin:

Throughout the northern part of this State fires have been raging in the woods for many days, spreading desolation on every side. It is reported that hundreds of families have been rendered homeless by this devouring element, and reduced to utter destitution, their entire crops having been consumed. Their stock has been destroyed, and their farms are but a blackened desert. Unless they receive instant aid from portions not visited by this dreadful calamity, they must perish.

The telegraph also brings the terrible news that a large portion of the city of Chicago is destroyed by a conflagration, which is still raging. Many thousands of people are thus reduced to penury, stripped of their all, and are now destitute of shelter and food. Their sufferings will be intense, and many may perish unless provisions are at once sent to them from the surrounding country. They must be assisted now.

In the awful presence of such calamities the people of Wisconsin will not be backward in giving assistance to their afflicted fellow-men.

I, therefore, recommend that immediate organized effort be made in every locality to forward provisions and money to the sufferers by this visitation, and suggest to mayors of cities, presidents of villages, town supervisors, pastors of churches, and to the various benevolent societies, that they devote themselves immediately to the work of organizing effort, collecting contributions, and sending forward supplies for distribution.

And I entreat all to give of their abundance to help those in such sore distress.

Given under my hand, at the Capitol, at Madison, this 9th day of October, A. D. 1871.   LUCIUS FAIRCHILD.

BY THE GOVERNOR OF MICHIGAN.

STATE OF MICHIGAN, EXECUTIVE OFFICE,
LANSING, *Oct.* 9.

The city of Chicago, in the neighboring State of Illinois, has been visited, in the providence of Almighty God, with a calamity almost unequalled in the annals of history. A large portion of that beautiful and most prosperous city has been reduced to ashes and is now in ruins. Many millions of dollars in property, the accumulation of years of industry and toil, have been swept away in a moment. The rich have been reduced to penury, the poor have lost the little they possessed, and many thousands of people rendered homeless and houseless, and are now without the absolute necessaries of life. I, therefore, earnestly call upon the citizens of every portion of Michigan to take immediate measures for alleviating the pressing wants of that fearfully afflicted city by collecting and forwarding to the Mayor or proper authorities of Chicago supplies of food as well as liberal collections of money. Let this sore calamity of our neighbors remind us of the uncertainty of earthly possessions, and that when one member suffers all the members should suffer with it. I cannot doubt that the whole people of the State will most gladly, and most promptly, and most liberally respond to this urgent demand upon their sympathy; but no words of mine can plead so strongly as the calamity itself.

HENRY P. BALDWIN,
Governor of Michigan.

BY THE GOVERNOR OF IOWA.

To the People of Iowa:

An appalling calamity has befallen our sister State. Her metropolis—the great city of Chicago—is in ruins. Over 100,000 people are without shelter or food, except as supplied by others. A helping hand let us now promptly give. Let the liberality of our people, so lavishly displayed during the long period of national peril, come again to the front, to lend succor in this hour of distress. I would urge the appointment at once of relief committees in every city, town, and township, and I respectfully ask the local authorities to call meetings of the citizens to devise ways and means to render efficient aid. I would also ask the pastors of the various churches throughout the State to take up collections on Sunday morning next, or at such other time as they may deem proper, for the relief of the sufferers. Let us not be satisfied with any spasmodic effort. There will be need of relief of a substantial character to aid the many thousands to prepare for the rigors of the coming winter. The magnificent public charities of that city, now paralyzed, can do little to this end. Those who live in homes of comfort and plenty must furnish this help, or misery and suffering will be the fate of many thousands of our neighbors.

SAMUEL MERRILL, Governor.

DES MOINES, *Oct.* 10, 1871.

BY THE GOVERNOR OF OHIO.

CHICAGO, *Oct.* 12.

To the People of Ohio:

It is believed by the best informed citizens here that many thousands of the sufferers must be provided with the necessaries of life during the cold winter. Let the efforts to raise contributions be energetically pushed. Money, fuel, flour, pork, clothing, and other articles not perishable should be collected as rapidly as possible—especially money, fuel, and flour. Mr. Joseph Medill, of *The Tribune*, estimates the number of those who will need assistance at about 70,000.

R. B. HAYES, Governor of Ohio.

As great exigencies develop great men, and peculiar sorrows call forth the best elements of human nature, thus compensating men for labors and loss in some measure, glorifying mankind and bringing down God's richest blessings, so on the bosom of this mighty sea of trouble rose a light that brightened into perfect day, and the people of this and other countries put forth their energies to relieve distress and provide for the army of sufferers. No sooner was the melancholy news sent forth, than women began to cook, and night and day they filled their ovens with the best they could prepare, and sent it hot to the depots from whence it was conveyed to the desolate city. One man superintended the unloading of two hundred and fifty cars in four days, and this was but a moiety of the bounty. Everything that came seemed to be of the best quality, and the poor were never treated to such a feast. In the midst of all the terror, confusion, dust, and smoke, arrangements were extemporized for receiving and disbursing supplies. The school buildings and saved church edifices were thrown open, and the citizens received the provisions and gave them out. Cushions were freely used for beds, and the poor homeless wanderers rested in God's sanctuaries. In the Second Baptist basement hundreds found good sleeping accommodations, and thousands were fed. While the outside public were so grandly generous, the sufferers found their more fortunate citizens absolutely unselfish and noble in their devotion and care. The loftier traits of Christian character shone forth conspicuous through the gloom. This was all the more marked, inasmuch as their own spared homes were exposed to fire every moment, or to pillage, until Sunday a week after the fire. Saturday the rain fell in copious showers, but even on that night the alarm was great, as may be gathered from the following description in one of the papers:

"The storm which swept over this city on Saturday night was the severest visitation of that character which we have encountered this season. Early in the evening a pretty stiff breeze blew from south-south-west. As the hours wore on, the wind veered around to the westward and gradually increased in strength. Toward midnight a perfect hurricane from the north-west prevailed. The reflection on the drifting storm-clouds of the burning coal along the docks struck terror to the hearts of the dwellers in the far-western portion of the city, who imagined that the glare was due to another outburst of the fire. Each house had its anxious watchers, who kept a steady look-out towards the east lest the fiery destroyer should stealthily approach and devour the dry remnant of the city. The solidity of those blocks which front bleak stretches of prairie was put to a severe test all through the night. No sleep came to quiet the unstrung nerves of the excited inmates, for the houses and everything about them rocked and rattled as if from the action of an earthquake. As morning approached the storm began to abate in violence, and the terrible light of the sky gradually faded away. When day broke full and clear, the wind had almost entirely subsided, to the intense gratification of weary sentinels.

"It was most fortunate that no incipient fires made their appearance in any distant portion of the West Division. It is terrible even to imagine the result of such a calamity, with water so scarce and a frightful storm raging. No power on earth could have saved us from utter annihilation. Happily but slight damage was done on land by the wind, though what disasters followed on the lake is not yet definitely known. It is feared that marine casualties have been numerous. Several dangerous walls among the south-side ruins were blown down during the night. Beyond the demolition of the frail steeple of the San Francisco church, on the corner of Twelfth street and Newberry avenue, which fell with a loud crash about midnight, nothing serious occurred on the west side."

Sunday was a day of perfect loveliness, and the people gathered in multitudes

UNDER THE SHADOW OF THE SANCTUARY.

"Those places of worship in the South Division which escaped the sad fate of so many of the finest monuments to architectural skill in the city, were crowded to overflowing during the services yesterday morning. A hundred uncovered heads could have been seen on the sidewalks fronting the few remaining churches which rear their spires heavenward in that blighted section. At the hour for the services to commence it was impossible to gain entrance to the auditoriums, and late-comers had to content themselves with what they could see and hear through open doors and windows.

"Those long lines of fashionably-attired Christians who were wont to exhibit themselves on the avenues on other Sabbath mornings were not visible yesterday. The raiment of the church-goers was as subdued as their feelings. Earnest, thankful prayer substituted itself for ostentatious display, and reverential attention for the thoughtless demeanor of other times. The services at the churches were of a dual character—sorrowful and joyful—sorrow for the unparalleled disasters of the past eventful week, and joy that so much of this great city has been spared from the fury of the flames. The sermons were based on the most appropriate texts, and in the great majority of instances were brimful of sound wisdom and practical suggestions to the troubled people.

"The congregations of some of the devastated churches assembled on the still smoking bricks, and offered up fervent thanks for the preservation of their lives and homes.

"Many an eye was dimmed with tears as little incidents in former Sabbath meetings were recalled to point out more forcibly the vast differences between now and then. The most impressive of those gatherings was that held on the ruins of Dr. Ryder's church. A large number were present, and were visibly affected.

"Mr. Cheney preached at Grace Church to a large congregation, composed of his own parishioners and outsiders unchurched by the fire. His topic was of course the lesson of the great calamity. He inculcated patience, hope, and charity, but most especially economy. We must, for a long time to come, dress plainly, live coarsely, and be generous to the very extreme of our means.

"The discourse was eloquent and abounded in practical suggestions.

"The goodly number of the Church of the Unity, Rev. Robert Collyer, met on the ruins of their late beautiful temple. The ladies and gentlemen were not fashionably dressed, and some of them not even comfortably, considering the fresh wind that blew in from the prairies upon them. The pastor stood in front of the arch of entrance, upon an ornamental stone fallen from the cornice. His congregation gathered in a semicircle in front of him. The scene was like a convention of early Christians in the Catacombs. Words of significance were read from Isaiah 54th and 65th. Then the congregation sang the 100th psalm, 'Before Jehovah's awful throne,' the pastor lining it. The hymn sung was, 'Awake our souls, away our fears.' The sermon was a tearful effort to be courageous under overshadowing discouragements. He only hovered on the edges of the great subject uppermost in everybody's mind. The speaker said that he had been trying to find some altitude of soul, some height of sentiment from which he could look down and thank God for what had occurred. At some future time he might be able to accomplish it. He could not thank God now. The sorrow was too near. After this expression, the speaker enumerated the few things which were left to be thankful for, and expressed the opinion that a more glorious future for the church and the congregation might arise from this dreadful past. He said that he should stay with his people through their bitter trial, and consider any offer of a position elsewhere not exactly as an insult, but as something resembling it.

"A list of the insurances on the edifice was read. It amounted to $105,000, of which at least $75,000 will be recovered. A place of meeting will be at once obtained, and regular Sabbath services will be held in the future.

"St. James's Church is one of the historical edifices of the city. It has also been noted for benevolence, as much as twenty or thirty thousand dollars having in single instances been collected at its Sunday services. Services were held yesterday at the ruins, the pastor, Mr. Thompson, officiating, and the attendance being good. The excellent choir furnished the music without organ accompaniment. The sermon was brief and delivered in a faltering voice to weeping, broken-hearted auditors. At a meeting of the vestry, immediately succeeding the service, Hon. I. N. Arnold made a brief address, speaking of what the church had done for others, and saying that outside aid in rebuilding would be gratefully received. A committee of five were appointed to attend to immediate and necessary business."

R. L. COLLIER said :—

"I have been busy in a more sacred ministry than that of arranging precise and careful thoughts for this occasion. I have thrown together this morning such reflections as have come to me. I thank God that our church still stands, and hope it will morally stand far more than ever before.

"I have heard not a little speculation about the moral significance of our great calamity, and men who meant better have unwittingly accused God of a great wickedness when they have intimated that it was a judgment of Heaven because of the ungodliness of our city.

"1. First of all, judgments of Heaven are never retrospective, but always prospective—that is, they are never of the backward glance, but always of the forward. This calamity, as all calamities, has a meaning, and its purpose is to work out God's unchanging will and beneficent design. The individual and temporary good or ill that may come of it will depend wholly upon the spirit with which we receive it.

"The chief element visible to our eyes by which the fire was brought about was the great drought. There has not occurred a great fall of rain for more than two years, and the whole region is a tinder-box. Our city of shanties and sheds was in a fit condition for the mingled furies of flame and wind.

"As to the fire being a judgment, in the sense of a punishment from Heaven because of the sinfulness of the people, I remark :

"God's way is otherwise. He disciplines without destroying, and builds up without pulling down. No such punishment could possibly do any good if it were only received as a wilful infliction of the rod of Heaven.

"2. Then there was no reason why Chicago should have been made an example for the rest of the world. Of course, we were a people of great worldliness and selfishness, of great boasting and parade; but certainly no city of the Christian world has ever done more, according to its means, for schools, churches, and charities.

"The poor have been systematically provided for, and freely educated in school and church. There have been from the first saintly men and women whose cry has gone up to God, and he has heard them.

"3. The judgment is meant to look *forward*, not *backward*.

"We have chiefly magnified the rights of individuals rather than of society. We have been shockingly short-sighted, in the boundaries of our fire limits, in permitting so many or any wooden buildings within the limits of the city, and to-day the fire limits should be the city limits.

"We have given full sway to drinking, gambling, and licentious houses, and have by our moral laxity invited to the city, and harbored in it a criminal population almost equal to that of London, which is the worst on the face of the earth.

"We have thus done less to reform this very population, when in our power, than almost any other city. Our Bridewell and jail have cried aloud to heaven for help and redress.

"We have had the experience of the whole world back of us, and yet, in building a great city and centre of civilization, we have given the work into the hands of greedy real estate speculators, and have selfishly taken care of our own concerns.

"We have drifted, too, into the hands of a set of tricky politicians, the spirit of which is illustrated by our present City Council, and the only recognized aristocracy of the city is a set of ignorant and recently enriched social swells and snobs.

BURNING OF THE CROSBY OPERA-HOUSE.

"Now, I say the judgment of our calamity is to teach us to cure these evils. We must learn, shortly, economy in our homes and business management. I am not hoping to see again such elegant residences and business blocks—I certainly never desire to. Europe knows better than we in these matters. Let our civic buildings and monuments, our school buildings and churches, our public libraries in each section of the city, our colleges of the learned professions, be grand and impressive as may be. In these we can illustrate our genius for beauty and sacrifice. When our business and domestic expenses are less, we can have more to give to public uses.

"What is lost?

"1. Our houses. Thousands of families are houseless and penniless.

"2. Our business. This is temporary.

"3. Our money. This is a great misfortune, but one which we can repair.

"We have not lost—

"1. Our geography. Nature called the lakes, the forest, the prairies together in convention long before we were born, and they decided that on this spot a great city should be built—the railroads and energetic men have aided to fulfill the prophecy.

"2. We have not lost our men—noble, generous, and of genius.

"3. We have not lost our hope. This city is to be at once rebuilt, and the glory of the latter house shall be greater than that of the former.

"Our duty.—We are in the poetry of the fire as yet. There is a dreamy, hazy romance about it. Stern reality will come to us more and more all winter. The temptation will be to greater selfishness on the part of those who have anything left. We must share to the last cent with the needy. Keep courage up, and give to others. Our churches must go on, and in them we must work as never before.

"God is on our side, and has left us something to do, something to hope for, something to love."

Here we may introduce the magnificent appeal made in Boston by Rev. E. E. Hale, at a meeting of citizens held to consider our calamity.

Rev. E. E. Hale being introduced by the Mayor, spoke substantially as follows:

"MR. MAYOR AND GENTLEMEN:—It is but a single word that I have to say here. I have simply to remind you that this is no mere matter of voting in which we are engaged. I have to remind you that these people, our people in Chicago, by their munificence, by their generosity, by their strength, by their public spirit, have made us debtors to them all. [Applause]. There is not a man here the beef upon whose table yesterday was not the cheaper to him because these people laid out that world-renowned and wonderful system of stock-yards. [Applause]. There is not a man here the bread upon whose table to-day is not cheaper because these people, in the very beginning of their national existence, invented and created that mavellous system for the delivery of grain which is the model and pattern of the world. [Applause]. And remember that they were in a position where they might have said they held a monopoly. They commanded the only harbor for the shipping of the five greatest States of America and the world, and in that position they have devoted themselves now for a generation to the steady improvement, by every method in their power, of the means by which they were going to answer the daily prayer of every child to God when praying that He will give us our daily bread, through their enterprise and their struggles. We call it their misfortune. It is our misfortune. We are all, as it has been said, linked together in a solidarity of the nation. Their loss is no more theirs than it is ours in this great campaign of peace in which we are engaged. There has fallen by this calamity one of our noblest fortresses. Its garrison is without munitions. It is for us at this instant to reconstruct that fortress, and to see that its garrison are as well placed as they were before in our service. Undoubtedly it is a great enterprise; but we can trust them for that. We are all fond of speaking of the miracle by which there in the desert there was created this great city. The rod of some prophet, you say, struck it, and this city flowed from the rock. Who was the prophet? what was the rock? It was the American people who determined that that city should be there, and that it should rightly and wisely, and in the best way, distribute the food to a world. [Applause]. The American people has that duty to discharge again. I know that these numbers are large numbers. I know that when we read in the newspapers of the destruction of a hundred millions of property those figures are so large that we can hardly comprehend them. But the providence of God has taught us to deal with larger figures than these, and when, not many years ago, it became necessary for this country in every year to spend not a hundred millions, not a thousand millions, but more than a thousand millions of dollars in a great enterprise which God gave this country in the duty of war, this country met its obligation. And now that in a single year we have to reconstruct one of the fortresses of peace, I do not fear that this country will be backward in its duty. It has been truly said that the first duty of all of us is, that the noble pioneers in the duty that God has placed in their hands, who are burned and suffering, shall have food; that by telegraph and railroad they shall know that we are rushing to their relief; that their homeless shall be under shelter, and their naked clothed; that those who for these forty-eight hours have felt as if they were deserted, should know that they have friends everywhere in God's world. [Applause]. Mr.

President, as God is pleased to order this world there is no partial evil but from that partial evil is reached the universal good. The fires which our friends have seen sweeping in their western horizon over the plains in the desolate autumn, only bring forth the blossoms and richness of the next spring and next summer.

"I can well believe that on that terrible night of Sunday, and all through the horrors of Monday, as those noble people, as those gallant workmen, threw upon the flames the water that their noble works—the noblest that America has seen—enabled them to hurl upon the enemy, that they must have imagined that their work was fruitless, that it was lost toil, to see those streams of water playing into the molten mass, and melt into steam and rise innocuous to the heavens. It may well have seemed that their work was wasted; but it is sure that evil shall work out its own end, and the mists that rose from the conflagration were gathered together for the magnificent tempest of last night, which, falling upon those burning streets, has made Chicago a habitable city to-day. [Applause]. See that the lesson for this community, see that the lesson for us who are here, that the horror and tears with which we read the despatches of yesterday, shall send us out to do ministries of truth and bounty and benevolence to-day. [Applause]."

It was in this spirit that men everywhere looked upon the woful disaster and its relation to other communities, and a more appreciative people never lived than the Chicagoans, who poured out their thankfulness to God and implored His divinest blessings on the benevolent self-sacrificing public. All jealousies seemed buried and forgotten, and our great rivals—Milwaukee, St. Louis, and Cincinnati—were profuse and generous beyond precedent in their donations for our benefit. Engines were despatched, provisions and money flowed forth from their noble marts, and thus our sorrow and burden became theirs, and we were brothers in distress. The feelings of her citizens were well expressed in the *Tribune*, which said:

"Amid the general gloom, the public distress, and the widespread wreck of private property, the heart of the most impoverished man is warmed and lightened by the universal sympathy and aid of his fellow-countrymen. There were cities that looked upon Chicago as a rival. Her unexampled success had provoked hostility,—amounting at times to bitterness. In the ranks of municipalities Chicago stood pre-eminent, and that eminence had drawn upon her the prejudices, and often the ill-natured jealousies of her supposed rivals. But the fire ended all this. Hardly had the news reached those cities before our sorrows were made theirs. The noble-hearted people did not wait for details; they suspended all other business, each man giving of his money and his property to be sent to Chicago. Before the fire had ceased its ravages, trains laden with supplies of food and clothing had actually reached the city. St. Louis and Cincinnati, Milwaukee, Detroit, Pittsburgh, and Louisville were active, even while the fire was burning, in providing for the relief of devastated Chicago. Every semblance of rivalry had disappeared. Not an ungenerous or selfish thought was uttered—everywhere the great brotherhood of man was vindicated, and our loss was made the loss of the nation.

"In the light of this experience, how absurd are the criminations and controversies of men. The hospitality and humanity of those in our city who have retained their homes, toward their less fortunate neighbors, though marked by every feature of unselfish charity, has failed even to equal the zealous efforts and generous actions of the people of the country, who have laid aside all other business to feed the hungry, clothe the naked, and give shelter to the roofless of Chicago.

"The national sympathy for us in our distress has shown that in the presence of human suffering there are no geographical lines, no sectional boundaries, no distinction of politics or creeds. The Samaritans have outlived the Levites, and there has been no such thing as passing by on the other side. The wine and oil have been distributed with a lavish hand, and the moneys have been deposited to pay for the lodging of the bruised and homeless.

"Words fail to express the grateful feelings of our people. Men who braved the perils of the dreadful Monday, who witnessed the destruction of all their worldly goods, and who with their families struggled for life upon the prairies during the awful destruction, and bravely endured it all, could not restrain the swelling heart or grateful tears when they read what the noble people of the country had done for Chicago; how the rich and the poor, whites and blacks, all—men, women, and children—had done something to alleviate the distress and mitigate the suffering of fellow-beings in far-off Chicago. How true it is that 'one touch of pity makes the whole world kin.' In some cities the contributions have exceeded an average of a dollar for each member of the population, and in the abundance that has been given unto us the aggregate is largely made up from the prompt offerings of the humble and the poor as well as of the rich. Future statisticians may compute in tabular array the commercial value of the donations to Chicago; but only in the volume of the recording angel will be known the inestimable blessings of that merciful, generous, humane charity which this calamity has kindled in the hearts of the whole American people.

"In due time there will be a formal and complete acknowledgment of donations, public and private; but in the meantime let the nation rejoice that underneath all the conflicts in which men are forever engrossed there is a latent spark of universal brotherhood, which needs but the occasion to develop into the most genial warmth. Property may be lost, wealth may be obliterated, but that people must be great who have hearts in which charity for human suffering cannot be stifled under any possible event."

Early in the period of want the more notable contributions were as follows:—

A. T. Stewart, of New York, $50,000; City of Brooklyn, $100,000; New York Board of Trade, $13,000; Gold Room, $7,000; Corn Exchange, $28,000; Produce Exchange $5,000; Stock Board, $50,000; A. Belmont, Brown Brothers, Jessup & Co., and Duncan, Sherman & Co., of New York, $5,000 each; Fisk & Hall, $10,000; District of Columbia, $100,000; W. W. Corcoran, Washington, $3,000; President Grant, $1,000; Philadelphia Commercial Exchange, $10,000; Rochester, N. Y., $70,000; Troy (N. Y.) Board of Trade, $10,000; London, Canada, $5,000; Hamilton, Canada, $5,000; Montreal, $20,000; Springfield, Mass., $15,000; Pittsfield, $5,000; Holyoke, $2,000; Albany (N. Y.) Board of Lumber Dealers, $6,000; Buffalo, N. Y., $100,000; Elmira, $10,000; Syracuse, $31,000; Niagara Falls, $10,000; City of Baltimore, $100,000, besides private subscriptions of $10,000; Robert Bonner, New York, $50,000; Spragues, of Providence, R. I., $10,000; Cincinnati Elastic Sponge Co., of Cincinnati, 100 sponge mattresses; the newsboys and bootblacks of Cincinnati, the proceeds of two days' labor; the Jane Coombs' Comedy Company, the proceeds of entertainment; Carl Pretzel, the proceeds of a lecture; every one in the Interior Department, one day's wages; Washington hackmen, one day's fares; Stone, of the New York *Journal of Commerce*, $5,000; Peoria, $75,000, and much food; Utica, $20,000; Worcester, $50,000; Toronto, $10,000; St. Joseph, Mo., $8,000; New York City, in all up to October 11, $450,000, and immense quantities of provisions, clothing, etc.; Liverpool, cargoes of provisions; J. S. Morgan & Co., London, $5,000; Dayton, $20,000; Lawrence, Kan., $13,000; New York dry goods houses, $20,000; Indianapolis, $75,000, and much provisions;

Louisville, $70,000 in public and private subscriptions, and much besides; St. Louis, $300,000, and unlimited quantities of provisions, etc.; Cincinnati, $200,000, and much of every needful thing; Milwaukee the first to help us; Berkeley street, Boston, $10,000; Baltimore Episcopal Convention, $2,000; Baltimore Corn Exchange, $7,000; Albany City, $12,000; Memphis, $40,000; Mr. Shaw, of Pittsburgh, $5,000; other private subscriptions at Pittsburgh, $40,000; Kansas City, $26,000; Tennessee Legislature, $5,000; Evansville, $16,000; Boston Hide and Leather Exchange, $10,000.

Herewith come the munificent offerings of foreign countries:

The Common Council of London unanimously agreed to forward 1,000 guineas immediately to the Mayor of Chicago. Appropriate resolutions of sympathy were passed.

The Lord Mayor received contributions from private individuals of upward of £7,000 sterling.

Baring, Morgan, Rothschild, Brown, Shipley & Co., of London, the Great Western Railroad of Canada, and the Grand Trunk Railroad, subscribed £1,000 each. The Liverpool Chamber of Commerce voted £5,000. The American Chamber contributed $13,000. Mass meetings to secure further aid were held all over England.

The Edinburgh Chamber of Commerce unanimously requested the calling of a meeting to organize relief.

A committee of the chief merchants of Southampton have opened subscriptions, and called upon the citizens generally to contribute.

At Berlin, the President of the Police heads the lists for the relief fund.

At Frankfort-on-the-Main, the leading banks and merchants took active interest in the relief movement in securing subscriptions.

In the world's history there was never such an outpouring, so spontaneous and immense—not one more sincerely appreciated. All these actual gifts were heaped upon us in the day of adversity, and at the same time banks and insurance companies proffered sympathy and cheering words. So vast were the losses that nobody thought securities of any value, and were ready to sell out their policies for five or ten cents on a dollar. Gradually the mists rolled away, and better tidings came, which served to brace up and sustain the flagging spirits of men who had lost great sums or little. Men spoke bravely to each other and gave assuring views of the future of Chicago. Thousands fled from the doomed city to towns in the vicinity, giving up all, and removed to their former homes. Indeed they could do nothing else, as they were little better than beggars. The majority began to look about them for new business places, or for sites for homes, for work, and opportunities of recovering their losses. It was felt that the importance of the city in a commercial view had not been over-estimated, and that business must seek this centre, and men live here. If the men who are here, and have lost, do not seize the opportunity, others will pluck the golden fruit, for a great city must rise on these ruins. Slowly but steadily the tide of hope rose, till the volume bore all upon its bosom, and every one set to work to remove the débris and rebuild their fortunes. In their confidence they began to suggest preparations against a recurrence of another similar disaster. Gross errors were brought to light by the searching element, which tried every man's work of what sort it was. The architecture of the Post-Office and Custom-House building, which, proving to be a sham and a fraud of the worst kind, has involved the loss of an immense sum of money.

The vault in the Sub-Treasury office, in which Collector McClean had deposited all the funds pertaining to his department, was built upon the second story. It rested upon two iron pillars built from the basement, with two iron girders of great strength and weight connected with the wall. A third girder connected the two pillars, forming a framework. A heavy fire-proof vault was built upon this foundation, and proved to be about the weakest in the city to resist the fierceness of the fire. There were in the vault at the time of the fire $1,500,000 in greenbacks, $300,000 in National Bank notes, $225,000 in gold, and $5,000 in silver; making a total of $2,030,000, of which $230,000 was in specie.

In an old iron safe which was left outside the vault was deposited $35,000, consisting of mutilated bills and fractional currency. This safe was regarded with scorn and deemed unworthy a place in the vault. But like the little fishes in the net, its insignificance saved it. When the building caught fire, and blazed with fervent heat, the miserable iron pillars melted, and the immense vault, with its fabulous treasures, fell to the basement, burying the insignificant safe and its mutilated contents. The consequence was that the contents of the latter were saved, while $1,800,000 in currency was burned to ashes and hopelessly lost.

The specie was scattered over the basement floor and fused with the heat. There are lumps of fused eagles valued at from $500 to $1,000, blackened and burned, but nevertheless good as refined gold. The employés have been compelled to rake the ruins of the whole building, and have recovered altogether about five-sixths of the whole amount. It is probable that many days will pass before they will be able to find the remainder.

It is a fortunate circumstance that only a week ago $500,000 in gold, and $25,000 in silver, had been shipped from the city.

The building was, as before stated, a fraud of the most barefaced description, and consequently an everlasting disgrace to the country. That a vault containing treasure to the amount actually lost should be supported only on two iron pillars, which gave way and let it fall in ruins, and should yet make a boast of being fire-proof, is a piece of irony the most acute.

But this vault was only one of the frauds. The fire-proof doors of the Post-Office vault, in which were stored the records, proved frailer still. The hinges of the massive portals which were to protect the government records were only affixed to a single brick. When, therefore, the walls expanded with the heat, the sturdy doors fell out of their own weight, each hinge carrying with it the single brick to which it held, while the remainder of the wall was as firm as possible.

Of course all the records were hopelessly ruined.

This vault was fire and burglar proof. Experts are not the only persons who can judge of the value of a vault whose doors had such a feeble hold.

The building is one of a large number built in the same way; and the condition of the lower vault suggests great weakness in those erected in other cities. It is probable that the Government will order an inspection of all existing vaults. The accompanying views upon the events of the time and the future Chicago were published, and deserve consideration and preservation. The unexpected fury of this fire must put in suspicion all precautions commonly used.

"The spirit displayed by the business men of this city in rebuilding is astonishing, and deserving of the highest praise after a calamity so terrible as the recent conflagration. That Chicago will rise again, and not only resume her old position, but become in time the first city on this continent, seems to me to be as certain as the perpetuation of our government and the increase of our population.

"It should be borne in mind at this time that there were certain defects in the plan of Chicago, arising from the rapidity of its construction, which seemed beyond remedy, except at enormous cost; but now it is possible, by considering the subject in time, and taking advantage of the experience of other cities, to make such rearrangements as will make the plan and accommodations of this city suitable for the metropolis of America.

"The present burnt district, on the south side, is, by universal consent, to become the centre of the city, and every consideration indicates that it should be so. Were the whole city to be laid out anew, the natural features of the country and the railroad communications would point to the south side as the centre. The business operations will commence here, and radiate, as heretofore, to the south, west, and north, but more to the south, owing to the fact that the communication is uninterrupted by natural obstacles. Into this centre hundreds of thousands of people will pour daily, coming from the residence portion of the city, the suburbs, and the whole country.

"There is always, in great cities, an immense amount of time lost in going to and from business, and in the absence of proper accommodations for doing business after the business centre is reached. Persons familiar with the city of New York understand this fully. Two or three hours of the day are consumed in travelling to and fro, and, owing to the crowds in the streets, the contracted markets and places of exchange, the time required to transact business is doubled and trebled.

"Now, the points which seem to me to be considered at this time and be fully provided for, are:

"1. The laying out of certain lines for steam communication from the centre of business to the suburbs, to be so arranged as not to obstruct the street travel, or be interrupted by it. This most essential element of a modern metropolis can never be secured or arranged for so well as at present.

"2. The arrangement of commodious and central depots for the great lines of railroads centering in the city.

"3. A commodious levee along the river for public docks, a grand market, and a grand plaza, where all can go without paying tribute. Instead of having buildings built close down to the river bank, let there be an open space on each side of the river devoted to the above purposes.

"4. The great leading lines of business should be consolidated or concentrated on certain streets running north and south. There should be a financial centre, a dry goods centre, a hardware centre, etc.

"5. An open square for public meetings and out-door business. The Court-House square suggests itself at once. Let the Court-House go further south and leave the present square open.

"Let it be surrounded by banks, brokers' offices, etc., and there will be room for everybody. These suggestions are hurriedly thrown out, but they should be considered, and a committee representing all interests should be appointed to draw up a scheme by which these desirable results can be secured. In the rebuilding of the city these matters can all be arranged for the benefit of all.

"The business portion of Chicago had already become overcrowded with the street cars, omnibuses, other vehicles, and foot-passengers. The limit of capacity had almost been reached.

"You believe in Chicago's future, and a few minutes' reflection will convince any one that more space is needed for the future, and that concentration and co-operation on the part of business men is necessary to make the best use of the ground now available. Very truly yours,

"D. C. HOUSTON,

"Major U. S. Engineers, Brevet Colonel, U. S. Army.
"CHICAGO, *October* 13, 1871."

The general prevailing opinion became so favorable to this view that temporary places were provided on city land for present use, in order that where permanent buildings should be erected they might be of the most substantial nature and enduring quality. This was strongly contended for in a leading editorial of the *Tribune:*

"The futility of locking the stable-door after the horse is stolen is proverbial. Equally futile would any suggestions as to the best preventive of fires seem after the city is burnt up. Any hints, therefore, which may be made on this subject, in these columns, must be taken as referring to the new Chicago which has already commenced to grow up from the ruins of the old Chicago. The cause which operated most fatally to render the catastrophe of Sunday night complete is a matter of no question among those who are acquainted with our city. It was the large area of inflammable buildings, lumber-yards, and other tinder-boxes with which the multitude of really noble buildings of central Chicago were surrounded. The magnificent piles of marble which lined our business streets, and of which we had begun to be so justly proud, had been seen and admired by so many visitors from abroad that the complete destruction with which these palaces of art met on that fatal night has excited, even outside of Chicago, no less astonishment than sorrow. Chicago had, up to within a very few years, the reputation of being the most wretchedly-built city of its size in America. The miles of marble stores and churches, and public buildings, through which the visitor of the last year or two has been driven in "doing" Chicago, have dissipated this unfavorable opinion of the outside world, and drawn to our city a great measure of credit for its business architecture. But this architecture had its weak points, and these have now been made painfully and vividly apparent.

"The fault of the fire, however, lies more with the public itself than with the architects. We have been too good-natured toward those who have, to save a few hundred dollars of their expenses, persistently kept in jeopardy the safety of the whole community by maintaining in the heart of the city great numbers of the most inflammable structures. It was the thousand or so of dry pine shanties and rookeries between the lake and the river and south of Monroe street which did the business for

Chicago on that terrible night. With these huddled around them, and emitting vast clouds of burning brands, which the hurricane forced into every cranny and through every window, the fine stone rows of the avenues and of the principal streets could no more resist the raging element than the chaff can resist the whirlwind. There may have been, and doubtless were, occasional weaknesses in the construction of the later-built stores and public edifices—a too fragile cornice, or windows too much exposed—but the fact that buildings, for which everything possible to architecture had been done to make them fire-proof, went with the rest, tells plainly that the only fault—the grand fault to which the general destructiveness is traceable—was in allowing the fire so much material on which to feed until it became too great for human power to resist. We had spent hundreds of thousands of dollars in spasmodic efforts to exorcise the fire-fiend from our limits, and yet we were all the while furnishing him with the material and the space with which to organize for his deadly work. We had been industriously feeding him on the only rations whereon he could thrive.

"Let these rations be cut off from this time forward. One of the first duties which the Mayor and Common Council should attend to is the enactment and strict enforcement of a comprehensive ordinance for the protection of the city against all future general conflagrations. In the business quarter now devastated there must, of course, be some temporary structures thrown together for the accommodation of business until better quarters can be provided. But the permits for these should be strictly confined to a certain limit of time—say six months from this date. It should then be ordained by the Council that the fire limits, within which no frame building, lumber stack, or other inflammable structure shall be erected, shall be extended very considerably, so as to embrace all sections of the city which are now, or are likely to become, central. And the ordinance should contain a rigid prohibition against roofs, facings, or cornices of wood, or of such flimsy material as to be easily penetrated or displaced.

"It should be ordained, further, for the encouragement of thorough building in all parts of the city, that no frame building or out-building, of no matter what dimensions, shall be erected within fifty feet of any brick, stone, or iron structure, and that all livery-stables, planing-mills, factories, foundries, shops, or other buildings, wherein furnaces, steam-boilers, or other machinery or apparatus requiring much fire, or endangering explosions, shall be built of brick, stone, or iron, and that no division walls therein shall be of wood.

"To these precautions should be added a system of water-basins, or low reservoirs, to be supplied with water, independent of the general pumping works—perhaps by direct inflow from the lake or river—perhaps from artesian wells. It will not take any extravagant outlay to obviate, by such means, the possibility of any such calamity in the future as the failure of the water supply while a conflagration is yet raging.

"Other precautions will doubtless suggest themselves to practical men on a careful examination of the subject. None should be omitted which are necessary to make Chicago the most indestructible city in the world. Our fire record has been hitherto—even before the late calamity—the worst in America. Let it be henceforth the best. We must not, while suffering the manifold curses of the great fire, lose any of the blessings, of which the greatest are unquestionably the lessons and the opportunity which it affords us for fortifying against future calamities of the kind. We cannot expect that we will not have our daily quota of half a dozen or more incipient fires. We cannot be sure that severe droughts will not come, followed by gales like that of last Sunday night. But we *can* take care that those exigencies, over which the city as a community has no control, are guarded against by all the measures which *are* within our control. San Francisco has suffered grievously by fires, which raked her from west to east, leaving nothing but ruin in their track. She is subject, during a considerable period of every year, to both droughts and gales quite as severe as those which contributed to our present misfortune; but she is now able to defy them all, having, by the means similar to those which we have now suggested, secured a system of fire-proof buildings—fire-proof streets, we might say—which are not only the pride and trust of all her citizens, but the admiration of all visitors. It is important that the burnt district of Chicago be rebuilt as speedily as possible; but paramount to that and all else is the necessity that it be built permanently and well. Chicago must rise again; and not only must she rise, but *rise to stand* as long as the world revolves."

If deep moral lessons could be conveyed and impressed by any calamity, it would certainly seem that this was the dispensation for such a schooling as men never got before. The North Division was thoroughly ruined, only Ogden's house and the Grant Place M. E. church remaining. Here, on this burnt district, Pandemonium seemed to reign on Sundays; here were the breweries and distilleries. Hence the opposition to Sabbath laws. In the South Division all the brothels, gambling-hells, and theatres were swept clean, as with the besom of destruction.

All the monuments of human energy and skill were levelled and destroyed. Now, will men rage and thirst for riches as they have done, when at one fell swoop the fire demon has melted their idol? Will vice and crime riot as they have done, eating out the very vitality of the city? In the presence of death and woe will men forget the better part? How insignificant seemed man as we stood by the dead in the Morgue! Mere pailfuls of charred bones and flesh indicated the existence of those who but the day before were full of lusty life. Oh! helpless man, call upon God, the living God. Here lay the body of a beautiful young girl, of perhaps two and twenty. This poor victim has a wealth of rich brown hair, and brown eyes; she is four feet in height, and possesses a handsome figure. She must in life have been exceedingly lovely. Not being burned at all, she suffocated in the smoke, as did many of the other victims whose remains were afterwards consumed by the flames. A father lying on his face was recognized by his motherless children as they looked upon his head. We turn from these sad relics of humanity to gaze on the wreck of wealth around us. No city can equal now the ruins of Chicago, not even Pompeii, much less Paris.

Tens of thousands have come in to view these remains of a once proud metropolis, to which no description is adequate. They are bleak and lonely. It is a phantom city.

The little one-story frame shanty, in the rear of which was the barn in which the fire originated, on De Koven street, stands to-day alone and uninjured. The flames swept around it on every side, igniting everything else, while that miserable structure stands—a monument of the place where the fire commenced.

Under the light of the sun, wandering among the ruins of a day, the beholder cannot dispel the illusion that he is the victim of some Aladdinic dream, and that he has been transported with the speed of light, by the genius of the lamp or ring, and set down among the ruins of the Titanic ages. Arabia Petra looks upon us from the stone walls of the Post-Office, and the Catacombs of Egypt stare at us from the embrasure-like windows of the Court-House wings. Cleopatra's Needle and the Tower of Babel find duplicates in the water-tower and the smoke-stacks of ruined factories. Tadmor of the desert, with its sandy tumuli, appears on every hand in the crumbling piles of brick and mortar; the walls of ancient Jerusalem arise in the ruins of the great Central and Rock Island depots, and the pillared ruins of Cairo and Alexandria in the roofless front of Honore Block. The puzzler Sphynx is doubly reproduced in the one-time green lions of Ross and Gossage; while the Parthenon, the Acropolis, and the gladiatorial arena of ancient Greece and Rome find their counterpart in the fire-built ruins of last week's palaces. Here all time is reproduced in a moment. The destroyer works by earthquake, by storm, by the attrition of the ages, and by fire. Time works slowly, and takes a thousand years in which to make an ornamental ruin; fire works with lightning speed, and sets before our eyes the ruins of a world in the compass of a single night.

A night of more grandeur can scarcely be imagined than that of our ruined city after nightfall. As far as the eye can reach to the north, east, and south, the smouldering flames, scarcely perceptible during the day, give just enough light to render indistinctly visible the ruined walls of the one-time busy palaces, teeming with life and traffic—now not even a fit abiding-place for bats and owls. Away in one direction appear the walls of a marble-front row on Wabash avenue, the spectre windows of which are lit up by the blazing ruins on the other side, looking like the fire-demon with a hundred burning eyes, crouching for a spring across the South Branch, to bring destruction on the remainder of the doomed city. Looking away through the iron stays of one of the few remaining bridges, to the northward, an immense heap of burning grain and coal lights up the background, against which everything is clear-cut and definite—a disjointed skeleton stretches its bare and bony arms toward heaven, as if chained in an attitude of supplication by the fire-fiend. Here and there blue, red, and green lights flit like spectres and hobgoblins over the graves of buried commerce. Ever and anon a falling wall pitches headlong to the earth with a heavy, deadened thud, like the drum-beat of the destroying angel, calling a rally of his sooty cohorts for a fresh and final charge. Against this threatening host a wall of stout hearts is the only thing opposed.

Soon all this scene will be changed and the ruins disappear. To some places a ruin is a God-send, as travellers find in the Old World. Here we want no such mournful mementoes, and the people say let us put away the doleful spectacle as soon as possible. The following suggestion is certainly original, and appeared in the journals:

"Chicago will be rebuilt. Nature designed this site for the great internal city of the world, and time will remove every trace of our present unparalleled calamity. When that time comes mankind will be incredulous as to our present greatness or losses. It is possible now to build a monument that will stand for ages. Let the safes which are rendered worthless by the fire be collected and piled into a pyramid in one of our public parks. It would be higher than the dome of the Court-House, and would be in the future the greatest curiosity of the city.

"The prevailing spirit of owners of real estate may be fairly indicated by the way in which a Vermonter, who had just arrived, viewed the situation. He was standing on Wabash avenue, in front of his particular pile of bricks, and thus manifested himself: 'When I heard of it I thought I would come out and see about it. I made my money here, and I lost part of it *there ;* I've got some left, and by to-morrow night I'll have a brick block started.' This seemed to be the general sentiment, and the only regret was the inopportuneness of the season and the lack of skilled labor to carry on the immense amount of business necessary."

God helps those who help themselves, and the world will lend their aid to us when they witness the determination with which our city rises again.

> I saw the city's terror,
>   I heard the city's cry,
> As a flame leaped out of her bosom
>   Up, up to the brazen sky!

And wilder rose the tumult,
    And thicker the tidings came—
Chicago, queen of the cities,
    Was a rolling sea of flame!

Yet higher rose the fury,
    And louder the surges raved
(Thousands were saved but to suffer,
    And hundreds never were saved),
Till out of the awful burning
    A flash of lightning went,
As across to brave St. Louis
    The prayer for succor was sent.

God bless thee, O true St. Louis!
    So worthy thy royal name—
Back, back on the wing of the lightning
    Thy answer of rescue came.
But alas! it could not enter
    Through the horrible flame and heat,
For the fire had conquered the lightning,
    And sat in the Thunderer's seat!

God bless thee again, St. Louis!
    For resting never then,
Thou calledst to all the cities
    By lightning and steam and pen.
"Ho, ho, ye hundred sisters,
    Stand forth in your bravest might!
Our sister in flame is falling,
    Her children are dying to-night!"

And through the mighty republic
    Thy summons went rolling on,
Till it rippled the seas of the Tropics
    And ruffled the Oregon.
The distant Golden City
    Called through her golden gates,
And quickly rung the answer
    From the city of the Straits.

And the cities that sit in splendor
    Along the Atlantic Sea,
Replying, called to the dwellers
    Where the proud magnolias be.
From slumber the army started
    At the far resounding call,
"Food for a hundred thousand,"
    They shouted, "and tents for all."

I heard through next night's darkness
    The trains go thundering by,
Till they stood where the fated city
    Shone red in the brazen sky.
The rich gave their abundance,
    The poor their willing hands;
There was wine from all the vineyards,
    There was corn from all the lands.

At daybreak over the prairies
    Re-echoed the gladsome cry—
"Ho, look unto us, ye thousands,
    Ye shall not hunger nor die!"
Their weeping was all the answer
    That the famishing throng could give
To the million voices calling
    "Look unto us, and live!"

Destruction wasted the city,
    But the burning curse that came
Enkindled in all the people
    Sweet charity's holy flame.
Then still to our God be glory!
    I bless Him, through my tears,
That I live in the grandest nation
    That hath stood in all the years.

Strangers perceive and acknowledge that this point is naturally designed for a great city, and the testimony of our sister city St. Louis is a generous recognition of our geographical supremacy. Said the *Missouri Republican:*—" Chicago, though stricken in purse and person as no other city recorded in history ever has been, is not crushed out and destroyed, and her complete restoration to the place and power from which she is temporarily removed is only a question of time. It would be sad, indeed, if a conflagration, though swallowing up the last house and the last dollar of a great commercial metropolis, could fix the seal of perpetual annihilation upon it, and declare that the wealth and prosperity which once were should exist no more forever. Such might be the case, perhaps, were there none other save human forces at work; but into the composition of such a city as that which the demon of fire has conquered, enter the forces and the necessities of nature. Chicago did not become what she was, simply because shrewd capitalists and energetic business men so ordained it. That mighty Agent, who fashions suns and stars, and swings them aloft in the boundless ocean of space, marks out by immutable decree the channels along which population and trade must flow. When the first settlers landed at Jamestown and Plymouth, and began to hew a path for civilization through the primeval forest, it was as certain as the law of gravitation, that if this continent were destined to be a new empire, fit to receive the surplus millions of the eastern hemisphere, and contribute to the progress and enlightenment of mankind everywhere, there must and would be a few prominent centres, so to speak, around which the vast machine could revolve. Those centres were determined by the geography and topography of the country; and when the advancing tide of immigration touched them they began to develop as naturally and irresistibly as the flower does beneath the genial influences of sunshine and showers. For practical purposes neither Jamestown nor Plymouth were of any special consequence; therefore the one has ceased to exist altogether, and the other remains an insignificant town. But the inner shore of Boston harbor, the island of Manhattan, the site of Philadelphia, Baltimore, Cincinnati, New Orleans, St. Louis, and San Francisco, furnished the required facilities, and we see the result to-day. Nature declares where great cities shall be built, and man simply obeys the orders of Nature.

"The spot where Chicago river empties into Lake Michigan belongs to the same category as those we have mentioned. It was designed and intended for the location of a grand mart to supply the wants of the extreme north-west—that portion of the central plateau lying on the line and to the north of the Union Pacific Railway, and the western part of the British possessions. The trade from these sections seeks an outlet there, and finds it better and more available than anywhere else. This fact was settled before the first brick was laid in Chicago; was settled when Chicago rose to the rank of the fifth city in the republic, and is settled just as firmly now, when, to all human appearances, her destruction is wellnigh accomplished.

"Natural advantages, then, must compel the reconstruction of Chicago, even though every foot of its soil passes out of the hands of the present proprietors. And if we examine what the fire has spared, it will be found that the nucleus of a new and rapid growth is not wanting. Nor more than twenty per cent. of the lumber supply has been consumed, thus affording ample material for building; the largest elevator and perhaps one or two of the smaller ones are safe; the stock yards are uninjured, and with these avenues for business open, business itself is sure to come speedily. Indeed, it is announced that several vessels received full loads of wheat from the elevators as early as Wednesday, and departed on their accustomed voyages to eastern ports. There is also good reason to believe that at least one-half the insurance will be paid, and as this cannot be much less than $100,000,000, money will not be lacking. If we add to these resources the railway lines converging to that point, which represent an aggregate capital of $200,000,000, and remember that every railway is directly interested in the process of reconstruction, and will aid it in all possible ways, it may not be difficult for even the most incredulous to see why and how Chicago must grow again. That she is absolutely ruined or permanently disabled is a sheer impossibility which no sensible person will for a moment credit."

It may here serve to show that all is not lost, and to convey some impression of the extent of losses, to append the statement of liabitities and resources of insurance companies doing business in Chicago:—

NEW YORK CITY AND STATE.

Companies.	Gross Assets.		Losses.
Ætna, City	$442,709		$200,000
Adriatic, City	246,120		5,000
Agricultural, Watertown	550,843		......
Albany, Albany	264,978		......
Albany City, Albany	396,646		Suspended
American, P., City	741,405		25,000
American Exchange, City	277,350		15,000
Astor, City	405,571		500,000
Atlantic, City	556,179		250,000
Beekman, City	261,851		Suspended
Buffalo City, Buffalo	370,934		500,000
Buffalo Fire and Marine, Buffalo	473,577		500,000
Buffalo German, Buffalo	270,081		5,000
Capital City, Albany	293,766		......
Citizens, P., City	684,798		25,000
Clinton, City	392,704		3,000
Columbia, City	451,332		3,000
Commerce, Albany	692,877		10,000
Commerce Fire, City	249,372		15,000
Commercial, City	306,002		5,000
Continental, P., City	2,538,038		800,000
Excelsior, City	335,744		Suspended
Exchange, City	183,959		......
Firemen's, City	369,961		15,000
Firemen's Fund, City	173,477		100,000
Fireman's Trust, City	226,269		20,000
Fulton, City	363,002	Ad	700,000
Germania, City	1,077,849		225,000
Glenn's Falls, Glenn's Falls	571,123		10,000
Guardian, City	279,688		40,000
Hanover, P., City	700,335		225,000
Hoffman, City	235,242		10,000
Holland Purchase, Batavia	171,496		......
Home, City	4,578,008	Ad	2,000,000
Howard, P., City	783,351		275,000
Humboldt, City	251,186		10,000

Companies.	Gross Assets.	Losses.
Importers' and Traders', City	$302,589	$22,500
International, City	1,329,476	400,000
Irving, City	321,745	Ref's risks.
Jefferson, City	411,155	47,500
Kings County, City	262,573	30,000
Lafayette, L. I. City	214,751	7,500
Lamar, City	551,402	200,000
Lenox, City	240,801	30,000
Long Island, P., City	334,002	....
Lorillard, City	1,715,909	800,000
Manhattan, City	1,407,788	500,000
Market, P., City	704,634	Susp'd.
Mechanics, L. I., City	218,047	22,500
Mechanics' and Traders, City	460,002	....
Mercantile, City	273,399	100,000
Merchants', City	442,690	15,000
Nassau, L. I., City	391,518	....
National, City	232,671	15,000
New Amsterdam, P., City	432,638	40,000
N. Y. Central, Union Sp'gs	201,864	....
New York Fire, City	392,278	15,000
Niagara, City	1,304,567	225,000
North American, City	770,305	250,000
North River, City	467,426	....
Pacific, City	443,557	12,500
Peter Cooper, City	295,724	....
Phœnix, L. I., City	1,890,010	350,000
Relief, City	310,908	10,000
Republic, City	683,478	225,000
Resolute, City	252,452	75,000
Schenectady, Schenectady	93,737	Wound up.
Security, City	1,880,333	Ad. 1,000,000
Sterling, City	247,027	7,500
Tradesmen's, City	423,181	25,000
Washington, P., City	774,411	400,000
Williamsburgh City, City	539,692	70,000
Yonkers and N. Y. City	863,963	300,000
Western, of Buffalo	582,547	600,000

MASSACHUSETTS COMPANIES.

Companies.	Gross Assets.	Losses.
Eliot, Boston	672,212	12,000
Hide and Leather	419,000	700,000
Independent	646,000	Suspended.
Lawrence, Boston	262,502	12,000
Manufacturers'	1,480,464	350,000
Merchants'	958,000	10,000
National	821,844	500,000
People's, Worcester	887,750	300,000
New England Mut. Marine	1,030,973	700,000
Washington, Boston	935,975	25,000

OHIO COMPANIES.

Companies.	Gross Assets.	Losses.
Alemania, Cleveland	285,000	25,000
Andes, Cincinnati	1,203,000	300,000
Cleveland, Cleveland	530,000	175,000
Globe	178,143	25,000
Home, Columbus	637,947	150,000
Sun, Cleveland	301,340	75,000

GREAT FIRE IN CHICAGO.

MISSOURI COMPANIES.

Companies.	Gross Assets.	Losses.
American Central, St. Louis	$254,875	$350,000
Anchor	121,974	27,000
Boatmen's	51,788	20,000
Chouteau	21,808	25,000
Citizens'	271,000	25,000

CONNECTICUT COMPANIES.

Ætna, Hartford	5,762,635	2,000,000
City, Hartford	544,237	225,000
Charter Oak, Hartford	251,951	200,000
Connecticut, Hartford	405,069	Suspended.
Fairfield County, Norwalk	216,358	30,000
Hartford, Hartford	2,737,510	1,200,000
Merchants', Hartford	540,096	350,000
Phœnix, Hartford	1,717,947	700,000
Putnam, Hartford	785,788	425,000

RHODE ISLAND COMPANIES.

American	374,069	400,000
Atlantic	326,614	275,000
Hope	211,673	150,000
Merchants	372,199	13,000
Narragansett	792,947	33,000
Providence, Washington	415,149	550,000
Roger Williams	279,946	100,000
American, New Jersey	300,000	10,000

Wheeling, West Virginia, pays in full. Sun, of Cleveland, will pay in full; Pacific, Peoples', Firemen's' and Union Insurance Companies, of San Francisco, promise to pay in full; Baltimore Companies announce they will pay in full.

MAINE COMPANIES.

National, Bangor	$241,000	$17,500
Union, Bangor	421,000	5,000

MICHIGAN COMPANIES.

Detroit Fire and Marine	273,000	30,000

WISCONSIN COMPANIES.

Brewers' Protective	183,681	75,000
N. W. National	191,202	90,000
St. Paul Fire and Marine	280,000	60,000
Aurora, Covington, Ky	163,000	35,000

FOREIGN COMPANIES.

Commercial Union	4,000,000	65,000
Imperial	5,438,665	150,000
Liverpool and London and Globe, Eng	20,136,420	2,000,000
North British and Mercantile	4,104,593	2,000,000
Queen	2,347,495	Nothing
Royal	9,274,776	93,000

PENNSYLVANIA COMPANIES.

Franklin	3,087,000	500,000
Alps, Erie	265,524	12,000
Boatmen's, Pittsburgh		18,000
Eureka, Pittsburgh		18,000
Artesian		17,000

Companies.	Gross Assets.	Losses.
Allemania		18,000
Monongahela		12,000
Pittsburgh		10,000
Union		5,000
Western		5,000
Federal		7,500
Alleghany		2,500
Merchants' and Manufacturers'		6,000
Enterprise, Philadelphia	611,000	125,000
Insurance Company of North America	3,050,000	600,000

When steamboats or railway trains, for instance, for many years pursue their roads in safety, the awful crash of an accident becomes the exception, nor does it deter the travelling community from running the same risk with a feeling of comparative safety. In the first place, there seems to be no rule in fire insurances of the amount of risk taken as to the proportion of capital paid up or held. Thus, for instance, some of the very best offices have a liability of nearly forty times their capital.

The Ætna company gives her statement on the 1st of January, 1871: Gross assets, $5,782,635; amount of risk on 1st of January, 1871, $237,874,573; yet this office is perfectly able to meet its liabilities. The total capital of all the insurance companies in the United States is:—

In the State of New York, companies' assets	$53,722,665 41
Mutual companies in State of New York, assets	2,575,077 36
Companies in other States, assets	23,171,101 00
Mutual companies in other States, assets	5,696,226 22
Total assets of fire insurance companies	$85,065,060 06

The amount of risk on the 31st of December, 1869, was:—

New York joint stock fire insurance companies	$2,714,198,776 31
New York mutual fire insurance companies	42,504,145 00
Companies from other States	1,740,650,887 97
Mutual fire insurance companies	33,748,782 41
Total amount of risk	$4,530,658,591 69

or twice the amount of the national debt, with assets of $85,000,000.

Considering that for the last generation the insurance companies have really only been called upon twice to make good a loss of over $10,000,000 at one time and in one place, viz., the fire in '35 and '45, we must confess that, as a general thing, fire insurance is a lucrative business, as there is no business that can do fifty times the amount of its investment in a year. The above figures do not include the foreign offices, which insure very heavily. The American branch of the London and Liverpool and Globe Insurance Company had, on December 31, 1869, $90,936,126 fire risks, and the risks during the year written, besides this, was $220,302,506, or a total of $311,238,632.

These gigantic figures certainly remind one of the distance to some planetary body, or the amount of yards of cotton fabrics manufactured in Manchester, yet all of this immense property upon which the prosperity of a whole nation depends, has very justly been looked upon as safe and secure. It must, however, not be supposed that the surviving insurance companies will very long feel the loss sustained in Chicago, as it can easily be seen by our very figures, that the increase of premium, which some have already put in force, of only thirty per cent., will give the total corporations in the United States $12,000,000 additional premiums, and consequently profits. The drygoods store in Maine, and the cotton-press in New Orleans, will alike be called upon to contribute to the loss of the insurance offices sustained by the Chicago fire.

On the week following the fire the National Banks resumed business as usual, and an immense number of men were again set to work, and hope animated all faces. The labor of removing rubbish and tottering walls seems Herculean to one riding over the streets along which the columns of flame rolled like swollen torrents of lava; but persistent skilful effort will soon accomplish wonders, and rear again the stately buildings and restore all the magnificence.

HISTORY OF THE

Fair she rose,
Lifting high her stately head,
Victor-crowned,
Stretching strong and helpful hands
Far around;
Full of lusty, throbbing life,
In the strife
Dealing quick and sturdy blows.

Sudden swept
Through her streets a sea of fire;
Roaring came
Seething waves, cinders, brands,
All aflame;
Blood-red glowed the brazen sky;
Far and nigh
Smoke in wreaths and eddies crept.

Oh! the cries
Shrill, heart-rending! Oh! the hands
Frantic wrung!
Oh! the swaying buildings vast!
Pen or tongue
Ne'er the awful tale can tell,
How they fell
Underneath the dizzy skies.

. . .

Low she lies,
Bowed in dust her stately head,
Desolate;
Yet by all her glory past,
Let us wait,
Stand beside her firm and true;
Built anew,
Watch her, help her upward rise.

NARRATIVE OF REV. T. W. GOODSPEED, OF QUINCY, ILL., AN EYE-WITNESS.

THRILLING DESCRIPTION OF SCENES, INCIDENTS, ETC.

It being announced that Rev. T. W. Goodspeed, of the Vermont Street Church, who was present in Chicago at the time of the fire, and had witnessed many of its scenes and incidents, would give a narrative thereof at his church, an immense crowd was early in attendance, filling all the space in the building, while hundreds of others were unable to gain admittance. Mr. Goodspeed took no text, giving simply a narrative of what he saw. He commenced by saying:—

It was my fortune to be in Chicago when it was destroyed. I do not propose to give you a complete history of the conflagration. You are getting that from day to day through the newspapers. Many have said to me, " Tell us all you saw." This great calamity is in all hearts. We are not prepared to speak of or listen to anything else; and I have thought there was a sufficient reason for giving up this service to telling my congregation what I saw of this unparalleled conflagration. Sympathizing with this feeling, Mr. Priest has given up his service to be with us, as has also the congregation of the First Church. I fear you will be disappointed in listening to me, as I design to tell you only what came under my observation, and there were a thousand things I did not see.

The Chicago river runs directly west from the lake almost a mile. It then branches north and south. That part of the city lying south of the main river, and east of the South Branch, is called the South Side. That part lying north of the main river, and east of the North Branch, is the North Side, and all west of the two branches the West Side. Each of these divisions is about one-third of the city.

You are aware that the great fire of Saturday night, which destroyed several blocks, was on the West Side, near the South

Branch of the river. The fire of Sunday night and Monday began also on the West Side, near the scene of the other, destroying, with that, forty blocks on the West Side; swept across the South Branch, destroying a mile square of the South Side—the entire business portion of the city—crossed the river and laid in ruins almost the whole of the North Side, about 400 blocks.

Sunday evening I preached in the Second Baptist Church, which is nearly a mile west of the South Branch. We stopped in the study about half an hour after service, and started for my brother's home a few minutes after nine. It was then that we first saw the fire, a mile to the south-east. We continued to watch it from time to time till eleven o'clock, when, supposing it under control, we retired.

We were aroused a little before four in the morning. Hurrying on my clothes, I went out. The fire had got far up on the West Side of the South Branch, and had evidently crossed the river to the South Side, and was beyond all control. The wind was blowing fiercely from the south-west. The whole city was lighted up by the flames almost like day. As I hastened toward the river I noticed that the stars were all obscured as effectually as if the sun were shining, and the moon gave a feeble, sickly light. It was almost gray, altogether unlike itself.

As I proceeded the streets became more and more crowded. The whole West Side was gathering and crowding toward the river. I stopped to rouse my brother, but he had long been gone. A woman stopped me on Washington street and said, "My husband's place of business is destroyed, and we are ruined."

Reaching the river, I found that a large part of the South Side was still unharmed. Here I saw the massive blocks of the South Side in flames, and saw vessels being towed north to escape the fire. I followed the South Branch up to where it joined the North Branch and the main river, and looked down the latter to the lake. Three or four blocks away the fire had crossed the river. Wells Street Bridge was burning. The spectacle was grand and awful beyond description. Great billows of flame swept clean across the river, while countless myriads of sparks and burning brands filled the air.

Proceeding, I crossed the Kinsie Street Bridge to the North Side. Here I met the fugitives—thousands of people, indeed, were going both ways—spectators to see, fugitives to escape. The streets were filled with merchandise and furniture. Women were everywhere guarding their household goods. The air was filled with a thousand noises. The screaming of the steamers, the whistle of the tugs, the cries of children, the shouting of men, the howling of the wind, the roar of the flames, the crash of falling buildings.

I went on as far as Wells street, and the wind was here a hurricane. The buildings on Water street and the south bank of the river caught, and almost instantly they were one vast volcano, throwing up great volumes of flame that were caught up and carried bodily across the stream. The river seemed a boiling caldron. We stood under the great elevator at the Wells street depot and saw on one of them a man wetting the roof. He had hose, and must have saturated the entire building with water, yet within fifteen minutes the building was aflame. I returned to the West Side. The fleeing people were carrying off articles of every description. Two men were wheeling away the Indian figure that had stood before their cigar store. One man was hurrying off with two whiskey bottles. I stopped again to look down the main river toward the lake. The scene was even more magnificent and awful than before. This was indeed the grandest spectacle of all. The whole length of the river was then one broad sheet of fire.

With every fresh blast of wind great billows of fire would roll across toward the doomed North Side, as if filled with a mad desire to sweep it away in ruin. Then for a moment they would subside and show the three bridges wreathed in flames (the water apparently boiling underneath them), the black walls of the buildings on either side, and here and there tongues of flames shooting out from doors and windows and roofs. Then again two walls of fire, extending a mile away to the lake, would flame up toward heaven for a moment, to be caught by the gale and tumbled in fiery ruin to the ground, or carried in great masses of fire to spread the conflagration. Going on from here I took my stand on Lake Street Bridge. The line of fire extended a mile or more down the South Branch. Several bridges had already been consumed. The great coal-yards were beginning to burn, and almost all the magnificent blocks of the South Side were in flames. From the slight elevation of the bridge, I could see almost two square miles of fire.

Looking toward the north-west, and seeing how directly toward the water-works the flames were rushing, it crossed my mind that they would be destroyed. I turned and hastened to my friend's house, a mile on the West Side, and immediately tried the water. I was too late, it would not run, and the great city of 300,000 people was without water.

Before seven o'clock I went to another friend's house and found him just returned from saving his books, and what merchandise he could. He had got into his place of business by the back way, and had been driven away by the swift demon of destruction. I went to another friend's house to inquire if his store was safe. He had visited the fire at half past-ten and gone home confident it was under control. At three he had tried to reach his business place, and been driven back by the fire that raged between him and it. I got into his buggy with him and we started to find it. Reaching Twelfth street, which runs across the South Branch, a mile and a quarter south of the Court-House we found the street crowded with people and vehicles, and all pressing toward the South Side. It was a little after seven o'clock, and of course daylight. We made our way to Wells or La Salle street, and tried to go up, but the flames stopped us. We went on to Wabash avenue, and found it to be so crowded as to be utterly impassable. We crossed to Michigan avenue, fell into the stream of travel, and worked our way up to the Michigan Avenue Hotel. My friend asked me to hold his horse five minutes, while he went to see what he could find. Left to myself I had time to look about me. I despair of describing the scene to you. It beggars description. It was here that my friend Sawyer, who is with me in the desk, joined me. His clothes covered with dust, his hair filled with dust and cinders, his eyes red from smoke, his face black, so unlike himself that I hardly knew him. Michigan avenue was burning from within a block of where we stood a mile away to the river. The magnificent residences and great business houses were going up in flames and down in blackness before our eyes. Great volumes of smoke rolling away before the gale concealed the North Side from view. But at every break or lift of the smoke, the great Central Depot could be seen all in flames. The fire was creeping away out on the piers, and had reached one of the immense elevators that stood near its end, and the flames were soon reaching up one hundred and fifty feet into the air. Every moment we expected to see the great Central Elevator, standing very near the burning one, fall before the conflagration that had devoured everything else in its path. But the wind seemed to veer suddenly to the south, and remained there an hour, and the great elevator was saved; with one exception, the only one on the South Side north of the line of fire. A steamer had reached the mouth of the river, but here the fire caught her, and I saw it run from one end to the other in little lines of light, and so over the rigging till the ship was all ablaze.

Meantime I was in the midst of the wildest confusion I had ever witnessed. The open space between Michigan avenue and the lake was filled with every variety of household goods and merchandise. There must have been the furniture of a thousand families crowded into this narrow space. Rich and poor, white and black, were together. Over every pile of goods stood some one to guard it. Meantime other fugitives were every moment crowding into the already overcrowded space, and seeking room for their goods as well. Thousands of people pressed along the walks and filled the open spaces—some coming to see and others fleeing. The avenue was for hours one solid mass of teams. Up and down the street they pressed endlessly, going up empty and returning full. At length the press became so great that the street was completely blockaded, and the police began to turn the still on-coming multitude of vehicles backward. They chose the spot where I stood to accomplish this. Then began cursing and shouting; the teamsters insisting that they must go on, every one of them having valuable property just ahead; and the police insisting that to save men's lives they must turn back. The more determined teamsters went through in spite of the police, who were strangely inefficient. The more timid or reasonable tried to turn back in a street where there was hardly room to move forward. One backed into my buggy wheels as I crowded the sidewalk and waited; another ran into one of the shafts. Twenty feet ahead of me a horse tried to run away, starting directly toward me. He ran about ten feet and smashed two buggies. A rod to my left a driver ran against a buggy wheel and crushed it, regardless of the other's load. I grew more and more nervous, expecting every moment to have the horse and buggy ruined. Two hours and a half passed and still I waited. I had plenty of time to look about me.

Every variety of vehicle passed me, loaded with every variety of article. I saw one of our former citizens, Mr. Pearson, carrying one end of a long glass case filled with his goods—hair done up in many forms. A dozen or twenty cows picked their way among the wagons. A woman found her way across the street, when there chanced to be an opening, leading a great black dog. The confusion was beyond all description. Up and down the Michigan Central track locomotives were constantly moving, drawing heavy trains, or alone, and, it seemed to me, blowing their unearthly whistles all the time. The fire-engines, a block away, added theirs, which were worse still. The voices of the police calling to the teamsters, the responses and often curses of the drivers, their impatient yells to one another, the cry of distressed citizens to the expressmen, the voices of the crowd, the roaring of the gale, the howling of the conflagration, the crackling of burning houses, the crash of falling walls, the ringing of bells, the shouts that greeted some new freak of the flames, and suddenly the sullen thunder that told us buildings were being blown up only a block away. The conflagration of the great day will hardly bring a confusion worse confounded.

The fire still made progress towards me until the people in all the houses above and below me removed their goods and fled. Again came the thundering and shaking of the earth that accompanied the blowing up of a building. It seemed ominously near. I could see the fire on the Wabash Avenue Methodist Church, and was sure it was going, and that was behind me. At length the vast crowd, men and teams, precipitated themselves down the avenue like a falling avalanche, and the cry went up that the building on the corner just above us was to be blown up. Waiting no longer I joined the fleeing multitude and made my way as fast as possible a block farther away. After three hours my friend returned; his coat gone; his face so black and his eyes so nearly put out, that, for a moment, I did not know him. He took his horse, to my great relief, and I proceeded up the Avenue toward the Central Depot, to see what good I could do. On beyond Terrace Row I went, and had the whole horrible scene before me. Not long, however, could I see it. The magnificent

Terrace Row was in flames, and the air was filled with smoke, and dust, and cinders, and live coals, and faggots of fire. The middle of this great row fell first, the ends following, covered in one black cloud of smoke, and ashes, and dust. It was almost past endurance.

Meanwhile the inflammable material in this narrow space caught fire in a hundred places. Beds, pillows, quilts, carpets, sofas, pianos, furniture, and it seemed to me that everything must be burned. With a small tea-chest I spent hours bringing water from the lake, helping to extinguish numberless incipient fires which broke out continually among the heaps of goods. I returned home at 3 P.M., having had nothing to eat since 6 o'clock Sunday evening. Helping to carry a mirror up stairs, I asked a woman on the way down to give me a drink from a full pail she carried, and she refused. In the evening, Monday evening, I took my station in the cupola of a four-story building to view the fire and watch, and for hours witnessed a scene which no language can describe.

Mr. Goodspeed visited the scene of the fire the next day and described many interesting scenes which he witnessed, most of which have become familiar to our readers. We regret that our space only allows of the foregoing imperfect synopsis of the address, but we must make room for the following thrilling incident:—

While Madison street, west of Dearborn, and the west side of Dearborn were all ablaze, the spectators saw the lurid light appear in the rear windows of Speed's Block. Presently a man, who had apparently taken time to dress himself leisurely, appeared on the extension built up to the second story of two of the stores. He coolly looked down the thirty feet between him and the ground, while the excited crowd first cried jump! and then some of them more considerately looked for a ladder. A long plank was presently found and answered the same as a ladder, and it was placed at once against the building, down which the man soon after slid. But while these preparations were going on there suddenly appeared another man at a fourth story window of the building below, which had no projection, but was flush from the top to the ground—four stories and a basement. His escape by the stairway was evidently cut off, and he looked despairingly down the fifty feet between him and the ground. The crowd grew almost frantic at the sight, for it was only a choice of deaths before him—by fire or by being crushed to death by the fall. Senseless cries of jump! jump! went up from the crowd—senseless, but full of sympathy, for the sight was absolutely agonizing. Then for a minute or two he disappeared, perhaps even less, but it seemed so long a time that the supposition was that he had fallen, suffocated with the smoke and heat. But no, he appears again. First he throws out a bed; then some bed-clothes, apparently; why, probably even he does not know. Again he looks down the dead, sheer wall of fifty feet below him. He hesitates, and well he may, as he turns again and looks behind him. Then he mounts to the window-sill. His whole form appears naked to the shirt, and his white limbs gleam against the dark wall in the bright light as he swings himself below the window. Somehow—how, none can tell—he drops and catches upon the top of the window below him, of the third story. He looks and drops again, and seizes the frame with his hands, and his gleaming body once more straightens and hangs prone downward, and then drops instantly and accurately upon the window-sill of the third story. A shout, more of joy than applause, goes up from the breathless crowd, and those who had turned away their heads, not bearing to look upon him as he seemed about to drop to sudden and certain death, glanced up at him once more with a ray of hope at this daring and skilful feat. Into this window he crept to look, probably for a stairway, but appeared again presently, for here only was the only avenue of escape, desperate and hopeless as it was. Once more he dropped his body, hanging by his hands. The crowd screamed, and waved to him to swing himself over the projection from which the other man had just been rescued. He tried to do this, and vibrated like a pendulum from side to side, but could not reach far enough to throw himself upon the roof. Then he hung by one hand, and looked down; raising the other hand, he took a fresh hold, and swung from side to side once more to reach the roof. In vain; again he hung motionless by one hand, and slowly turned his head over his shoulder and gazed into the abyss below him. Then gathering himself up, he let go his hold, and for a second a gleam of white shot down full forty feet, to the foundation of the basement. Of course it killed him. He was taken to a drug store near by, and died in ten minutes.

HAIR GOODS!

F. CAMPBELL,

Having re-opened at No. 112 Twenty-Second Street, wishes to inform the Ladies of Chicago and vicinity, that he has the only complete Stock of

HAIR GOODS AND HAIR JEWELRY

IN THE CITY.

DON'T FORGET THE NUMBER,

112 Twenty-Second Street,

Between Michigan and Indiana Avs.

Map Showing the Burnt District

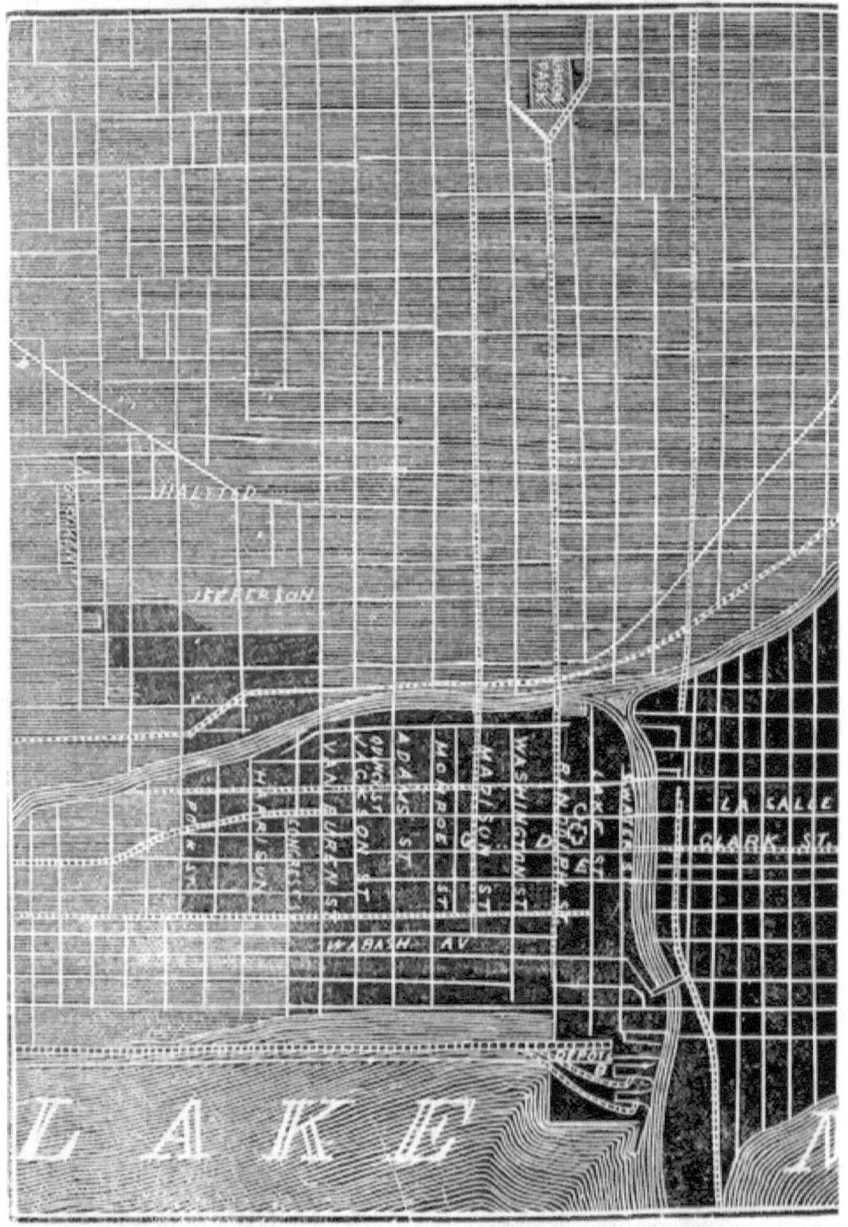

Mayhon, Daly & Co., Importers of Millinery an

Map Showing the Burnt District & the Business Portion of the City.

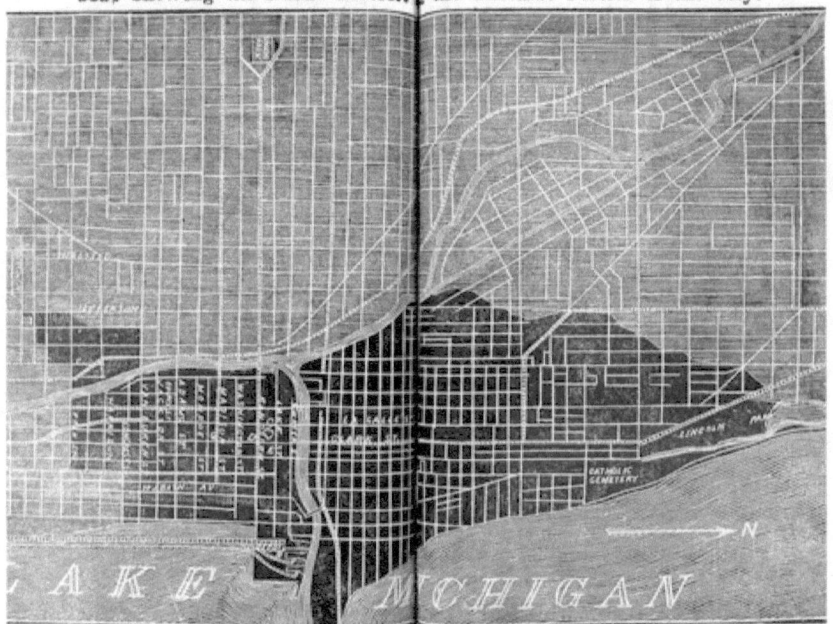

Mayhon, Daly & Co., Importers of Millinery and Fancy Dry Goods, on Michigan Av. near Monroe St.

The Babcock Fire Extinguisher

Played a conspicuous part at the time of the Conflagration and since. One of these Engines was used, and actually saved the only Building that was saved by the aid of any fire apparatus during the Fire. We now speak of the Lind Block, corner of Randolph and Market Streets, occupied by Messrs. Fuller Finch & Fuller, and Z. M. Hall. This valuable apparatus and self-acting method of Extinguishing Fire is now attracting much attention, and we notice our Firemen are enthusiastic as to its availability to extinguish fire before it assumes the shape of a Conflagration.

The Machines can be procured at the factory, corner Washington and Clinton Streets, or at 656 Wabash Avenue,

Babcock Extinguisher Co.

THE Great Conflagration,

A COMPLETE ACCOUNT

OF THE BURNING OF CHICAGO.

CONTAINING

Descriptions of the Scenes, Incidents, and Accidents of the Fire.

WITH A

BUSINESS DIRECTORY

AND

List of the Principal Business Houses

IN THEIR PRESENT LOCATIONS.

CHICAGO.
PUBLISHED BY THE WESTERN NEWS COMPANY.
1871.

FURNITURE

COMPANY,

86, 88, 90, and 92 West Randolph Street.

Factory in full Operation. Office Desks and other Furniture.

Van Schaack, Stevenson & Reid,

849, 851 and 853 Wabash Avenue,

COR. 18th STREET,

Late 90, 92, and 94 Lake Street,

Wholesale Druggists,

Have taken the Old Baptist Church, and are now laying in a Large Stock.

COME AND SEE US.

CONTENTS.

THE ORIGIN OF THE FIRE.
Its Commencement, Progress, Incidents, and Occurences,................... pp. 5–9

ITS RAPID PROGRESS
Through the West, South and North Divisions of the City................ pp. 9–27

THE TERMINATION OF THE FIRE
In the South Division... pp. 27–29

LOSS OF LIFE,
And number of Persons missing.. p. 29

UPRISING OF THE CONTINENT.
Contributions both public and private in United States and Europe......... pp. 29–35

REMARKABLE SCENES AND INCIDENTS.
Accidents, Heroisms, and Hair-Breath Escapes........................... pp. 35–59

INTERESTING FACTS AND STATEMENTS.
Survey of Losses by Streets.. pp. 59–63

ESTIMATE OF THE AGGREGATE LOSS
By the Chicago Conflagration... pp. 63–79

CHICAGO AS IT WAS.
Describing the appearance of the City before the Fire,.................. pp. 79–83

CHICAGO AS IT IS.
Showing its present appearance of ruin and devestation,................ pp. 83–87

CHICAGO AS IT WILL BE.
Depicting the future glory and prosperity of the City,................. pp. 87–93

FIRES OF HISTORY.
The Great Conflagrations of Ancient and Modern Times................... pp. 93–97

DIRECTORY
Of the City and County Offices, Banks, etc., etc.,..................... pp. 97–99

CATALOGUE OF THE PRINCIPAL BUSINESS HOUSES
Of the new Chicago and their present location.......................... pp 101–107

INDEX
To Advertisements... p. 108

☞ ALL RIGHT! ☜

THE ILLINOIS CENTRAL R. R.

Is Running Trains Regularly from the Depot, foot of 22d St. as follows:

9:20 A. M. | For ST. LOUIS, KANSAS CITY, CAIRO, MEMPHIS, VICKSBURG, MOBILE and NEW ORLEANS.
Daily, Except Sundays.

5:15 P. M. | For CHAMPAIGN and all WAY STATIONS between CHICAGO and CHAMPAIGN, also for PEORIA, CANTON, KEOKUK and WARSAW.
Daily, Except Sundays.

8:10 P. M. | For ST. LOUIS, KANSAS CITY, CAIRO, MEMPHIS, LITTLE ROCK, VICKSBURG and NEW ORLEANS.
Daily, Except Saturdays.

No Change of Cars from Chicago to St. Louis.
TIME AS QUICK AS BY ANY OTHER ROUTE.

NO CHANGE OF CARS FROM CHICAGO TO CAIRO
From 100 to 150 Miles shorter, and **HOURS** Quicker than any other Route.

ELEGANT DRAWING ROOM SLEEPING CARS ON NIGHT TRAINS.

Baggage Checked to all Important Points.

☞ Transfer made in Chicago by Parmelee Omnibus Line, as usual.

For Through Tickets and Information apply at the Depot, foot of 22d Street, Chicago, and at the principal Railroad Offices throughout the United States and Canadas.

W. P. JOHNSON, General Passenger Agent. **A. MITCHELL,** General Superintendent.

The Great Conflagration.

PHENOMENAL CHICAGO.

It has long been a distinguishing characteristic of Chicago, that all her undertakings and accomplishments were phenomenal. Her modes of action were original and sensational, both as regards individuals and the body corporate. She took counsel of no precedents in anything she did. When she wanted to raise the grade of her streets, she elevated the city upon screws, and reposed it upon higher foundations. When she wished to provide accomodations for the national convention of a political party, she erected a vast "wigwam," which was a marvel of its kind, eclipsing all of its predecessors in every part of the republic. When convenience demanded easier and speedier transit from bank to bank of the river, she burrowed tunnels underneath the stream. When a supply of fresh and pure water became a necessity of our rapidly augmenting population, she carried an immense viaduct out miles from the shore, and gathered a pellucid stream from the far-off bosom of Lake Michigan. When the river became the recepacle of the sewerage of 350,000 people, and generated an insufferable stench, she carved out a connection with the Mississippi, turned into the channel the crystal floods of the lake, and created a perennially flowing and purifying current, sweeping away the whole accumulation of impurities, and permanently transforming a cess-pool into a stream of cleanliness. Even her crimes were phenomenal. Her criminals were hunted down with a detective sagacity that was extraordinary and astonishing, as witness the case of Ziegenmeyer. Her suicides were bizarve in the extreme, as witness the self-destruction of the man who inhaled death at the end of a gas pipe. Her accidents were beyond the level of the common-place, as witness the crushing fall of the Court House roofs. A miracle of materiel developement, of commercial activity, of far-reaching forecast, of tireless energy, of prompt execution, of growing population, of accumulated wealth, of advancing influence, Chicago had become a phenomenon among cities. And when, on the woful Sunday night of our Black October, she departed partly to the skies in flame and smoke, and partly to the earth in ashes and ruins, she maintained her phenomenal reputation, and signalized her exit by a conflagration, which outvies every one of history in all that is wierdly sublime, appalling terrible and amazingly destructive.

R. T. CRANE, *President.* C. S. CRANE, *Vice President.*
S. W. ADAMS, *Secretary.* G. S. REDFIELD, *Treasurer.*

(THE CRANE BROS.)
North=Western Manfg. Co.

Works : Jefferson and Des Plaines Streets,

(Between Lake and Randolph.)

CHICAGO.

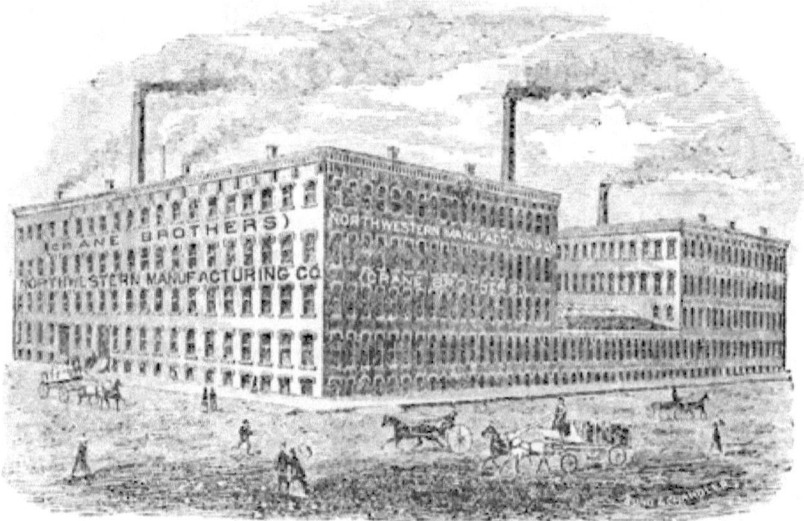

GENERAL OFFICES AND SALESROOMS,

No. 10 North Jefferson Street,

BRANCH STORE, 100 WASHINGTON ST.

MANUFACTURERS OF

WROUGHT IRON PIPE

MALLEABLE IRON FITTING, AND

STEAM WARMING AND VENTILATING APPARATUS.

Brass and Iron Goods for Steam and Gas Fitters and Engine Builders. Steam Engines and Steam Pumps, General Machinery, etc., etc.

Steam Freight and Passenger Elevators.

MALLEABE IRON CASTINGS MADE TO ORDER.

☞ Circulars and Prices of Goods not given herein sent on application.

BEFORE THE CONFLAGRATION.

Several important atmospheric peculiarities marked the period just previous to the great fire. For weeks there had been no rain throughout the vast region of the Northwest. In various parts of Wisconsin and Michigan, the woods had been parched into a sort of tinder, and in places among them, the flames had been raging with dangerous and wide-spread fury, involving in their lurid path, towns, settlements, and farms. During three nights, no dew had fallen in this city. Our lumber yards, our frame buildings, our shingle roofs, and wood-work of every description in our palatial structures had become dry as kindlings. The atmosphere seemed not to contain an atom of moisture. Clouds of dust ascended from our streets with every passing gust, and at every rattling by of a vehicle, so weather-scorched were our thoroughfares. Our brave and energetic firemen had been almost worn out, the evening previous, in fighting down a fire, which in itself amounted to a conflagration. And, to complete the list of fatalities, a heavy gale was blowing from the South-west, ready to feed combustion with all its forces, and render nugatory the most heroic effort.

COMMENCEMENT OF THE LURID MARCH.

We need not occupy room in recounting the particulars of the great fire which occurred on Saturday night—and which the public thought a terrible disaster—for the one of the following night and its succeeding day throws that into insignificence. The first mentioned was itself a consuming tornado of flame, which lasted for appalling hours, destroying about twenty acres of buildings and lumber piles, on the West side, between Clinton, Adams and Van Buren Streets, and the South Branch, and involving the loss of several lives. The scene of that conflagration was visited during Sunday by thousands of spectators, who reviewed the spectacle of desolation with manifest sadness, little dreaming, however, that a broader, wider, more complete devastation was so soon in store for the city, and for very many of their own homes and business houses—a destruction of life and property compared with which that of Saturday night was but the crackeling of a juvenile bonfire.

When, about nine o'clock in the evening, the fire alarm sounded, the general impression was that the former fire had broken out in a new place, and that it would be extinguished with little trouble. Nobody had the remotest fears of the actual result. Even when the flames began to spread, lighting up the heavens far and near, and the disaster threatened to be quite serious, was there any considerable apprehension that the lurid march would cross to the South side. Indeed the origin of the conflagration was ludicrously insignificant. A sick calf lay in a trumpery stable belonging to a trumpery frame dwelling, on DeKoven street, between Jefferson and Clinton, and thither the owner had gone with a kerosine lamp to look after the ailing brute. This lamp was set down in the straw, and accidentally overturned, the spilled contents starting up into an instant blaze, which quickly involved the whole structure. At the moment, a little presence of mind and some energetic action might have sufficed to end the danger on the spot. As it happened, the flames, under the stimulus of the stiff gale then blowing, speedily spread to the adjacent buildings. Suddenly the fire assumed such proportions as to make it necessary to call out the whole fire department without delay. But despite the most vigorous efforts of the entire force, the lurid flames leaped from roof to roof, and building to building, rapidly enveloping block after block in their consuming embrace. The exertions of the firemen, worn down and jaded as they were by the previous night's rough toil, seemed utterly inadequate to stay the onward career of the devouring element, and ere long it

CHICAGO
Type Foundry,

72 West Washington Street.

We desire to inform our friends that we are located as above, and have opened our office for business.

Having recovered from the recent disastrous Fire, we are happy to inform the Printers and Publishers throughout the Northwest, that they will find us as above, where we will be happy to see our friends, and will, in a short time, be able to fill all orders with usual Dispatch.

MARDER, LUSE & CO.

H. HARTT.   J. W. OSTRANDER.

H. HARTT & CO.,
Printing Press Machine
SHOP,

AND DEALERS IN

PRINTING PRESSES,

70 & 72 West Washington Street,

Are prepared to fill all orders in their Line promptly, and at old prices.

became apparent that the city was doomed to suffer the most appalling visitation of the fire-fiend that it ever had experienced. All the combined energies of the firemen, policemen and citizens could accomplish was to prevent the flames from moving further West than Des Plaines street. The fire, having started in a neighborhood where there were numerous lumber yards, planing mills, and other wooden structures, fed hastily upon these light combustibles, and spread with incredible rapidity. All the heavens were lighted up with a lurid glare. From various quarters poured forth a thick suffocating stream of blackish smoke, glittering with blazing brands and spangles of cinders the moment it touched the purer atmosphere. Meanwhile the gale had increased in severity, and the conflagration raged with intensified violence. That part of the city now seemed but the almost boundless crater of an inextinguishable volcano, as viewed by the near spectator. Vast volumes of flame shot up to an immense hight into the air, and appeared at times to have been detached by the fury of the wind, and precipitated forward over entire blocks and even squares, kindling new fires to feed other like flame volumns, to be hurried hence on their mission of devastation. Showers of cinders descended upon all the dwellings and factories and streets in the path of the onpouring current.

PROGRESS OF THE CONFLAGRATION.

It was now a little after 10 o'clock. The fire had already made fearful havoc. A vast tract, perhaps 30 or 40 blocks on the West Side, north and south of Jackson street, was one great field of fire. As yet, the people on the East Side felt themselves comparatively safe. They had little apprehension that the fire would cross the river. The light from the burning city illuminated the heavens with a fearful glare. The streets were filled by an excited multitude. People from the West Side were fleeing from their burning homes. The noise of the roaring tornado of flames as it swept onward in its career of devastation rose above the tumult and din of the great houseless multitude that fled before its devouring fury.

Up to this time the inhabitants on the East Side had been hopeful. They relied largely on the character of their great iron and stone front buildings. The track of the fire-fiend was already nearly a mile in length and half a mile wide. A vast multitude, hurried from their burning homes, were crossing the river before the advancing columns of flame. The wind whistled and howled through the streets, and the bright light of the fire every moment grew brighter. The heat in the vicinity of the fire became intense, as the winds fanned the glowing timbers to a whiter heat.

Still in the lower part of the city in the vicinity of the great hotels and business the feeling among the people was more that of commisseration for the sufferers on the West Side than of apprehension for their own safety. They did not as yet fully believe that it would cross the river. Still the wind roared through the streets, and still the flames blazed and crackled among the timbers of fast consuming dwellings and shops along Jackson street, and north of that street on the West Side. The crowds in the streets, in the eastern part of the city, were every moment growing larger; the noise was increasing. It was now fully evident that the fire engines could do nothing to resist the onward march of the flames.

By this time, nearly the entire population of the city had been aroused, and the streets for a mile or two surrounding the scene of the disaster were thronged with excited, swaying humanity, and with all descriptions of vehicles, pressed into the service for the hasty removal of household goods and personal effects. Every street resembled a second-hand furniture store, goods of all descriptions being loaded and unloaded here, there, everywhere, that promised refuge, in promiscous confusion. Invalids and cripples were car-

J. BAUER & CO.,

MANUFACTURERS OF

Improved Agraffe

SQUARE AND UPRIGHT

PIANOS

AND

Musical Instruments

OF ALL DESCRIPTIONS.

650 Broadway, New York,

270 and 614 Michigan Avenue.

FORMERLY AT

No. 69 WASHINGTON STREET, (Crosby Opera House.)

CHICAGO.

ried away on improvised ambulances; aged women and helpless infants were hastily borne to places of temporary or permanent safety; people who were utterly overcome with excitement and fatigue were seen sleeping on lounges, trunks and tables, in the midst of the crowds that were surging with emotion; empty houses were forcibly broken open and taken possession of by houseless wanderers, made desperate by the awful surroundings, in some instances, as many as five families tumbling into the same building.

THE FIRE CROSSES THE RIVER.

It was now a little after 11 o'clock. The roaring furnace along the West Side up to the river, extending from Jackson to Adams street, represented a miniature hell. Men forgot the flight of time—moments, under the terrible suspense and apprehension, lengthened into hours. Some buildings in the neighborhood, on the East Side, were proclaimed to be on fire. Jackson street bridge was already a mass of rolling flames. Then the hearts of the people on the East Side sank within them for very horror. They now fully realized the magnitude of the peril. The gale, in a steady, blustering current, was blowing great sheets of blaze down into the heart of the business part of the city. Strong men trembled, women shrieked, and children became frantic.

In an incredibly short space of time, the conflagration had reached Wells street, and with another mighty leap involved the buildings on La Salle. From Jackson street northward, the fire column seemed to bound forward successively to Adams, to Monroe, and on towards Madison street. One of the finest quarters of the city was now swallowed, as it were, in a vortex of fire. No words could photograph the tumultuous and appalling scene at that moment of universal terror and despair.

STREET SCENES.

It was now midnight. The heavens were lighted up with a lurid glare, the vast surging multitude swaying to and fro, while above the roar of the wind, and the crackling of the flames, rose the confused noise of shouting men and wailing women. Merchants were gathering up their most valuable articles, such as books and papers; landlords were arousing their guests, and advising hasty departures; men, loaded with the most precious articles of the household, followed by awe-stricken women and frantic children, were rushing away from the fire-demon as rapidly as the thronged condition of the streets would admit; women, separated from their families, gave utterance to shrieks that rang out clear and shrill above the horrible roar of the devouring flames and the wild moan of the wind as it swept the fiery deluge along in its march to ruin.

Vast smoke clouds hovered over all the central and northern part of the city. The fire-light, reflected back from the dense smoke, shone with a baleful red glare that was truly awe-inspiring. Strong men grew powerless, and became frantic in face of the appalling calamity.

A little after 12 o'clock the guests of the large boarding-houses in the neighborhood of State and Adams streets, were turned horrified into the streets to swell the vast multitude already abroad.

MILLIONS TOPPLE INTO RUINS.

Still onward swept the sea of flame, remorselessly consuming everything which fire could destroy that lay in its path. And, not only did the conflagration march Northward and Eastward, but they also made slow but steady progress Southward, against the driving force of the gale, involving many of the finest residences on Wabash and Michigan avenues, and all the other buildings located between Harrison street and the main river,

STARK & ALLEN,

IMPORTERS OF

WATCHES,

AND

MANUFACTURING JEWELERS

363 WABASH AVENUE.

Sammons, Clark & Co.

MANUFACTURERS OF

Cornice and Picture Frame

MOLDINGS,

Square, Oval, Arch Top and Rustic Picture Frames,

IMPORTERS OF

Mirror Plates, Chromos,

AND ENGRAVINGS.

Wholesale Dealers in Backing Cords, &c., &c.

Escaped the late Fire unharmed, and continue Business as usual. Price Lists and Cuts of Mouldings sent on application. Address,

SAMMONS, CLARK & CO.,

197 & 199 South Clinton St., Chicago.

in the South division. Among the more prominent structures destroyed within this area, besides dwellings, were the following: the Armory, the Gas Works, the Wabash Avenue Methodist Church, the St. Paul's Church, the First and Second Presbyterian, the New Jerusalem Temple, the Palmer, Bigelow, Orient, Everett, Tremont, Sherman, Briggs, Metropolitan, St. James, Adams, Massasoit, City Nevada, and Clifton hotels; the Chamber of Commerce, the Court House and Jail, (which contained the offices and records of all the city officials); the four principal telegraph offices; the Crosby Opera House, McVicker's Theatre, Hooley's Opera House, the Dearborn Theatre, the Michigan Central and Union depots, all the banks in the city except two small ones located in the West division; Farwell, Metropolitan, and Crosby's halls, several bridges and viaducts, and all the newspapers and job offices on the South side.

This devastated area extended from Harrison street North to the river, and from the South Branch east to Lake Michigan, taking in every building, with three exceptions—the Lind Block at Randolph bridge, church on the corner of Harrison street and Michigan avenue, and a new structure on the corner of LaSalle and Monroe. The Michigan Southern and Rock Island passenger house, together with the Michigan Central and Illinois Central freight depots, were swept away, including one of their elevators. The principal offices of the Chicago, Burlington, and Quincy, and of the Chicago and Northwestern Railroads were also utterly destroyed. From the latter not a scrap of paper outside of the safe was rescued. This completeness coupled with swiftness, of destruction, is one of the most remarkable features of the occasion. Fire-proof structures, or what were so esteemed, crumbled to pieces as easy as those of brick. Stone-work, both sand and limestone, melted down, for the most part, into a disintegrated mass.

The ground burned over on the West side, was about one mile in length, from DeKoven street to Van Buren, and perhaps a quarter of a mile in length, bordering along the river for most of the way, and consuming the Chicago and Alton Railroad freight house, together with all freight cars in their yards.

SCENES OF THE BURNING.

While this wholesale wreck of property was going on, the wind at times blew almost a hurricane, and it seemed but the work of a moment for the fire to enter the south ends of buildings fronting on Randolph, Lake and Water streets, and to reappear at north doors and windows, shooting forth in fierce flames. The conflagration appeared literally to melt its way from street to street. Often the long tongues of fire would dart clear across some thoroughfare, igniting the houses on the opposite side, when both sheets of flame would pour together toward the centre, uniting and presenting a solid mass of combustion, completely filling the open space, and shooting upward a hundred feet or more into the air above the roofs in their mad career; and thus was street after street filled with flame and fire, accompanied by a roar which can be equalled only by combining the noise of the ocean when its waters are driven, during a tempest, upon a rocky beach, with the howl of the blast. Huge walls toppled and fell into the sea of fire without, apparently, giving a sound, as the roar of the devouring element was so great that all the minor sounds were swallowed up. The fall was perceptible to the eye if not to the ear. If the reader will recall to his mind the fiercest snow storm in his experience, and imagined the snow to have been fire, as it surged hither and thither before the fury of the fiend, he will be able to form a faint conception of the flames as they raged through the streets of our doomed city. Many of the buildings situated along South Water street buried their red-hot rear walls in the waters of the river into which they plunged with a hiss like to nothing earthly, throwing up a billow of seething water, which would

ST. CAROLINES COURT HOTEL.

Elizabeth cor. Washington Street
CHICAGO.

This new and elegantly furnished Hotel with all modern improvements, offers the only first class accomodations for families in the City:

JAMES L. BURNS, Proprietor.

KIRK, COLEMAN & CO.

Manufacturers, Importers, and Dealers in

IRON, NAILS, STEEL,

SPRINGS, AXLES,

Wagon and Carriage Materials,

CARRIAGE TRIMMINGS &c.,

34 South Canal St,   CHICAGO.

gradually subside, until other walls would follow in their turn. The heat was so intense at times from some of the burning buildings, that they could not be approached nearer than an hundred and fifty feet, which accounts for the manner in which the fire worked back South, generally in the very teeth of the blast.

RUSHING TO THE RESCUE.

Long before the conflagration reached the vast proportions described, a new element of uproar was added to the general confusion. It being Sunday, proprietors and employes of the business section were, for the most part, enjoying the comforts of home in dwellings far distant from spectacular drama of the fire-king. Those who saw the flames supposed them the remains of Saturday night's fire, and having implicit confidence in the fire department, were unconcerned spectators; but between 11 and 12 o'clock a rumor got abroad that the disaster had overtaken the very heart of Chicago. Then ensued a scene of the wildest excitement. Every available horse and vehicle was brought into requisition to hurry proprietors and their friends to the point of peril. For several hours the main thoroughfares leading from the outskirts toward the scene of the conflagration were thronged with galloping horsemen urging their steeds to the top of their metal; by wagons and buggies and hacks, rattling along at break-neck speed; and by pedestrians out of breath, yet pushing their panting way with what strength and swiftness could be put forth by agonizing anxiety and overstrained resolution. But what a harrowing spectacle met the gaze of these new comers! The Board of Trade building, the Court House, the Western Union Telegraph and Associated Press Offices, with hundreds of other structures, stately with architectural grandeur and opulent with contained wealth, were masses of fire, from which the flames ascended, with a sullen roar, into the very skies. Worse than all, the fire-engines were powerless to save. Indeed, when the conflagration first crossed over to the East side, all these instruments of protection, save one, were in the West division, where had been their properly assigned place of duty until the arrival of that catastrophe.

A REAL BLESSING.

The large fire on the West Side, which occurred on Saturday night, has since been regarded as a positive god-send, for, had it not been for the vacant ground occasioned by it, two squares in width, the conflagration would have swept unhindered to the Northward, and destroyed in its path the principal manufacturing district of the city, and the the business portion of the West division. As it was, this vacant ground was the means of checking the onward sweep of the flames west of the river, although, on its way to the South Side, it reduced to ruins the lofty elevator which so nobly had withstood the fire of the previous evening. Thus it was that the blasted and desolated district which had been accounted a great calamity proved to be really a blessing in disguise—a sort of insurance against further disaster.

NORTH SIDE IN FLAMES.

While much of the South division was helplessly awaiting the approach of destruction, the deluge of fire had rolled on until it encountered the main river, where many persons had hoped its devastating strength would be effectually and finally stayed; but it leaped across this watery barrier at a single bound, and, like some tidal wave of flame, resumed its consuming progress. This sudden transit of the devouring element was preceded by a half-crazed multitude thronging across the Rush street bridge to the aid of their imperiled families and to the rescue of their household effects. Many driven

COLLINS & BURGIE,
STOVE MANUFACTURERS,

Being among the very few whose Manufactory escaped destruction, by the great Conflagration, are in full operation, and as usual

MANUFACTURING AND DEALING IN

Cook, Parlor & Heating Stoves

ALSO, SOLE MANUFACTURERS FOR THE NORTHWEST OF

Prindle's Agricultural Steamer and Farmers' Boiler,

FOCHT'S PATENT PULLEY BLOCKS,

With or without Wick's Semi Metallic Faced Sheave,

Clark's Patent Tuyere Iron,

CONCEDED TO BE THE BEST IN USE.

Stable Fittings and Fixtures, Ornamental, Convenient and Durable.

NOTT'S PATENT KITCHEN SINKS,

Unsurpassed in utility and finish. Address Orders for Sinks to S. L. BIGNALL & CO., 232 Lake Street

Particular attention given to orders for Light and Fancy Castings, and Castings for Patterns where Models are furnished.

STOVE WORKS AND OFFICE, COR. JEFFERSON AND VAN BUREN STREETS, CHICAGO, ILLINOIS.

UNION SCREW AND BOLT CO.,

Cor. Van Buren and Jefferson Sts., Chicago.

SOLE MANUFACTURERS OF

Lag Screws, Cider Press Screws, Bench Screws,

Cheese Press Screws, Bridge Bolts, Skein Bolts,

JACK SCREWS, SCREW HINGES,

WITH FORGED UPSET THREAD

MANUFACTURERS ALSO OF

CARRIAGE BOLTS, AGRICULTURAL BOLTS, SPLICE BAR BOLTS,

Machine Bolts, Plow Bolts Tire Bolts,

SET SCREWS, &c., &c.,

With Forged Thread either raised or reduced, or with common cut Thread.

SEND FOR PRICE LIST.

upon Water street by the onrushing fire, suddenly found themselves cut off from all ordinary means of exit, and were forced to seek an unwilling refuge in the river, where it is believed that quite a number must have escaped roasting alive only in death by drowning.

Panic soon spread wide and far throughout the North division. The same infatuation which had made thousands of residents on the South Side feel unapprehensive of danger, and caused them to spend golden opportunities in sight-seeing that should have been devoted to diligent preparations against the coming catastrophe, seems to have lulled into financial security the mass of the population on the North Side. Hence, when the great peril was at their very doors, large numbers were almost as much startled as if a conflagration had broken out in their very midst without a spark of warning. Hundreds, even of those who lived near the river, were taken so unawares that they escaped barely with their lives and the clothes on their backs, and rushed away from their homes, half demented, in every direction which seemed to promise expedient refuge from the scorching heat at their heels, following sometimes almost at their own pace.

So soon as the flames had spread beyond the loftier and more substantial business structures, and had entered upon the long and broad stretch of frame dwellings and retail stores, the progress was frightfully rapid, seeming to pursue the frightened inhabitants with the menace of fate itself. Many comfortable residences, with all their contents, were abandoned to the march of destruction, the tenants glad to escape on any terms. In various instances, fathers and husbands had ventured over to the South Side as spectators, and had been cut off from timely return, and women and children had thus been left to battle with the peril alone. It required an incredibly brief space of time to destroy all avenues of passage across the main river. La Salle street tunnel early ceased to be available, for it sucked in a broad sheet from the south, and poured forth from its hither entrance a vast volume of suffocating smoke and heat, as if it had been some huge chimney. All the bridges above and below this artery of travel were soon involved in the general wreck, and both sides of the river, from the branches to the lake, were walls of living fire. This broad destruction cut off large numbers from access to their homes, and drove them panic-stricken to the lake shore for precarious refuge.

When the fire had passed Kinzie street, the terror was something indescribable. Every imaginable kind of conveyance, even hearses, were employed to hurry away to places of safety such remnants of household furniture and personal effects as could be snatched from the general wreck. Many were summoned from beds where they had been quietly sleeping, and suddenly confronted with the peril of the hour, often escaping only in their night garments. The Nicolson pavement in the streets was on fire in every direction reached by the conflagration. For a long distance in advance of the flames, which rolled on like billows, showers of sparks, intermingled with blazing brands, were whirled aloft by one eddy of the breeze, only to be precipitated by another upon roofs dry as tinder, where they first sent up curling whisps of blue smoke, and then gushed forth in spurts of dark red flame,

THE STRIDES OF DESTRUCTION.

In this way, solitary building were often ablaze half a dozen squares ahead of the main line of the fire. This separate havoc opened new lines of march for the devouring element, which spread forward and laterally, leaving tracks of desolation in the midst of otherwise untouched districts. Indeed, the fire on the North Side did not move on in solid column as it had done in the South Division, but broke into sections, some of which advanced more rapidly than the others, the whole spreading afterward, and involving

D. B. FISK & CO.,

WHOLESALE DEALERS IN

Millinery and Straw Goods,

LADIES' FURNISHING FANCY GOODS

AND TRIMMINGS,

57 West Washington Street,

Near Tunnel Entrance.

Orders Solicited and Satisfaction Guaranteed.

J. H. SMALL.   H. GRAINGER.

JOHN H. SMALL & CO.,

STATIONERS

AND

Blank Book Manufacturers,

No. 27 South Canal Street,

FORMERLY 117 DEARBORN STREET,

CHICAGO.

everything in a mass of ruins. All that was spared in its earlier stages was one corner of Kinzie street, a few houses between Market street and the bridge, one elevator (Newberry's), a few lumber-yards, and a coal-yard or two. With these exceptions, the conflagration swept along the North Branch to the Gas Works, taking every stick and stone that lay in its way. It worked with the wind and against it, with frightful impartiality. It held a direct northward course to Division street bridge, near the Gas Works, where there are some large vacant lots, rather damp, and without any combustible surroundings. At this point it took an oblique turn eastward, toward Lincoln Park, leaving the Newberry School, on North avenue, and sweeping along to Lincoln avenue, to Dr. Dyer's new house, where, on that side, it halted, having burned itself out. It left a couple of frame buildings in front of the park entrance, sparing the fine park itself, hardly a shrub being injured. Not so with the old cemeteries, Protestant and Catholic. The grass on the graves was burned, the wooden crosses were consumed, and the gravestones were splintered into dust. Trees were withered like dry leaves, hardly a skeleton remaining, while furniture, piled there for safety by the earlier fugitives, served only to make a funeral pyre. The very pest-house, down on the lake shore, was burned to the ground, the miserable patients being obliged to seek in the water the fate from which they fled. The affrighted fugitives in the cemeteries escaped madly toward the park, while the air resounded with their cries and lamentations. Meantime the conflagration swept eastward to the lake, consuming everything that lay in its path. By this time dawn was beginning to tinge the horizon, and with its coming, the great Water Works, the pride and the protection of the city, were discovered to be charred and promiscuous ruins.

REFUGEES AND VICTIMS.

To describe this fire in its details through the North Division would be utterly impossible. It was like a battle, where all was din, smoke, confusion, and turmoil. Each individual of the vast fleeing tide can tell a different story of peril and escape. Before that awful front of flame, the streets yet unburned were packed and jammed with myriads of human beings of every age, sex and condition. It reminded one of a disastrous retreat, the baggage blocking up the highways, while the very horses were burned to death beneath the loads of household goods crowded upon their wagons. Hundreds of the affrighted animals ran away, mad with pain and terror, crushing in their flight men, women and children. The principal lines of retreat for the North Side community, living west of Clark street and North of Oak street, were over Erie and Indiana street, Chicago avenue and North avenue bridges. They retired to the prairie in the neighborhood of the rolling mills, or else took refuge with their terrified and trembling friends in the West Division. The North Side, taking a line from Canal street north, was completely annihilated. The little portion that escaped belonged more properly to the northwestern section.

On Erie street and Chicago avenue the loss of life was fearful. The bridges were choked with fugitives and baggage. The wagons became entangled, and the frightened people either plunged into the river and were drowned, or else fell down never to rise, suffocated by the frightful smoke. The scene was enough to unnerve the stoutest heart.

DESTRUCTION OF CHURCHES AND SHADE TREES.

Through the hellish splendor of mingled gloom and fire the tall church steeples loomed proudly against the fiery firmament. The first spire that went down was that of the Holy Name—Roman Catholic—Church, on State street. The crash was fearful and was only exceeded by the terrific noise produced by the falling of the North Presbyterian

LATE, No. 50 LAKE STREET.

DEALERS IN

Leather & Findings

35 and 37 South Canal St.,

CHICAGO.

GEO. A. MISCH & BRO.

MANUFACTURERS OF

Stained, Enameled,

EMBOSSED, CUT AND GROUND GLASS.

Office, Corner Canal and Lake Streets,

Manufactory, N. Wells St., bet. Division and Schiller

GEO. A. MISCH.
ADOLPH MISCH.
CHICAGO.

FILL ALL ORDERS AS BEFORE THE FIRE.

Church, on Cass street, a moment later. It was a sad sight to see the beautiful little church of Robert Collyer succumb to the pitiless enemy, and the hardly less beautiful German Catholic Church of St. Joseph met the same untimely doom. And sad was it to see the fine rows of stately trees which formed the shade of the North Side streets go down like grass, withered and blackened. The marble can be replaced and the stone can be laid afresh, but many a long year must pass ere we shall see again the maples, and poplars and elms.

LANDMARKS GONE.

Those of the North Side inhabitants who lived in the section lying between Clark street on the west and the Lake on the east, and between Chicago avenue on the north and the river on the south, were the last to suffer. They expected that the flames would pass them, as they had already burned up to the Newberry school before Rush street was engulphed. This hope, like so many others, was doomed to be of short duration. Very soon the cry arose that Rush street bridge was burning, while the large reaping machine factory of C. H. McCormick was discovered to be a blazing ruin. Presently the old Lake House, built in 1837, and situated on Michigan, near the corner of Rush street, shot up a column of flame, which proclaimed that the fiend had seized upon it.

FLEEING FOR LIFE.

This was the signal of a general stampede. The roughs that infested the lower streets, near the river, broke into the saloons and drank what liquor they could find. Many of these ruffians were draymen and wharfrats, and their conduct was ruffianly in the extreme. Hell seemed to have vomited these wretches forth as fitting denizens of the fiery air around them. The robbers broke into and sacked many houses, the inhabitants thereof being only too glad to get away at any price. Retreat to the north was cut off, for already the flames had fired the water works and were burning the pier at the foot of Superior street. The destruction of Rush street bridge precluded a southward flight, and, besides, the South Side was one ocean of fire. Everything was burned on a line with Rush street, and that was already beginning to go. Language cannot portray the scenes that ensued. Everything was placed on some kind of vehicle, horses were let loose from their stables, children were flung into carts with their half crazy mothers, the lower orders were raging drunk, while the respectable people were wholly demoralized. For a time it looked as if the final day had come for all these thousands, for the fire was rushing down upon them like an avenging spirit. On most faces was depicted terror, on the fewer calm indifference or detestable brutality. Women cried out for aid to save their little ones. Their entreaties were disregarded or else were made the the theme of ribald jokes by the inebriated ruffians from the purlieus of North Water and Kinzie streets. Happy were those women and children who had husbands and fathers to protect them. Where were all these affrighted beings tending to? The cry of "To the sands! To the Sands!" was heard on every side, and to the sands everybody fled as by common intuition.

PERILOUS LIFE AMONG THE "SANDS."

The "Sands" have long been notorious in the annals of the city. They used to be infested with the vilest of vile rookeries until Long John Wentworth, when he was Mayor of Chicago, became a justifiable incendiary and burned them all out. Since then they have been almost deserted. They are that portion of the lake shore lying between St. Clair street and Lake Michigan and between the North Pier and the Water Works. A more desolate place could hardly be imagined. The sand there has been drifted into small mountains, which half conceal knots of miserable shanties, wherein the Arabs of

M. GLASSBROOK,

IMPORTER OF

HUMAN HAIR

AND

ORNAMENTAL HAIR MANUFACTURER,

At Wholesale and Retail.

145 TWENTY-SECOND ST.

ORDERS BY MAIL PROMPTLY AND FAITHFULLY ATTENDED TO.

DIEBOLD & KIENZIE'S

Celebrated Fire and Burglar Proof

SAFES.

The fearful ordeal of fire which has visited Chicago, among other things has tested thoroughly the comparative value of the different Safes.

We refer with just pride to the record of the DIEBOLD and KINIZE Safes in this terrible test, which in almost every case have preserved their contents in excellent condition. No other Safes in the fire were so uniformly successful in protecting their contents. We are constantly receiving testimonials from the leading business men of Chicago who used these Safes, which we invite those requiring Safes to examine at our office,

D. S. COVERT, Gen'l Agt.

446 STATE STREET.

the North Side used to dwell. In most parts these houses reached nearly to the water's edge. In a few places there was an extent of some hundred yards in width. The place might have been comparatively safe from the fire, only that at the foot of Erie street was the large wooden bath house, dry as tinder, and along the southern section, toward the pier, stretched an immense varnish factory, an oil refinery, and a long range of sheds in which pitch and tar were stored in large barrels. All this made the situation anything but pleasant, and very far from secure. All the space, unoccupied by houses and lumber was on that eventful morning crowded with trunks, bedsteads, mattresses, pianos, chairs, tables, bundles of clothing, feather beds, people, horses, wagons, and almost everthing that goes to make up a large city. Besides, there were numerous barrels of whisky which had been rolled down from the hell shops further up by the dissolute wretches.

Day was just breaking when the conflagration had reached the edge of the sands. The gale continued to drive with fury, and the sand and smoke combined to pelt the very eyes out of the wretched thousands crowded on that desolate place. Soon the smoke became so dense that the sands were dark as at midnight. The strongest constitution could not look that wind in the teeth and remain alive. The people fled down to the very water, while the flames bust through the dense smoke and leaped after them. The fiery brands fell amid the furniture and bed clothing, soon setting the entire shore in a blaze. Hundreds of horses broke from their owners and ran into the lake; the wagons which were run into the water for safety, took fire where they stood and burned to the water's edge. Scores of horses perished in the waves, which, even against the wind, leaped upon the shore like mad things of life.

At 9 o'clock on Monday night, thirty-six hours after the breaking out of the conflagration, the varnish factory and the rest took fire, raising a wall of flame between the people and the west. All now gave themselves up for lost. The brands came down by thousands, causing the water to hiss where they fell. The clothes of women caught fire from this fatal shower, and one old woman, named McAvoy, was burned to death before she could be rescued.

The smoke grew more dense every moment and the sense of suffocation was dreadful. Women screamed in utter despair, while the poor children were stricken mute with terror. A number of people were smothered in the bath house. Thousands threw themselves on their faces in the hot sand, while hundreds rushed into the lake up to their necks. The final day could not have brought more terror with its dawn. The great fear was that the north pier itself would go, in which event hundreds, if not thousands, of people must have perished. Fortunately, between the varnish factory and the foot of the pier there lay a broad expanse of sand, and the people on the pier used their hats and a few buckets to extinguish the brands that continued to fall upon the structure. At 11 o'clock that morning the factory was burned out, the pier was saved, and the people began to hope. There was no food and no prospect of any. Five large steamers—Goodrich's— were standing out near the crib in the lake, and a score of schooners were lying to, under bare poles, watching the tableau on shore. Not a sail ventured to approach the sands. The afternoon wore away and the evening shadows were coming to lend a deeper gloom to the smokewreaths when a fleet of tug boats, sent down by the Mayor, came to the relief of the unfortunates. Most of them were taken off and landed, up through the heated river, at Kinzie street bridge, while the others slept that night on the shore, guarding the few household articles that remained to them. The wreck of home comforts lay along that sorrow-laden beach, and some human beings lay there dead. When the sun went down that Monday night, the 10th of Obtober, 1871, he set upon a waste of ruined homes, the lost treasures of grief-wrung hearts, all that remained of world-renowned Chicago.

SAFES
AND
BANK LOCKS,

The terrible ordeal through which these Safes here recently passed, have fully demonstrated their great superiority over all others. Up to this date, October 19th, one hundred and twenty-three have been taken from the ruins, that have preserved their contents in good condition, and in many of them the contents were uninjured.

Such a record and such a test need no comment from us.

We have already contracted for the re-building of our spacious store, at the old stand, Nos. 147 and 149 Dearborn Street, and expect to occupy it by December 15th, with a splendid assortment of

SAFES & VAULT WORK.

In the mean time our Offices and Salesrooms will be at 66 West Madison Street, where we will use every exertion to supply the great demand for our work.

Hall's Safe and Lock Co.,

66 West Madison St., Chicago.

DAYLIGHT SCENES ON THE WEST SIDE.

Standing in a safe spot near the junction of the North and South Branches, the beholder surveyed a waste of ruin and flame extending to the lake in front, and on either hand far beyond what it was possible to see. The conflagration was still raging fiercely, and flames still shot up from various quarters of the wilderness of devastation, over which it had so remorselessly swept. Blowing strongly, the wind bore the breath of miles of fire, and was oppressive with its heat and suffocating with its smoke.

Just as the blood-red sun rose above the horizon, the object of central solicitude was the Lake street bridge; for now the danger of the conflagration crossing to the West Side was confined to that spot. In the presence of a multitude of helpless spectators, strung up to the highest pitch of anxiety, the fire was steadily working from various quarters toward the bridge, near which stood two wholesale drug houses, filled with the most combustible and heat-maintaining materials. The flames seemed literally to melt through walls in their progress. Soon the southeast corner was converted into a maelstrom of fire. Broad jets of blaze burst from doors and windows, extending half way across the street, their scorching power being distinctly felt across the river by the onlooking multitude. Yet, within forty feet of this furnace, the firemen maintained their position with unflagging resolution, and fought back the further spread of the flames. Presently the conflagration enveloped the lofty structure on the northeast corner, and the lines of approach were kept thoroughly wet by a stream poured thereon from a hose on the bridge. These combined efforts proved successful, and the baffled conflagration was happily prevented from resuming its devastating march in the West Division, to the infinite relief of the people. Meantime the sun, a blood-red ball, shorn of his beams, hung in the sky partially obscured by the pall of smoke, and glaring down upon the scene of ruin like the eye of some malignant and exultant fiend.

ALONG THE LAKE SHORE.

The intense heat of the fire in the city had forced the vast multitude collected along Michigan avenue back to the furthest verge of the beach, and southward into Lake Park and even down to Cottage Grove. The day dawn found not fewer than 75,000 people exposed to the wind and mist of the lake, who had been but a few short hours before surrounded by the comforts of home.

It is now impossible to describe the scene presented by these now houseless, homeless, and in many cases penniless people. Hither had been brought the old, the infirm, and the sick, rescued from burning homes. It was indeed a pitiable sight to see the pale, emaciated, and suffering men, women, and children, removed from comfortable couches, and laid out in the open air with perhaps only a blanket or two under them, and only the smoke-hazed sky for a covering above them. The amount of suffering thus entailed upon the helpless sick cannot be estimated.

A SLEEPLESS NIGHT AND HOPELESS DAWN.

All night the fire fiend continued its dread work of devastation. Strangers had been hurried from their quarters in the hotels and compelled to take their chances in the general chaos into which everything was thrown by the untoward calamity to the city.

All night the hurrying throngs had been driven before the fast-traveling flames. Goods taken from burning houses to localities supposed to be safe were soon endangered again, and had to be removed to still more remote sections of the city, or abandoned at last as a prey to the flames. Suddenly, enveloped in dense clouds of suffocating smoke, great crowds rushed into the lake or the river. The number of lives thus lost must have

COGSWELL & CO.,

Late 120 Lake Street,

JOBBING JEWELERS,

ORDERS SOLICITED.

LORD, SMITH & CO.,
Wholesale Druggists.

We shall resume business at once in commodious quarters on Dearborn Park, Fronting on Washington Street, just east of our old Store.

A continuance of the patronage of our friends throughout the west is earnestly solicited.

LORD, SMITH & CO.

been great. Reliable persons state that they saw numbers of people throwing themselves into the lake to escape a more horrible fate by being strangled by the stifling clouds of hot smoke from the raging cauldron of fire on the south side of the river.

If the night had been one of alarms and ceaseless anxiety to scores of thousands, the dawn found them hopeless and despairing. The wind, which had been blowing from the first a breeze that amounted almost to a gale, seemed to gather strength with the coming day, and careered over the doomed city, creating whirlwinds of fire which seemed to clutch every object and reach far out in quest of more food to appease its insatiate fury.

No pen can adequately describe the awful sublimity of the scene. The light from the first buidings which had fallen a prey to the flames had not faded away before the advance columns of fire were two miles away in the North Division, leaving in its track nothing but glowing fires and drifting ashes.

EXTORTION AND PLUNDER AMONG THE RUINS.

No sooner was the extent of the disaster known abroad than the ghouls of the race, who ever haunt scenes of disaster and misfortune, began to gather. Thieves mingled with the great stricken multitude and busily plied their vocation, even in that dire hour of calamity. Villians seized upon the fleeing inhabitants as they came from their blazing homes, and endeavored to take what little remained to them saved from the general wreck. Hackmen and express drivers and carmen seemed to have lost all conscience, and charged fabulous sums for conveying a load from the scene of destruction to a safe distance. Men who had large sums of money, endeavoring to convey it away to places of safety, were beset by thieves, even in the street, in the garish light of their consuming houses, and robbed of their remaining all.

One instance is known of a hackman exacting from a distracted husband $250 to convey his invalid wife from his burning home to a place of safety. Twenty-five dollars was regarded as a very moderate charge for an express wagon to take a load ten squares, and $50 and $100 were frequently demanded and paid for the use of a wagon and team of two horses for half an hour.

When the fire was raging along La Salle, Clark, and State streets, and sweeping onward towards Washington and Randolph, towards the north, the great commercial houses were thrown open and an attempt made to save the most valuable goods. The harvest of the thieves began at this time. The police had lost control. Those intent on profiting by the fire now went in with great zest. They loaded themselves with the richest goods, and sought a place of concealment.

THE CONFLAGRATION STAYED.

It is proper to narrate how the flames were stayed in their progress southward. At the corner of Clark and Harrison streets the Jones School was burned. A wooden primary on the same lot escaped destruction. Why it escaped would be curious to know. The flames, as if weary of the awful race they had run, did not cross the street. At the corner of Fourth avenue and Harrison street the Jewish Synagogue burned fiercely, but the Otis block of brick buildings on the northeast corner of the street did not burn. At the corner of Third avenue and Harrison, men with chains pulled down a wooden residence, which, though it was consumed, did not burn fiercely. At the corner of State and Harrison, O'Neil's brick block was blown up by powder, and prevented the further spread in that direction. At the corner of Harrison and Wabash the Methodist Church stood as if defying the flames, and as though it uttered with the voice of authority, "Thus far shalt thou go, and no farther." The flames did not cross Wabash avenue

SHANDREW & DEAN,

STATE AGENTS,

NORTHWESTERN

MUTUAL

LIFE INSURANCE COMPANY.

OFFICE.

19 South Green Street, Chicago.

Weed Sewing Machine,

196 WEST MADISON ST.

Are now prepared to fill Orders as formerly, from their new Office, as above.

GIVE US A CALL.

We Guarantee Satisfaction in every Case.

WEED SEWING MACHINE,

196 West Madison St.

was saved, the Michigan Avenue Hotel standing upon the corner like the huge battlement of a fortress that had withstood a siege. By noon the fire had ceased in its progress southward, and, except by uncertain rumor (and during all the fire many-tongued rumor spread its baleful tales more rapidly than ran the wild fire), no one south of Harrison street knew the desolation which reigned in the North Division. Nor was it known that the city's situation had excited the active sympathy of its neighbors, and that steam engines had upon the wings of steam flown to our rescue.

The lake front was filled with household goods piled in the utmost confusion. Weary watchers stood guard about their little all, and hundreds of people homeless and without property of any kind were lying about exhausted. The last was a grievous annoyance, but the roar of the fire was a positive terror which drove minor considerations from the mind. From the lake front the destruction of the palatial block of residences known as Terrace Row was watched with intense interest. Its burning, although occurring in the day time, when the spectacular effect of fire is greatly lost, was one of the remarkable scenes of the great tragedy. If it alone had burned, all the rhetoric at the command of the writers on the press would have been used in its description.
south of Congress street, one block north of Harrison, and the south side of Congress

LOSS OF LIFE.

When the flames were raging and block upon block of solid stone melted into nothingness, it was feared that the destruction of life would be something unparalleled. It was well known that many people roomed in the lofty buildings in the business portion of the city, and that some kept house there, but the greater number by far were single men and abandoned women, who hired sleeping rooms, and lived a wandering life, obtained food here to-day and there to-morrow. This class was in imminent danger of being caught near the roof of the lofty structures to which they usually betook themselves, and, even if awake and active, of being suffocated by the smoke ere they could find their way to the pavement. How many such fell victims to the flame is not known now, and never can be. Fire that melted granite would leave nothing of human bone and muscle, and the spirits of those who perished in the awful conflagration passed to the land of the hereafter amid no cries save their own, and their bodies perished from off the face of the earth. As soon as the ruins were in a condition to be visited, bodies of the dead were looked for with horrible interest. A superficial examination brought to view in various parts of the city the charred and, for the most part, unrecognizable remains of ninety persons. A morgue was erected on Milwaukee avenue, whither the bodies were borne. Here they were viewed by thousands, many drawn to the hideous spectacle through morbid curiosity, others because they feared to find the remains of friend or relative, who in the fearful confusion were separated from them. The Coroner held an inquest upon the bodies, and they were soon consigned to their last resting place. The whole number of deaths, on the lowest estimate made by competent authority, is 200. The yet unreported missing, together with the known dead, make an aggregate of one thousand persons.

UPRISING OF THE CONTINENT.

It is now a positive certainty that Chicago is to be rebuilt, and the indications are that the city will rise from its present ruins greater than ever before. This conclusion was arrived at immediately after the great catastrophe, and the secret of it all is exactly here: Chicago saw that the world at large had the fullest confidence in her ability to reconstruct herself; that the country would be greatly disappointed if the representative city of the energy of the age lagged in the slightest degree in the fulfillment of her manifest

HAYES, GIBBONS & CO.,

Late at 105 & 107 State Street, now at

No. 434 State Street,

IMPORTERS, MANUFACTURERS AND JOBBERS

MILLINERY, STRAW GOODS,

FRENCH FLOWERS, FEATHERS & LACES.

Orders solicited and Promptly Executed.

HODGE & HOMER,

Wholesale and Retail Dealers in

BUILDERS' HARDWARE,

MECHANICS' TOOLS AND AGRICULTURAL IMPLEMENTS.

We are one of the few firms left by the fire and we have a complete stock of BUILDERS' HARDWARE, CUTLERY, MECHANICS' TOOLS, SHOVELS, SPADES, PICKS, Etc., Etc.; also, a good stock of REVOLVERS and AMMUNITION, at Wholesale and Retail, all of which will be sold at the lowest market price. Give us a lift.

duty; and that the world was willing to assist Chicago in her endeavors. It was this which inspired our city to a grander effort than she had ever made before. When she saw the contributions from Europe and the whole of America pouring in so bountifully, she could not help showing herself worthy of them.

Chicago could not feed the fugitives from the fire without impoverishing the citizens who still retained a portion of their possessions; and so the people of America sent in supplies without limit, and 100,000 refugees were plentifully supplied with the necessaries of life. Chicago could not afford house room for so many wanderers; and, therefore, car-loads of building material and thousands of greenbacks came in, with which barracks were erected for the accommodation of the sufferers. No detail was omitted in this work of benevolence. A cargo of nails came from Springfield, and lumber came from the North, where other devastating fires bade fair to destroy the source of supply of this same material.

When the people of Chicago saw the stupendous quantities of provisions, of blankets, of lumber, of everything that could be of use in the present emergency, they could not but take heart, and, while earnestly thanking these friends in need, resolved that their bounty should not be wasted, nor their confidence betrayed. Therefore, we see brick walls already going up on the burned district, although it is the last of October, and likely to be an inclement building season; therefore we see business firms and banks resuming—or rather continuing—on every hand. This most generous aid from abroad has produced an air of cheerfulness among all classes of citizens, and has done wonders in the restoration of public confidence.

It is impossible to give statistics of the aid that has been rendered. In the first place no written record has been kept of the arrivals and in the second, the contributions have not by any means ceased, and the sum totals of supplies sent in to date would not even approximate to the real amount transmitted. We can only state that the quantity sent in has been stupendous. The quarters from which munificence was least expected have been most munificent. St. Louis and Cincinnati, whom we have maligned for twenty years have sent in their offerings by millions. New York, whose interest we were beginning to combat, and a portion of whose commerce we were just striving to obtain, has sent us $2,000,000. The lists of subscribers to the relief fund in the metropolis, as published in the journals of that city, are most interesting. "A widow and her two boys" give $10 each—a mite which, perhaps, shall provide shelter for another widow and her children. Robert Bonner, who remembers when he was without a dollar, and in, possession only of the meagre clothing upon his person, gives $10,000 for impoverished printers and journalists in Chicago, who have been placed in a similar situation by the fire. It is useless enumerating instances of this spontaneous generosity in the metropolis, for it would require many volumes to record them.

The city of Cleveland, 400 miles from Chicago, sent us twenty-three car-loads of supplies within twenty-four hours after the reception of the news of the disaster in that city. One car-load was on its way to this city from Cleveland before a single hour had elapsed after the first telegram had been received. Milwaukee sent the first car-load, Cleveland the next. Milwaukee suffered by the fire largely by way of the destruction of commercial interests, and was still more directly injured by conflagrations at her very door. Milwaukee depends very largely for support upon the lumber regions of Northern Wisconsin, and the loss of these immense pine districts was necessarily the loss of Milwaukee. Besides, thousands of people in Northern Wisconsin were driven from their homes into a bleak wilderness by these same devastating conflagrations, and Milwaukee,

C. C. COLLINS

BOY'S
CLOTHING

792 Wabash Avenue,

Burned out at 74 Randolph St.

COBB, ANDREWS & CO.

WHOLESALE AND RETAIL

BOOKSELERS and STATIONERS

469 Wabash Avenue,

Blank Books, Diamond Paper, Envelopes, Pencils, Pens, Arnold's Inks, Copying Books, Copying Presses, Drawing Paper, And Office Stationery of all kinds.

COBB, ANDREWS & CO.,
No. 469 Wabash Avenue.

MAYHON, DALY & CO.,

IMPORTERS OF

MILLINERY,

AND

Fancy Dry Goods,

Michigan Av. near Monroe,

———————

Orders filled on day of receipt, at our usual Low Prices.

he metropolis of the State, was called upon to provide them shelter and food. This she
did without stint, and had enough left to feed the suffering of Chicago, her old and successful commercial rival.

Old feuds and differences were everywhere forgotten in this work. St. Louis was scarcely exceeded in the amount sent by New York herself. Cincinnati held mass meetings and sent relief without limit. Many were the instances where towns in the country sent aid out of all proportion to their size and resources. In one case, such a number of immense boxes of bread, crackers, blankets, etc., came from a small city in Ohio that the clerks who had been receiving goods of this kind all day, were astounded, and, knowing nothing better to do, sent a message by telegraph thanking the citizens of the town in question for their marvelous generosity, on behalf of the citizens of Chicago. Every town, and every agricultural community, throughout the length and breadth of the country, sent food without stint, and, what was needed sorely, timber to shelter the houseless and blankets to cover them.

Detroit, Milwaukee, Indianapolis, Lafayette, Peoria and other cities generously sent fire engines, which were our sorest need during the day immediately succeeding the great disaster.

Nor was generosity limited to our own country. There was a spontaneous uprising of the whole world to help us. England, never behind in a work of genuine charity, sent us money to the extent of hundreds of thousands of pounds sterling. Within a day after the reception of the news in Great Britain, a cargo of food was on its way from Liverpool to Chicago. Public meetings were held in all parts of the three kingdoms, at which there was little speech-making and much aid-giving. The merchants of London gave liberally of their opulence. They knew that London was long ago visited by a precisely similar calamity, and they also knew that very little aid had been rendered from any quarter on that occasion. London was rebuilt in spite of the cold world, but Chicago must not have that obstacle to her recovery. Dublin sent us more than £15,000 sterling. The continent of Europe was not behind. Germany in particular gave largely by way of subscriptions, and the mercantile organizations in her leading cities sent lists scarcely exceeded by those of our brothers in England.

The Springfield (Mass.) Republican tells of a contribution which, weighed in the philosopher's scales, is the largest sum yet given to the Chicago relief fund. A little Irish boy in that city had no money, but he possessed a toy whip, the pride of his heart, dear as the apple of his eye, and this he sold for ten cents, and cast his mite into the treasury of charity. Was Stewart's $50,000, or Bonner's $10,000, dearer to its owner than this poor boy's one possession?

But our poverty-stricken language falls far short of its task when it attempts an intelligent account of this uprising of a world. Language, with a stretch of its tension to utmost limit, can describe the appalling scenes of that evnetful Sunday night; it can how palaces fell before the mighty hurricane of fire, and how great marble columns ished in the midst of that furnace heat; but it is incompetent to deal with so vast a subject as the spontaneous union of the whole world in deeds of charity to the suffering inhabitants of a single city. It is true that no record of this munificence has been kept upon paper, and that history will never be able to tell how much was given; but the story of this great charity is recorded in the hearts of our citizens and in heaven. Not a loaf of bread nor a single cracker has failed of its purpose; and if the gratitude of our citizens is not expressed it is because it is inexpressible.

The distribution of these copious supplies has been an easy matter. The Mayor turned it over soon after the disaster to the Relief and Aid Society, and that organization, by

MATHEWS & MASON,

(LATE BROWN & MATHEWS,)

TAILORS

FORMERLY 93 WABASH AVENUE,

Now Located 659 Wabash Ave

☞ Stock complete—Business continued as formerly.

BROWN & PRIOR.

GENTS FURNISHING GOODS,

MANUFACTURERS OF THE

CELEBRATED SAM BROWN SHIRT,

LATE 93 WABASH AVENUE,

NOW LOCATED AT 659 WABASH AVE.

Clifton House,

REMOVED TO N. W.

Cor. of Washington and Halsted Streets.

☞ FIRST CLASS IN EVERY RESPECT

W. A. JENKINS, Prop'r.

H. F. KITTREDGE, Clerk.

parceling the work out to able and willing gentlemen, has easily solved the problem of distribution. The different receiving depots have witnessed busy scenes for the past week, and the pouring in of supplies has been watched with delight by those who have the matter in charge, as well as by the thousands in need of sustenance. The arrangements of the Relief and Aid Society have been so perfect that probably very few articles have been misappropriated, and it is certainly better that many who do not deserve aid should receive it than that a single hungry person should suffer. The churches, at which the bulk of the fugitive population is fed, make requisitions on the distributing depots for the amounts needed, and all the hungry are supplied. The scenes at the churches to-day, which are all to-day fulfilling only a part of their legitimate duty, are often interesting. The paupers are fed at rough board tables by the young ladies of the different church societies, and so universal is the desire among the charitable women of the city to serve in this capacity that many applications are daily rejected by the committees having the distribution in charge. The poor found comfortable quarters and abundant food in the churches, and, thanks to the kindness of our friends abroad, begin to think there might be worse happenings than burnings. Temporary barracks have been erected on several squares on the West Side—those on the square bounded by Madison, Ada, Washington, and Elizabeth streets being able to accommodate several thousand people.

This, then, is what Europe and America have done for us: One hundred thousand people, who were homeless, shelterless, and without a morsel of food on the 9th of October, have found themselves, on the 14th, with comfortable quarters in which to live, warm clothing, abundance to eat, and no prospect of suffering during the coming winter. When this is made known nothing more can or need be said. It is a marvel which will forever stand out upon the page of history, the feature of paramount interest in the great Chicago disaster of 1871.

REMARKABLE SCENES AND INCIDENTS.

A PERILOUS EXODUS.

Perhaps the most fearfully thrilling scene of the great conflagration was that in the eastern section of the North Division. When it became apparent that all hope of saving the city was lost, after the flames had pushed down to the main branch of the river, the citizens of the North Side, who were over to see the principal theater of the fire, thought it time to go into their own division, and save what they could. Accordingly, they beat a rapid retreat toward the tunnel and bridges. The former of these thoroughfares were impassable at 3 o'clock. Clark street had not been open for some time, and State street was in a blaze from one end to the other. Rush street bridge was now the only means of getting away from the South Side, and over that bridge the affrighted fugitives poured in thousands. The latter jumped the river with miraculous swiftness, and ran along the northern section, from Dearborn street to the North Branch, like lightning. So rapid was the advance of the fiery element, driven by the heavy gale from the southeast, that the people were glad enough to escape unscathed. Everything was abandoned. Horses and wagons were merely as a means of flight. Few people in the direct course of the fire thought about saving anything but their lives and those of their families.

HOME SHUTTLE
SEWING MACHINE.

This unequalled Machine uses a straight needle, makes the Lock Stitch (alike on both sides,) has a self-adjusting Tension, works equally well on Silk, Linen, Woolen and Cotton Goods; with Silk, Linen and Cotton Thread.

In Simplicity, Strength and beauty it is unapproachable; a successful combination of UTILITY, and ECONOMY, and it is the only Practical, Low-priced Lock stitch SEWING MACHINE ever invented,

Do not pay enormous prices when you can buy of us at the following rates, MACHINES WARRANTED to work as well as any in the market:

PRICE LIST:

Plain Machine	$37.00
Half Cabinet	42.00
Full "	75.00
Silver Plated, extra	10.00

We have a full line of Attachments.

We invite every one to call and make a personal examination of the merits of the HOME SHUTTLE.

JOHNSON, CLARK & CO.,
General Agents,
242 WEST MADISON STREET.

LIBERAL TERMS TO AGENTS.

HEMMED IN.

The conflagration having reached Chicago avenue, took an eastward turn, and cut off from flight, northward, all who remained in the unburned section, lying between Dearborn street and the lake. The inhabitants of that district flattered themselves that their homes might escape the general destruction. But the fire was not to be cheated in that way. The gale changed its course in a few minutes more toward the east, and the entire quarter of the city specified became a frightful pen, having a wall of fire on three sides, and the fierce, rolling lake on the fourth. Then followed a scene which surpassed anything that ever took place on this continent. The houses were abandoned in all haste. Wagons were loaded with furniture, clothing and bedding. Mothers caught up their infants in their arms. Men dragged along the aged and helpless, and the entire horror-stricken multitude bent their course to the "Sands."

DESTRUCTION OF THE TRIBUNE BUILDING.

One block in all the vast business section remained at daylight, the Tribune block. The Custom House and Honore block, in Dearborn street, had burned, and those who had fought the flames here thought, at last, this block could be saved. A patrol of men under Sam Medill swept off the live coals and but out flames on the sidewalks, and another lot of men, under the direction of Hon. Joseph Medill, watched the roofs. At half-past seven o'clock this appeared safe, and most of the men went to get a rest or food. A number went to sleep in the Tribune building, but there was a change of wind. The flames reached Wabash avenue, State street and Michigan avenue, and soon McVicker's Theater caught fire. In a few moments the Tribune was in flames, and at the last moment the sleeping men were aroused and rescued from the flames. By ten o'clock in the forenoon this remaining block was in ashes. Now was to be seen the most remarkable sight ever beheld in this or any country.

SUFFERING HUMANITY.

There were from 50,000 to 75,000 men, women and children fleeing by every available street and alley to the southward and westward, attempting to save their clothing and their lives. Every available vehicle was brought into requisition for use, for which enormous prices were paid, and the streets and sidewalks presented the sight of thousands of persons and horses inextricably commingled; poor people, all color and shades, and every nationality, from Europe, China and Africa, mad with excitement, struggled with each other to get away. Hundreds were trampled under foot; men and woman were loaded with bundles and their household goods, to whose skirts were clinging tender infants, half dressed and barefooted all seeking a place of safety. Hours afterwards these might be seen in vacant lots or on the streets, far out in the suburbs, stretched in the dust.

PITIFUL SIGHTS.

One of the most pitiful sights was that of a middle aged woman on State street, loaded with bundles, struggling through the crowd, singing the Mother Goose melodies, "Chickery, Chickery, Craney Crow," "I went to the well to wash my toe," &c. There were hundreds of others likewise distracted, and many rendered delirious by whiskey or beer, which, from excess of thirst in the absence of water, they drank in great quantities, and spread themselves in every direction a terror to all they met.

A FEARFUL ALTERNATIVE.

At one time, after the fire had been raging in the centre of the city, and while the fire was raging on the south side of the river a considerable number of persons were cut off

AIKEN, LAMBERT & CO.,

Formerly 34 Dearborn Street.

Fire compels us to temporarily locate at

88 W. Washington St.

Manufacturers of and Wholesale Dealers in the Celebrated

AIKEN, LAMBERT & CO.'S

GOLD PEN,

FINE JEWELRY,

GOLD AND SILVER PEN AND PENCIL CASES,

TOOTH PICKS, &c.

Our New York House gives us facilities for filling all orders in our line on short notice, and we hope to be favored.

LET THE WEST REMEMBER CHICAGO SUFFERERS.

AIKEN, LAMBERT & CO.,

88 West Washington Street.

from crossing and could not retreat on account of the flames. The water or the fire was the alternative presented. Not long did they hesitate, and the whole party were soon struggling in the river. It is not known if all safely reached the shore; but one brave fellow seized a little girl, plunged in and safely crossed with his precious burden.

ONE POOR MAN

crawled for refuge into a water main lying in the street near the water works, but the fire fiend found him even there before he could get his body wholly in safety, and robbed him of his life.

FRUSTRATED RUFFIANS.

A banker had a cash-box in his hand, containing $50,000, which he was endeavoring to convey away. Three desperadoes seized upon him with the intention of robbing him. To prevent it he threw the box with its valuable contents into the fire, rather than yield it to these ghouls of disastrous fate.

FILIAL PIETY.

A man residing on one of the small streets running from North State street to the lake, had lost his father on Saturday. The coffin was in the house, and so rapid was the progress of the flames on Monday morning that he was unable to save anything else, and to repeated the story of Anchises, pious Æneas and blazing Troy. He carried out the coffin on his shoulders, and, safety on shore being impossible, anchored it in the lake with a rope and stone.

ANOTHER COFFIN STORY.

Early on Monday morning a strange procession was seen coming over Lake street bridge. An undertaker's establishment being in peril, the proprietor (sure of a market for his wares) seized the largest and costliest of his caskets, loaded two express wagons therewith, then grasped one himself in both arms, and followed the carriages, succeeded in turn by about a dozen employes of all ages, each of whom wrestled with a coffin. The procession, ghastly and ludicrous withal, reminded one of the inmates of the city grave-yard compelled to take up their coffins and walk out of the way of the march of modern improvement.

MEANING WELL.

An old man from Iowa no sooner heard of the conflagration than he took instant passage for the city to succor his son's family. It was his first visit to Chicago, and it is to be presumed he was ignorant of our geographical position. Still he meant well, so well, indeed, that on being informed at a way station that the people were suffering from a scarcity of water, he alighted from the train, purchased a cask, filled it with water, and brought it to the city in triumph. It did not transpire, but is likely to have been the case, that a philanthropic expressman charged him $100 to convey it from the railroad station.

GUTTERS OF LIQUOR.

At the distilleries near Madison street bridge, where the stronger liquors were unfitted for such a purpose, the spectators could see, for it seemed for hours, a steady stream of alcohol, from stills, vats, and casks, pouring into the river. On the North Side the streets in some places literally ran with beer and spirits. Men bailed the tide up with their hats, and scooped it up in the palms of their hands to drink. In some places the fire communicated with these streams and ignited them for hundreds of feet with the rapidity of trains of gunpowder. Stories were rife of men drunken to excess falling

BOSTON SQUARE DEALING

ONE PRICE

Clothing House,

Burned at 147 and 149 S. Clark St.

NOW LOCATED

WEST BRANCH,

Thompson's Block,

229 Madison St. cor Peoria.

SOUTH BRANCH,

22nd. St. near State St.

SQUARE DEALING FOREVER.

Terms offered by no concern in the world, viz:

All Goods can be returned (if not Soiled) and the Money Refunded good naturedly.

THAT IS WHAT WE MEAN BY SQUARE DEALING.

into these streams of liquid fire and being roasted to death. At the fancy grocery stores heaps of canisters of potted meats, oysters, fruits, etc., were to be seen lying in the ruins, burst open at the ends by the action of the fire or the air within. Hundreds of people made a luscious feast on Tuesday upon these, and on the site of Stanton's store, corner of Clark and Madison streets, almost every person carried a canister out of which he picked roasted oysters or cooked tomatoes, with a fork improvised from a stick or a piece of telegraph wire.

FIRE AND MARRIAGE.

On Monday a high city official was accosted in the street by a clergyman, followed by a youth and maiden, who all asked him at once, in the name of Heaven, if they couldn't get a marriage license. The young couple desired, it seemed, to espouse each other, and when the swain reached the Court-House he found that the office of the County Clerk was not there. He rushed madly about, asking the policemen, the firemen, everybody, if they could tell him where he could get a marriage license. No one knew and no one seemed interested. In tears he returned to the would-be bride, and they, with the clergyman, went down town to see what could be done. The city official, moved by their tears and protestations, told them that he was very sorry, but—"Oh, good Mr. City Official," said the bride, can't you give us a permit, or a pass, or anything?" The city official, being in a hurry, and being, further, noted for his obliging disposition, told them that he hadn't any passes with him at the time. "But," said he, kindly, "just go ahead, and I'll make that all right." He hadn't any power to issue a license, but that made no difference; everybody was satisfied, the clergyman (who is connected with a West Side church of prominence) married them, and the happy couple went to see the ruins of Lill's brewery, next day, as a wedding trip. It is a question in that remorseful city official's mind as to whether he has not been guilty of malfeasance of office, at the very least.

A NARROW ESCAPE.

Mrs. A. J. Crnswold, the wife of the well-known organist, was compelled to flee from her house on Ohio street, and was so hotly pursued by the flames that she was compelled to take refuge in the lake, with her children, one about three years old and the other an infant. Numerous other cases of people seeking refuge in the lake or the river are recorded, and others are known to have fled to the sand-hills nearer Lincoln Park, and there, throwing themselves flat on their faces, to have remained until the fiery sirocco went by, leaving them almost suffocated and with the clothing on their backs burned to cinders.

MR. MILLIGAN'S TROTTER.

Peoria sent a steam fire engine to the relief of Chicago, and in one of the narrow streets it was so nearly surrounded by the flames that the men had given up hope of saving it, and were about being forced to seek their own safety in flight. At this juncture, Mr. Milligan, of the firm of Heath & Milligan, came along with his roadster. Perceiving their peril, in a moment he had hitched the fast trotter to one side of the pole. The men caught the tongue, pole and wheel, and with a cheery shout, out they whirled through the smoke and cinders at a four-minute gait. The Peorians saved their steamer, and vow that they will get up a subscription and purchase Milligan's sorrel if the city has to issue more bonds.

A SEA OF FIRE.

The basins at one time were literally seas of fire. Some large furniture dealers had thrown large quantities of furniture into the water, hoping to save their goods. Streams

JEWELRY

Wholesale and Retail.

A. B. VAN COTT & CO.,

Late 107 Lake Street, have opened at

461 Wabash Avenue,

And are now receiving new goods from the East. The greater portion of our stock being destroyed; we will, soon have a fresh stock of desirable goods.

Orders from the trade will receive as heretofore prompt attention.

A. B. VAN COTT, & CO.,
461 WABASH AVENUE.

EDWARD ELY

657 WABASH AVENUE,

Draper and Tailor,

AND MANUFACTURER OF

SHIRTS,

(*Extra Durable and Perfect in Fit.*)

Wedding Outfits a Specialty.

ESTABLISHED IN CHICAGO IN 1854.

Clergymen 10 Per Cent. off.

of petroleum and of liquor had in other places trickled from the docks. The intense heat of the fire had set fire to these lighter liquids as they floated on the water, and the newly-varnished furniture, almost as inflamable, burned rapidly. As each piece rose and sunk in the slowly swaying water, the swelling or decadence of the flames and their crackle or hiss afforded a strange picture to the eye and odd music to the ear.

THE COMING MAN

Early on Monday afternoon, a reporter for the Evening Post met an elderly man on Wabash avenue, in an excited and lachrymose humor. He was shouting at the top of his voice; "I know there is! I know there is!" "I know there is what?" asked the reporter. "A man who could stop this fire if he wanted to by just saying one word. Oh, where is he? Why doesn't he speak? Oh, where, where is he?" The reporter vainly endeavored to ascertain the mysterious individual's name, but the excited individual did not know it, and went along on his quest, bellowing tearfully, "Where is he? Oh, where is he?"

WHAT THEY SAVED.

It was almost as ridiculous as melancholy to watch the long stream of people who poured out of the tenements on Adams street, Van Buren street and the alleys near the river, both on the West and South Sides, and to notice what each bore. On Adams street the perambulators outnumbered every other article saved. About every third person wheeled one, and about every seventh perambulator contained a baby. One man in his shirt sleeve, and with but one boot, wheeled a child's carriage, in which was a baby, perhaps eighteen months old, astonished at its sudden awakening and the crowd, and sucking lustily at a green paper lamp-shade. These, alone, evidently remained of all his Lares and Penates. Another, perfectly frenzied with excitement, rushed along Harrison street, waving over his head the handle of a bronzed earthernware pitcher, and shouting at the top of his voice. The woman, with hardly an exception, carried a bundle in one arm and a baby in the other, and had their shawls thrown over their heads. Perhaps a couple of older children clung, frightened and crying, to their skirts. When the hotels were menaced, out poured from each a long string of guests, each with a valise in one hand and dragging behind him a trunk. The fate of these amateur baggage-smashers is wrapped in mystery, as hardly a traveling trunk was anywhere to be seen on Tuesday.

A NEW USE FOR CIDER.

One building on the West Side, which was saved after desperate exertions, owes its preservation to an agent rarely, if ever, used before for such a purpose, and which in efficacy was a formidable rival to the Babcock. The roof was covered with wetted blankets, and when water for this purpose failed, two barrels of cider were employed with success. The flames retired, and the proprietor on the roof carroled a joyous paean. "A little more cider, too,"

BURIED THE HATCHET.

The fire has wrought many changes among business men—some separated, and others brought together. Among the latter we may mention Wm. Eden and A. M. Delight, between whom for many years there has existed a deep feeling of business rivalry. The former manufactured the well-known "Exoral," for the hair, and the latter the equally well-known "Spanish Lustral." The storm of fire found them both unprepared for such an emergency, and swept their magnificent establishments out of existence. But before the embers were cold they had shook hands, joined fortunes, bought the lease of a store

WALSH & HUTCHINSON,

WHOLESALE

MILLINERY,

616 WABASH AVENUE.

Being among the first to rise from the ruins, we beg to announce we are again in the field with a full stock of

Ribbons, Silks, Velvets, Laces, Flowers, Feathers, Straw Goods, &c.,

To which we invite the attention of the Trade.

N. SHERWOOD & CO.,

WHOLESALE

TEAS,

No. 812 STATE STREET,

Formerly 58 Michigan Avenue.

We are glad to inform the public that we are again prepared to supply our patrons with goods at as close figures as ever. Notwithstanding the entire loss of our heavy Stock in store, the interruption of business was slight, as we had a large stock of our own importation still remaining in Bonded Warehouse, and heavy invoices in transit, giving us a complete stock with which to continue business.

We would say to those wishing to buy goods from this city, that their wants can be supplied without looking further, as Chicago Merchants are determined to hold all their old trade, if careful buying and selling at close figures will do it.

Our buyer is now in China and Japan markets, and will forward us new Teas by every steamer. Greater effort, if possible, than ever, will be made to make it for the interest of the trade to deal with us.

N. SHERWOOD & CO.

on Canal street, just north of Randolph, in the heart of the new business center, and are now in full blast, with more business than they can do. Their old friends are invited to call.

MONUMENTS OF MERCY.

The most remarkable feature of what is left in the districts of the great fire are the buildings that escaped destruction. A new five-story stone building, which was all completed except putting in the windows, on the corner of La Salle and Monroe streets, is a marvel. Its exterior is perfect and its interior not even smoked, notwithstanding the fact that the terrible flames raged around it on all sides. Its preservation is truly a mystery. Equally wonderful was the preservation of the extensive glass-covered greenhouse and conservatory of Mr. E. B. McCagg, on the North Side. Notwithstanding the total destruction of all the buildings on all sides of this little oasis in the great desert of ruin, there it smiles before the observer in all its wonderful loveliness—not even a crack in all its oval glass-covered roof—the prints and flowers inside as fresh and beautiful "as if nothing had happened." Yet Mr. McCagg's fine brick residence, only a few feet from it, is a mass of ruins. Two blocks distant stands the large house of Mahlon D. Ogden, a wooden building, which, notwithstanding the total destruction of all the large churches and other fine edifices around, it stands there isolated and unharmed—even the wooden outhouses unscorched, and the grass fresh. These and Elevator B, of the Illinois Central Railroad Company, are the only really remarkable escapes of the great conflagration; and it is very difficult for any man to explain satisfactorily how and why they were spared. "There are more wonders in heaven and earth than are dreamed of in our philosophy."

THRILLING INCIDENT IN THE WASHINGTON STREET TUNNEL.

While the conflagration was raging in the South Division, on that memorable Sunday night, a thrilling incident occurred in the Washington street tunnel, which, we believe, has not yet been mentioned publicly. Several of the bridges over the South Branch being on fire, the tunnel was resorted to by thousands of people who desired to pass from one division into the other. Those going into the South Division were mostly persons who had offices and places of business "down town." Those going the other way were terrified residents of the South Side, rushing into the West Division for safety. At a moment when the passage-way was filled with pedestrians, rushing wildly in either direction, the gas suddenly gave out, and all were left in total darkness. A terrible panic, a collision, and the trampling to death of the weaker by the stronger, seemed inevitable. But, strange as it may seem, everybody in that dark recess seemed at once to comprehend the necessity for coolness and courage. Not a man lost his presence of mind, but all, as with one accord, bore to the right, each calmly enjoining upon others to be cool and steady, and to march steadily on till the end of the light could be reached. Rapidly, but without confusion, the two columns moved on through the thick darkness with almost military precision, the silence being broken only by frequent shouts of "right," "right." There was no collision, and no one was harmed, but all reached the ends of the tunnel in safety, and then for the first time in almost ten minutes breathed freely.

The incident was one of the most thrilling imaginable, and will never be forgotten by those who participated in it. Had there been any considerable number of women and children in the crowd, the result might have been horrible, and to many lives, fatal; and even with none but men in the tunnel, it seemed almost miraculous that all should keep their presence of mind.

The Finkle & Lyon Manufacturing Co.'s
'VICTOR'
Sewing Machine

The "VICTOR" is the simplest, most durable and complete Family Sewing Machine now in use, and is in every respect reliable and *first class*, contains all the latest improvements and inventions, doing every variety of Family Sewing without the complications of springs, cog wheels, or delicate and troublesome adjustments.

The "VICTOR" is the only lock-stitch machine that has a straight "self-setting" needle, which cannot be set wrong.

The "VICTOR" has the simplest and most easily-threaded Shuttle, which is moved by a Shuttle-carrier that prevents soiling thread and wearing the shuttle.

The "VICTOR" has a positive Tension and Thread-Controller, enabling it to pass from heaviest to lightest materials, or to cross seams, without change of tension.

The "VICTOR" is so constructed that all wear is taken up by adjusting screws, permitting it to run much longer without repair than any other shuttle machine.

The "VICTOR" Sewing Machine has taken First Premiums at numerous State and County Fairs.

The "Great Northwestern Exposition" at Minneapolis, in Minnesota State Fairs in 1869, 1870 and 1871, awarded to the Finkle & Lyon Manufacturing Co., Highest Premiums and Silver Medal for Best Family Sewing Machine.

Wherever introduced, the "VICTOR" has met with universal favor, and has far exceeded the most sanguine expectations of its friends and patrons, its sales more than doubling in the last year.

Each Machine is sent out complete (without extra charge) with Drop Feed, new style Hemmer and Feller, Quilter, Braider, extra Needle Plate, Screw Driver, Oiler, Bottle of Oil, 12 assorted Needles, 6 Bobbins, Gauge and Screw, Wrench and Instruction Book.

Price List "VICTOR" Sewing Machines.

Plain Table, Oil Finish,	$65 00
Box Cover	70 00
" " with Extension Leaf and Castors	75 00
" " with Chest, four Drawers	80 00
" " with Chest, four Drawers and Extension Leaf	85 00
Folding Cover, moulded base	85 00
Cabinets	100 00 to 150 00
Pearl and Half Pearl Machines, additional	10 00 & 15 00

RELIABLE AGENTS WANTED.

THOMAS BARROWS & CO.,
GENERAL WESTERN AGENTS,
No. 73 South Halsted Street, Chicago.
Before the Fire 101 Washington Street.

W. L. BATES & CO., Agents for Michigan.
J. L. BARROWS & CO., Agents for Iowa.

THE BRUTE CREATION CRAZED

The horses, maddened by heat and noise, and irritated by falling sparks, neighed and screamed with affright and anger, and reared, and kicked, and bit each other, or stood with drooping tails, and rigid legs, ears laid back, and eyes wild with amazement, shivering as if with cold. The dogs ran wildly hither and thither, snuffing eagerly at every one, and occasionally sitting down on their haunches to howl dismally. When there was a lull in the fire, far-away dogs could be heard barking, and cocks crowing at the unwonted light. Cats ran along ridge-poles in the bright glare, and came pattering into the street with dropsical tails. Great brown rats, with bead-like eyes, were ferreted out from under the sidewalks by the flames, and scurried hither and thither along the streets, kicked at, trampled upon, hunted down. Flocks of beautiful pigeons, so plentiful in the city, wheeled into the air aimlessly, circled blindly once or twice, and were drawn into the maw of the fiery hell raging beneath. At one bird-fancier's store on Madison street, near La Salle, the wails of the scorched birds as the fire caught them were piteous as those of children.

A THRILLING INCIDENT AND A NARROW ESCAPE.

When the fire crossed from the South to the North Side, at Wells street, and the Galena depot and buildings in its vicinity were on fire, some seven or eight men were on the roof of Wheeler's elevator, on which a shower of cinders, and burning shingles, and patches of flaming felt roofing from other buildings was thickly falling. Lookers-on felt and knew that the efforts to save the building were useless. Still the men persisted in their endeavors to the last. All at once the roof was in flames in several places. All but four of the men made their escape down through the interior of the building, but these four were in such a locality that their retreat was cut off. One portion of the roof after another falls in, the men are huddled together on the northwest corner of the brick wall, sixty feet from the ground, and the whole interior of the structure is a roaring gulf of flame. No hook and ladder company or fire engine has yet arrived on the North Side, and only two or three men, their escaped comrades, are at the foot of the wall. No other human aid is near them, although Lake street bridge and its viaduct, across the river, are covered with thousands of spectators, thrilled with a hopeless horror. And now the lives of these four men depend, not upon minutes, but upon seconds. Their comrades below make vain efforts to cast up to them a stout rope. Then one of the men runs away and soon returns with a small line, to which a piece of brick is attached and thrown over the wall, and the men eagerly draw up the rope. An agony of suspense, silent, breathless, intense, pervades the multitude of people at the bridge, for, ever and anon, with the puffs and blasts of wind, huge sheets of flame intervene between us and the men which seem to have enveloped them. Then the flames lift again, and we see that the men are still there. They fasten the rope to some inner projection. There is a row of windows all along the side of the building just below the top of the wall, and each window, *except one*, is a roaring furnace of flame. That *one* is where their rope passes. It so chanced that the rope could be secured nowhere else. Then the men go down the rope, one after another, the last one has passed the window, and the flames almost immediately after burst out of that window also, and his feet have scarcely touched the ground when the burning rope parts and comes down. Then the shout of joy that went up from the thousands on the bridge may be imagined, but it cannot be described.

RAPACITY OF EXPRESSMEN.

A wholesale grocer, residing on the North side, was absent from the city. His wife, a delicate woman, finding the flames suddenly upon her house, snatched up a silver cake

CHAS. W. STEVENS,

Late 150 Dearborn Street,

NOW, 564 WEST MADISON STREET,

"GREAT CENTRAL"

Cash Photographic Warehouse,

Photograph Goods of every description at usual Low Prices.

SEND ALONG YOUR ORDERS.

BARNES HOUSE.

The Largest Hotel left in Chicago.

Cor. of Randolph and Canal streets, near Randolph street Bridge.

W. K. SWALLOW, Proprietor.

H. H. HAMLIN, } Clerks.
HENRY LANGDON, }

SALOON, BARBER SHOP AND BILLIARD ROOM ALL IN THE HOUSE.

basket and a valuable little clock, took one of her two children in her arms and another by the hand and fled. As she sped before the pursuing fire, she found her strength failing, and begged the driver of a passing express wagon, lightly laden, to help her in her extremity. He would, for the clock. She submitted to the exaction, was carried three blocks, and then forced to get down. The cake basket bought her another ride of about the same distance, and then she was forced to finish her flight on foot, her means of satisfying the rapacity of drivers being exhausted. Finally, more dead than alive, she reached a place of safety.

KEEPING OPEN HOUSE.

On Monday evening, a knot of men, from 35 to 40 years of age, stood on Michigan avenue, watching the fire as it sought its way southward, in the teeth of the wind. They were looking grimy and dejected enough, until another, a broad shouldered man of middle height, with a face that might have belonged to one of the Cherryble brothers, shining through the overspreading dust and soot, approached them, and clapping one of their number on the shoulder, exclaimed cheerfully: "Well, James, we are all gone together. Last night I was worth a hundred thousand, and so were you. Now where are we?" "Gone," returned James. Then followed an interchange from which it appeared that the numbers of the group were young merchants worth from $50,000 to $150,000. After this, said the first speaker, "Well, Jim, I have a home left, and my family are safe. I have a barrel of flour, some bushels of potatoes and other provisions laid in for the winter; and now Jim I'm going to fill my house to night with these poor fellows," turning to the sidewalks, crowded with fleeing poor, "chuck full from cellar to garret!" The blaze of the conflagration revealed something worth seeing in that man's breast. Possibly the road to his heart may have been choked with rubbish before. If so, the fire had burned it clear, till it shone like one of the streets of burnished gold, which he will one day walk.

COMMON OCCURRENCES.

The experience of Mr. Lambert Tree and family was in part that of many. Perceiving that his own house could not escape, Mr. Tree, with his wife and child and aged father, went to the residence of his father-in-law, Mr. Magee. The Magee residence occupied the centre of a large enclosure, and was therefore regarded as a place of probable safety. But the very fact that of its isolation from surrounding buildings soon revealed that it was the most dangerous retreat that could have been chosen. The conflagration enveloped it completely on all sides before the house took fire. On the side opposite to the approaching flames, the square was enclosed by a high board fence, without openings. On the front, the flames had already cut off all possibility of retreat. The only way of escape was toward the northeast, over the fence already mentioned; a barrier which three aged persons, a woman already fainting in the dense smoke, and a little child half suffocated, could not possible scale. The fence, too, was on fire. The house was already enveloped in a shower of burning fire-brands. A horrible death seemed to be the inevitable doom of the entire party.

At this terrible juncture, a portion of the burning fence fell to the ground, opening a gateway from the fiery cul de sac. Through this opening, Mr. Tree dragged his fainting wife and child, fled toward the lake. In the flight from the premises, the party became separated. Nothing more was seen of Mr. and Mrs. Magee until, on the following day, they were found on the prairie northwest of the city. In their flight they had taken a different direction from the others, and had no choice but to hasten on before the advancing fire until beyond the line of its horrible path. The aged couple passed the night of Monday on the open prairie.

Furniture!

Furniture!

AT WHOLESALE AND RETAIL,

99 West Madison Street,

CHICAGO, ILL.

—C. B. 1855—X 1866—B. O. & C. A. 1871—

E. A BOWEN,

Sign Writer,

(FORMERLY ON DEARBORN STREET,)

43 W. Washington St., near Clinton St,.

ALL SIGN WORK AT OLD PRICES, OR LESS.

In an open space, sheltered by the walls of Lill's brewery, Mr. Tree and his family, with some of their neighbors, again supposed themselves to be in a place of safety. But from the refuge they were also driven by the advancing flames. The intense heat drove them to the beach and even into the water in which many men, women, and children stood for an hour, throwing water over their clothing to prevent it taking fire from the flames and sparks which a fierce wind drove toward them.

ONE OF THE WORST FEATURES

of Monday night was the agonizing appeals of wives for missing husbands; daughters and sisters for absent fathers and brothers, and children for their parents. The station houses were beseiged by tearful, despairing searchers for relatives and acquaintances who had not been seen nor heard of since the preceding night, and, as soon as it was known that dead bodies were being brought into the various municipal head-quarters remaining, the anxiety and terror increased tenfold.

NORTH SIDE INCIDENTS.

The interesting incidents attending the fire on the North Side were innumerable.

Mr. C. H. McCormick, the great reaper manufacturer, slept out on the prairie.

A musically disposed individual, probably filled with despair as well as melody, on Tuesday commenced playing on a piano standing on the street near to Lill's brewery and continued the occupation for several hours.

Dr. Weiner, a well-known North side physician, was seen during the progress of the fire, rushing up North Clark street on horseback, with a game cock under each arm.

On one of the streets, a cat, being rather too warm to be comfortable, rushed up a fallen lamp where it stuck and was roasted.

As an instance of the suffering of those who were burned out on the North side may be mentioned the case of an newly-married couple, who were driven from their home along with the fire to the prairie, remained out in the drenching rain that followed, and two days afterward walked miles over to the South division to get their first mouthful of bread.

A woman, after saving $300 from her house, attempted to return to the building to save something else; but when she came again she was in flames, and the only way that her husband could save her was by tearing off her clothes; not a shred of clothing being left on her. Her nakedness, however, was finally covered with a blanket. Her eldest daughter was in the same plight,

Three Protestant ministers and a Chatholic priest slept under the sidewalk at North avenue bridge one night.

A woman living on Ontario street, between Market and Franklin brought out her two children, aged 5 and 7 safely, and then went for a baby. The children followed her back and none came out alive.

The Quinn brothers went into their house while it was untouched by the fire to secure some clothing, but in getting out had to jump through the windows.

Mr. Malcomb, who died about two hours before the fire reached his residence, was burned almost beyond recognition.

THE KEY TO THE POSITION.

At one time on Monday, "the key to the position," as regards the spread of the flames in the South Division, was to keep the fire from striking the Palmer House. The walls of the Bigelow House had fallen. This house stood on the northwest corner of Dearborn and Quincy, and after the walls had fallen, the low frame house on the northeast corner

Mabley & Co.,

THE GREAT

CLOTHIERS

OF THE WEST,

AND THE

Chicago One-Price Clothing Store,

AT 122 WEST MADISON STREET.

JOHN HUGHES & SON,

PLUMBERS,

GAS FITTERS,

AND DEALERS IN

Plumbers' Goods,

No. 245 West Madison Street,

CHICAGO, ILL.

of Dearborn and Quincy stood intact. But the engine stationed at this point continued playing upon the ruins of the Bigelow House, when not a single spark issued therefrom, instead of taking up a position about a block or two further to the southwest, on the corner of Van Buren and Wells streets, where the small frame building was burning, and the only one on fire then in that part of the city. Judge Trumbull and other citizens urged that the engine be removed and made to play on this building, but, in the absence of the captain, the engine was not removed until too late. The fire in fifteen minutes swept the Palmer House, and the result was the loss of all the houses in the space lying between Quincy and Congress street, and Wells street and the lake.

CHICAGO PLUCK AND PRIDE.

The most hopeful and characteristic sign during all the terror and ruin of Sunday night was the pride displayed by many in the extent of their calamity. Chicago was ruined, true; but in her ruin she was Chicagoish. Like Ajax, she fell with the light of heaven around her. It is in this spirit that the magnificent bankrupt for millions looks down on the insolvent whose balance sheet does not require four figures for the sum total. But the frame of mind finding expression in these words is not of kin to that in which hypochondriacs glory in their diseases. These are the outspeaking of a hearty egotism, which no calamity can overcome; of a self-reliance which nothing can destroy. In memory of this honorable pluck the new city might change its name, emblem and motto. The Garden City has no significance now. Let the name be the Phœnix City, the emblem a Phœnix, springing glorious from the flames, and the motto, "Resurgam," for Chicago will rise again.

CUSTOM HOUSE VAULTS PROVED WORTHLESS.

The Custom House, the walls of which are standing, proved to be worthless as a place of safety for Government money and Government treasure. The vault in the subtreasury office was upon the second story. It rested upon two iron pillars built from the basement, with two iron girders connected with the wall. A fire-proof vault was built upon this foundation, and proved to be the weakest in the city. In the vault at the time of the fire were $1,500,000 in greenbacks, $300,000 in National Bank notes, $225,000 in gold, and $5,000 in silver, making a total of $2,130,000, of which $300,000 was in specie. A little safe containing $50,000 was saved, it having been buried away from the heat by the ruins of the vault. The specie was scattered over the basement floor and fused with the heat. Lumps of fused eagles, valued at from $500 to $1,000, blackened and burned, but now as refined gold, are in the ruins. The employees have recovered about five-sixths of the amount.

All the vaults of the building were shams of the thinnest kind, and as many of the United States buildings are constructed on the same plan, the Government will doubtless have them inspected.

THE GREAT LEVELER.

An instance to show the leveling process of the fire. A gentleman who had $65,000 annual income from stores situated in the burned district of the South Division has not to-day $1 of income, and his family is talking of taking boarders to help pay the winter's expenses.

A WATER-PIPE TURNED INTO AN OVEN.

Even the surroundings of the water-works were not without their tragedies. A man employed in a foundry on the corner of Van Buren and Clinton streets, who had been on a spree for some time, was overtaken by the fire, and thinking, perhaps, that the heat

J. B. SHAY,
DRY GOODS,
NOTIONS, FANCY GOODS &C.

Wholesale and Retail.

241, 243 & 245 West Madison St.,

Thompson's Block,

Between Peoria and Sangamon Sts.

Resumes business in this new and convenient locality.

My STOCK IS COMPLETE IN EVERY DETAIL, shall continue the business with duplication of our past success.

Will have the Goods to meet the wants of all, and trust by RENEWED EXERTION and LOW PRICES, to continue to merit in the future as in the past the GOLDEN OPINION of all our patrons.

OUR JOBBING DEPARTMENTS are now in complete working order, shall be happy to see all our old customers and hosts of new ones,

All Orders sent will be Promptly Executed.

NEW GOODS CONSTANTLY ARRIVING.

of the approaching fire would not prove to be so intense and destructive as it actually was, crawled into a large water-pipe lying on the ground and was roasted to death. When fully awake to his mistake, probably all he saw at either end of his last refuge was a flame of fire.

THE CAR TRACKS.

North, along Clark street, and on the branch tracks along Chicago avenue, Division street, Larrabee street, Sedgwick street, and Clybourne avenue, the horse-car tracks were more or less injured; the tracks in some places being doubled up to a height of three feet. The tracks of the Northwestern road along North Water street, and extending between the government pier and the Ogden slip, were still more damaged, many of the ends of the rails being thrown eight or ten feet from their original position. In many sections of the track the rails have assumed a zigzag course.

THE LAST BUILDING TO BURN

was "Terrace Row," a palatial block of private residences on Michigan avenue, extending northward from Harrison street. Its destruction required two or three hours, as nothing remained in its rear to accelerate the work. About eighteen hours from the first discovery of the fire on De Koven street, the last wall of "Terrace Row" fell. In the South Division, north of a diagonal line reaching from the east end of Harrison street to Polk street bridge, there remained two buildings unharmed, one the large business block immediately north of Randolph street bridge, and the other an unfinished stone structure at the corner of Monroe and La Salle streets. The entire business portion of the city was obliterated. Two-thirds of the territorial area of the city was unscathed, but Chicago as a great business mart, the proud commercial center of the growing West, was no more. Was ever devastation more complete?

A FRIGHTFUL SCENE.

While Madison street, west of Dearborn, and the west side of Dearborn, were all ablaze, the spectators saw the lurid light appear in the rear windows of Speed's block. Presently a man, who had apparently taken time to dress himself leisurely, appeared on the extension built up to the second story of two stores. He looked cooly down the thirty feet between him and the ground, while the excited crowd first cried "Jump!" and then some of them more considerately looked for a ladder. A long plank was soon found, which answered the same as a ladder, and it was placed at once against the building, down which the man soon slid.

But while these preparations were going on, there suddenly appeared another man at a fourth-story window of the building below, which had no projection, but flush from the top to the ground—four stories and a basement. His escape by the stairway was apparently cut off, and he looked despairingly down the fifty feet between him and the ground. The crowd grew almost frantic at the sight, for it was only a choice of death before him. Senseless cries of "Jump! Jump!" went up from the crowd—senseless, but full of sympathy, for the sight was absolutely agonizing. Then, for a minute or two, he disappeared, perhaps even less, but it seemed so long a time the supposition was that he had fallen, suffocated with smoke and heat. But no, he appears again. First, he throws a bed, then some bed clothes, apparently; why, probably even he does not know. Again he looks down the dead, sheer wall of fifty feet below him. He hesitates, and well he may, as he looks behind him. Then he mounts to the window sill. His whole form appears, naked to the shirt, and his white limbs gleam against the dark wall in the brigh light as he swings himself below the window.

LIND'S BLOCK.

The only remaining building in the whole of the business portion of the City North and South Side.

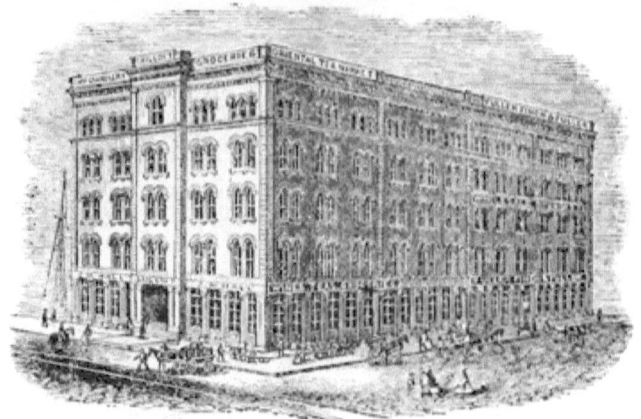

Which is occupied as follows: By Z. M. HALL, WHOLESALE GROCER, 259 & 261 Randolph St.---Keeps a full stock of TEAS & GROCERIES, and Manufacturers of ROASTED AND GROUND COFFEES AND SPICES.

JOHN DAVISON,
PROPRIETOR OF THE
Chicago Oakum Works;
ALSO, DEALER IN
CORDAGE, ANCHOR CHAINS,
Tackle Blocks &c.,
30 SO. MARKET STREET,
LIND'S BLOCK.

☞ See next page for Occupants of same Building.

Somehow—none can tell—he drops and catches upon the top of the windows below him of the the third story. He stoops and drops again, and seizes the frame with his hands, and his gleaming body once more straightens and hangs prone downward, and he drops instantly and accurately upon the window sill of the third story. A shout, more of joy than applause, goes up from the breathless crowd, and those who had turned away their heads, not enduring to look upon him as he seemed about to plunge to sudden and certain death, glanced up at him once more with a ray of hope at this daring and skillful feat. Into the window he crept to look, probably, for a doorway, but appeared again presently, for here was the only avenue of escape, desperate and hopeless as it was. Once more he dropped his body, hanging by his hand.

The crowd screamed, and waved for him to swing himself over the projection from which the other man had just been rescued. He tried to do this, and vibrated like a pendulum from side to side, but could not reach far enough to throw himself upon the roof. Then he hung by one hand, and looked down; raising the other hand, he took a fresh hold, and swung from side to side again to reach the roof. In vain. Again he hung motionless by one hand, and slowly turned his head over his shoulder, and gazed in the abyss below him. Then, gathering himself up, he let go his hold, and for a second a gleam of white shot down fully forty feet to the foundation of the basement. Of course the fall killed him. He was taken to a drug store near by, and died in ten minutes. His name was P. P. Dewey, dealer in real estate, 125 Dearborn street.

THE ONLY BUSINESS BLOCK LEFT.

Standing solitary and alone within the limits of the fire district is the Lind block, at the corner of Randolph and Market streets. That locality will henceforth assume many aspects of historical interest, and we present, on another page, a wood-cut of that landmark as it now appears. Only there, were wholesale stocks saved untouched by the general wreck.

Fronting south are the stores occupied by Z. M. Hall, the well-known grocer, who was fortunate enough to save his large assortment complete, and to be able to resume business at the old stand, with a full line of goods, so soon as the scene of dismay and confusion came to an end.

The Market street front, embodying the stores made so conspicuous and so generally known by the large number of gilt signs displayed on the outer walls, advertising Eastern medicines, were and still are occupied by Fuller & Fuller, the only wholesale drug house in Chicago which entirely escaped the tornado of fire. These gentlemen had on hand an extensive stock of everything in this line of business, and are as ready to and capable of filling orders to any amount as they were before the conflagration, since not a single article of their immense assortment suffered the slightest injury.

Adjoining them toward the north, is located the well known firm of Henry W. King & Co., also unscathed, whose high and deserved reputation throughout the Northwest as clothing dealers, must guarantee them the continuance of their old patronage and of their customary prosperity.

These three wholesale houses tower aloft amid the wide-spread scene of desolation with a sort of columnar significance—monumental piles of brick and mortar, around which must cluster for many long years the most eventful and emotional recollections, after the ruins and vestiges of the burnt district shall have utterly disappeared from sight, and been replaced by a resurrection of buildings and commercial activity.

Wholesale Dealers in Flour, and

COMMISSION MERCHANTS,

No. 28 MARKET STREET,

Lind's Block.   **Chicago.**

FULLER & FULLER,

22, 24 and 26 Market Street, Chicago,

Importers and Wholesale Dealers in

Drugs, Medicines,

PAINTS, DYE STUFFS, CHEMICALS,

Window Glass, Putty, Soap Makers' Stock, Tanner's Stock, Etc., Etc.

We are happy to inform the public, that our establishment was entirely uninjured by the late fire. Orders filled with our usual promptness.

WRIGHT & BEEBE,

Commission Merchants

No. 20 MARKET STREET, Lind's Block,

N. T. WRIGHT,
G. T. BEEBE.   **CHICAGO, ILL.**

SCENES ON WABASH AVENUE.

As the fire commenced spreading up the avenue, a wild scene of confusion ensued. The street was crowed with vehicles of all descriptions, many drawn by men, who found it impossible to procure draught animals. The sidewalks were filled with a hurrying crowd, bearing in their arms and upon their backs and heads clothing, furniture, and so on Ladies dressed in elegant costumes, put on with a view of preserving them, and with costly apparel of all kinds thrown over their arms and shoulders, staggered along under the unwonted burden. Poor woman with mattresses upon their heads, or weighed down with furniture, tottered with weary steps up the crowded street. Nearly every one wore a stern expression, and moved on without a word, as if they had braced up their minds to endure the worst, without manifesting any emotion. Occasionally, however, the wail of women and children rent the air, bringing tears to the eyes of those who witnessed the manifestations. Poor little children shivered in the cold night air, and looked with wide open eyes upon the scene they could not comprehend. Ludicrous incidents were of occasional ocurrence, lighting up with a sort of horrible humor the terrible realities of the situation. Women would go by with dogs in their arms, their pets being all they had saved from the ruins of their homes. An octogenarian ran in a yard, with a large cat enfolded in his feeble embrace. Men dragging wagons wore green veils over their faces to protect their eyes from the blinding dust.

Drunken men staggered among the crowds, apparently possessed of the idea that the whole affair was a grand municipal spree, in which they were taking part as a duty that should be discharged by all good citizens. Trucks passed up street loaded with trunks, on which sat ladies in costly garb, and with diamonds on their fingers. But one day before they would have scorned the idea of riding in anything less imposing than a luxurious landau or coupee; but their pride was leveled in the presence of the universal imminent danger, and they were thoroughly glad to get the humblest cart in which to place themselves and their valuables.

A HORRIBLE TRAGEDY:

At the intersection of Randolph and Market streets was a large building (Cullom's), used for offices. The janitor resided on the fourth floor, with his family, consisting of a wife and four children. By some means they were unable to escape. Surrounded by the fire they ascended to the roof. The babe was in the mother's arms, and another child—a little boy—clung to her skirts. Two girls were clasped in the arms of the father. Their shouts were but faintly heard over the howl of the winds and the roar of the flames. At last the heat became so intense that the woman was overcome, and fell to the roof. The father wildly threw out his hand, then staggered, writhed, and sank by his wife's side. That was all of that tragedy. It froze the blood of those who witnessed it, who yet could extend no helping hand, but were forced to hurry on to places of safety for themselves.

INTERESTING FACTS AND STATEMENTS.

A SURVEY OF LOSSES BY STREETS:

No better idea of the losses can be obtained than can be got by going over a little in detail the area swept by the fire in the South Division. As yet, and for weeks and months to come, no one will be able to enumerate these losses accurately and elaborately.

HARRIS'
Safe Factory,

60 and 62 So. Canal St.

The record of these Safes during the recent Fire is one that has no superior, and parties interested in the matter have only to inquire to ascertain the noble record they have made for themselves.

Vault Doors
AND
BURGLAR CHESTS.

AGENT FOR SARGENT & GREENLEAF'S

Patent Combination & Key Locks.

Beginning, not with the point where the fire commenced, but at the main branch of the river, for convenience, let us enumerate the streets and, as far as possible, recall what was on them, what was bought and sold and stored there, and by whom they were occupied.

And first, South Water street was swept with destruction's besom, from the South Branch to the lake. Here went down the Lumber Exchange, several elevators with their contents, almost innumerable houses stored with flour, with apples and butter, with lard and pork, poultry, farm products, garden vegetables, and on the east half of the street on both sides were wholesale houses stored from cellar to attic with groceries, coarse and fine, with the products of Europe, the wines of Burgundy and the Rhine; coffee from South America, the West Indies, and the Orient; teas piled high like a Canton storehouse; whisky, the distilled essence of thousands of acres of Illinois corn. These, with all that was left of the Fort Dearborn buildings, were wiped out, for the entire length of the street, with the peculiar paraphernalia of the street, the skids, the clogged and choked sidewalks, through which buyers wended sinuous. Where, now, oh, consigners from the Northwest, are the products of your labor? You may come in thousands, as you already have, to look after them; but they are consigned where no consignee or purchaser will ever see them—into oxygen and hydrogen, thin air.

While pursuing its resistless way along this street, eating through the vegetables, and poultry, and fruit, and provisions of the Northwest more rapidly than the carnivorous tooth of time, aided by the forces of decay, the fires were also sweeping across the river.

Next take Lake street. This street, which for twenty years has stood as the great business street of Chicago, was totally destroyed from end to end, from the lake to the river, with the contents of the houses. The principal hide and leather houses occupied the west end; next came several heavy hardware and cutlery establishments, farm implement establishments and toy shops, some of the largest silver and plated ware establishments, clothing houses, large retail dry goods houses, and below Dearborn street both sides of the street were occupied for about a quarter of a mile with palatial marble-fronted rows where goods were only sold at wholesale; tall buildings whose shadows fell entirely across the street and terminated somewhat up the fronts of the opposite side. These, containing millions of dollars' worth of goods of all kinds, the labor of the loom, from sunny France, from Italy, from India and China, and the shops of Old and of New England, were all consigned at last to the general limbo of total destruction. At the foot of this street stood several fine hotels, the Adams, the Richmond, and Massasoit Houses, and the great railroad union depot, a marvel of magnitude and art, whose picture graces some of the school geographies. These, with the freight buildings and the warehouses beyond almost to the mouth of the harbor, containing freight, and stores, and grain in quantities that nobody knows, and probably never will, in the aggregate, were all consumed.

Then Randolph street followed. The Lind block stands at the bridge, the solitary structure left out of all that was valuable, beautiful, or grand on the street. This was the street where the large hotels stood, the Sherman house, the Briggs house, the Metropolitan, the Matteson, and several others. A large number of furniture establishments and toy establishments occupied the west end of the street, while the east end was devoted, like Lake street, to wholesale houses, including the great auction house. The Museum, the Northwestern Engraving Company's building, and several wholesale grocery establishments together with a miscellaneous business, comprising retail establishments, banks, etc., which were all consigned to ruin with the rest.

REED'S TEMPLE OF MUSIC.
81 Sixteenth Street.

This well-known establishment, with its contents, was burned in the late Fire, but fortunately, was fully insured in good Eastern Companies. The new establishment occupies two entire floors of one of the finest brick buildings in the City. A large and complete Stock of

ONE HUNDRED CHICKERING

PIANOS

Are now arriving, which will offer the best opportunity that can be found in the West for those wishing to purchase.

The Messrs. Reed's are determined to re-establish their Business on a basis as extensive as before the Fire, and make their establishment now, as then, the

GREAT LEADING PIANO HOUSE OF THE WEST.

☞ Every one is invited to call and see them at their new place, as above.

WHITE & ROSSMAN,

Wholesale and Retail Dealers in

STOVES,

HEATERS, RANGES,

AND

House Furnishing Goods,

Formerly 200 East Lake street,

NOW LOCATED AT

No. 146 WEST MADISON STREET.

Western Agency for Imperial Stove Works,
HICKS & WOLFE, Proprietors, Troy, N. Y.

THE GREAT CONFLAGRATION. 63

Washington street, from the tunnel to the lake, comprised many of the best buildings in the city. It was largely devoted to banks, offices, insurance, and real estate dealers. On this street was the Second Presbyterian church, the Union bank building, the Merchants' insurance building, the Nevada house, the Opera house, St. James hotel, the first National bank, the Board of Trade and a large number of other equally fine blocks almost all of which were marble fronts.

Then all on Madison street from the lake to the bridge. Some of the famous buildings on this street were Farwell Hall, McVicker's theatre, the Morrison block, *Tribune* building, *Staats Zeitung* building, and St. Mary's church. The entire street was built up with blocks such as cannot be excelled in any city.

Monroe street, from river to lake, having upon it the Lombard block, the Post office, the *Prairie Farmer* building, and a large number of the finest blocks in the city; Adams street with its cheaper buildings at the west end, its Academy of design, with most of the works of art therein contained, its temple of Swedenburg, the South side reservoir, and many other buildings; Quincy street, with its Pacific hotel, fast approaching completion, and its Palmer house, the pride of everybody, with its palaces and its dens of infamy and shame. Jackson street, from the residence of the rich and elegant Trinity church on the east to the less pretentious houses of the working class farther west, to the hundreds of dens and holes of darkness at the west, were illuminated and oxygenized.

Van Buren street, with its bridge, the magnificent railway depot, St. Paul's church, the Academy of Science building, and its blocks of fine residences and acres of poor ones were annihilated.

Congress street, with its elegant Second Congregational church. Harrison street, with its freight-house, the Jones school building, and everything else, except the Methodist church on Wabash avenue and the houses on Michigan avenue fell before the flames. And this was the most southern street which was burned from end to end, from the lake to the river.

The east and west streets only comprise in their description a larger portion of the houses burned.

On State street, stood the magnificent book stores of Griggs & Co., Keen & Cooke, and the Western News Company, Field & Leiter's wholesale dry goods house, besides many large wholesale and retail houses, jewelry establishments, and furniture houses.

On Dearborn street stood the *Times* and *Journal* newspaper offices, the Dearborn theatre, and a considerable number of banks and large office blocks. La Salle street was built up with many of the finest buildings to be found in the city. It was largely occupied by insurance agents, real estate brokers, lawyers, etc. Between Washington and Randolph streets stood the Court House, which of course, shared the general ruin.

These details are only given to aid the reader in obtaining a proximate idea of the losses. Little was saved except from those houses which were not attacked by the flames until several hours after it was seen to be inevitable that the city was doomed.

Immense quantities of goods were piled upon the lake park and on the grounds of the Chicago Base-Ball club—pyramids of clothing, boots and shoes, dry goods, and furniture from the rich dwellers along Michigan avenue—all of which finally fell a prey to the destroyer.

A WESTERN MERCHANT'S ESTIMATE OF THE AGGREGATE LOSS BY THE CHICAGO CONFLAGRATION:
[From the New York Express, Oct. 12.]

Ten thousand houses burned, of which 2,000 were business houses, and 8,000 dwellings.

HENRY M. SHERWOOD,

MANUFACTURER AND DEALER IN

School, Church and Office Furniture,

GLOBES, MAPS, CHARTS, INK WELLS, SLATING FOR BLACKBOARS, ETC.,

103, 105, 107 Canal St.

HENRY M. SHERWOOD,   (Near Madison Street Bridge.)
GEO. SHERWOOD,
C. W. SHERWOOD.   CHICAGO.

Geo. & C. W. Sherwood, SCHOOL BOOKS, 103 S. Canal St.

H. L. DAHL,

MERCHANT TAILOR.

201 W. Madison St.

(Formerly 202 South Clark St.)

CHICAGO.

I still live and am prepared to fill all orders promptly. A choice Stock on hand.

2,000 business houses at $25,000.............................	$50,000,000
8,000 dwellings averaging $6,000.............................	48,000,000
Engines and machinery attached.............................	2,000,000
Total loss in houses alone.................................	$100,000,000
Of business houses probably ten contained $1,000,000 each ...	10,000,000
20 valuables at $500,000 each.............................	10,000,000
40 contents worth $250,000 each...........................	10,000,000
200 worth $100,000 each...................................	20,000,000
500 averaging $30,000 each................................	15,000,000
Remaining, 670, and averaging $10,000 each................	16,700,000
Furniture and other contents of 8,000 dwellings averaging $2,000..	16,000,000
Lumber yards, railroad stock and craft.....................	2,300,000
Total goods and wares, lumber, railroad stock and vessels..	$100,000,000
Aggregate loss by fire....................................	200,000,000

We do not think this an excessive estimate, and it comes from a very careful business man of the West, who knows whereof he writes. To this loss of $200,000,000 in property is to be added the immense loss in arrested improvements, works stopped, and corresponding or worse calamities incidental to the greatest misfortune of the times. But among all the people we know of, the citizens of Chicago will bear their losses in as manly a way as the very best. They have shown patience, pluck, courage and hope, with a becoming sorrow and resignation, and there is no better capital than this to begin a new life.

CHICAGO TIMES' ESTIMATE.

The aggregate loss has been variously guessed to be two, three, four, five, and so on to eight or nine hundred millions of dollars. One will meet in an hour's walk among the ruins twenty intelligent men who will avow that not a dollar less than $500,000,000 of property has been destroyed. This is nonsense. At the most liberal estimate, $500,000,000 would cover the value of every particle of property of every kind that ever existed within the corporate limits of Chicago. It is certainly not all destroyed, nor a half, nor a third of it

A careful calculation will show that $150,000,000 is a liberal estimate for the value that has been destroyed by the conflagration. The valuation of property for city taxation for the present year was in round numbers as follows:

REAL ESTATE (INCLUDING BUILDINGS.)

South Division...	$110,000,000
West Division..	87,000,000
North Division...	38,000,000
Total...	$235,000,000

PERSONAL PROPERTY.

South Division...	$40,000,000
West Division..	8,000,000
North Division...	5,000,000
Total...	$53,000,000

The judgment of the most trustworthy experts is that the assessed valuation of real property is rather over than under two thirds of the actual cash value, upon an average of the whole city, while that of personal property is rather under than over one-third

Western Star Metal Co.

BRASS FOUNDERS,

AND

FINISHERS,

No. 17 South Canal Street

CHICAGO.

J. E. ALDRICH & CO.,

MANUFACTURERS OF

FURNITURE,

Rear of Nos. 11, 13, 15 & 17 S. Canal,

Near Randolph St.,   CHICAGO.

FINE CABINET WORK TO ORDER.

of the actual cash value. Adding one-third to the real property and two thirds to the personal, and the total value of all property in the city of Chicago before the fire was $469,000,000. How much of this value still remains? How much of it has the fire destroyed?

Assessment District No. 1 included all the South Division north of Twelfth street. The total valuation of land and buildings in that district was $64,000,000—about $40,000,000 for the former and $24,000,000 for the latter. Much the greater part of the personal property of the South Division was in that district—probably $35,000,000; total, $99,000,000. Deducting $40,000,000 for the land, and the loss, if everything else were destroyed, would be $60,000,000, according to the Assessor's valuation; or if this be equal upon an average of real and personal estate to one-half the actual cash value (which is believed to be quite within the fact), an actual loss of $120,000,000. Similarly, the actual loss in the North Division is found to be in the vicinity of $30,000,000. But from this calculation must be deducted all that unburnt portion of Assessment District No. 1 between Twelfth and Harrison streets, and a small unburnt district in the northwest corner of the North Division. From it must also be deducted the value of all personal property saved from the fire. To it must be added the loss in the burnt district of the West Division. Thus, while the calculation does not assume the character of precision it furnishes a trustworthy approximation, showing that $150,000,000 will cover the entire destruction of property by the conflagration.

HOMELESS POPULATION OF THE BURNT DISTRICT.

The following table will show the number of people who lost their homes. The figures are taken from an official list. Of the wards the Third and Sixteenth were partially destroyed; the others have totally disappeared:

First Ward	8,103
Second Ward	13,449
Third Ward	3,500
Sixteenth Ward	8,380
Seventeenth Ward	18,814
Eighteenth Ward	18,805
Nineteenth Ward	9,237
Twentieth Ward	14,522
	96,810
West Side (about)	2,500
	99,310

The partially burned wards and the portion of the West Side destroyed are figured approximately, a large margin being left on the hopeful side. The figures may therefore be relied upon as the closest to the facts that can be made. In round numbers, 100,000 persons have been rendered homeless.

CITY BUILDINGS DESTROYED.

The loss to the city as a corporation is considerable, and includes many fine buildings, the most notable of which was the Court-House. The old Bridewell buildings, mere shanties, were swept away. The Armory was consumed. Of school-houses, the Jones, erected in 1844, at the corner of Polk and Clark streets; the Kinzie, on Ohio street; the Ogden, on Chestnut street; the Division street school and the Lincoln are all gone. Of engine-houses, the Rice, the Titsworth, and all stationed on the

THE HARTFORD FIRE INS. CO.

THE IRON-CLAD
"OLD HARTFORD"
NEVER SURRENDERS!

Tested by the storms of 61 Years, and still is Sound.

Pays from her surplus of

$1,800,000
HER LOSSES BY THE GREAT CHICAGO FIRE

Leaving her magnificent capital of

ONE MILLION

untouched and **QUARTER OF A MILLION SURPLUS** to spare'

Get the Best. Get Hartford Policies.

Chartered, 1810.   Capital. $1,000,000.

Agencies in all prominent Localities in the United States and Dominion of Canada.

G. F. BISSELL, Gen'l Agt.
PRESENT OFFICE :
CORNER WASHINGTON & GREEN STS.
Office Building to be immediately rebuilt, 49 La Salle St.

North Side. The magnificent Water Works buildings, with the gigantic engines stationed there, were badly damaged, but it is thought they may be repaired. The bridges gone are those at Polk, Van Buren, Adams, Wells, State, Clark, and Rush streets. The pavements in the burnt district are nearly useless, but as they were built by special assessment the loss is not immediately upon the corporation.

A PARTIAL LIST OF THE PUBLIC HALLS, BLOCKS, BUILDINGS, HOTELS, CHURCHES, CHARITABLE INSTITUTIONS, ACADEMIES, SCHOOLS, ETC., DESTROYED BY THE FIRE.

The Chicago Evening Journal of Oct. 13 contained the following philosophic view of the ruins of the great conflagration. It said:

Now that the smoke of the burnt district has cleared away and the general confusion—at first so confounding, has very considerably subsided, we are able to take a birds, eye view of the general loss, which we give below:

PUBLIC HALLS AND BLOCKS, ETC.

Aiken's Museum, Andrews' Building, Andrews & Otis' Building, Arcade Building, Arcade Court, Berlin Block, Blake's Building, Blaney Hall, Boone Block, Bowen's Building, Burch's Block, Calhoun Block, Foltz's Hall, Chamber of Commerce Building, Chicago Mutual Life Insurance Company, Chicago Times Building, City Armory, City Gas Works, Court-House, City Water Works, Cobb's Block (No. 1), Cobb's Building, Cobb's Block (No. 2), Commercial Building, Commercial Insurance Company's Building, Crosby's Building and Crosby's Opera-House, Custom-House and Post Office, Democratic Hall, Dickey's Building, Dole's Building, Drake's Block, Ewing Block Exchange Bank Building, Farwell Hall, Fenian Hall, Firemen's Hall, Flanders' Block, Ætna Building, Fullerton Block, Gallup's Building, Garrett Block, German House Turner Hall (Clark street), Germania Hall, Hartford Fire Insurance Building, the finest insurance building in the West; Health Lift Building, Holt's Building, Honore Block, Illinois Central Railroad Land Department Building, Jackson Hall, Keep's Building, Ke t' Building, King's Block, Kinzie Hall, Larmon Block, Light Guard Hall, Lincoln Block, Link's Block, Lloyd's Block, Lombard Block, Loomis Building Lumbermen's Exchange, McCarty's Building, McCormick's Building, McKee's Building, Magie's Building. Major Block, Marine Bank Building, Masonic Temple, Mechanic's Building, Mercantile Building, Methodist Church Block, Metropolitan Hall Block, Monroe Building, Morrison Buildings, New Turner's Hall, Newberry Block, North Market Hall, Norton Block, Odd Fellow's Hall, Old Board of Trade Buildings (South Water street), Oriental Buildings, Otis Block (La Salle street), Otis Building (State street), Pardee's Building, Phenix Building, Pomeroy's Building, Pope's Block, Portland Block, Post Office Building, Purple's Block, Raymond Block, Reynolds' Block Rice's Building, Scammon's Building, Shepard's Building, Sherman House Block, Smith, Nixon & Ditson's Hall, Smith & Nixon's Block, Sons' Hall, Speed's Block, Staats-Zeitung Building, Steele's Block, Stone's Building, Taylor's Block, Teutonia Hall, Trade Assembly Hall, Tribune Building, Turners' Building, Tyler Block, Uhlich's Block, North Division City Railway Stables, Baer's Bloc Herting's Building, Union Building, Volk's Building, Walker's Block, Warner's Hall and Block, Washington Block, Wheeler's Building, Wicker's Building, Witkowsky Hall Building, Workingmen's Hall, Wright Bros.' Building, Bryan's Block.

In addition to the above were a large number of elegant buildings recently completed, or in process of erection, representing a valuation approximating millions of dollars.

HASKIN, MARTIN & WHEELER,

MANUFACTURERS OF

FINE SALT,

AND DEALERS IN

Fine, Coarse and Dairy Salt, Cements, Stucco, &c.

Utica Cement Company

MANUFACTURERS OF

BLACK BALL BRAND

Utica Cement.

HASKIN, MARTIN & WHEELER, Agents,

Office temporarily No. 686 So. Canal St.,

CHICAGO, ILL.

---

79 SOUTH HALSTED ST. 79

Gas Fitting and Plumbing.

BAGGOT & ALMY,

FORMERLY OF 163 and 165 LAKE ST.,

ARE STILL ALIVE

We are ready to attend to all work in the Plumbing and Gas Fitting line. No advance in Price. All work warranted. Do not fail to call at

79 S. Halsted Street.

CHURCHES.

North Baptist, Olivet Baptist, (colored), Swedish Baptist, North Star Baptist, Mariners' Bethel. New England Congregational, Lincoln Park Congregational, Church of Our Saviour, (Epis), Church of the Ascension, (Episcopal), Cooper's Independent, St. Ansgarius (Swedish Episcopal), St. James (Episcopal), Trinity (Episcopal), Trinity Mission, Evangelical Association of North America, Evangelical Second Church, Free Evangelical, English Lutheran (Ontario street), First German Evangelical Lutheran, St. Paul's Evangelical Lutheran Trinity, First German United Evangelical Lutheran St. Paul's Illinois Street Independent Mission. Jewish Church of the North Side, Kehileth Benai, Shalom (Jewish), First Methodist, Wabash Avenue Methodist (scorched), Grace Methodist, Grant Place Methodist, Dixon street Methodist, Van Buren street German Methodist, Clybourn avenue German Methodist, First Scandinavian Methodist, Grace Scandinavian Methodist, Huron street Bethel, Bethel African Methodist, Quinn's African Methodist Chapel, First Norwegian Evangelical Lutheran, Swedish Evangelical Lutheran, First Presbyterian, Second Presbyterian, Westminster Presbyterian, Fullerton Avenue Presbyterian, North Presbyterian, Orchard street Presbyterian, Bremer street Independent Mission, Newsboy's Independent Mission and Home, Erie street Presbyterian Mission, Burr Presbyterian Mission, Tammany Hall Mission, Catholic Cathedral of the Holy Name, St. Mary's Catholic Church and University, the Catholic Ecclestical Palace, St. Louis' Catholic, St. Joseph's Catholic, St. Michael's Catholic, Church of the Immaculate Conception, St, Rose of Lima Catholic, Convent and Academy of St. Francis Xavier, Convent of the Sisters of Charity (North Side), Convent of Notre Dame, House of the Good Shepherd, Convent of the Sisters of the Good Shepherd, Convent of the Benedictine Fathers, Convent of the Benedictine Nuns, Convent of the Redemptionist Fathers, Swedenborgian Temple of the New Jerusalem, North Swedenborgian Mission, Unitarian Church of the Missiah, (R. L. Collier), Unity Church (Robert Collyer's), St. Paul's Universalist.

BANKS.

Chicago Clearing House ; First, Second, Third, Fourth, Fifth, Cook County, Commercial, City Manufacturers', Merchants' Mechanics', Loan and Trust, Northwestern, Traders', and Union National Banks ; International Mutual Trust Company ; Merchants' Savings, Loan and Trust Company ; Commercial Loan Company ; Farmers', Merchants' and Mechanics' ; State Savings Institution ; Real Estate, Loan and Trust Company ; Union Insurance and Trust Company ; Hibernian Banking Association ; Chicago Building and Loan Associations ; Swedish Commercial ; National Bank of Commerce ; Marine Bank.

PRIVATE BANKERS.

J. M. Adsit, A. C. & O. F. Badger, Baldwin, Walker & Co., H. Clausenius & Co., Ullman. Wrenn & Co., Cushman & Hardin, Folansbee & Son, Henry Greenebaum & Co., Greenebaum & Foreman, Lunt, Preston & Kean ; Mayer, Leopold & Steiner ; Meadowcroft Brothers, Nichoff & Co., Louis Sapieha, J. R. Shepherd & Co , Lazarus Silverman, A O. Slaughter, Geo. C. Smith & Bro., Snydacker & Co , James B Storey & Co., Wilkins & Stone, Ferd. S. Winslow, Collins & Ullman.

HOTELS.

Adams House, American House, Brevoort House, Briggs House, Central House, City Hotel, Clarendon House, Clifton House, Continental, Eagle, European (Dearborn street), European (State street), Everett, French (Wells street), French (Kinzie

WM. B. PHILLIPS, President.   ANDREW MOODY, Vice Pres't.   GEO. E. CHURCH, Sec'y

GOSS & PHILLIPS MANUF'G CO.

MANUFACTURERS OF

Sash, Doors, Blinds,

STAIR RAILING, POSTS, BALUSTERS,

MOULDINGS, FLOORING, SIDING, &c.

DEALERS IN LUMBER, LATH, SHINGLES.

Principal Office, cor. Clark & 12th Sts.

Factories { COR. CLARK & 12th STS.
{ COR. 22d & FISK STS.

CHICAGO.

☞ The above cut represents our Establishment cor. Clark and 12th sts. Our Establishment cor. 22d and Fisk streets is fully as extensive—the cuts of which were all lost in the great Fire.

street), Fort Dearborn House, Garden City, Girard, Hatch, Hess, Garni, Howard House, Haber House, Illinois House, Jervis House, Palmer, Bigelow, Ogden House, Laclede, Mansion House, Massoit House, Matteson House, Moulton House, Metropolitan Hotel, Michigan Central Railroad Hotel, Bethel Home, Nevada, New York, Orient, Potomac, Raymond House, Revere, Rock Island, Schall, Sherman, St. James', Tremont, Washington, Western Eagle, and Wright's.

In addition to the above, should be mentioned at least a dozen other structures in course of erection and completion, representing a valuation of several hundred thousand dollars.

RAILWAY DEPOTS.

Great Union Central Depot, (including the Illinois Central, Michigan Central, and Chicago, Burlington & Quincy), Southern Michigan and Rock Island, Northwestern (Wells street).

TELEGRAPH COMPANIES.

Western Union, Metropolitan, Great Western, Atlantic and Pacific.

EXPRESSES.

Adams', American Merchants' Union, United States. Brink's.

NEWSPAPERS, ETC.

Evening Journal, Tribune, Times, Republican, Post, Mail, Ledger, Democrat, Agerdyrkning and Oeconomic, American Churchman, American Messenger, Americanischer Botschafter, Baptist Quarterly, Baptist Teacher, Catholic Weekly, Chicago City Directory, The Chicago Mercantile Journal, Commercial Bulletin, Commercial Express and Produce Reporter, Daily Law Record, Daily Programe, Daily Record, Dispatch, Druggists' Price Current, Dry Goods Price-List, Journal of Commerce, Legal News, Office Directory, Railway Review, Real Estate Journal, Union (German), Staats Zeitung, Child's Paper, Child's World, Dagslyet, Daily Commercial Report and Market Review, Der Deutche Arbeiter, Der Hausfreund, Evening Lamp, Hemlandet, Hemlandet Ratta, Home Circle, Volks Zeitung, Catholische Wochenblatt, Little Corporal, Live Stock Reporter, Macedonian and Record, Methodist Publishing House, National Baptist, New Covenant, News from the Spirit World, Northwestern Review, Publishers' Auxiliary, Railroad Gazette, School Festival, Sunday School World, Svenska Amerikanaven Advance, Art Review, The Arts, Bright Side, Courier, The Chronicle, Congregational Review, Fremad, Herald of the Coming Kingdom, Land-Owner, Inside Track, Liberal, Interior, Juxbruder, Life-Boat, Lyceum Banner, National Prohibitionist, Observer, Pharmcist, Prairie Farmer, Religio-Philosophical Journal, Skandinavian, Spectator, Standard Reporter, Western Odd Fellow, Western Rural, Soldiers' Friend, Westliche Unterhallings Blaeter, Workingman's Advocate, Young Reaper, and the following

MAGAZINES.

Lakeside Monthly, Manford's, Home Journal, Medical Examiner, Bureau. Chicago (Mrs. Rayne's) Missionary, Mystic Star Monthly, Sunday Scholar, Sunday School Helper, Sunday School Teacher, Voice of Masory.

LIBRARIES.

Historical Society, Law Institute, Metropolitan Hall Library Association, Young Men's Christian Association, Union Catholic, together with many others of great value.

ADAMS EXPRESS CO.,

55 W. Washington St.,

CHICAGO.

Lightning Line

TO AND FROM

NEW YORK, BOSTON, BALTIMORE,

WASHINGTON, PHILADELPHIA & NEW ENGLAND STATES,

—VIA—

Pittsburgh Ft. Wayne & Penn. Central Rail Roads.

JOHN L. HOPKINS, Agent.

GLOBE MUTUAL LIFE INS CO.,

OF NEW YORK.

PLINY FREEMAN, President.

All Books, Receipts and Papers belonging to the Northwestern Department were saved from the Great Chicago Fire.

To men of ability out of business and who desire permanent and profitable employment, Mr. McKindley offers a CAPITAL CHANCE in the following Card.

The GLOBE is one of the Standard Companies of the country and in too well known to need comment.

The *Globe Mutual Life Insurance Company* of New York, wish to engage men of intelligence, integrity and business ability, to solicit applications for Life Insurance in Michigan, Indiana, Illinois, Iowa, Wisconsin, Minnesota and Nebraska on liberal terms.

Agencies in all parts of the above States can be formed into Districts of from three (3) to ten (10) counties

To Agents thoroughly conversant with the business, rare inducements will be offered.

Agents make contracts at this office with, and work directly for the Company in the above territory.

Address, with references, J. G. McKindley, Manager Northwestern Department.

23 SOUTH HALSTED ST. near Washington,

CHICAGO, ILL.

CITY SCHOOLS.

Dearborn, Jones, Kinzie, Franklin, Ogden, Newberry (scorched), Pearson Street Primary, Elm Street Primary, North Branch Primary, La Salle Street Primary, Third Avenue Primary.

INDEPENDENT SCHOOLS.

Holy Name, St. Mary's, St. Joseph's, Immaculate Conception, First Lutheran, First United German Lutheran, St. Paul's Second and Third, Italian School, German and English.

ACADEMIES AND SEMINARIES.

Academy of Sciences, Christian Brothers, Holy Name, St. Francis Xavier, Bryant & Chase's Commercial, Dearborn Ladies' Seminary, Dyhrenfurth's Commercial, Goldbeck's Conservatory of Music, Law Department of the University of Chicago, Rush Medical College, College of Pharmacy, Homeopathic Academy of Medicine, Charity Dispensary, Hahnemann Medical Dispensary, Bennett Medical and Surgical College.

HOSPITALS.

Women and Children's, Protestant Deaconess', Small Pox, Alexian Brothers', United States Marine Hospital, Jewish.

ASYLUMS.

Newsboys' and Bootblacks' Home, Nursery and Half-Orphan, St Vincent, House of Providence, St. Paul's Presbyterian Orphan Asylum, St. Mary's and St. Joseph's Orphan Asylum, Charitable Eye and Ear Infirmary.

IRREPARABLE LOSSES.

The losses by the destruction of buildings, goods, and commercial paper and property by the great fire are not the only great losses. Treasures of literature, science and art were consumed which can never be restored or replaced, and which no insurance risks can ever give back to us.

Among these are the invaluable collections of books, pamphlets and manuscripts in the Historical Society's well-filled rooms; the priceless scientific collections in the rooms of the academy of sciences; the vast collection of curiosities, wonders and valuables in Colonel Wood's Museum; the oil paintings in the Opera House and Academy of Design Art Galleries, and in the score of artists' studios; the choice art collections and libraries in the private residences of wealthy citizens on the South Side avenues and on the North Side; the libraries of the Library Association and the Young Men's Christian Association; and the vast stocks of fine books and pictures in the great State street book-stores; and other losses only apparently less important because less generally known.

The value of many of these rare treasures of literature, art and wonder, cannot be computed by money considerations. They were beyond price, beyond the power of purchase, and are beyond the power of human wealth or ability to replace.

HOW CHICAGO RESUMES BUSINESS.

To the Editor of the New York Tribune:

SIR: As a little indication of the go-ahead spirit of Chicago, I send you a copy of the first and only telegram received by the American News Company, since the fire, from their house in Chicago, the Western News Company, dated Oct. 11, 1871:

Send two cases steamboat cards.

FOLEY'S
Billiard Hall,
AND
SAMPLE ROOM,
Cor. Canal and Randolph Streets.

Under Barnes House.

CHICAGO, ILL.

ESTABLISHED 1857.

W. BARROW,
Premium Wig Maker,
And Manufacturer of Hair Goods,

143 West Madison St., Chicago,

Late, No. 103 Madison Street.

GRAY & BARROW,
Importers and Manufacturers of
HUMAN AND IMITATION HAIR GOODS,
(LATE No. 77 CLARK STREET,)

No. 143 WEST MADISON STREET,

J. GRAY.
W. BARROW.
CHICAGO.

$500 worth of Faber's pencils
$300 worth of Eagle pencils.
One case each, 5 and 6, in German S. S. pencils.
One cask Arnold's quarts.
$18,000 worth of school books, assorted.
200 gross Gillott's 303 pens.
100 gross Gillott's 404 pens.
50 gross Gillott's 170 pens.
100 gross Estabrook's pens, assorted.
One cask Arnold's pints and half pints.

Not one word about fire or other calamity; simply business, nothing more, nothing less. This "move on" spirit made the old Chicago, and will make the new, grander and more beautiful.

SINCLAIR TOUSEY,
President of the American News Company.

New York, Oct. 11, 1871.

An estimate made by the Western News Company, about eighteen months ago, gives the following as their current sales of each edition of the periodicals named:

Ledger, 25,000 copies; New York Weekly, 16,000; Saturday Night, 14,000; Harper's Weekly, 5,500; Chimney Corner, 5,000; Western World, 3,500; Fireside Companion, 3,500; Harper's Bazar, 3,000; Day's Doings, 3,000; Frank Leslie's Newspaper, 2,500; Police News, 2,500; Appletons' Journal, 2,400; Waverly Magazine, 2,300; Sporting Times, 1,800; Hearth and Home, 1,000; Spirit of the Times, 500; Nation, 200; New York Citizen, 75; Harper's Monthly, 7,000; Godey, 4,000; Atlantic, 2,000; Peterson, 2,000; Our Young Folks, 1,500; Putnam, 750; Galaxy, 700; Our Boys and Girls, 500; Overland, 250; Lippincott, 200; Riverside, 200.

BIRTH AND DEATH.

On some unhappy women the throes of child-birth fell at this supreme hour. One lady, a guest at a hotel, was wrapped in a blanket by her husband, who bore her tenderly away through the crowd and flames. She lay there, silent, and he thought that she had, perhaps, fainted. Still pursued by the fire, he hurried northward, and it was only at Lincoln Park that he paused, and unfolded the covering only to find that Love had carried Death in its arms.

Another woman, in the pangs of maternity, could only crawl, with her hour old babe, to the door of her house, where she was found, stark and dead, with her child in her lap, naked. It was removed by a pitying woman—whither?

Out on Lincoln Park during that awful Monday night, three children were born only to die. Of the mothers, two survived; but the third succumbed to the cold and exhaustion.

PHIL. SHERIDAN'S PLUCK.

One of the very few men in Chicago who did not lose heart or head in presence of the calamity was General Sheridan. He was everywhere and always cheery and self-possessed. Nowhere was he of greater service than in conducting the blasting operations at the corner of Harrison and State streets. It was owing to him, indeed, that the fire was checked here. Through a fiery rain of falling sparks he passed into the centre building of a large terrace, a man on each side of him bearing a barrel of powder. The powder was placed in the cellar, the fuse attached, the men retired.

LAKE SHORE AND MICHIGAN SOUTHERN RAILWAY.

THIS RELIABLE AND POPULAR LINE,

OFFER THE SAME

First Class Accommodations

TO THE TRAVELING PUBLIC AS BEFORE THE FIRE.

4 EXPRESS TRAINS,

DAILY ARRIVE AND DEPART FROM THE

New Depot on Polk Street,

With that Regularity which has made the

LAKE SHORE LINE

The Favorite Route with the Public.

Through Tickets and Berths in Sleeping Coaches

CAN BE PROCURED IN

New Depot on Polk Street,

AND AT S. W. COR. OF CANAL AND MADISON STS.,

AND PASSENGER STATION 22d ST.

CHAS. F. HATCH,   F. E. MORSE,
Gen. Sup't, Cleveland, O.   *Gen. Western Pass. Agt., Chicago, Ill.*

THE GREAT CONFLAGRATION.   79

The General stood alone on the steps, waving the crowd back and shouting at the top of his voice, "Back! back, all of you for your lives!" When the street had been cleared, he gave the signal, the match was applied by the soldier, who hastily retreated, the General walked slowly away, last of all, and only to a short distance. A loud explosion, and the ring of falling masonry ensued, and when the smoke cleared away a great gap was opened in the path of the advancing fire, and its progress was checked. But this was not sufficient. To the width of the street it was desired to add the width of a house at the corner. The owner protested and entreated, but in vain. What availed petty private interests in a moment of such peril. "The house shall go down, by ——," said Sheridan, "pull away, boys." A hundred willing hands were instantaneously at work, there was a crackle and a crash, and the building melted into a mass of shapeless ruin. South Chicago was saved.

CHICAGO AS IT WAS.

A half a century ago there was nothing of Chicago save a marsh lying at the foot of Lake Michigan, with prairies at its back. Indians gathered there, because thence they could conveniently reach the Southern and the Western rivers and the great lakes. A few whites came at irregular intervals to trade with the red men, and forty years ago there was written, " The village presents no cheering prospects. As a place of business it offers no inducement to the settler." In 1795 the Potawatamies had ceded to the United States a tract of land six miles square, at the mouth of the Chicago River.

In 1804 the United States erected thereon Fort Dearborn, which was destroyed during the War of 1812, and rebuilt, sheltering, in 1832, 800 inhabitants, and the taxes in that year were $150. In 1833 the United States expended $30,000 in dredging out the Chicago River, and in 1834 a freshet swept away the bar at the mouth of the river, opening the stream to the largest lake craft. There was nothing of this description, however, in the vicinity of Chicago at that time. Two years later the population was 4,000. In 1849 the first locomotive came and halted ten miles below the city. Lake commerce had grown beyond all calculation; the Indians were disappearing; the arrival of one locomotive had revolutionized sentiment on the subject of railroads, as well as the methods of magnifying traffic. The marshes were already partially drained; the canal joining the Chicago and Illinois river was in active operation, and the trade in coal and stone had gained considerable importance. The population from 1840 to 1871 has been as follows: 1840, 4,855; 1850, 29,963; 1860, 110,973; 1870, 299,227; 1871 (Edward's report), 334,270.

THE RAPID GROWTH OF THE CITY.

The rapid growth of Chicago in wealth, population, commerce, and all the elements which go to make up a prosperous commonwealth, has been one of the marvels of our age. The first white child born within what are now the corporate limits of the city of Chicago is yet in the prime of life, while the mere collection of huts which existed at the time had expanded into a city of nearly a third of a million population, busy with the pursuits of a hundred trades, abounding in public and private palaces, rich in the treasures of art, and possessing all the refinements and elegancies of

HEATH & MILLIGAN,

MANUFACTURERS OF

WHITE LEAD

ZINC,

AND

COLORS,

170 and 172 Randolph St.

☞ Until the completion of our New Store, we shall be at

103 West Randolph st.

civilized life. Passing, in its marvelous career, the older cities of the continent, it has pushed steadily forward for the front rank, until it stood fourth in population and importance, exceeded only by New York, Philadelphia, and Brooklyn.

The causes which have contributed to this rapid development are various. We became the depot from which the productions of our rich and boundless prairies were sent over the lakes to the older Eastern cities, while the returning craft brought the products of Eastern manufactories, together with thousands of immigrants who sought homes among us. Capital, energy, and forethought soon began that network of railways which have gone on expanding, until Chicago has become the focal point for nearly ten thousand miles of road, reaching by its connections nearly every point of the habitable globe. Into its granaries the product of the vast arable plains around us have been gathered, and numerous parallel railways, and an immense marine carry them onward to the sea.

The following is a summary of the various branches of trade which have ministered to the city's wealth and population. The total exhibits the receipts and shipments of the articles named, for the year 1870, together with the total valuation of receipts.

The estimated value of the receipts of the articles named for the year 1871 is as follows:

Article.	Value.	Article.	Value.
Flour	$ 8,000,000	Iron ore	$16,000,000
Wheat	18,000,000	Shingles	2,500,000
Corn	13,000,000	Lath	1,000,000
Oats	4,000,000	Highwines	6,000,000
Pork	2,000,000	Boots and shoes	8,000,000
Dressed hogs	6,000,000	Drugs and chemicals	4,000,000
Live hogs	45,000,000	Hardware	5,000,000
Tobacco	6,000,000	Jewelry	6,000,000
Cattle	22,000,000	Dry Goods	35,000,000
Coal	8,000,000	Groceries	53,000,000
Lumber	16,000,000		

The total trade is estimated at $400,000,000, showing an increase of some nine per cent. on a gold basis over that of the previous year. We had before the fire seventeen large grain elevators, having an aggregate capacity of 11,580,000 bushels, the largest accommodating 1,700,000 bushels.

To carry on this immense traffic, eighteen banks were in operation, with an aggregate capital of $10,000,000, with nearly $17,000,000 of deposits. The total amount of checks passing through the Clearing-House during the year 1870 was $810,000,000.

To accommodate this traffic, and the vast travel, not less than one hundred passenger trains and one hundred and twenty freight trains arrived and departed daily, while full seventy-five vessels loaded and unloaded every day at our wharves.

For the municipal year of 1870-71 the assessed valuation of the city was $277,000,000, of which $224,000,000 was real and $53,000,000 personal. This, however, represents scarcely more than a half of the actual value, which was in excess of $500,000,000. The taxes collected for that year were $3,000,000, besides nearly an equal amount for special improvements, grading, paving, and curbing. The personal property was classed as follows: Individual personal property, $43,647,920; bank personal property, $7,511,600; vessels, $1,183,430.

The area of the city, according to the last arrangement of the boundaries, including parks, public squares, etc., was about 35 square miles, or 22,400 acres. The number of dwellings, according to the last enumeration, was nearly 60,000, of which about 40,000 were wood.

Burned out Oct. 9.   Printing Office running Oct. 11.

CULVER, PAGE, HOYNE & CO.,

11, 13, 15 North Desplaines St.,

CHICAGO,

JOBBING STATIONERS,

BLANK BOOK MANUFACTURERS,

AND JOB PRINTERS.

Our Printing Office and Bindery are now in full operation.

Orders for BLANK BOOKS promptly filled.

BLANK BOOKS CAREFULLY REBOUND.

100 CASES PAPER RECEIVED OCTOBER 21.

Shipments of General Stationery daily received.

Shall be ready to fill all orders from the trade promptly about first of November.

LEGAL BLANKS.

We respectfully announce to Attorneys, Public Officers, etc. that sample sheets of our Blanks were preserved in our vaults and are now being reprinted as rapidly as possible.

CHICAGO AFTER THE FIRE.

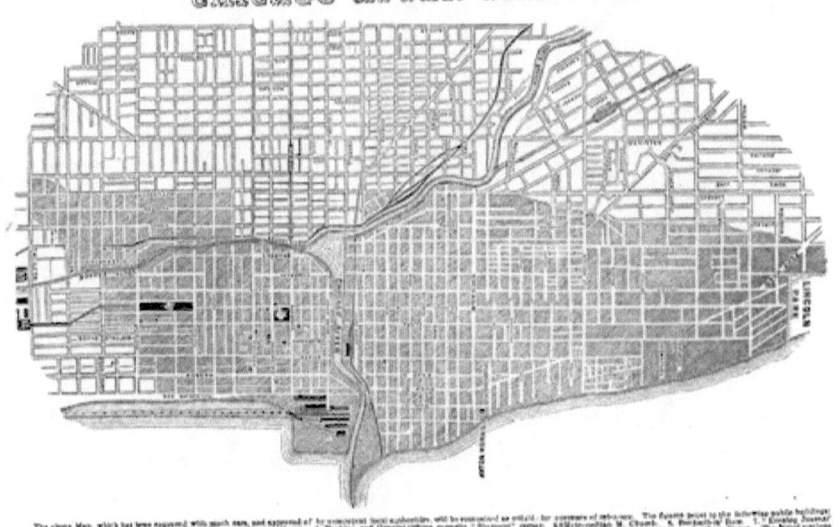

Chicago had thus become a miracle of material development, and had achieved a reputation known wherever civilization existed. By rapid stages, it had advanced to the position of the railroad city of the railroad State of the Union. It had become the center of the grain trade of the Northwest, and had invented the elevator system to accommodate this immense agricultural interest. It had grown to be the emporium of the pork-packing business of the entire country. Its relations to the hide and leather industry had assumed vast proportions, which were becoming still more important and vital. It had grasped and securely held the chief market for the sale of all descriptions of agricultural labor-saving machinery. It was gradually, but surely, wresting from the East supremacy in the tea trade, the finer qualities being already imported to this point, and distributed therefrom, to all parts of the interior of the continent. In groceries; in drugs; in oils; in dry goods; in crockery; in hardware; in stoves; in hats, boots and shoes; in ready-made clothing; and in a variety of other lines of business, Chicago had already secured a broad and expanding market, and was rapidly gaining the ascendency. Direct importations from foreign countries were daily gathering new strength, promising the day soon when this city would be entirely independent of all tide-water marts. The horizon of our future was aglow with the brightest promises. With every local and surrounding advantage on our side, we stood where New York city had stood in 1840, as regards population, and at the same rate of increase, the year 1900 promised to give us inhabitants to the number of three millions

Its elevators, its bridges its tunnels, its water-works, its changed current of the river, its commercial fleet, its railroad communications, its lumber yards, its push and vim, had become a wonder wherever the efforts of enterprise were heralded and appreciated. Chicago was everywhere a name synonymous with all that is progressive, sagacious and successful.

CHICAGO AS IT IS.

JUST AFTER THE FIRE.

To eyes that see no further than the present, Chicago is nothing more than one vast net work of prostrate ruins, contemplating while hope itself may feel discouraged. A track one mile wide and five miles long presents one vast stretch of ashes and *debris*. Where are the traces of architectural stateliness? Where are the proud structures, the magnificent stores and business palaces, which so lately had been the glory of Chicago? Vanished as if before the wand of an enchanter Nothing left were to indicate their character—nothing but the repulsive opposite of their greatness and beauty. Here, where stood, a proud, exulting city—here, where throbbed the the heart of its commercial energy—is nothing but a rugged, chaotic expanse of desolate destruction—an unsightly broken plain, still hot with unsubdued flame, and rolling upward a dun, colored cloud of smoke. Here and there are walls in which are large gaps, and the jagged peaks rise with bleak uneven profile, while between such stark sentinels are wide spaces covered with that bleak *debris* which only a tempest of flames can leave behind. The lines of streets are obliterated, for so intense has been the action of the heat, and the force of miles of simultaneous flame, fanned by a wind-storm, operating with all the intensity of some stupendous blow-pipe that houses had not merely crumbled and fell, but burst open and scattered the materials of construction on all

THE GREAT FIRE CAUSES NO DELAY TO THE
TRAINS

OF THE

MICHIGAN CENTRAL

AND

Great Western R'ys.

Four Passenger Trains Leave Chicago Daily,

FROM THE FOOT OF

TWENTY-SECOND STREET,

AS FOLLOWS:

6.13 A. M. Mail stops at all Stations—Sundays excepted.

9.13 " Day Express—Sundays excepted.

5.28 P. M. Atlantic Express Daily This Train has Pullman Car attached through to New York

9:13 " Night Express—Saturday and Sunday excepted

Sunday Train Leaves 5.28 P.M.

Through Tickets

AND SLEEPING CAR accommodations can be obtained at Company's Office, N. W. cor. Canal and Madison Streets (West side) and at Depot.

W. K. MUIR,   **SARGENT,**
Gen'l Supt. Great Western R'ys.   Gen'l Supt. M. C. R. R

HENRY C. WENTWORTH,
Gen'l West. Pass. Agent.

sides, in promiscuous confusion, the lighter wooden stuff of the interior having been torn up into the air as by an awful suction, and shed abroad from a great height. Walls had fallen inward, walls had fallen outward, as if melted or uprooted.

THE DE KOVEN LANDMARK.

As if to mock the pride of architecture and ordinary notions of security, one squalid little hovel alone remains intact in all the broad expanse of desolation, where the conflagration first began its devouring march. A warped and weather-beaten shanty of two rooms, perched on thin piles, with tin plates nailed half way down them, like dirty pantalets. There is no shabbier hut in Chicago, nor in Tipperary. But it stands there safe, while a city has perished before it and around it. It was preserved by its own destructive significance. It was made sacred by the curse that rested on it—a curse more deadly than that which darkened the lintels of the house of Thyestes. For out of that house, on that ever memorable Sunday night, came a woman with a lamp to the barn behind the house, according to one account, drunken and aimless; according to another legend, to milk the cow with the crumpled temper, that kicked the lamp, that spilled the kerosene, that fired the straw, that fired the stable, that burned Chicago. And there to this hour stands that craven little house, holding on tightly to its miserable existence.

OUT ON THE PRAIRIES.

Destitute, shivering wretches, lately tenants of comfortable homes, and owners of property, lie huddled on the ground, exhausted with tense feelings and overstrained exertions. Near by each stricken group is the little pile of damaged personal effects— the insignificant remnants of their worldly possessions—rescued from the maw of destruction. Few have anything to eat, and no lips have touched water for hours. Many are prone at full length, thoroughly tired and sound asleep. Others sit crouched on the bare earth, and peer with sleepy, furtive eyes through the smoke-filled atmosphere at the not far-distant wilderness of ruins. In some places, the pains of parturition have seized some suffering women, and the cries of the new-born infant mingle with the murmurs of the wind. Death, too, has set his seal on some eyes, and the prostrate forms, pulseless and cold, lie stretched beside the living. Despair is in many a heart. A rain has swept over the sorrowful scene—a rain welcome to all at first, for it supplied moisture for parched throats, and purified a suffocating atmosphere; but pernicious in   nd, for it drenched everybody to the skin, and chilled the frame of every victim.

Many in the vast throng of anxious spectators of the awful scene had been startled by the first alarm, and left their homes supperless; but the night passed and the day came again, bringing no prospects of breakfast. The sun mounted toward the zenith, and yet the gnawings o   er were not appeased. The scene became pitiable in the extreme. Thousands   who had never known what it was to want even for the luxuries of life, now   ried for bread they could not get. Men with haggard look and bloods   by exertion and anxious care, unrefreshed by slumber or food, mov   stless air, and if spoken to frequently returned for an answer a   stare, as if reason and the power of utterance had vanished togethe

The day wore slowly away, and sti   ken no food. The cries of the children became more boisterous; won   rong men bowed in unutterable agony. The gale had blown clou   smoke into their very

11

Chicago & Alton R. R.

THE ONLY FIRST CLASS ROAD IN THE WEST.

(See Classification of Railways by Board of Railway Commissioners.)

Chicago, Alton & St. Louis Thro' Line

Louisiana, Mo. New Short Route from CHICAGO to KANSAS CITY.

THE SHORTEST, BEST AND QUICKEST ROUTE FROM

CHICAGO TO ST. LOUIS Without Change of Cars.

THE ONLY ROAD RUNNING

3 EXPRESS TRAINS TO ST. LOUIS DAILY, and a Saturday Night Train. **11** and making the time in **HOURS**

The only Line running PULLMAN PALACE SLEEPING CARS between

Chicago and St. Louis.

CLOSE CONNECTIONS In St. Louis for all points in Missouri, Kansas, Colorado and California.

The DIRECT ROUTE and the ONLY ALL RAIL ROUTE to Memphis, Vicksburgh, Mobile, New Orleans, and

ALL POINTS SOUTH.

AVOID a long Steamboat Transfer of TWENTY-FIVE MILES, and changes of Cars by taking this Route.

PULLMAN PALACE CARS RUN on THIS ROUTE ONLY from CHICAGO to NEW ORLEANS, with but one Change.

LOUISIANA, MO. NEW SHORT ROUTE FROM CHICAGO TO KANSAS CITY,
Via Chicago and Alton and Northern Missouri Railroads, passing through Joliet, Bloomington and Jacksonville Ill., and crossing the Mississippi, at Louisiana, MO.

THE BEST SHORT ROUTE FROM CHICAGO TO KANSAS CITY WITHOUT CHANGE OF CARS.

CLOSE CONNECTIONS in Union Depot, Kansas City, with all Western Roads for Kansas, Colorado, New Mexico and California; and in Chicago

WITH TRAINS OF ALL ROADS FOR THE EAST AND NORTHWEST.

Elegant Day Cars and PULLMAN PALACE SLEEPING CARS run through from
Chicago to St. Louis and Ch **to Kansas City**
WITHOUT **E.**

Pullman Palace Dining and rs on all Day Trains.
The ONLY LINE running the .ICAGO & ST. LOUIS
and CHIC .S CITY.

JAMES CHARLTON,   J. C. McMULLIN,
General Passenger   General Superintendent,
Ch   Chicago.

faces, and enveloped and covered them up, until they scarcely wore the semblance of human beings.

It is amid these forlorn groups, scattered over a wide expanse, that relief parties from the city soon move, bringing wagon-loads of provisions to succor the sufferers by those two miserable nights of hunger and cold. As they satisfy appetite and quench thirst, hope gleams in weary eyes, and partially recuperated nature once more turns to the tasks of life with almost instinctive purpose. Little by little they were removed from their open, unsheltered bivouac, terrible in its remembrances, and supplied with temporary homes, where they once more face the realities of the future with resolute hearts, and put their hands to the duties of the hour. Charity meantime proceeds with her work of mercy and benefaction, until all the outlying victims of the conflagration are safely housed, fully fed, and comfortably clad.

ORGANIZED RELIEF.

Contributions of money and food soon pour in from every direction. Churches become depots of supplies, whence the needy flock and are comforted. The railroads munificently offer to carry away, without charge, the destitute to places where they can find work or friends. School-houses are thrown open to the homeless. Rows of tenements are hastily run up on various open lots. Employment is secured for those able to work. In a few days all suffering that can be relieved by such means is brought to an end.

THE WORK OF RESTORATION.

The wonderful people of Chicago are already upon their feet. Banks are doing business as usual. Insurance companies are adjusting losses. Numerous temporary structures and some first class buildings are already taking the place of recent ruins. Contracts are being let for the erection of hundreds of buildings of the most imposing, costly, and substantial kind. The Water Works are again supplying the whole city with its accustomed abundance. The gas companies are rapidly getting into condition to fulfil their former relations to the public. All the daily newspapers are revived. The railroads are in full operation. Business men who have been burned out, with a large number of corporations, have opened new centers of trade and offices in the West and South Divisions, until they can can return to their old locations. Canal and Clinton streets, with Lake, Randolph, Washington, Madison, and Monroe, toward the South Branch, are now the great thoroughfares of commerce, loud with the hum and bustle of traffic, thronged with drays, wagons, and carriages, thick with coming and going pedestrians. All is life, vigor, cheerfulness, and hope once more. Nobody doubts, nobody hesitates. Everywhere the city, Phœnix-like, is preparing to rise from its ashes. Confidence in the future is even exultant. Indomitable Western pluck is master of the situation. Resumption of business is the order of the day.

CHICAGO AS IT WILL BE.

WHAT IS LEFT TO BEGIN WITH.

Chicago has still all the elements of a great city except the mere buildings. She has her river harbor, which has been dredged and enlarged, and her piers and breakwaters, which have been constructed at an enormous expense. These can not be

W. J. JEFFERSON.   T. J. WROE.

JEFFERSON & WROE,

General

Job Printers,

No. 463 South Clinton Street,

Are prepared to fill Orders for all kinds of Printing with usual dispatch. Their old customers, hotel men, and others, are invited to call and see them.

W. F. HUNT,

DEALER IN

Rags and Old Metals

78 and 80 West Van Buren Street,

Chicago, Ill.

extemporized in any other place. She has her light-houses for the security of navigation. She has her expensive tunnel under Lake Michigan for supplying a city thrice her recent magnitude with pure water, with an extensive ramification of mains and subsidiary ducts wholly unimpaired; and all the gas mains that feed the city exist still in as perfect condition as before the fire; she has her extensive system of sewerage, which, being under ground and constructed of non-combustible materials, has not been consumed. She has the grading to her streets, and eighty to hundred miles of paving in fair condition throughout the burnt district, with the excavations of her cellars and vaults. She has the outlying vegetable gardens and milk dairies for supplying her tables. Her vast cattle yards were untouched by the flames. The destruction of her great railroad depots will scarcely obstruct travel and traffic, as passengers can be received and landed, and freight taken and delivered, in the open air, until the depots are rebuilt. Her water communications are untouched, and her commercial fleet is as numerous to-day, and as ready and efficient and potential, as ever it was. Her geographical position, which made her the entrepot and emporium of the Northwest, possesses all the natural advantages, with nearly all of those superadded by the hand of enterprise. The people of this whole section, who found it to to their interest to trade with Chicago before, will still find their account in coming here, if the goods are here to buy, and if the means are provided here for receiving and shipping the produce of the country, as assuredly they will be.

And what is, perhaps, the most important of all her remaining advantages and sources of resuscitation, Chicago has not lost her shrewd, enterprising, energetic, indomitable men of business. They can more easily re-establish themselves in Chicago than they can form new connections elsewhere. They will not break from their creditors in the East, nor from their customers in the West. The vast, magnificent Northwest must still be furnished with goods and they will continue to furnish the supply. New men in new cities have not their business acquaintances, and can not build stores and collect stocks as quickly as the Chicago merchants can build and renew them. Chicago will restore herself before competitors can come into the field.

The Chicago of Oct. 9 may be likened to a strong, active man stunned. Consciousness is now returning; the stiffened limbs are recovering their lost action; the warm blood is again coursing through the veins and arteries; the man is again erect, inspired with new energies, looking to the future, and determined to forget the past. Its geographical location gave Chicago a stamp of greatness. Commerce and finance pointed it out as one of their favorite centers. This fact attracted energy, industry, enterprise, and capital. The men who built Chicago are still bustling about the ruins. Past opportunities for business success in Chicago were nothing as compared to future ones. The business men of to-day will remain, to be joined by thousands of others, all inspired by a common interest,—that of not only restoring the City of the Lakes to its former grandeur, but increasing it tenfold. The wand of a grater than the genii of Aladdin's palace will soon be busy around the charred ruins. Its magic touch will fashion the blackened, ragged walls into towering structures, and with its enchantment in time substitute living vernal offerings for the heaps of dead ashes. There is no Marius to stalk, like a specter, among the ruins of this our Carthage, but tens of thousands whom no calamity can dishearten, to build the city anew, more Cyclopean in its massiveness, more æsthetic in its architecture, more secure in its durability, more utilitarian in its progress, more powerful and far-reaching in its influences.

The growth of Chicago—a city which has risen like an exhalation on the south-

Pittsburgh, Ft. Wayne & Penn.
RAILROAD.

Trains leave from cor. Madison & Canal Sts., CHICAGO, as heretofore,

9:00 A. M. EXPRESS, entire train, with Pullman Palace Cars through to New York, without change

5:15 P. M. EXPRESS, with Pullman Palace Cars through to New York, without change.

9:00 P. M. EXPRESS, with Pullman Palace Cars through to New York, without change.

5:30 A. M. MAIL, stops at all Stations between Chicago and Pittsburgh.

3:45 VALPARAISO ACCOMMODATION.

Tickets for sale, and Sleeping Car Berths secured at **43** Madison St. in Sherman House, and at Depot, cor. Madison & Canal Sts., Chicago.

F. R. MYERS, *Gen'l Passenger & Ticket Agt.* W. C. CLELAND, *As't Passenger Agt.*

Oct. 1871.   J. N. McCULLOUGH, Gen'l Manager.

Pittsburgh, Cincinnati
AND ST. LOUIS RAILWAY.

Trains leave old Milwaukee Depot, Cor. Canal & Kinzie Sts., Chicago, as follows:

Express, Except Sunday.   (VIA PAN-HANDLE ROUTE.)
7:20 A. M.   Indianapolis, Richmond & Cincinnati.

Express, Except Sunday.   (VIA LAFAYETTE ROUTE.)
8:40 A. M.   Indianapolis, Cincinnati & Louisville.

EXPRESS, Except Sunday.   VIA PAN-HANDLE ROUTE.
12:40 P. M.   COLUMBUS AND EASTWARD.

EXPRESS, Except Saturday.   (VIA LAFAYETTE ROUTE.)
7:25 P M.   Indianapolis, Cincinnati and Louisville.

EXPRESS, Except Saturday.   (VIA PAN-HANDLE ROUTE.)
7:25 P. M.   COLUMBUS AND EASTWARD.

EXPRESS, Except Saturday.   (VIA PAN-HANDLE ROUTE.)
***7:55 P. M.**   Indianapolis, Richmond and Cincinnati.

4:10 P. M.   Except Sunday.   Dolton & Lansing Accom.

10:10 A. M.   Except Sunday.   Dolton Accom.

F. R. MYERS,   W. C. CLELAND,
Gen'l Pass. & T. Agent, Pittsburgh.   Ass't Gen. Pass. Ag't, Chicago.
J. N. McCULLOUGH, Gen'l Manager, Pittsburgh.

* Passengers for Columbus and Eastward leaving Chicago at 7:55 P. M. overtake and can change at Logansport to train leaving Chicago at 7:25 P. M.

WM. KERR & CO.,

MANUFACTURERS AND DEALERS IN

Wisconsin Lime

CEMENT,

Plaster, Plastering Hair,

&c., &c.

96 WEST LAKE ST.,

CHICAGO.

western shore of Lake Michigan—has been regarded by travelers and economists as one of the chief marvels of recent times. It is a phenomenon which never had a parallel, but which will be eclipsed by the more astonishing miracle of the reconstruction of the burnt emporium from its ashes. Forty and two years was this wonder in building, and yet it will be reconstructed in three years. It will rise again from its ruins as if by magic, and the marvel of its original growth will be forgotten in the greater marvel of its sudden new creation. If there was any place on the earth's surface where there was concentrated, within a few square miles, the most wonderful evidences of human enterprise, activity and vigor, and where life was most intense and hopeful and where the thought of destruction, or even of possible repression of growth, was most absolutely banished, it was in that area of which the Chicago Court House was the center, and where the soft-made earth seemed to groan beneath hundreds or proud edifices, worthy of a world's metropolis, and to quake under the mighty pulsations of the greatest commerce ever transacted in a city of like dimensions. This gigantic realization is to be reproduced, only more magnificent in proportions, more vigorous in strength, more enterprising in spirit, more sagacious in forethought, more solid in prosperity.

The hopeful and confident anticipation rest upon the most solid grounds. In the first place, the city remains, except the consumed buildings, machinery, and stocks of goods. There are the hundreds and hundreds of outlying cities and villages scattered through the West; there are millions and millions of acres of productive farms; there are the thousand and thousands of miles of railroad radiating in all directions from that great center; there are the millions of tons of shipping on the great lakes which have been accustomed to sail from Chicago laden with grain, and to return laden with goods and lumber. These are what made the greatness of Chicago, and they will quickly renew it. Chicago has grown only because these have grown. Chicago was a marvel only because the West was a miracle. It has taken Chicago forty years to reach the greatness it had before the fire, because it has taken that length of time to bring the Western prairies under cultivation, to build up the tributary Western towns, to construct the Western railroads, to cover the Western waters with their fleets of propellers and sailing vessels. All these still exist, forming the materials and the machinery for a vast commerce, which must be transacted from some Western center. The destruction of the Western farms, towns and railroads would have been fatal to Chicago, but the burning of her buildings is not fatal, and will be only a transient impediment to her wonderful growth.

There is not the slightest danger of the transfer of her grain trade and her various business to other lake cities. At present the other lake cities have not facilities to accommodate it; their elevators, warehouses, mercantile establishments, banks, etc., being proportioned to the business they already possess. To transact in addition the business of Chicago, they would need an enormous increase of structures, accommodations, and capital. But these can be replaced in Chicago as quickly as they could be built at Milwaukee and other lake ports, and nobody will invest money for them elsewhere with the certainty that Chicago will be rebuilt as speedily as multitudes of busy hands can do the work. The lake commerce will always tend to one great center, and there is no other center which possess such natural advantage as Chicago. These have been increased by costly artificial advantages which it has required thirty years of persistent industry to create. All the great railroad lines have been constructed with a view to Chicago as a starting point and a terminus. It might be easy

HERRING'S SAFES
IN THE GREAT FIRE.

CHICAGO, Oct, 17, 1871.

MESSRS. HERRING & CO.:

GENTLEMEN—In the ever memorable fire of the 8th and 9th instant, which destroyed some TWENTY THOUSAND buildings, including the entire wholesale business portion of this city, we had our valuable books, papers, etc., enclosed in HERRING'S SAFES, which, owing to the intensity of the heat and the want of water, lay imbedded in the ruins for days before they could be got at, and, notwithstanding the unparalleled trial, they have proved equal to our expectations, preserving our property when every thing else was swept away.

- Day, Allen & Co.
- Tappan, McKillop & Co. (2 safes.)
- Union Insurance and Trust Company (2 safes.)
- Wenge, Kirtland and Ordway.
- John V. Farwell & Co.
- H. H. Husted.
- Gale & Blocki.
- Armour, Dole & Co.
- Brinkworth & Leopold.
- Field, Benedict & Co.
- A M. Wright & Co
- Giles Bro. & Co.
- Warner & Felix
- Van Schaack, Stevenson & Reid.
- Heath & Milligan.
- Haskin, Martin & Wheeler.
- W. H. Hoyt & Son.
- Loomis & Foilett.
- Charles Cleaver.
- Tenney, McClellan & Tenney.
- A. E Neely & Co.
- Stanton & Co.
- George Armour.
- L. A. Willard.
- Singer & Talcott.
- James S. Kirk & Co.
- J. C. Mitchell.
- L P. Wright.
- A. F. Dickinson.
- D. Herfurth & Son.
- Holland, Frear & Wilson.
- Dyer & Payne.
- Doggett, Bassett & Hill.
- Carter, Becker and Dale.
- Louis Faessler.
- Frear Stone Manufacturing Company.
- Shandrew & Dean.
- Geo. W. Hannis.
- Ingram, Corbin and May.
- W. M. Hoyt & Co.
- G. Beckwith.
- Bradner, Smith & Co.
- Taylor & Thomas.
- F. E. Spooner, Agent Union Line Company.
- Union Akron Cement Company
- Northwestern Manufacturing Company.

A LARGE ASSORTMENT OF

HERRIN'GS
PATENT CHAMPION SAFES,

BANK SAFES,
DWELLING HOUSE SAFES,
VAULT SAFES.
EXPRESS CHESTS. &c.

Constantly on hand at our Factory and Warerooms,

Cor. 14th st. & Indiana ave.

to build a new town, if that were all; but not easy to reconstruct the railroad system of the West with a new point of convergence.

Milwaukee, Toledo, and some other places will no doubt do an additional business up to the limit of their facilities, in moving what has not been burnt of this years' grain crop. But they will not venture to erect a single new elevator with reference to next year's business. Before the next grain crop is threshed, Chicago will have as many elevators as she possessed the day before the fire. There will be no difficulty in restoring all the buildings and machinery before the end of July, nor perhaps before the opening of navigation in the spring. It would be sheer waste of money to build them at other ports when they are certain to be rebuilt with the utmost speed and energy on their old sites.

The city will surely rise with renewed greatness and magnificence and power. Of course, all parts of the restoration will not go on simultaneously. Buildings for the accommodation of commerce and travel will be first reconstructed, and probably most of the elevators, railroad depots, warehouses, hotels banks, and many of the stores will be replaced within a year. There will be no difficulty in obtaining capital for enterprises which are not entative or experimental, but absolutely certain to bring in handsome returns. The buildings can be mortgaged: and the land on which they stand can be mortgaged to pay the cost of construction.

On the Fourth of July, 1876, the American people will signalized the centennial celebration of Independence Day; and the sojourners in Chicago, who shall, on that occasion, sally forth from his comfortable and even luxurious quarters in the most magnificent and celebrated hotel in the interior of this continent, in search of vestiges of our late conflagration, will be able to view only stately piles of brick and mortar and stones—long avenues flanked by lofty buildings, and thronged with pedestrians and vehicles—and his ears will be assailed with the hum of commerce, the whir of machinery, and the commotion of enterprise, where he expected to find conspicuous traces of Sunday night's calamity. Should he, in his extended search, come upon anything of columnal significance, marking the black ruins that once existed, it will be in the shape of some memorial purposely set up by our citizens, not any sign of guant desolation left perforce.

FIRES IN HISTORY.

THE GREAT CONFLAGRATIONS OF ANCIENT AND MODERN TIMES.

Fire has ever been at once the greatest blessing and scourge of the human race. While ministering to human wants, it has never failed to give to war redoubled horrors, and invest peace with uncertainty and dread. The dreadful scenes at the fall of Troy are invested with a lurid, ghastly splendor, when Homer describes the demoniac flames bursting from the devoted city, roaring and battling with the clouds, while the Greeks, frenzied with victory, and maddened by their ten years' absence from their wives and children, rush through the blazing streets and murder the Trojans in their ancestral halls. When Alexander returned from Hydaspes, and entered Persepolis, the mysterious and wonderful capital, he revenged himself for the Grecian cities which had been ravaged with fire and sword one hundred and seventy years before by burning the city, of which the sublime Chebelminar, or Forty Pillars, alone remain to bear actual evidence of its former greatness. A century later the world was appalled by the conflagration that swept Carthage into oblivion. In her last melancholy struggle with Rome, Æmilanus, the besieging general, carried fire to be applied to the houses as the only means of gaining a footing within the walls. The city was allowed to burn six days, when the flames were extinguished. On her final subjugation, Rome's inexorable decree, "*Carthage delenda est*," was carried into effect. The city was set on fire, and in many quarters at once. The renewed conflagration raged with incredible fury for seventeen days. Here, unlike at Chicago, the flames were assisted rather than resisted by man; but so vast in extent, and so filled with treasure was the African metropolis, that for twenty-three days the smoke of her burning palaces and warehouses ascended.

In time Rome herself was burned. The flames raged for six days and seven nights, and out of fourteen quarters only three escaped unharmed. The origin of this dreadful calamity is involved in doubt, although the frequent occurrence of minor fires in Rome lends probability to the assumption that it was due to accident. So common was conflagrations in Rome that Crassos amassed much of his great wealth by speculating on these calamities. When a fire broke out he would hasten to

SWEET, DEMPSTER & CO.,

59 & 61 West Washington St.,

HAVE RESUMED BUSINESS,

And are prepared to offer to the trade an ENTIRE NEW STOCK OF

HATS, CAPS,

FURS, GLOVES, MITTENS, &c.,

AT THE VERY LOWEST PRICES.

Orders promptly and carefully filled.

J. MANZ,

𝔈𝔫𝔤𝔯𝔞𝔳𝔢𝔯 𝔬𝔫 𝔚𝔬𝔬𝔡,

165 W. Madison Street,

CHICAGO,

(FORMERLY AT REYNOLDS' BLOCK, CORNER OF DEARBORN AND MADISON STREETS,)

Again in full working order, and prepared to take any orders for Engraving on Wood, which will be executed in the best style of the art at low rates and on short notice.

ORDERS SOLICITED.

the scene with a gang of slaves, and would induce the affrighted householders to part with their burning property at considerable under its value. He would then employ his slaves in arresting the flames, and afterward would have the buildings repaired. In this way he became landlord of a great part of Rome.

Constantinople has suffered most of all places from fire. Early in he reign of Justinian it was the scene of the greatest conflagration known in history, and to the present day the Turkish capital retains its proverbial liability to the ravages of fire

The great fire of London broke out at one o'clock on Sunday morning, Sept. 2, 1666, at the house of one Farryner, a baker, in Pudding-lane. Fish-street Hill. Whether it originated in accident or design is a point on which historians by no means agree, while all concur in representing it as at once more destructive in its progress, and ultimately productive of more beneficial effects, than any conflagration recorded in history. The part of the city where it began consisted of narrow lanes and passages, and the houses were principally of wood. The fire soon spread to the adjacent houses, and defied the power of water poured from buckets, for the engines could not be brought to bear upon it successfully on account of the narrowness of the streets. It was then suggested to the Lord Mayor, who arrived on the spot at three o'clock in the morning, that it would be advisable to pull down several houses to interrupt the progress of the flames, but he refused so prudent a measure, and is said to have expressed his opinion of the fire in a flippant and indelicate terms. By eight o'clock in the morning it had reached London Bridge and there divided. The main body of the flames pressed forward into Thames street, which was filled with combustible material that augumented the fire considerably, which raged with great fury the whole day; and struck the inhabitants with such terror that, says Lord Clarendon, "All men stood amazed as spectators only, no man knowing what remedy to apply, nor the magistrates what orders to give."

On Monday the winds changed and spread the flames over places deemed quite secure the day before. Grace Church street and parts of Lombard and Frachurch streets were in flames, and the fire was then burning in the form of a bow. The night of Monday was more fearful than the preceding one the fire shone with such fearful blaze that the streets were as light as noonday. The Cathedral of St. Paul's was entirely consumed. On Tuesday night the fire continued, sweeping away Ludgate Hill, the Old Bailey, the whole of Fleet street, and the Inner Temple, and threatening even the Court at Whitehall, which now began to be alarmed, and gave directions to blow up several houses with gun powder. On Wednesday morning, when the inhabitants of Westminster and the suburbs were preparing for flight, the wind fell, and the fire was stayed. Thirteen thousand and two hundred dwelling houses, 89 churches and 400 streets were destroyed in this conflagration, which is, perhaps, the only one commemorated by a monument. The extent of the ravages covered 436 acres, and the value of the property destroyed was estimated at $50,000,000

London rapidly recovered from this disaster, and in four years had rebuilt, in an improved style, the greater part of the burned district. The inherent vitality in great cities ought to be full of promise to Chicago, which, unlike London, has at her command all the great improvements introduced within recent years for facilitating the construction of buildings

The burning of Moscow was perhaps more remarkable in its character and ultimate effect than any other conflagration recorded. It changed at one stroke the fortunes of Napoleon, and delivered Russia from the invader. Napoleon had advanced with successive victories 2,000 miles from his capital, and at length entered the Russian capital with 200,000 men, when the city was fired. The French soldiers shot the incendiaries, bayoneted them, tossed them into the flames, but still the gangs plied their work The fire continued with unabated fury for three days, until nothing was left of Moscow save the remembrance of its former grandeur.

The fire in Liverpool in 1842, the great fires that have taken place within the last twenty years in London, and the dreadful scenes last April in Paris, may be regarded as among the principal conflagrations that have occurred in Europe during this century.

The conflagrations of American cities have so far not equalled in extent the great European burnings, but still have entailed vast losses and created great suffering. The most fearful fire that ever devasted New York city broke out on the night of the 16th of December, 1835, in the lower wards. The flames raged fiercely for three days, laying waste the business part of the city, and consuming 648 houses and stores, with $18,000,000 worth of property, among which were the marble Exchange, in Wall street, hitherto deemed fire-proof, and the South Dutch Church in Garden street. Some buildings were finally blown up by gunpowder, and the work of ruin thus arrested. This calamity was soon followed by the commercial distress of the winter of 1837, but the elasticity of the city was not long depressed by these misfortunes. A reaction took place before many months had passed, and business revived more briskly than before.

GAGE BROTHERS & CO.,

WHOLESALE MILLINERY

And Straw Goods.

961 Indiana Avenue, between 20 & 21st Streets,

CHICAGO,

(Formerly at 78 Lake Street.)

Orders promptly filled, Stock full, Goods all new and Cheap.

FRANCIS DODD.   FRANKLIN J GUTH

DODD & GUTH,

Manufacturers of

Shirts and Fine Underwear,

Dealers in Mens' Furnishing Goods,

LIST OF PRICES AND INSTRUCTIONS FOR SELF-MEASUREMENT SENT BY MAIL.

REGULAR DISCOUNT TO THE TRADE.

109 West Madison St., Chicago.

Goods can be returned at our expense, that prove unsatisfactory.

Four years later 46 buildings were burned, entailing a loss of $10,000,000. In 1845 a fire broke out in New street, then extended to Broad street, where a building in which saltpetre or other explosive material was stored, blew up, carrying six or seven buildings with it, and shaking the whole city like an earthquake. After raging all day, the flames were extinguished about midnight. In a section nearly bounded by Broadway, South William street, Exchange place, and Beaver street, 208 buildings had been destroyed, causing a loss of about $6,000,000.

In other parts of New York State fires of great magnitude have occurred. In August, 1849, 24 acres were burned over in Albany, and 600 buildings, with a number of steamboats, were destroyed. The fire of April 10, 1845, consumed 200 houses in Brooklyn, causing a total loss of $860,000. In Troy a fire in 1820 destroyed the business part of the city. Another fire (Aug. 25, 1854) destroyed 300 buildings; and again on May 10, 1862, property valued at $3,000,000 was burned, including 671 buildings, among which were many public edifices.

San Francisco has been in special degree scourged by fire. The first great fire was on Dec. 24, 1849, and the estimated loss was $1,000,000; the next was on May 4, 1850, loss $3,000,000; the third on June 14 of the same year, loss $3,000,000; the fourth on May 2, 1851, loss $7,000,000; the fifth on June 22, 1851, loss $2,000,000—making a total of $16,000,000 lost by fire fire within 18 months by a city whose population did not then exceed one-tenth of the present population of Chicago.

The city of Washington, which was burned down by the British during the war of 1812-14, was visited, in 1836, with a fire which reduced to ruins the general post office and patent office, and consumed 10,000 valuable models and drawings.

Pittsburgh was the scene of conflagration on April 10, 1845, which destroyed 1,000 buildings, and entailed a loss of $6,000,000.

In Philadelphia the fire of July 9, 1850, destroyed 400 buildings.

St. Louis endured a similar calamity in July, 1849, leveling 418 buildings, and destroying 25 steamboats. The total loss was over $6,000,000.

In the fire at Portland, Maine, July 4, 1866, 1,600 buildings were reduced to ruins. The loss was $9,000,000. The value of the property insured did not exceed $4,000,000.

The British Provinces have had some extensive fires in their cities. At Quebec, 1,500 houses were burned, and a vast amount of property was consumed on the 28th of May, 1845. One month afterward, 1,300 buildings were destroyed in the same city, in all amounting to two-thirds of the whole city. In June, 1846, the whole city of St. John's, Newfoundland, was destroyed by fire, and 6,000 people were rendered homeless.

DIRECTORY.

Amid an uprooting of old landmarks so complete, and changes of location so numerous, so simultaneous, and so anomalous, we have encountered extraordinary difficulties in compiling an accurate and reliable directory. Offices of wholesale houses are to be temporarily found in private residences. Banks have resumed business in the most unexpected localities. Firms are to be found in basements or in second floor rooms, that used to require whole structures for the accommodation of their business. Indeed, if a nitro-glycerine explosion had scattered the signs of the burnt district, and the owners had set up business again at the places where these signs had fallen to earth again or lodged, there could hardly be a more promiscuous and novel distribution of business localities. The same may be said of the offices of city and United States officials.

We have done the best we could amid so many impediments, and present below a directory which, if not always accurate and reliable, will prove useful for reference, and supply a want greatly urgent at the present time.

OFFICES OF THE UNITED STATES, COUNTY AND CITY GOVERNMENT, HOTELS, RAILROADS, AND BANKS.

UNITED STATES OFFICES.

Custom House, United States Depository, Marshal, Commissioner, Pension Agent, District Court Appraiser, Assessor of Internal Revenue, Collector of Internal Revenue, will be found at Congress Hall, Congress street.

Postoffice, Burlington Hall, State and Sixteenth streets, soon to be removed to Plymouth Church, corner Wabash avenue and Eldridge court.

COUNTY OFFICES.

The County Clerk, Circuit and Superior Clerks, County Treasurer, and Courts of the

SIDDONS'
Patent Fire-Proof Iron Roofing,
GALVANIZED IRON CORNICES,
WINDOW CAPS &
ORNAMENTAL GALVANIZED IRON WORKS.

JOHN SIDDONS & SON,
90 Main st. Rochester, New York.

No argument is needed to convince an intelligent public of the importance of good buildings. To secure such without too great an expense, has been the labor and study of years. Experiments with different materials have been more or less satisfactory, but no cheap roof has yet been found to answer the purpose fully. Iron, for roofing, has been conceded by those best informed in such matters, to be the best material for roofing, taking cost, durability and protection against the elements into account. The desideratum was to so construct the iron roof that it would fully answer the purpose required.

Siddons' Patent Iron Roofing is so constructed as to overcome all objections heretofore met in the construction of iron roofs. It has been thoroughly tested in every particular, and has given the most entire satisfation where it is used. An experience of twenty-five years in the manufacture of roofs, has enabled the inventor to understand fully what was wanted and what difficulties had to be overcome.

Our Roofs are so put on that expansion and contraction are provided for in all directions of the sheet.

We also make a specialty of Galvanized Iron Work, for Cornices, Window Tops, Dormal Windows, and all kinds of Ornamental Work, such as is usually used on buildings.

Address, **C. R. OTIS**, Chicago.

Record generally, will be found in the High School building on Monroe streeet. This is the county's headquarters generally.

CITY OFFICES.

The Mayor and city officers generally are located at the corner of Hubbard court and Wabash avenue.

Board of Public Works, Masonic building, corner of West Randolph and Halsted streets

Board of Education, No. 271 West Randolph street.

Police headquarters are at the Union Street Station.

Headquarters of the First Precinct at church, corner of Third avenue and Polk street.

COMMERCIAL.

Board of Trade, 51 and 53 South Canal street.

Lumber Exchange, southwest corner of Lake and Market streets.

THE BANKS.

First National, 644 Wabash avenue.
Merchants' Loan and Trust Company, 544 Wabash avenue.
Third National, 436 Wabash avenue.
Fourth National, 475 Wabash avenue.
Fifth National, 449 Wabash axenue.
Union National, 534 Wabash avenue.
National Bank of Commerce, 532 Wabash avenue.
Northwestern, 536 Wabash avenue.
City National, Bishop Block, West Randolph.
Traders' National, 447 Wabash avenue.
Merchants' National, 225 Michigan avenue.
Cook County National, 681 Wabash avenue.
Illinois State National, 101½ West Randolph.
Merchants' National, 281 Cottage Grove avenue.
Manufacturers' National, 532 Wabash avenue.
Cushman, Hardin & Co., 57 Calumet avenue.
Merchants', Farmers' and Mechanics' Savings Bank, 64 South Halsted street.
Merchants' Savings, Loan and Trust Company, 414 Wabash avenue.

THE HOTELS.

Sherman, corner Clinton and Madison.
Tremont, the old Michigan Avenue, corner of Congress.
Briggs, West Madison street, near the bridge.

NEWSPAPERS.

Tribune, No. 15 Canal street.
The Evening Post, business office No. 101½ Randolph street.
The Times. 105 West Randolph street.
The Republican, 21 Clinton street.
Evening Journal, No. 13 Canal street.
The Staats Zeitung, business office No. 101½ Randolph.
The Evening Mail, Lind's block, South Division.

RAILROADS.

Chicago, Burlington and Quincy, and Illinois Central, at the ruins of the old depot.

The following railroad offices have been established at No. 308 Wabash avenue Offices of the Chicago and Southwestern Railroad, offices of the Decatur and State Line Railroad, office of the Solicitor of the Chicago and Northwestern Railroad, and office of the Solicitor of the Chicago, Rock Island and Pacific Railroad.

Trains on the Chicago, Rock Island and Pacific Railroad leave the depot, corner Clark and Twenty-second streets, at 10 A. M., 4:30 P. M., and 10 P. M.

The Pullman Palace Car Company, corner of Eighteenth street and Prairie avenue.
Erie and North Shore Line, 769 Wabash avenue.
Merchants' Dispatch, 218 West Randolph street.
Goodrich's steamers, dock foot of Michigan avenue.
Union Steamboat Company, west end of Lake street bridge.
Blue Freight Line, 769 Wabash avenue.
Baltimore and Ohio, corner of Sixteenth and State.
Northwestern, Halsted, near Kinzie.

TELEGRAPHS.

The Pacific and Atlantic Telegraph offices are situated at 345 Clark street.
Western Union, 358 Canal.
Fire Alarm Telegraph Office, southwest corner of Canal and Washington streets.

EXPRESSES.

Adams Express Company, 55 West Washington streets.
American Merchants' Union Express, corner of Green and Randolph streets.
United States Express, Washington near Canal.

CHICAGO
Homeopathic Pharmacy

No. 704 State Street,

In Complete Running Order,

DEALERS IN HOMEOPATHIC MEDICINES,

Surgical Instruments,

Galvanic Batteries, Fountain Syringes,

&c., &c.

Agents for Voltaic Armor Bands and Soles.

☞ During the recent calamitous Fire, it was observed by thousands that the rapid spread of the Conflagration was owing largely to immense sheets of Composition or Felt Roofing, which, becoming ignited, were borne through the air by the wind, setting fire wherever they dropped---in many instances many blocks in advance of the fire itself. We are glad to see that merchants and builders are giving this matter serious consideration, and will largely adopt in their new buildings a fire-proof roofing. Such is SIDDONS' PATENT FIRE-PROOF IRON ROOFING, a description of which is given in our advertising pages. Mr. C. R. Otis, the Chicago Agent, will be happy to confer with parties desiring to place on their buildings this celebrated roofing.

BUSINESS DIRECTORY.

A

American Express Co, Washington st, near Canal
American Sewing Machine Co, 133 South Peoria st
Andrews, A H, office desks, &c, 119 West Washington st.
American Mutual Express Co, cor Green and West Randolph sts.
Adams' Express Co, 55 West Washington st.
Allen & Mackey, carpets, 744 State st.
Aiken, Lambert & Co, jewelers, 88 West Washington st,
American Fire Insurance Co, 487 West Madison s .
American Powder Co, 1064 Indiana av
Adams, Blackmer & Lyon, publishers, 201 West Washington st.
Appleby, R B, frames and mouldings, 15 South Halsted st.
Atwater & Co, agricultural implements, 51 and 53 North Jefferson st.
Arctic House, 95 Canal st
Ætna Sewing Machine Co, 159 Milwaukee av.
Andrews, A H & Co, office desks, cor Washington and Jefferson sts.
Barlow & Wells, 201 West Washington st.
Aldrich, A E & Co, furniture, rear 11, 13, 15 and 17 South Canal st.

B

Boal, C F & Co, grocers, cor Harrison court and Michigan av.
Bonsfield, Poole & T Althrop, 1405 Wabash av
Bliss, Moore & Co, grocers, 604 Wabash av.
Bittinger, J & Bro, dried fruits, 392 West Harrison st.
Boynton & Co, 139 Park av.
Bowen, Hunt & Winslow, dry goods 128 Michigan av.
Buret, A W & Co, Continental Ins Co, N. Y, 393 Wabash av.
Bowen, E A, sign painter, 43 Washington st.
Bowen Bros, 360 Wabash av.
Baldwin S S, gold and silver plating, 356 Wabash ave.
Boyd, Chas I, money broker, 386 Wabash av.
Boylington, architect, cor Van Buren st and Wabash av.
Board of Public Works, cor Halsted and Randolph sts.
Brick, U S Machine Works, cor Monroe and Clinton sts.
Bohanon & Purington, fruit, etc, 60 Madison st.
Belding Bros & Co, 716 Michigan av.
Buck & Rayner, druggists, 819 State st.
Bangs Bros, stoves, 1135 Prairie av.
Byrne & O'Brien, 47 and 49 Miller st.
Bless Sewing Machine Co, 142 West Twelfth st.
Baker & Baker, 343 State st.
Barker & Illsby, stoves, 674 State st.
Barnes, A S & Co, 515 State st.

Bowen, E R & Son, gloves, 15 Center av.
Boynton & Co, contractor, cor Clark and Madison sts.
Board of Education, Randolph, bet Sangamon and Morgan sts.
Brigham & Jones, saddlery hardware, 14 West Randolph st.
Blackburn Bros, leather findings, 27 South Canal st.
Blanchard, Borland & Co, lumber commission, cor Lake and Market sts.
Bernauer, B, 66 Lake st.
Barnes House, cor West Randolph and Canal sts.
Blenis House, cor Canal and West Randolph sts.
Brinks' City Express, 37 East Randolph st.
Briggs, Spencer & Co, hardware, 1022 Wabash av.
Burley & Tyrrell, crockery, 367 Wabash av.
Bullock Bros, boots and shoes, cor Twenty-first st and Wabash av.
Bassett & Hammond, hats and caps, 196 West Madison st.
Blanchard, Rufus, maps, 132 Clark st.
Barlow & Wells, 201 West Washington st.
Beiersdorf, J, furniture, 350 Wabash av.
Beckwith, C H & Sons, wholesale grocers, Michigan av. and Monroe st.
Barnum & Richardson, car wheel manufacturers, 67 to 71 West Madison st.
Butler, E W & Co, paper warehouse, 22 and 24 Desplaines st.
Blatchford, E W, Chicago Lead and Oil Works, 66, 68, 70 South Clinton st.
Blandy's engines and sawmills, 36 Canal st.
Bell, R L, ties, wood, bark, etc, 30 Canal st.
Butts, G C & Co, 73 West Lake st.
Bliss & Sharp, druggists, 154 Twenty-second st.
Boston Square Dealing Clothing House, retail, Madison, cor Peoria st.
Boston Square Dealing Clothing House, Twenty-second st, near State st.
Botsford & Son, wholesale hardware, 461 Wabash av.
Briggs House, cor West Madison and Canal.
Bradstreet & Son, mercantile agency, 36 Canal st.
Bradner, Smith & Co, paper dealers, 619 State st.
Bauer, J & Co, pianos, 270 Michigan av.
Bradley & Sidley, machine oils, 60 West Lake st.
Brituell, Terry & Belden, wholesale hardware, 57 West Lake st.
Butler, J W & Co, paper, 13 West Jefferson st.
Butters, W A & Co, auctioneers, 3 and 4 Dearborn Park.
Burton & Pierce, cor Eldridge ct and Michigan av.
Bonte, A C P, pictures, looking glass, etc, 155 West Indiana st.
Bryan, Thos B, fidelity safe depository. 139 Randolph st.
Board of Public Works, 204 West Randolph st.

Brown & Prior, gents furnishing, 659 Wabash av.
Baggott & Almy, gas fitting and plumbing, 79 South Halsted st.
Barrow, W, 143 West Madison st.
Bowen, Ira P & Co, crockery, 107 Wabash av.

C

Collins & Burgie, stoves, cor Jefferson and Van Buren st.
Chicago Gas Light & Coke Co, 1st Baptist church, cor Wabash av and Hubbard court.
Cragin, H B & Co, tinners stock, 122 Michigan av.
Coly & Farwell, 114 and 116 Michigan ave.
Cossitt, F D & Co, grocers, cor Monroe st and Michigan av.
Cook, G C, wholesale grocer, 299 Michigan av.
Cunard Line Steamers, office 376 State, room 12.
Chase, F B & Hild, sign painters, 109 Randolph st.
Case & Savin, lamps, etc, 15 South Canal st.
Clement, Morton & Co, wholesale clothing, 125 Michigan av.
Crerc, Adams & Co, railway supplies, 164 Michigan av.
Cook County National Bank, cor Harrison and Wabash av.
Corn Exchange National Bank, 364 Wabash av.
Connecticut Mutual Insurance Co, 377 Wabash av.
Clapp, Wm B & Bro, silver-plate ware, 356 Wabash av.
Cahn, Wampold & Co, clothing, 474 Michigan av.
Chase, Hanford & Co, oils, etc, 479 Canal st.
Campion, Safford & Co, 460 West Adams st.
Colburn, L J, confectionery, 1045 Wabash av.
Crane, H E & Co, builders, cor State and Jackson sts.
Church's Housekeepers' Resort, 1221 State st.
Collins & Ullman, 1234 Prairie av.
Cornell, W, 662 West Madison st.
Connell, D, ornamental plasterer, 343 Center av.
Cass, Chapman & Co, architects, Clark st.
Cone, S, jeweler, 369 South Clark st.
Chicago Manufacturing Co, 213 and 215 Lake st.
Cooper, C & G & Co, wholesale hardware, 10 and 12 Randolph st.
Chicago Daily Union, cor Market and Randolph sts.
Clark & Edwards, printers, 198 West Randolph st.
Cummings, S & Co, 266 West Madison st.
Cohen, N, Center av, near Twelfth st.
Coggswell & Co, jewelry, 318 West Madison st.
Cragin H B & Co, cor Michigan av and Washington st.
Culver, Page, Hoyne & Co, jobbing stationers, 11, 13, 15 North Desplaines st.
Chicago Scale Co, 36 West Washington st.
Chadwick, dry goods, 237 West Madison st.
Clifton House, cor West Washington and South Halsted sts.
Chicago Shot Tower Co, 64 South Clinton st.
Coggswell, Chas P, machinery, 37 and 39 Canal st.
Chicago Foundry, cor Monroe and Canal sts.
Chicago Lumber Co, cor Lake and Market sts.
Counties, R H, teas and spices, 817 State st.
Chandler, H H, advertising agency, 49 South Canal st.

Commercial National Bank, 532 Wabash av.
City National Bank, N E cor Clinton and Washington sts.
Cobb, Andrews & Co, paper and stationery, 469 Wabash av.
Coen & Ten Broeke, carriages, cor Ann and West Randolph st.
C & G Cooper & Co, machinery, 10 and 12 Randolph st.
Chase C E & Co, forwarding and Ins agency, cor Randolph and Halsted sts.
Campbell, Nye, wholesale fish depot, 21 Jefferson st.
Chandler & Boynton, hides, pelts, etc, 49 South Canal st.
Childs, S D & Co, engraver and die sinker, 253 Kinzie st.
Chicago Plate and Bar Mill Co, 752 Wabash av.
Coggswell & Co, jewelers, 318 West Madison st.
Callaghan & Crockeroft, law books, 121 West Randolph st.
Chicago Lime Co, 800 State street.
Cannon, M T, merchant tailor, 514 Wabash av.
Chicago Newspaper Union, 13 North Jefferson st.
Chicago Scale Company, 34 and 36 West Washington st.
Clinton Wire Cloth Co, 781 State st.
Commercial Agency of Tappan, McKillop & Co, 35 and 37 South Canal st.
Chicago Academy of Music, 800 Wabash av.
Cross, Steele & Cass, 289 West Madison st.
Chicago Mercantile Journal, 463 South Clinton st.
Chicago Type Foundry, 72 Washington st.
Collins, C C, boys' clothing, 792 Wabash av.

D

Draper, N C, teas, syrups, etc, 49 West Lake st.
Dana, Hyde & Co, teas, syrups, etc, 49 West Lake st.
Dane, Westlake & Covert, 87 West Lake st.
Dunlop, Reade & Brewster, printers, 7 and 9 Jefferson st.
Drake, A, wall paper and painting, 175 West Madison st.
Day, J L, tailor, 265 Madison st.
Dana, Hyde & Co, merchants, 49 West Lake st.
Dunham & Holt, 20 South Market st
Downs, A G & Co, dry goods, cor State and Archer av.
Dixon & Hamilton, architect. 829 State st.
Doggett, Bassett & Hills, boots and shoes, 522 Wabash av.
Dean Bros, & Hoffman, book manuf, 31 South Clinton st.
Day, Allen & Co, wholesale grocers, 631 Michigan av.
Diebold & Kenzies, safes, 446 State st.
Duraud Bros, & Powers, wholesale grocers, cor Washington and Green sts.
Doane, J W & Co, wholesale grocers, 148 Calumet av.
Douglass, Frank, machinery depot, 58 South Canal st.
Dennison & Co, tags, 14 Canal st, A L Hale & Bros building.

DIRECTORY TO PRINCIPAL BUSINESS HOUSES. 103

Dawson, John, oakum works, 30 Market st.
Dahl, H L, merchant tailor, 201 West Madison st.

E

Evening Journal Office, 13 South Canal st.
Electric Watch Company, 67 West Madison st.
Eldorado Cook Stove Company, 991 Michigan av.
Evans & Co, 24, 26 North Jefferson st.
Evening Mail, cor Market and Randolph sts.
Edwards, Bluett & Co, clothiers, 47 West Madison st.
East India Tea Company, cor Madison and Halsted sts.
Erickson, boots and shoes, 470 State st.
Esway, A S & Co, bedding, 435 West Lake st.
Eclectic Life Insurance Co, Halsted and Randolph sts.
Esnay, Simmonds, 25 South Canal st.
Ely, W L & Co, 84 West Randolph st.
Eden & Delight, Canal, just N of Randolph st.
Ely, Edward, tailor, 657 Wabash av.

F

Field, Leiter & Co, wholesale and retail dry goods, cor. 18th and State sts.
Friedman, J, clothing, 671 Michigan av.
Frank & Co, clothing, 509 Wabash av.
Fowler & Carr, builders, 13 Egan av.
Flavels, G W, trunk store, 131 West Randolph st.
Forsyth, J F & Co, scales, 70 West Washington st.
Forsyth, James & Co, wholesale grocers, 154 and 156 Lake st.
Fuhring, F, drugs, 156 West Randolph st
Fuller & Fuller, wholesale drugs, 22, 24, and 26 Market st.
Fargo, C H & Co, Boot Manufacturing Co, 575 State st.
Faxon, E G L & Co, 654 Wabash av.
Folsom Bros & Co, 16 North Canal st.
Fisk, D B & Co, wholesale millinery and straw goods, 57 West Washington st.
Ford, David M, machine shops cor Clinton and Washington sts.
Freeman Bros, boots and shoes, 243 West Madison st.
Furst & Bradley, Garden City Clipper Plow Works 58 to 70 South Jefferson st.
Fairbanks, Greenleaf & Co, scales, 14 Canal st.
Ford & Co, 164 West Lake st.
Franklin Insurance Co, 165 West Washington st.
First National Bank, 446 Wabash av.
Farwell, F W, Babcock Extinguisher, 556 Wabash av.
Finkle & Lyon Sewing Machine, 73 South Halsted st.
Florence Sewing Machine, 15 Eldridge st.
Fitch, Williams & Co, 75 Calumet av.
Fitch, T S & Co, real estate, 421 Cottage Grove av.
Farrington, Brewster & Co, grocers, Michigan av, near Hubbard court.
Fairbank, Peck & Co, oils, cor Eighteenth and Blackwell sts.
Farwell, J V & Co Wabash av, near Sixteenth st
Farnum, Flagg & Co, boots and shoes, 266 West Madison st.
Fourth National Bank, 475 Wabash av.

Fifth National Bank, 449 Wabash av.
Follansbee & Son, bankers, 401 Wabash av.
Foley, billiard hall, cor Canal and Randolph st.

G

Gray Bros, 332 Michigan av.
Greensfelder, Rosenthal & Co. wholesale boots, etc, 133 Wabash av.
Goudy & Chandler, attorneys, 391 Wabash av.
Gregory, Campbell, 360 Wabash av.
Glaser, Rifield & Co, Michigan av, near Congress st
Gillespie, J M, 705 Wabash ave.
German Bank, 17 Milwaukee av.
Gottig, C H, cor Lake and Canal sts.
Greenebaum, Henry & Co. German Bank, 16 North Canal st.
Giles, J, show cases, 935 State st.
Glade & Sievers, 54 Lake st.
Gavin, John R, scroll sawing, 87 West Lake st.
Gilmore, A W, banker, 107 West Randolph st.
Gale & Blocki, drugs, 57 West Randolph st.
Gras, Wm & Co, tailors, 172 West Washington st.
Globe Theater, Wood's Museum, etc, Desplaines and Washington sts.
Gage Bros & Co, wholesale millinery, 961 Indiana av.
Goodspeed, J W, publisher, 292 West Madison st.
Garrick, John, 30 Canal st.
Gilbert, Hubbard & Co, cordage, twines, etc, 14 and 16 Market st.
Gibson Bros, 35 West Lake.
Gillett, McCulloch & Co, chemical works, 51 West Lake st.
Graff, M & Co, fruit, fancy dealers, 123 West Madison st.
Gould, Briggs, & Co, wholesale grocers, 41, 43 South Canal st.
Glassbrook, M, hair goods, 145 Twenty-second st
Giles Bros, jewelers, cor Wabash av and Twenty-second st.
Globe Job Printing, 45 West Washington st.
Gilbert & Sampson, 320 Michigan av.
Grand, Hotel, cor Canal and Madison sts.
Gray & Barrow, 143 West Madison st.
Globe Mutual Ins. Company, 23 South Halsted st.
Goss & Phillips, cor Clark and Twelfth sts.

H

Hibbard & Spencer, hardware and tinplate, 120 Michigan av.
Hall, Kimbark & Co, iron merchants, 118 Michigan av.
Hussey, Wells & Co, 1284 Wabash av.
Hale, Ayer & Co, iron, nails, 1 Park Row.
Hunt, Edwin & Sons, hardware, Michigan av, bet Monroe and Adams.
Hull, Sidell & Co, hops and malt, 9 Michigan av
Hibben & Co, 21 Archer av.
Harmon, Messer & Co, grocers, 125 Michigan av.
Hotchkiss, Eddy & Co, 167 Michigan av.
Henderson, C M & Co, boots and shoes, 337 Michigan av.
Harvey, H M, men and boys clothing, 385 Wabash av.

Hamlin, Hale & Co, dry goods, 288 Michigan av.
Heimedinger & Florek, 148 Twenty-third st.
Hall & Harlow, boot and shoe company, 1050 & Michigan av.
Hodges, J B, 577 State st.
Hopson & Co, 300 Michigan av.
Hanchet, livery stable, Hubbard court.
Holden, W H, 1050 State st.
Henry & Cunningham's Oyster Depot, 421 Clark st.
Hotchkin, Palmer & Co, 148 Twenty-fifth st.
Hibernian Banking Association, 146 Wabash av.
Heron, Hugh & Co, book publishers, 376 State st.
Hirsh, J M & Co, 88 West Washington st.
Haggart, S B & Co, stoves, 39 Lake st.
Hunt & Co, farming implements, 47 West Lake st.
Heath & Milligan, paints and oils, 103 West Randolph st.
Hodge & Homer, hardware, paints, oils, etc., 78 West Randolph st.
Hooker, H M, wholesale and retail hardware, 59 West Randolph st.
Hall, Z M, wholesale grocer, 259 and 261 East Randolph st.
Hartford Fire Insurance Co, cor Washington and Green sts.
Hineich & Sontag, 1269 Indiana av.
Halsey Bros, homeopathic pharmacy, 704 State st.
Hale, A L & Bro, furniture, Canal, bet Randolph and Lake sts.
Hart, Asten & Co, Bag Manufacturing Co, 5 and 7 West Madison st.
Haden & Kay, saddlery, etc, 47 West Randolph st.
Hayes, Gibbins & Co, millinery, etc, 434 State st.
Hartford Life Insurance Co, 659 Wabash av.
Home Insurance Co of N Y, 30 and 32 Clinton st.
Hallock & Wheeler, belting and rubber goods, 23 West Randolph st.
Haskin, Martin & Wheeler, cement, 686 South Canal st.
Hollister, E F & Co, carpets, 10 North Canal st.
Hanson, C H, engraver, 54 West Madison st.
Howe's trucks, etc, 57 North Jefferson st.
Home Shuttle Sewing Machine Co, 243 West Madison st.
Hall's Safe and Lock Co, 66 West Madison st.
Hobson, J W & Son, wholesale fish dealers, 60 South Canal st.
Hendrickson, J S, 163 Milwaukee av
Hartt & Co, printing presses, 72 Washington st.
Hunt, W F, rags and metals, Van Buren, bet Clinton and Jefferson sts.
Harris' safes, Canal, bet Randolph and Washington sts
Herring's safes, cor Fourteenth st and Indiana av.
Hughes, John & Son, plumbers, 245 West Madison st.

I

Inness Bros, 364 West Washington st.
Ingraham, Corbern & May, 127 Michigan av.
Inman Line Ocean Steamers, 39 West Kinzie st.
Indiana Pioneer Coal Mining Co, West Lake st.

Ivison, Blackman, Taylor & Co, school books, 273 West Randolph st.
Illinois Central R R Company, 510 Michigan av.
Imperial Insurance Co, London, 505 Michigan av.

J

Jenkenson & Keitz, 47 Twenty-sixth street.
Jordan, C H, undertaker, 56 South Curtiss st.
Jevne & Almini, paints, oils, etc, 669 State st.
Jones, R, paints and oils, 200 West Madison st.
Jenesen, E S, architect, 669 State st.
Johnson & Abbey, hardware, 534 South Canal st
Jones, J M W, Canal st, bet Washington and Madison sts.
Jefferson & Wroe, printers, 463 Clinton st.
Jones & Laughlin, 100 to 106 South Canal st.

K

King, H W & Co, wholesale clothing, 24 Market st.
Kinsley, H M, caterer, 114 Michigan av
Kersting, French boots, 99½ Twenty second st.
Keene, W B, Cooke & Co, Washington st, bet Wabash and Michigan avs.
Kern's lunch rooms, 117 South Clark st.
Kerr, Wm & Co, Wisconsin lime, 98 West Lake st.
Kelley, J W D & Bro, hardware, 959 Indiana av.
Kimball, W W, pianos, 610 Michigan av.
Keith Bros, hats and furs, wholesale, 916 Prairie ave.
Knickerbocker Life Insurance Co, cor Randolph and Halsted sts.
Kirk, Coleman & Co, iron, nails, etc, 34 South Canal st.
Kenley & Jenkins, oils, 34 North Canal st.

L

Lord & Smith, wholesale druggists, Dearborn Park.
Lorillard, P, 82 West Madison st.
Lunt, Preston & Kean, bankers, cor Halsted and Randolph sts.
Loring, E R, plumber, 98 Sixteenth st.
Lombard, Wm, for Cooper, Fellows & Co 311 West Randolph.
Lyon & Healy, music store, 287 West Madison.
Lyon, J W & Co, 197 Van Buren st.
Lusk & Blatherwick, com. merchants, 56 West Lake st
Lichtenberger, Chas, hides, etc, 136 West Randolph st.
Larrabee & North, hardware, 46 and 48 West Lake st.
Leavenworth, A, hardware, 216 West Lake st.
Luddington, N, 263 West Twenty-second st.
Lasher, G & Son, 28 West Randolph.
Libby, A A & Co, packers, 830, 840 State st.
Laflin & Rand, powder company, 595 Wabash av.
Laflin, G H & L, paper, 57 North Jefferson st.
Liverpool, London & Globe Ins Co. 5 West Madison st.
Leopold & Co, 373 Wabash av.
Lloyd, Lewis & Co, advertising agent, 59 West Randolph st.

DIRECTORY TO PRINCIPAL BUSINESS HOUSES. 105

M

Munn & Scott, elevator, 182 West Washington st.
Merchant & Carter, 15 Desplaines st
Marston & Peck, 592 Wabash av.
Millard & Decker, 24, 26 Jefferson st.
Merker Bros, 56 South Canal st.
Mayhon, Daly & Co, millinery goods, 126 Michigan av
McLennan & Frost, contractors and builders, 129 Michigan av
McAuley, Yoe & Co, wholesale books, etc, 198 Michigan av.
Merker, A B, American and Scotch Iron Pig, 376 Wabash av.
Manhatten, S M & C, 386 Wabash av.
Mathews & Mason, 659 Wabash av
Mosebark & Humphrey, boot and shoe store, 1050 Michigan av.
Miller Bros, warehouse North Pier, 629 Wabash av.
Manufacturers' National Bank, 454 Wabash av.
McNeal & Urbans, safes, Canal st, bet Madison and Washington sts.
McLeon & Collins, 56 State st.
Morrison & Colnell, 58 State st.
Merchants' Agency, 104 State st.
McIntyre & French, stoves and tinware, State st, cor Jackson st.
Markley, Alling & Co, hardware, 339 State st.
Miller Bros & Keep, hardware and cutlery, 28 and 30 State st.
Meadowcroft Bros, 5 North Canal st.
McDermott & Co, painters, 98 South Desplaines st
Morton, A V, dry goods, 463 West Lake st.
Mallory D D & Co, oyster depot, 114 West Randolph st
Munson & Co, jobbers, 14 Randolph st.
McLean, A B, 26 South Clinton st.
Myers, S H, 43 West Randolph st.
McGrath, J J, paper, 133 and 135 West Madison st.
Morrill, J F & Co, 139 Randolph st.
McDonald & Bro, 15 South Canal st.
Mabley & Co, clothiers, 122 West Madison st.
Mulefyt, A, carriage manufactory, 205 West Madison st.
Merchants', Farmers' and Mechanics' Savings Bank, 60 Halsted st.
Merchant & Holden, lime, 50 North Clinton st.
Merker Bros, Pocketbook Manufacturing Co, etc, 56 Canal st.
Mott, J R, headquarters of Board of Trade, 51 South Canal st
Maxwell, Wheeler & Co, 1000 Indiana av.
Mayo, A B, jeweler, 468 State st.
Mechanics' Savings Bank, 164 Twenty-second st.
Mandel Bros, 123 Twenty-second st.
Mercantile Agency, 373 Wabash ave.
Mitchell & Hathaw, bookseller, 58 South Canal st.
Mason, C & Co, boilers, cor Clinton and Carroll st.
Misch, George A & Bro, cor Canal and Lake st.
Manz J, engraver on wood, 165 W Madison st

N

National Loan and Trust Co Bank, 107 West Randolph st.
National Publishing Co, 181 West Madison st.
New England House, cor Harrison and Clark sts.
New Haven House, cor Halsted and Randolph sts
Northwestern Manufacturing Co, 20 and 22 South Jefferson st.
Norton & Faucher, tin and Japanned ware, 65 Canal st.
Neeley, Albert E & Co, River, bet Twenty-second and Twenty-third sts.
National Bank of Illinois, 704 Michigan av
Northwestern National Bank, 526 Wabash av.
North American Insurance Co, 511 Wabash av.
National Elgin Watch Co, cor Green and Washington sts.
Northwest Paper Co, 87 West Lake st.
Neage, Rutland & Ordway, Michigan av, opp hotel.
Niedert & Co, commission, 28 Market st.
Noble, W T & Co, looking glasses, etc, 595 State st.
Northwestern Mutual Life Insurance Co, 19 S. Green st.
National Bank of Commerce, 543 Wabash av.

O

Orvis, O D, frames, chromos, etc (wholesale), 381 Wabash av.
Ortmayer, Lenk & Co, 49 West Randolph st.
Ogden, Sheldon & Scudder, fire insurance, 62 South Canal st.
Oglesby, Barnitz & Co, paper warehouse, 318 Randolph st.

P

Pearce & Benjamin, Hyde Park House.
Page, M E & Co, 145 North Desplaines st.
Partridge, C W, dry goods, 123, 125, 127 State st.
Phelps, Dodge & Palmer, wholesale boots, etc, 861 Indiana av.
People's Fire Insurance Co of Springfield, 389 Wabash av.
Philadelphia Collar Co, 696 Wabash av.
Publishing Co, A B & L, 55 West Randolph st.
Prairie Savings Bank, 95 West Randolph st.
Prairie Farmer, 96 Randolph st.
Porter, F. Thayer & Co, furniture warerooms, 90 West Randolph st.
Phelps, Thos & Co, dry goods, 32 Randolph st.
Prestons, J, piano factory, 259 East Randolph st.
Page Bros, & Co, 55 and 57 South Canal st
Prairie State Savings Bank, 95 West Randolph st.
Phœnix Insurance Company, 51 Canal st.
Pugh Bros, machine works, cor Clinton and Van Buren st.
Protection Insurance of Chicago, 235 West Madison st.
Peoples Insurance Company, 30 West Madison st.
Parkhurst, S B, 132 West Madison st.
Parkhurst & Wilkinson, 70 South Canal st.
Price, Rosenblatt & Co, 176 Twenty-fifth st.
Pinkerton's Detective Agency, 55 West Washington st.
Pittsburgh, Fort Wayne and Chicago Ticket Office, under Sherman House.
Post, 101 West Randolph st.

R

Rathbone, John F, & Co, stoves and hollowware, 30 and 32 South Canal st.
Rathbone, John F, warehouse office, 32 Canal st.
Ritchie & Duck, 48 South Union st.
Ross & Gossage, dry goods, Madison st, near Peoria st.
Ruffner, F W, 82 West Madison st.
Richards, D M & Co, 48 Carpenter st.
Raynolds, C T & Co, 1222 Prairie av.
Reissig, Chas, florist, 114 Michigan av.
Ray, DeForest & Fisher, architects, 218 Wabash.
Richards, Crumbaugh & Shaw, 848 Wabash av.
Rothschild, S, 178 Twenty fifth st.
Reinhartt & Foreman, 733, Wabash av.
Rand, McNally & Co, printers, 108 West Randolph st.
Rock River Paper Co, 56 North Jefferson st.
Richards & Gooch, staple groceries, 597 State st.
Rigby & McHenry, 135 Twenty-second st.
Republican Office, 21 Clinton st.
Rice & Thompson, photograph goods,
Reed's Temple of Music, 81 Sixteenth st.

S

Sammons, Clark & Co, mouldings and frames, 197 and 199 Clinton st.
Sweet, Dempster & Co, 59 and 61 West Washington st.
Sprague, Warner & Co, 28 Canal st.
Sherwood, N, teas, 812 State st.
Smith, J L & Co, Illinois River Elevator, over Madison st bridge.
Shay, J B, dry goods, Tuompson's block, West Madison st.
Scales, J C, 184 West Lake st.
Spalding & Merrick, tobacco, 11 Michigan av.
Schwab, McQuade, Co, 618 Michigan st.
Sherman, Hail & Cook, 625 West Washington st.
Sherman House, cor Madison and Clinton sts.
Stark & Allen, jewelers, 363 Wabash av.
Sherman Marble Co, 217 Wabash av.
Stine, Kramer & Co, notions, hosiery, etc, 519 State st.
Summerfield, C & Co, 776 Wabash av.

Sherwood, Henry M, school furniture, 103 to 107 South Canal st.
Seeberger & Breakey, 716 Michigan av.
Stephens, Chas W, photographic stock, 564 West Madison st.
Schmitt & Tahner, 254 Fourth av.
Slade Bros, 66 Lake st.
Small, John H, stationer, 27 Canal st.
Singer Manufacturing Co, 213 South Halsted st.
Simpson, Norwell & Co, 1317 Indiana av.
State Savings Institution, 589 Wabash av.
Schuman & Co, leather findings, 30 West Madison st.
Star and Crescent Mill, Randolph st, near bridge.
Schulters, P, office 92 and 94 South Canal st.
Sawyer, C B & Co, boots and shoes, 854 Indiana av.
Star Chicago Bottling Factory, 162 and 164 Twentieth st.
Schaaf, J, 1130 Wabash av.
Sonne, Chas, 313 West Van Buren st.
Scammon, McCagg & Fuller, 464 Michigan av.
Surdam, S J & Co, 405 Michigan av.
Stover & Dollinger, groceries and teas, 97 West Madison st.
St Caroline's Court, Elizabeth, bet Washington and Randolph.
Snell, Taylor & Co, 365 Wabash av.
Stuart, J C, liquor importer, 199 West Madison st.
Swansea Silver Smelting Works, 49, 55 North Jefferson st.
Sharp, S W, 49 West Lake st.
State Street House, 413 State st.
Snyder & Ingraham, last factory, cor Clinton and Jackson st.
Smith & Nixon, pianos, 287 Madison st.
Stanton & Co, grocers, 857 Wabash av.
Sandmeyer & Klassen, 461 State st.
Staats Zeitung, newspaper, 191 West Randolph st.
Silverman, Lazarus, banker, 562 Wabash av

T

Tribune Office, 15 Canal st.
Tilotson Bros, 182 Michigan av.
Thatcher & Co, 52 South Park av.
Thayer & Tobey, furniture, 90 West Randolph st.
Taylor, N H, engraver, wood, 55 West Madison st.
Thompson, Steele & Co, 49 West Lake st.
Tolman & King, drugs, 53 West Lake st.
Terry & Belden, wholesale hardware, 57 Lake st.
Thompson & Sherwood, 62 Fullerton av.
Tuttle, Thompson & Wetmore, 459 Wabash av.
Tittsworth, A D, millinery, 97 West Madison st.
Tremont House, cor Michigan av. and Congress st.
Terwilliger, J M, McNeal & Urban's safes, Canal, near Washington.
Times Office, 105 West Randolph st.
Tappen, McKillop & Co, Canal, near Washington st.

U

Union Screw and Bolt Co, cor Jefferson and Van Buren sts.

United States Brick Machine Works, cor Monroe and Clinton sts.
United States Insurance, 96 West Washington st.
Uhlich House, cor Twenty-second and State st.
United States Express Co, Washington near Canal st.
Union National Bank, 543 Wabash av.

V

Van Schaack, Stevenson & Reid, wholesale drugs, cor Eighteenth and Wabash av.
Van Cott, A B & Co, 461 Wabash av.

W

Western Star Metal Co, 17 South Canal st.
Western News Co, 99 West Randolph st.
Welsh, T C, 91 South Peoria st.
Webster Bros, West Washington Union Park
Williams, J M & Co, 171 West Washington st.
Wetherell, H W & J M, 369 Wabash av.
Weber, T W & Co, 714 Wabash av.
Wells & Faulkner, wholesale grocers, 165 Michigan va.
Wiswall, Hasrue & Thompson, boots, etc, 131 Twenty-second st.
Warren, Keeney & Co, notary publics, 381 Wabash av.
Whitcomb, J S & Co, real estate, 336 Wabash av.
Wells, W D & Co, 618 Wabash av.
Wrenn, Ullman & Co, bankers, 674 Wabash av.
Wolf, F, liquor importer, 32 West Madison st.
Whitney Bros, 1454 Prairie av.
Willard, P H & Co, 107 Throop st.
Walter, Wm, 101 Washington st.
Wippo, Chas, furniture, 99 West Madison st.
Walter, Victor, 206 Third av.
White & Rossman, stoves, 146 West Madison st.
Welch & Burns, 143 Canal st.
Whitefield & Co, cor State and Eighteenth st.
Weed Sewing Machine Co, 196 West Madison st
Wilmarth, H M & Bro, 222 Michigan av.
Woods Museum Co, Globe Theatre, etc, Desplaines st.
Wheeler & Wilsons Sewing Machine Co, 338 West Madison st.
Wetherell, H W & J L, 369 Wabash av.
West & Co, 150 Twenty-second st.
Woodman, C L & Co, grocers, 61 South Clinton st.
Windett & A B Baldwin, 79 Aberdeen st.
Windheim, W F, 484 West Jackson st.
Wiser, A H & Co, 144 South Peoria st.
White & Rossman, 146 West Madison st.
Webster, Chas L, confectioner 87 South Halsted st
Wood's Hotel, cor Hubbard court and State st.
Wood, W A, harvesting Machines, office at St. Carolines Court Hotel.
Willoughby, Hill & Co, clothing, cor Madison and Peoria sts.
Walsh & Hutchinson, millinery, 616 Wabash av.
Wright & Beebe, commission, 20 Market st.

THE PRINTERS

have been scattered, their type and presses entirely consumed, but, with a few exceptions, are all getting on their feet again, and will be in running order this week. The following firms can be found at the places named:

Horton & Leonard, 10 North Jefferson st.
J S Thompson & Co, cor Washington and Canal sts.
Howard, White & Crowell, 11 South Canal st.
Blair & Sinclair, South State st.
Millard & Decker, 24 and 26 Jefferson st.
Spaulding & Lamonte, 906 Michigan av.
Rounds & Kane, 9 North Jefferson st.
Jefferson & Wroe, 463 South Clinton st.
Outway, Brown & Co, 107 South Peoria st.
Rand, McNally & Co, 108 West Randolph st.
Cameron, Amberg & Hoffman, 14 Randolph st.
Clark & Edwards, S E cor Randolph and Halsted sts.
P L Hamscom & Co, Madison, cor Peoria st.
Culver, Page, Hoyne & Co, 13 and 15 North Desplaines st.
J M W Jones, 68 South Canal st.
Guilbert & Clissold, 65 South Canal st.
Daley, Cowles & Co, 105 South Clinton st.
J W Middleton, Lake Park.
Hand & Hart, 52 West Madison st.
Oakley & Son, 64 Washington st.

The following firms have dissolved partnership: Dunlap, Reid & Brewster, Ottaway & Barlow, Mitchel, Lawrence & Fordham. Bassett Bros. sold out well to Rand, McNally & Co. Rounds & Kane will hereafter confine themselves to their extensive type foundry business, and leave printing severely alone.

The Chicago Type Foundry has come nobly to the rescue of Chicago printers. Tons of type are arriving daily, and every facility is afforded printers having fair credit before the fire to again resume business. Messrs. Marder, Luse & Co. lost everything except their good name, which, as an aid to re-establishing their extensive business, they have found better than riches.

INDEX TO ADVERTISERS.

A. H. Andrews, office and school furniture	Inside first cover.
Thos. Phelps & Co., dry goods	" " "
Walter A. Wood, mowing and reaping machines	" " "
C. H. Beckwith & Sons, wholesale grocers	Inside last cover
Chase, Hanford & Co., oils, paints, glass etc.	" " "
John F. Rathbone, stove and hollow-ware.	" " "
Hale & Bro., furniture	Outside last cover.
Dennison & Co., Tags	" " "
Thayer & Toby, furniture company	2
Van Schaack, Stevenson & Reid, wholesale druggists	2
Illinois Central Railroad	4
Crane Bros., Northwestern Manufacturing Company	6
Chicago Type Foundry	8
H. Hartt & Co., Printing press machine shops	8
J. Bauer & Co., pianos	10
Stark & Allen, manufacturing jewelers	12
Sammons, Clark & Co., picture frames and mouldings	12
St. Carolines Court Hotel	14
Kirk, Coleman & Co., iron, nails and steel, etc.	14
Collins & Burgie, stove manufacturers.	16
Union Screw and Bolt Company	16
D. B. Fisk & Co., millinery and straw goods	18
John H. Small & Co., stationers	18
Page Bros., & Co., leather and findings	20
George A. Misch & Bro., stained, moulded, cut and ground glass.	20
M. Glashbrook, importer of human hair.	22
Diebold & Kinzie, safes	22
Hall's Patent Safe and Bank Locks.	24
Cogswell & Co., jewelers	26
Lord, Smith & Co., wholesale druggists	26
Shandrew & Dean, life insurance.	28
Weed Sewing Machine Company	28
Hayes, Gibbons & Co., millinery, and straw goods	30
Hodge & Homer, builders hardware	30
C. C. Collins, clothing	32
Cobb, Andrews & Co., booksellers and stationers.	32
Mathews & Mason, tailors.	34
Clifton House.	34
Home Shuttle Sewing Machine.	36
Aiken, Lambert & Co., gold pens, fine jewelry, etc.	38
Boston Square Dealing Clothing House.	40
A. B. Van Cott & Co., jewelry	42
Edward Ely, tailor	42
Walsh & Hutchinson, millinery	44
N. Sherwood, teas	44
Victo. Sewing Machine, (Thos. Barrows & Co., Western Agents)	46
Chas. W. Stevens, photograph goods.	48
Barnes House.	48
Charles Wippo, furniture.	50
E. A. Bowen, sign writer	50
Mabbey & Co., clothiers	52
John Hughes & Son, plumbers	52
John B. Shay, dry goods	54
Z. M. Hall, wholesale grocer.	56
John Davison, Chicago Oakum Works	56
Henry W. Niedert & Co., commission merchants.	58
Fuller & Fuller, wholesale drugs	58
Wright & Beebe, commission merchants.	58
Harris safe factory.	60
Reed's Temple of Music.	62
White & Rossman, stoves	62
Henry M. Sherwood, school furniture.	64
H. L. Dahl, merchant tailor	64
Western Star Metal Company.	66
J. E. Aldrich & Co., furniture.	66
Hartford Fire Insurance Company.	68
Haskin, Martin & Wheeler, salt and cement.	70
Baggot & Almy, gas fitting and plumbing.	70
Goss & Phillips, sash, doors and blinds	72
Adams Express Company.	74
Globe Mutual Life Insurance Company.	74
Foley's Billiard Hall.	76
W. Barrow, wig maker	76
Gray & Barrow, hair goods	76
Lake Shore and Michigan Southern Railroad.	78
Heath & Milligan, white lead, zinc and colors	80
Culver, Page, Hoyne & Co., jobbing stationers	82
Michigan Central Railroad	84
Chicago and Alton Railroad	86
Jefferson & Wroe	88
W. F. Hunt, rags and old metals.	88
Pittsburgh and Ft. Wayne Railroad.	90
Pittsburgh, Cincinnati and St. Louis Railroad.	90
Herring's Safes.	92
Sweet, Dempster & Co., hats and caps.	94
J. Manz, engraver	94
Gage Brothers & Co., wholesale millinery	96
Dodd & Guth, shirts and underwear	96
Siddon's Fire Proof Iron Roofing	98
Halsey Bros., Homeopathic Pharmacy.	100
Edwards, Bluett & Co., clothing.	105

RAISED FROM THE RUINS!

WITH AN EYE TO BUSINESS.

50,000 worth of
MEN & BOYS' CLOTHING

Just received and will offer them to the Public at

LESS THAN OLD PRICES.

CALL AND SEE US.

EDWARDS, BLUETT & CO.,

45 & 47 MADISON ST. cor. Clinton,
376 STATE STREET, near Harrison.

(Formerly at 96 & 98 Randolph St.)

McNEAL & URBAN,

Manufacture

SAFES

AND

BANK LOCKS,

PATENT INSIDE BOLT WORK ETC.

The only Safe that could be opened after the great fire without cutting the door to pieces.

☞ One Hundred and Thirty-seven in the fire all preserving their contents.

J. M. TERWILLIGER, Agent,

Office:—**27** South Canal Street, CHICAGO.

www.ingramcontent.com/pod-product-compliance
Lightning Source LLC
Chambersburg PA
CBHW021158230426
43667CB00006B/449